Resistive Switching Systems for In-Memory Computation and Artificial Intelligence

AF786813

Online at: https://doi.org/10.1088/978-0-7503-6169-9

IOP Series in Next Generation Computing

Series editors

Prateek Agrawal

University of Klagenfurt, Austria and Lovely Professional University, India

Anand Sharma

Mody University of Science and Technology, India

Vishu Madaan

Lovely Professional University, India

About the series

The motivation for this series is to develop a trusted library on advanced computational methods, technologies, and their applications.

This series focuses on the latest developments in next generation computing, and in particular on the synergy between computer science and other disciplines. Books in the series will explore new developments in various disciplines that are relevant for computational perspective including foundations, systems, innovative applications, and other research contributions related to the overall design of computational tools, models, and algorithms that are relevant for the respective domain. It encompasses research and development in artificial intelligence, machine learning, block chain technology, quantum cryptography, quantum computing, nanoscience, bioscience-based sensors, IoT applications, nature inspired algorithms, computer vision, bioinformatics, etc. and their applications in the areas of science, engineering, business, and the social sciences. It covers a broad spectrum of applications in the community, including those in industry, government, and academia.

The aim of the series is to provide an opportunity for prospective researchers and experts to publish works based on next generation computing and its diverse applications. It also provides a data-sharing platform that will bring together international researchers, professionals, and academics. This series brings together thought leaders, researchers, industry practitioners, and potential users of different disciplines to develop new trends and opportunities, exchange ideas and practices related to advanced computational methods, and promote interdisciplinary knowledge.

A list of recently published titles published in this series can be found here: https://iopscience.iop.org/bookListInfo/iop-series-in-next-generation-computing.

Resistive Switching Systems for In-Memory Computation and Artificial Intelligence

Shaibal Mukherjee (F-JSPS, F-Humboldt Foundation, FInstP, FRSC, F-IETE)
Professor, Department of Electrical Engineering and Centre for Advanced Electronics, Indian Institute of Technology Indore, Khandwa Road, Simrol, Madhya Pradesh 453552, India

and

Director and Co-Founder, QuanTechL2M Innovations Pvt. Ltd., Indore, Madhya Pradesh, India

IOP Publishing, Bristol, UK

© IOP Publishing Ltd 2025. All rights, including for text and data mining (TDM), artificial intelligence (AI) training, and similar technologies, are reserved.

This book is available under the terms of the IOP-Standard Books License

No part of this publication may be reproduced, stored in a retrieval system, subjected to any form of TDM or used for the training of any AI systems or similar technologies, or transmitted in any form or by any means, electronic, mechanical, photocopying, recording or otherwise, without the prior permission of the publisher, or as expressly permitted by law or under terms agreed with the appropriate rights organization. Certain types of copying may be permitted in accordance with the terms of licences issued by the Copyright Licensing Agency, the Copyright Clearance Centre and other reproduction rights organizations.

Permission to make use of IOP Publishing content other than as set out above may be sought at permissions@ioppublishing.org.

Shaibal Mukherjee has asserted his right to be identified as the author of this work in accordance with sections 77 and 78 of the Copyright, Designs and Patents Act 1988.

ISBN 978-0-7503-6169-9 (ebook)
ISBN 978-0-7503-6167-5 (print)
ISBN 978-0-7503-6170-5 (myPrint)
ISBN 978-0-7503-6168-2 (mobi)

DOI 10.1088/978-0-7503-6169-9

Version: 20260101

IOP ebooks

British Library Cataloguing-in-Publication Data: A catalogue record for this book is available from the British Library.

Published by IOP Publishing, wholly owned by The Institute of Physics, London

IOP Publishing, No.2 The Distillery, Glassfields, Avon Street, Bristol, BS2 0GR, UK

US Office: IOP Publishing, Inc., 190 North Independence Mall West, Suite 601, Philadelphia, PA 19106, USA

This book is dedicated to all my school teachers, institute professors, colleagues, collaborators, students, friends and family members who have been with me; guiding, encouraging, loving and supporting me to overcome each and every hurdle of life. I am particularly grateful to the PhD students (Sanjay Kumar, Kumari Jyoti, Animesh Paul and Lokesh Kumar Hindoliya) of Hybrid Nanodevice Research Group (HNRG) and members (Mayank Dubey, Saurabh Yadav, Sumit Chaudhary) of QuanTechL2M Innovations Pvt. Ltd for their contributions and support. Last but not the least, I am grateful to the Almighty for His blessings in the form of a beautiful and loving family: my gorgeous wife Pallabi, our son Ishan, my parents and in-laws; who provided me with strength, unconditional love and affection, support, encouragement, blessings, advice and guidance to complete this journey.

Contents

Preface

Recently, there has been incredible interest in the translational and transformational research and developmental activities in the domain of resistive switching (RS) devices. Resistive random-access memory (RRAM) has garnered significant attention as a non-volatile memory solution for future memory-related processing, particularly in neuromorphic computing and image processing applications. It shows great potential as a replacement for traditional flash memory in data storage systems. The RS system offers a multitude of advantages over the existing memory systems in terms of simplistic device architecture and relative ease in the analog and logic implementations as compared to its counterparts. Additionally, RS systems exhibit ultra-fast memory switching capabilities, high stacking density, enabling efficient read and write operations, yielding swift access and storage of data. The RS device and system hold tremendous potential for revolutionizing data storage systems and providing more efficient and powerful memory solutions for non-volatile memory storage, digital logic circuits and operations, and neuromorphic applications. As researchers continue to explore the possibilities, the impact of RS systems is poised to be transformative, reshaping the landscape of memory technologies for years to come.

This book provides detailed information on neuromorphic system theory and its practical realization along with hardware-level implementations. This book targets broad and interdisciplinary domains ranging from the fundamental concepts of memristors and their importance in various domains, including neuroscience, complex logics, applied physics, computer science, materials science, and various engineering fields. A comprehensive review of analytical models and simulations of RS systems is provided with particular emphasis on neuromorphic designs and logic operations. Moreover, this also covers the hardware-level implementation of such RS systems and their applications in the field of nanotechnology, intelligent systems, large-scale optimization, and robotics. It is anticipated that this book will be a valuable and timely asset to academicians, researchers, and industry personnel at various levels of expertise, including postgraduate and doctoral students. Prerequisites to understanding this book are undergraduate-level courses in science and engineering such as electron devices and circuits, electromagnetic waves, digital circuits.

Chapter 1 outlines the fundamental concept of RS and detailed discussion on RS in various transition metal oxide (TMO) and two-dimensional (2D) transition metal dichalcogenide (TMD)-based systems. A detailed analytical and physical electrothermal modelling of nanoscale RS system is discussed along with their corresponding experimental validation. Chapters 2 and 3 detail selector memory device for crossbar arrays, essential for multibit data storage and the role of RS in brain-inspired computing. Chapters 4 and 5 deal with the impact of RS devices on in-memory computing and logic operations. These chapters also cover the multilevel conductance state programming functionality from the RS system and a comparative analysis of logic circuit implementation based on RS and complementary metal-oxide semiconductor (CMOS) systems. Chapters 6 and 7 elaborate vector-matrix operations in memory crossbar system and stochasticity in the devices owing to their architecture. Chapter 8 discusses the integration of the RS system at system-level. Chapter 9 explores the application of the RS system for image compression, biomedical and agriculture image processing to identify the various diseases in the living organisms and plants/crops, artificial intelligence (AI), edge detection and correction, and image construction.

In a nutshell, I hope the book can be a useful tool at the postgraduate and/or advanced undergraduate level of science and engineering degree programs as a textbook or major reference for courses such as advanced electronic circuits, materials science and engineering, nonlinear dynamical systems, mathematical modelling, computational science and AI applications. This book will be equally beneficial as a useful reference for a novice and an expert in the aforementioned domains.

Shaibal Mukherjee
Professor, Department of Electrical Engineering and Centre for Advanced Electronics, Indian Institute of Technology Indore
Khandwa Road, Simrol, Madhya Pradesh 453552, India
and
Director and Co-Founder, QuanTechL2M Innovations Pvt. Ltd., Indore, Madhya Pradesh, India

September 2025

Acknowledgments

Editing a book like this is only possible with the diligence and sincerity of many dedicated people. I am particularly grateful to the PhD students (Sanjay Kumar, Kumari Jyoti, Animesh Paul and Lokesh Kumar Hindoliya) of Hybrid Nanodevice Research Group (HNRG) and members (Mayank Dubey, Saurabh Yadav, Sumit Chaudhary) of QuanTechL2M Innovations Pvt. Ltd. for their tremendous contributions and support. This book also contains results from research work supported enormously by several funding agencies. Such work is partly supported by the TIH-IoT CHANAKYA Faculty Fellowship under Grant TIH-IoT/2024-05/HRD/CHANAKYA/SL/CFF-003, INAE India-Taiwan Programme of Cooperation in Science & Technology (2024/IN-TW/08 dated May 29, 2024) and India-Russia (ANRF-RSF) Bilateral Research of Cooperation in Science & Technology.

Author biography

Shaibal Mukherjee

Shaibal Mukherjee completed his PhD in Electrical and Computer Engineering, University of Oklahoma, USA in 2009 followed by his postdoctoral research work in the Center of Quantum Devices, Electrical Engineering and Computer Science, Northwestern University, USA. In September 2010, he joined IIT Indore and currently is a Professor in the Department of Electrical Engineering at IIT Indore. The Hybrid Nanodevice Research Group (HNRG) led by Shaibal at IIT Indore explores new physics of micro- and nano-structured materials, and to apply this knowledge in realizing advanced tools and devices for chemical, biological, optical, electronic and energy applications. He has published 145+ research articles in peer-reviewed journals, 110+ international conference proceedings, 11 book/book chapters and 16 patents (Granted: 14 and Filed/Published: 2). He is the recipient of various prestigious awards such as '**2025 Friedrich Wilhelm Bessel Research Award by Alexander von Humboldt Foundation**', '**2024 Microelectronic Engineering Journal Middle Career Investigator Award and Lectureship**', '**2024 TIH-IoT CHANAKYA Faculty Fellowship, IIT Bombay**', '**2023 Japan Society for the Promotion of Science (JSPS) Invitational Fellowship Award**', '**2021 JSPS Invitational Fellowship Award**', '**2020 DUO-India Professor Fellowship Award**', '**2019 DAAD Fellowship Award**', '**2018 Materials Research Society of India (MRSI) Medal**', '**2016 Young Faculty Research Fellowship (YFRF) under Visvesvaraya PhD Scheme for Electronics and IT**'. He is an Associate Editor for *IEEE Sensors Journal*, a senior member of IEEE, a regular member of Optical Society of America and Life Fellow of MRSI and Optical Society of India. He is a fellow of IoP, JSPS, Humboldt Foundation, RSC and IET. He is the founding Chair of IEEE Madhya Pradesh (MP) Section Electron Devices Society (EDS) chapter. He is also the Director, Co-Founder and Mentor of QuanTechL2M Innovations Pvt. Ltd.

IOP Publishing

Resistive Switching Systems for In-Memory Computation and Artificial Intelligence

Shaibal Mukherjee

Chapter 1

Introduction to resistive switching devices

1.1 Introduction

In recent years, there has been a sudden increase of interest in research and developmental activities in the domain of resistive switching (RS) devices [1]. Resistive random-access memory (RRAM) has garnered significant attention as a non-volatile memory (NVM) solution for future memory-related processing, particularly in neuromorphic computing and image processing applications [2]. It shows great potential as a replacement for traditional flash memory in data storage systems.

RRAM offers a multitude of advantages over the existing memories such as Static Random-Access Memory (SRAM) and Dynamic Random Access Memory (DRAM) in terms of simplistic device architecture and relative ease in implementation compared to its counterparts. Additionally, RRAMs exhibit ultra-fast memory switching capabilities, enabling rapid read and write operations, yielding swift access and storage of data. RRAMs are also highly energy-efficient and amenable to a high stacking density, providing with an increased storage capacity and efficiency [3]. RRAMs hold tremendous potential for revolutionizing data storage systems and providing more efficient and powerful memory solutions for non-volatile memory storage [4], digital logic circuits [5], and neuromorphic applications [6]. As researchers continue to explore the possibilities, the impact of RRAMs is poised to be transformative, reshaping the landscape of memory technologies for years to come.

1.2 Fundamentals of resistive switching

The concept of RS in memristive devices was initially proposed by Leon Chua in 1971 [1]. Capacitors, inductors, and resistors are the fundamental passive circuit elements that form the core building blocks of electrical circuits, each characterized by unique relationships. A capacitor stores electrical energy in an electric field

doi:10.1088/978-0-7503-6169-9ch1 © IOP Publishing Ltd 2025. All rights, including for text and data mining (TDM), artificial intelligence (AI) training, and similar technologies, are reserved.

between its plates, with its fundamental relationship expressed between charge (q) and voltage (V). An inductor, on the other hand, stores energy in a magnetic field generated by the flow of electric current through a coil, with its fundamental relationship involving current (I) and magnetic flux (Φ). A resistor establishes a direct relationship between voltage (V) and current (I), governing the flow of electrical energy in a circuit. In contrast, the memristor is recognized as the fourth fundamental circuit element as it relates electric charge (q) and magnetic flux (Φ) in a way that depends on the device's past states. This memory-dependent behavior completes the missing link in circuit theory by directly connecting flux and charge. Unlike the traditional passive circuit elements such as resistors, capacitors, and inductors, memristors, as RS devices possess the unique property of exhibiting a relationship between electric charge and flux that depends on their history [1]. This characteristic makes them distinct and has led to their classification as the fourth fundamental circuit element, as shown in figure 1.1. Voltage is defined as the rate of change of magnetic flux ($\mathrm{d}\Phi$) with respect to time ($\mathrm{d}t$). Resistance is calculated as the ratio of the change in voltage ($\mathrm{d}V$) to the change in current ($\mathrm{d}I$). An inductor relates to the change in flux ($\mathrm{d}\Phi$) with respect to the change in current ($\mathrm{d}I$), while a capacitor is the ratio of the change in charge ($\mathrm{d}q$) to the change in voltage ($\mathrm{d}V$). Current is determined by the rate of change of charge ($\mathrm{d}q$) flowing through a conductor over time ($\mathrm{d}t$). Similarly, a memristor is characterized as the ratio of the change in flux ($\mathrm{d}\Phi$) to the change in charge ($\mathrm{d}q$).

There are different types of RRAM such as conductive-bridge RRAM (CB-RAM) [4], interfacial RRAM (I-RAM) [5], and valence-change RRAM (VC-RAM) [6]. Each type has its unique operating mechanisms; however, they all share the common trait of RS while toggling from one resistance state to another. Among various RRAM technologies, I-RRAM devices are particularly favored for practical applications due to their RS

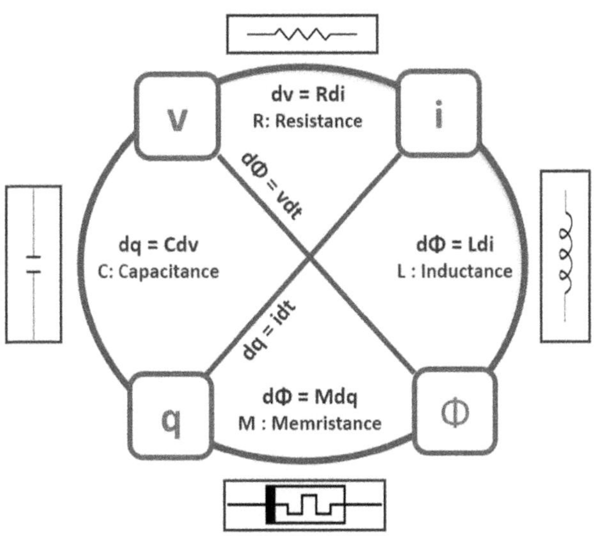

Figure 1.1. Relationship between fundamental circuit elements.

mechanisms, which rely on changes in electrical resistance at the interfaces between two distinct materials [7]. For example, this switching can occur at the interface between a metal electrode and a metal oxide layer, where the accumulation or depletion of oxygen vacancies effectively alters the device's resistance.

1.2.1 Introduction to resistive switching

In this section, we explore the fundamental concepts and terminology that form the building blocks of understanding resistive switching memristor devices. These concepts are essential for grasping the underlying principles and developments in the field of memristor technology. A memristor, short for 'memory resistor', is a two-terminal electronic component that stores information in the form of variable resistance. Unlike traditional resistors with a fixed resistance, a memristor can remember the amount of charge that has passed through it by adjusting its resistance accordingly. This unique property allows memristive devices to change their resistance based on their history of electrical activity, enabling them to function as memory elements [5]. In addition to their use in non-volatile memory and neuromorphic computing, memristors can also be applied in advanced electronic devices such as adaptive filters, which dynamically adjust their response based on input signals, and programmable logic devices, which can perform complex computations with reconfigurable hardware [6]. Furthermore, memristors have potential in secure hardware encryption for data security and in artificial intelligence hardware accelerators, where they can enhance the efficiency of machine learning algorithms by mimicking the adaptive behavior of neural networks [7]. Resistive switching refers to the phenomenon where a material can change its resistance between two or more distinct states when subjected to an external bias voltage. This change in resistance is non-volatile, meaning the material retains its resistance state even after the removal of the applied voltage. This characteristic makes RS devices highly promising for various applications, including memory devices [7], neuromorphic computing [8], image processing [9], and logic circuits [10]. These RS devices are made up of a simple structure consisting of metal/insulator (or semiconductor)/metal structure and when an electric signal is applied, their resistance undergoes change. The insulator layer in these devices typically consists of a specialized material that enables the movement of both electrons and ions [1].

Subsequently, the current–voltage (*I–V*) characteristics of an RS device as shown in figure 1.2, provide a graphical representation of how the device current changes in response to variations in the applied voltage, thereby demonstrating its resistive switching behavior. The *I–V* characteristics of an RS device demonstrate a hysteresis loop, primarily attributed to its low-resistance state (LRS) and high-resistance state (HRS) [11]. In an RS memristive device, the LRS and HRS represent two distinct binary states used in memory and computing applications. The LRS, or 'ON' state, occurs when conductive pathways are formed between the device's electrodes, resulting in low resistance and allowing a higher current to flow; this state typically represents a binary '1'. Conversely, the HRS, or 'OFF' state, occurs when these

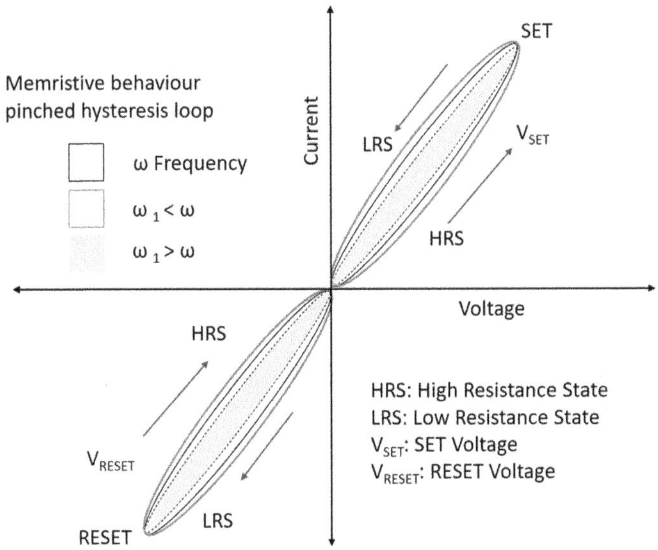

Figure 1.2. Resistive switching behavior.

conductive pathways are disrupted, leading to high resistance and reduced current flow, usually representing a binary '0'. The ability of a memristive device to switch between the LRS and HRS under an applied voltage makes it highly suitable for non-volatile memory, logic circuits, and neuromorphic computing, where such dynamic resistance changes are crucial for operation [12]. In the HRS, the device maintains a high resistance for a range of voltages, leading to significantly lower current flow as compared to that for the LRS. The hysteresis loop arises due to the bistable nature of the device, where it can exist in two stable resistance states under the influence of applied voltages. The *I–V* characteristics of an RS device with hysteresis loop behavior reflects the dynamic interaction between its LRS and HRS, offering insights into its resistance switching dynamics and potential applications in electronic devices [13]. In the HRS of the RS device, the curve appears as either a straight line or a slightly curved line, indicating a linear or weakly nonlinear behavior, respectively. In contrast, the *I–V* curve in the LRS exhibits a more pronounced nonlinear behavior, reflecting a change in the device's conductive properties. This part of the curve corresponds to the resistance of the device in the LRS. The presence of a hysteresis loop, a distinctive feature of RS devices, is a significant characteristic observed in the *I–V* curve. The memristor is a state-dependent system characterized by a pinched hysteresis loop that intersects at zero [14]. The area of this pinched hysteresis loop diminishes as the operating frequency (ω) increases, as shown in figure 1.2, which highlights the key characteristics, or 'fingerprints', of an RS-based system. Due to the inherent inertia of the device, it cannot respond swiftly to rapid changes in the excitation waveform. Consequently, it stabilizes at an equilibrium state, resulting in a reduced hysteresis loop area at higher sweep or ramp rates [14]. This behavior explains the pinched *I–V* hysteresis loop, which is clearly influenced by the rate of the bias sweep.

Analysing the *I–V* curve, as shown in figure 1.2, enables the determination of various crucial parameters that aid in comprehending and characterizing the device's performance. The I_{ON}/I_{OFF} ratio refers to the ratio of the current in the low-resistance state (I_{ON}) to the current in the high-resistance state (I_{OFF}). This ratio is crucial for determining the effectiveness of RS and the reliability of RS devices. The I_{ON}/I_{OFF} ratio is a pivotal metric in assessing the performance of RS devices. A high I_{ON}/I_{OFF} ratio ensures distinct and reliable switching states, essential for data integrity, noise immunity, and low power consumption. Evaluating RS characteristics, including the I_{ON}/I_{OFF} ratio, is fundamental for understanding and improving the endurance of RS devices, thereby enhancing their viability for various advanced applications in memory and computing technologies. RS characteristics facilitate the evaluation of the device endurance, a measure of the number of switching cycles the RS device can withstand while maintaining an optimal performance. On the other hand, retention of an RS device is the measurement of the ability of the device to maintain a stable resistance state over time, which can also be assessed through the *I–V* curve. Moreover, the switching characteristics provide information regarding the switching voltages required for transitioning between different resistance states. Retention in memristive devices, which refers to a device's ability to maintain its programmed resistance state over time, can be measured from the *I–V* curve by monitoring the current stability under a non-destructive read voltage. Initially, the device is programmed into either an LRS or a HRS using a voltage sweep, which is evident from the distinct currents on the *I–V* curve for each state. After programming, a small read voltage is applied periodically to measure the current without altering the device's state. By tracking the current over time, researchers can observe how it decays and determine the retention time defined as the duration for which the current remains within a specific percentage (such as 90% or 95%) of its initial value. A retention plot is created by plotting current versus time, showing the stability of the resistance state. The retention times for both the LRS (high current) and HRS (low current) are compared to evaluate the device's stability and reliability. A longer retention time for both states indicates better performance, making the memristor suitable for non-volatile memory applications. Analysing the retention characteristics from the *I–V* curve thus provides insights into the endurance and data storage stability of memristive devices.

Resistance switching: Resistance switching is a fundamental behavior observed in memristors, wherein the device can transition between high-resistance and low-resistance states. This switching occurs under the influence of an electric field or current. The ability to change resistance states is essential for the storage and manipulation of information in memristor-based devices, enabling non-volatile memory functionality.

SET and RESET processes: The SET process involves inducing a controlled change in the resistance state of a memristor, typically from a HRS to an LRS. Conversely, the RESET process refers to the reversal of this change, returning the memristor from an LRS to a HRS. The SET and RESET processes are critical for establishing reliable and controlled operation of memristive devices.

Conductive bridge: A conductive bridge is a crucial element within a memristor that forms during the SET process. It is a conductive path that enables the flow of electric current through the device, leading to the change in resistance. The formation and dissolution of this conductive bridge plays a pivotal role in the RS behavior of memristors.

Hysteresis: Hysteresis is a phenomenon commonly observed in memristors, where the *I*–*V* relationship exhibits dependence on both the present input and its history. In other words, the resistance of the memristor not only depends on the current voltage but also on the previous voltage levels experienced. This hysteresis effect adds a memory-like behavior to the device and is important in various memristor applications.

State variables: Memristors possess state variables that represent their internal state or characteristics. These variables, such as the resistance state or the size of the conductive bridge, play a crucial role in determining the behavior and performance of the memristor. Understanding and controlling these state variables are key to developing advanced memristive systems.

By gaining a comprehensive understanding of these basic concepts and becoming familiar with the associated terminology, readers will establish a solid foundation for comprehending the principles and advancements in memristor technology. This knowledge will enable further exploration of the vast potential and applications of memristors in various fields, including memory devices, computing architectures, and beyond.

In a filamentary RS device, conductive filament formation and rupture are key processes that occur during the SET and RESET operations on the application of an external bias voltage [14]. When an external bias is applied to an RS device, a conductive filament is typically created by the movement of ions or defects within the resistive material, as shown in figure 1.3(a). Under the influence of this external

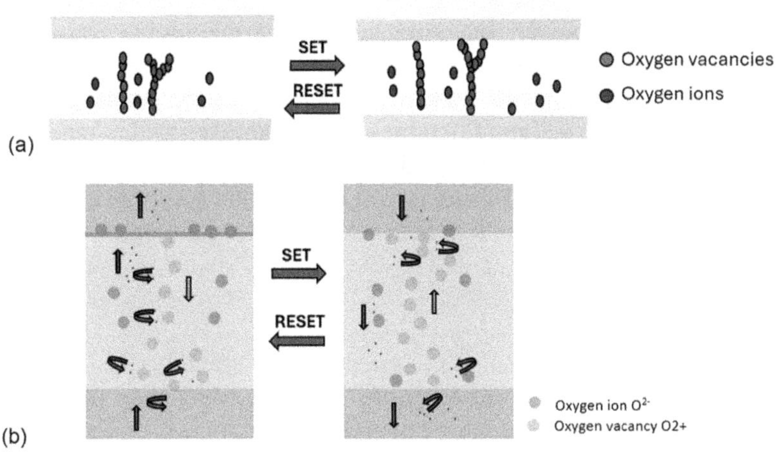

Figure 1.3. SET–RESET mechanism in (a) a filamentary RS device and (b) an interfacial RS device.

voltage, ions or defects within the material start to move, migrating towards regions of lower resistance or higher electrical conductance. As these ions or defects accumulate, they create a conductive path, essentially forming a bridge between the two electrodes of the RS device, and this bridge allows the flow of electric current, resulting in an LRS for the device. On the other hand, during the RESET process, due to the rupture of the conductive filament, the resistance state of the RS device transitions back to its HRS state. One common mechanism is the application of a high current or voltage pulse, which generates a significant and localized joule heating. Alternatively, the electro-migration effect can also play a role in the filament rupture process. Under the influence of the RESET voltage, ions or defects within the filament may migrate away from the conductive path, leading to its dissolution or rupture. Once the filament is disrupted, the device returns to its original HRS state, blocking the flow of current between the electrodes. Figure 1.3 (b) illustrates the Al/ZnO/Al memory cell in its HRS and LRS, focusing on the roles of oxygen vacancies, oxygen ions, and the AlO_x interfacial layer. While aluminum typically forms an ohmic contact with ZnO, the oxygen-rich region at the Al/ZnO interface creates an asymmetric Schottky barrier, limiting current flow. When a negative bias is applied, oxygen vacancies move towards the top electrode (TE), and oxygen ions migrate to the Al (bottom electrode, BE)–ZnO interface, forming an AlO_x layer and reducing current density, leading to the HRS. During the SET process, a positive voltage dissolves the AlO_x layer, increasing current and switching the device to the LRS. The SET–RESET cycles are governed by the movement of oxygen vacancies and ions, supported by redox reactions at the interface. Conduction in the ZnO bulk is driven by electron hopping through oxygen vacancy paths, with RS involving both bulk conduction and interfacial AlO_x layer formation/dissolution. Modifying interfacial properties exerts a significant influence on charge flow dynamics, thereby inducing changes in resistance within RS devices. These changes are contingent upon a multitude of factors such as the constituent materials, architectural configurations of the RS, and external stimuli. The confluence of these diverse factors engenders a spectrum of RS phenomena. Investigation into the interplay between these underlying mechanisms and influencing factors elucidates the intricacies of RS phenomena, facilitating comprehensive exploitation of RS devices. Systematic examination of these mechanisms enables researchers to tailor memristor materials and designs for targeted RS characteristics. Consequently, the interplay of these mechanisms alongside considerations of material composition, device architecture, and external stimuli manifests a broad spectrum of RS behaviors, offering avenues for advancements in memristor-based technologies.

1.2.2 Historical overview

This section presents highlights of the journey of understanding the fundamentals of RS in memristors, from early observations to the current state of the field. The interdisciplinary nature of memristor research, combining materials science, device engineering, and circuit design, has led to remarkable advancements and has the potential to reshape the landscape of future electronics [13–20] and in-memory computing technologies.

1.2.2.1 Early studies on resistive switching

The study of RS phenomena began in 1962 with T W Hickmott's observation of reversible resistance changes in thin film under applied voltage, marking the first step in this field [1]. The theoretical foundation for memristors was laid in 1971 by Leon Chua from the University of California, Berkeley, who introduced the concept of a memristor as a unique circuit element [1, 13]. This concept was further expanded by Sung Mo Kang from the University of California, Berkeley, in 1976, who described memristive devices and systems [14], outlining their properties and potential applications [14]. In 1980s no major advancement specific to memristor-based applications occurred, but in 1994 Strukov *et al* [16] from Hewlett-Packard (HP) Labs worked on the theoretical development of nanoscale devices that could potentially behave like memristors. Renewed interest emerged in 2000 when Beck *et al* demonstrated reversible and reproducible RS in strontium titanate ($SrTiO_3$), underscoring its potential for memory technology [15]. Significant advancements followed in 2008 when Strukov *et al* proposed a mathematical model for memristors, establishing them as the fourth fundamental circuit element that combines memory and resistance [16]. The same year, R Stanley Williams and his team at HP Labs reported the first experimental realization of a memristor using a thin film of titanium dioxide, which validated theoretical predictions and sparked new research avenues in memory storage and neuromorphic computing [16, 17]. From 2009 onwards, researchers have delved deeply into understanding the fundamental mechanisms underlying memristors, working to enhance their performance and extend their applications beyond non-volatile memory to include areas such as logic circuits and machine learning [18], as detailed in the following sections. Since 2015, there has been a strong focus on translating memristor technology into practical applications by developing scalable manufacturing techniques and addressing key reliability challenges. These efforts aim to pave the way for the commercialization of memristors, with the potential to revolutionize advanced memory, computing systems, and next-generation electronic devices [19–23].

1.2.2.2 Evolution of memristor materials

Memristor research has evolved significantly over the years, driven by a continuous exploration of new materials to optimize their performance and applications. The early years of memristor development, beginning in the 1960s [1], were marked by the use of oxide materials. T W Hickmott's pioneering work in 1962 introduced aluminum oxide (Al_2O_3) as a potential memristor material, which laid the groundwork for future studies [17]. By 2008, Strukov *et al* [1] demonstrated memristive behavior in strontium titanate ($SrTiO_3$), a key development in oxide-based memristors [18]. Other oxides, such as titanium dioxide (TiO_2), hafnium oxide (HfO_2), and zinc oxide (ZnO), were also explored for their memristive properties during this period [19]. The 2000s–2010s saw a shift towards chalcogenide materials, with Choi *et al* introducing amorphous chalcogenide ($Ge_2Sb_2Te_5$) as a promising material for memristors in 2009 [20]. This research expanded to include other chalcogenides, such as antimony sulfide (Sb_2S_3), bismuth telluride (Bi_2Te_3), and lead sulfide (PbS) [21]. The focus then extended to organic materials in the 2010s, with Ikeda *et al* demonstrating memristive behavior in organic compounds such as poly(3-hexylthiophene) (P3HT) and phenyl-C61-butyric acid methyl ester (PCBM) [15]. Subsequent research has also investigated other organic materials, including PEDOT, polyaniline, and carbon nanotubes (CNTs) [17]. In recent years, emerging materials such as two-dimensional (2D) materials, for example graphene, transition metal dichalcogenides (TMDs), and black phosphorus, and ferroelectric materials such as barium titanate ($BaTiO_3$) and lead zirconate titanate (PZT) have shown significant potential for memristor applications. Key research groups have driven these advancements, including Strukov's group [22] at Stanford University, Hui's group at the University of Michigan, IBM Research, and Wei Lu's group at the University of California, Berkeley, which has focused on 2D materials for memristors. When selecting memristor materials, researchers consider several critical factors, such as switching speed, endurance, retention, scalability, and compatibility with existing fabrication processes. The material choice often depends on the specific application and desired properties of the memristor device. As research continues, new and innovative materials are expected to emerge, further broadening the scope and potential of memristor-based technologies.

1.2.2.3 Recent advancements

In recent years, significant advancements have been made in the field of RS memristors [22]. Understanding RS effects has been essential for achieving consistent and reliable operation in small-scale memristor devices. Reliability issues have also been addressed to ensure the long-term stability and endurance of memristors.

The potential applications of memristors are vast and diverse; they have shown promise in non-volatile memories, neuromorphic computing, analog computing, and adaptive circuits, opening doors for exciting advancements in electronic technologies. Researchers have made significant progress in improving the performance of memristor devices by utilizing advanced fabrication and growth techniques. Key advancements in the material synthesis process include the use of experimental techniques such as atomic layer deposition (ALD), physical vapor deposition (PVD), molecular beam epitaxy (MBE), metal–organic chemical vapor deposition (MOCVD), direct current (DC) sputtering, dual ion beam sputtering (DIBS), and chemical vapor deposition (CVD) [25]. Here, we will discuss some of these techniques:

(a) DC sputtering system: The DC sputtering system, shown alongside a schematic diagram in figure 1.4(a) and (b), is used to deposit metal films such as aluminum, platinum or titanium, acting as the top or bottom electrode in RRAM. DC sputtering is a thin-film deposition technique widely used in material science and engineering to coat substrates with a thin layer of material. In this process, a vacuum chamber is first evacuated using a pumping system to create a low-pressure environment. A gas

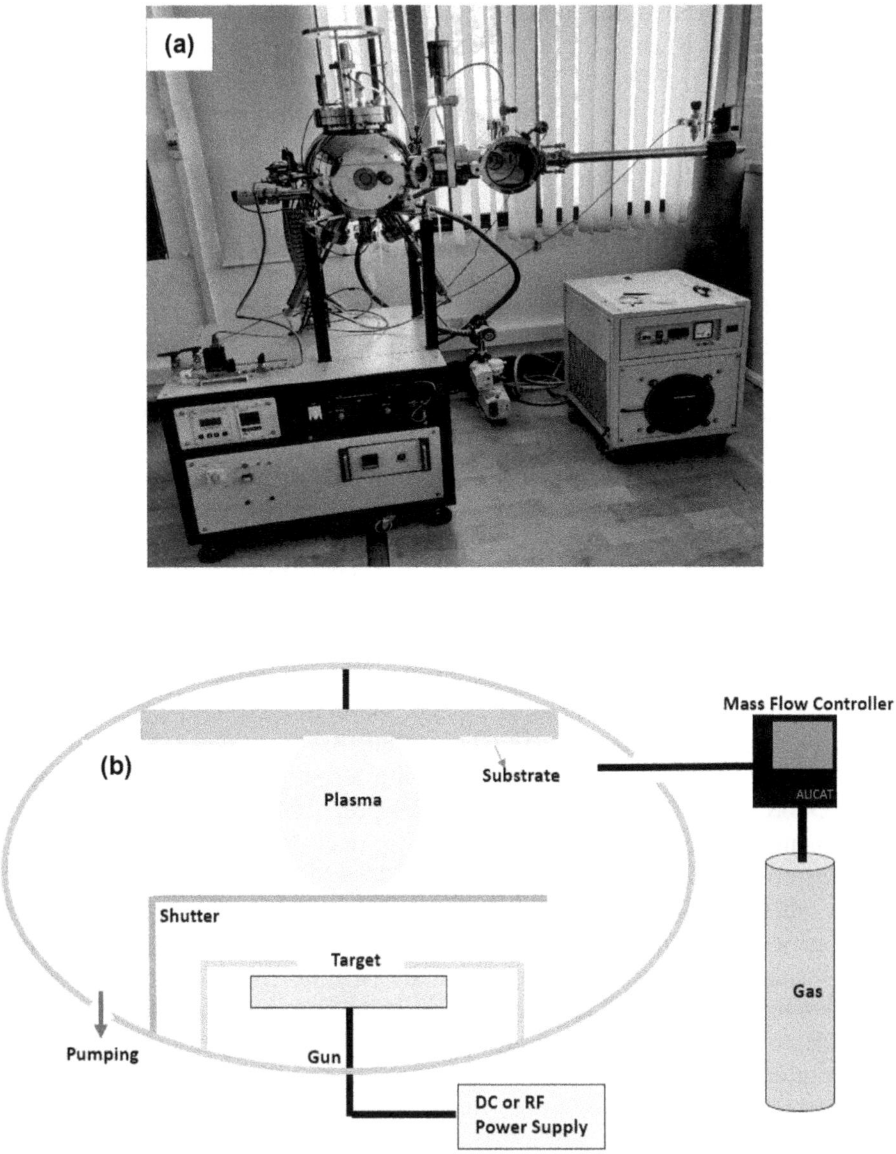

Figure 1.4. (a) A DC sputtering system. (b) Schematic of a DC sputtering system.

system, typically involving a gas cylinder (usually containing argon) and a mass flow controller, introduces an inert gas into the chamber at a controlled rate to maintain a stable pressure. Inside the vacuum chamber, a target material (the source of the thin film) is connected to a DC power supply, which creates a strong electric field between the target and the substrate holder. The substrate, placed on the substrate holder, is positioned opposite the target. When the DC power supply is turned on, it ionizes the inert gas, generating plasma of positively charged ions. These ions are accelerated toward the negatively charged target, causing the ejection (or 'sputtering') of atoms from the target surface. The ejected atoms travel through the vacuum chamber and condense onto the substrate, forming a thin film. A gun, positioned near the target, aids in the plasma generation, while a shutter can be used to control the deposition process by covering or exposing the target. Radio frequency (RF) power supplies can also be employed for sputtering insulating or non-conductive materials. The DC sputtering process is a controlled method for depositing thin films, with the gas flow, power supply, vacuum level, and other parameters carefully adjusted to achieve the desired coating characteristics. The process involves bombarding a metal target with ions in a vacuum chamber, causing metal atoms to be ejected and deposited onto the substrate as a thin film. The top electrode completes the electrical circuit in the device and enables RS behavior, crucial for data storage and processing. Precise control of the sputtering of metal ions ensures efficient and reliable contact formation with the semiconductor film, eventually realizing an efficient RRAM.

(b) Dual-ion beam sputtering (DIBS) system: The DIBS system, shown alongside a schematic diagram in figure 1.5(a) and (b), is a process used to fabricate semiconductor or dielectric film for an RRAM. The DIBS system involves two ion sources in which the first ion source bombards a target material causing atoms to be ejected and deposited onto a substrate, while the second ion source assists in controlling the properties of the thin film; the resulting thin film exhibits RS behavior essential for memristor operation. DIBS allows precise control over film properties and enables the development of efficient and reliable memristor devices for advanced memory and computing applications.

In the DIBS system, a vacuum chamber is maintained at a low pressure using a vacuum pump to create the necessary environment for sputtering. Inside the vacuum chamber, there are two ion sources: the deposition ion source and the assist ion source. The deposition ion source directs a primary beam of ions (usually argon) onto the target assembly, which contains the material to be deposited. When the energetic ions strike the target, they dislodge (or sputter) atoms from its surface. These sputtered atoms travel across the chamber and are deposited onto the substrate, which is held in place by a heater assembly. The heater maintains the substrate at a specific temperature, which helps control the film properties. To neutralize the ion beams and prevent charging effects on the substrate, a neutralizer is positioned near both ion sources. The assist ion source provides a secondary ion beam aimed directly at the growing film on the substrate. This secondary beam is used to modify the film properties by cleaning the surface, controlling the film microstructure, and enhancing adhesion. The crystal monitor measures the film thickness in real-time, ensuring accurate control over the deposition rate. The neutralizers associated with both ion sources release electrons to neutralize the ions, preventing any build-up of

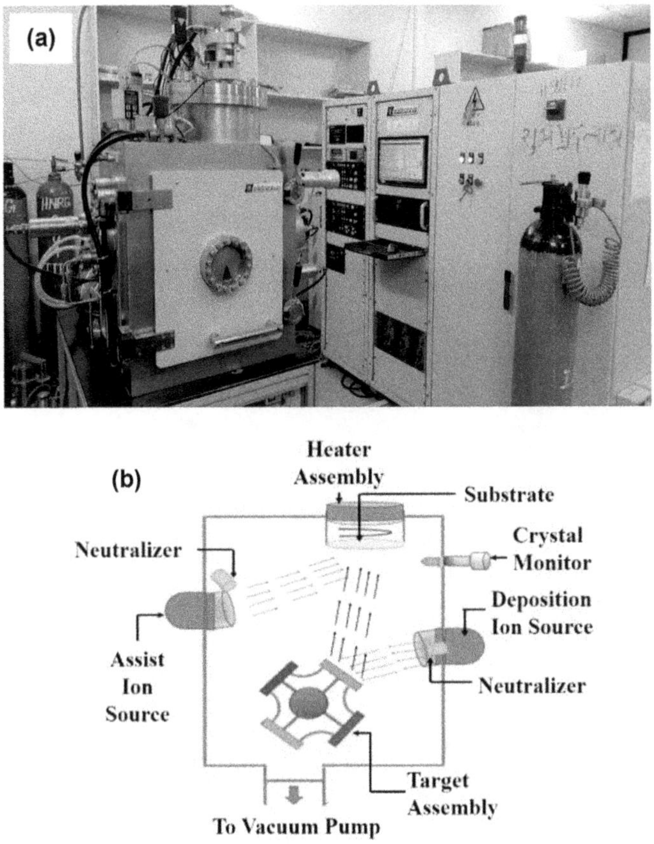

Figure 1.5. (a) A DIBS system. (b) Schematic of a DIBS system.

electrical charge that could interfere with the deposition process. The DIBS system allows for precise control over the deposition parameters, such as film composition, thickness, and microstructure, making it ideal for applications requiring high-quality thin films.

(c) Chemical vapor deposition (CVD) system: Researchers have explored the integration of RRAMs with other emerging technologies, such as two-dimensional (2D) and quantum materials, to enhance device performance and enable new functionalities [22, 26]. By leveraging advanced fabrication techniques and integrating memristors with other emerging technologies such as CVD, researchers are pushing the boundaries and opening new possibilities for RRAM-based devices and systems. The CVD system, shown alongside its schematic in figure 1.6(a) and (b), is used to grow thin films of semiconductor materials in memristive device fabrication. Precursor gases are introduced into a chamber, where they decompose and form the film on the substrate. The thin film enables RS behavior for data

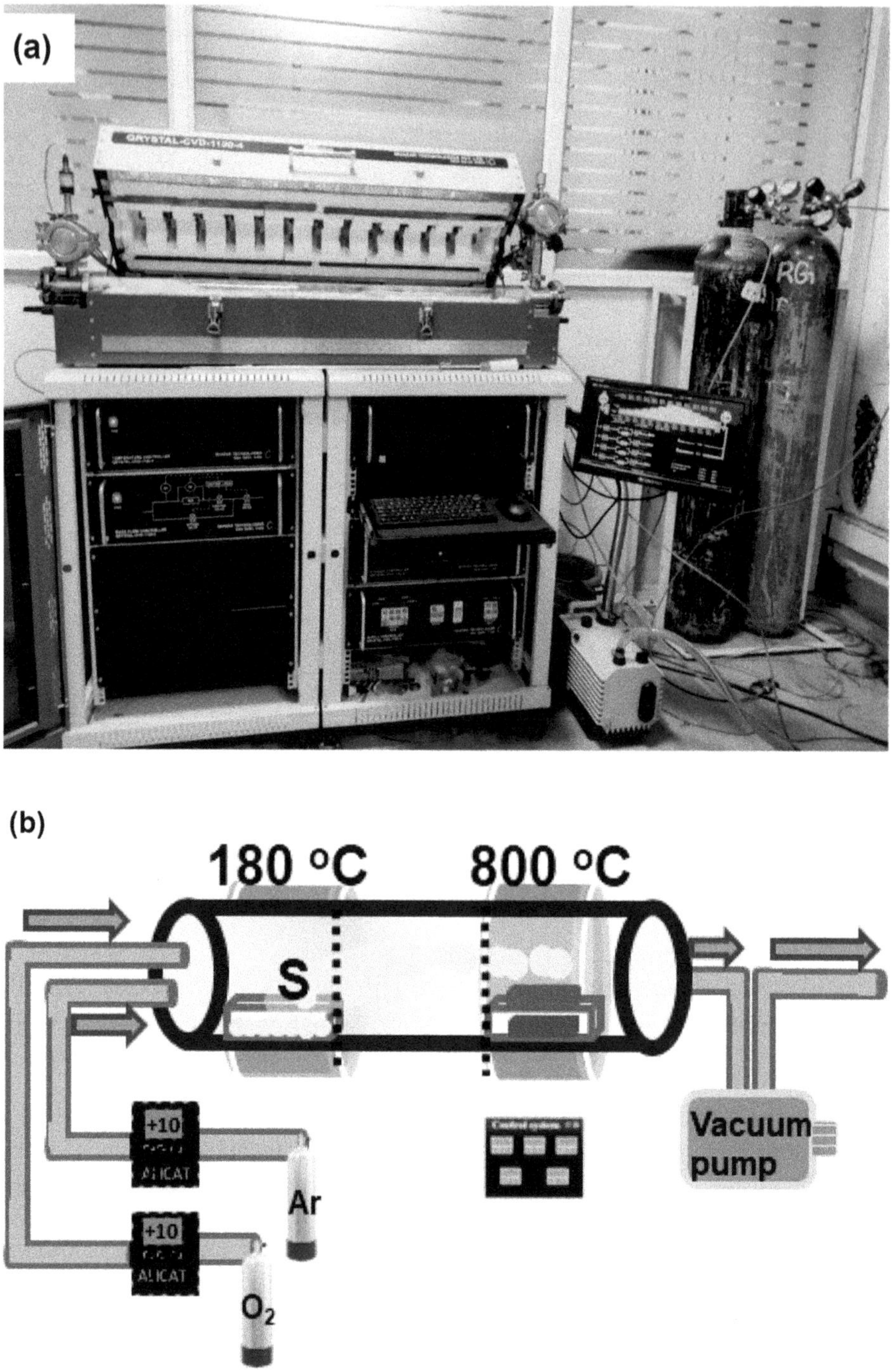

Figure 1.6. (a) A CVD system. (b) Schematic of a CVD system.

storage and processing. CVD ensures precision and uniformity, making it crucial for reliable memristive devices in advanced memory and computing applications.

CVD is a process used to produce high-quality thin films and coatings on various substrates. In a typical CVD system, a reaction chamber is designed to facilitate the chemical reactions that lead to the deposition of a desired material. The CVD process begins with the introduction of precursor gases, such as argon (Ar) and oxygen, through controlled inlets. These gases are transported into the chamber, where the deposition will take place. Inside the chamber, a silicon substrate is positioned in a heating zone maintained at a high temperature, typically around 800 °C. This high temperature is essential to activate the chemical reactions needed for the deposition. The substrate is heated uniformly to ensure consistent deposition across its surface. A precursor seed layer sample is placed at an optimized length from the gas inlets, where it begins to decompose or react due to the thermal energy. As the gases flow over the substrate, chemical reactions occur on its surface, resulting in the formation of a thin film. The temperature for S power deposition is set at around 140 °C to control the precursor reaction rate and the film growth.

1.2.3 Advantages and applications of resistive switching

RRAMs have garnered significant attention in recent years due to their unique electrical properties and potential applications in various fields. One of the key advantages of RRAM is its superior performance characteristics. It boasts fast read and write operations, low power consumption, and excellent scalability, making it an attractive solution for various applications, including mobile devices, Internet of Things (IoT) devices, and artificial intelligence systems.

These key advantages, making RRAMs an attractive choice for future data storage systems. First, RRAM has a simple structure, which makes it easy to incorporate into different circuit designs [23]. Second, RRAM devices have a fast-switching mechanism, enabling quick read and write operations. This speed greatly enhances the overall performance of memory systems based on RRAM technology. Moreover, RRAM devices have low power consumption, contributing to energy-efficient computing. This is particularly important in modern electronic devices that aim to minimize power usage and extend battery life. This results in increased storage capacity, which is beneficial for applications that require large amounts of data storage. RRAM is a promising candidate for the next generation of non-volatile memory, as it has the potential to replace conventional charge-based flash memory in data storage applications.

Moreover, the non-volatility of RRAM ensures that data remain intact even when power is disconnected, enhancing its suitability for data storage applications. In this subsection, we delve into the diverse applications of RRAM-based models across three primary domains: medical diagnostics, biometric systems [28], and face detection algorithms [29, 30]. First, in medical diagnostics, memristor-based models are applied

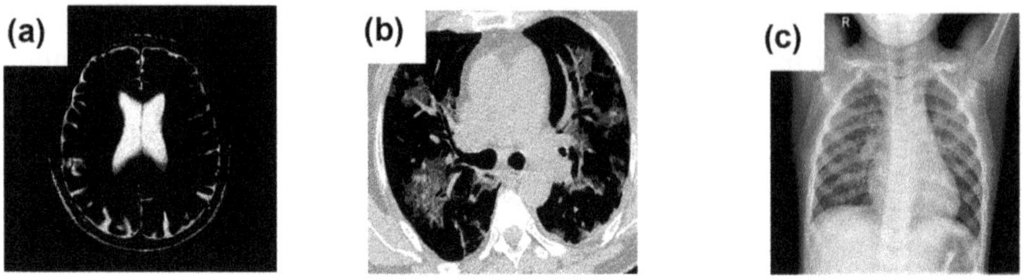

Figure 1.7. Applications of RS devices in medical diagnosis. (a) MRI. (b) CT scan. (c) Chest x-ray image.

to enhance the processing of various imaging modalities, including magnetic resonance imaging (MRI) (figure 1.7(a)), computed tomography (CT) scans (figure 1.7(b)), and chest x-ray images (figure 1.7(c)). In medical diagnostics [9], memristors are also advancing neural networks by mimicking synaptic connections, enabling the creation of efficient parallel processing algorithms that improve the accuracy and speed of medical diagnoses. Additionally, memristive sensors integrated into medical devices offer real-time disease detection and monitoring capabilities, revolutionizing healthcare systems. These sensors, characterized by their non-volatile memory and low power consumption, facilitate continuous health monitoring, which is crucial for the early detection of medical conditions and the enhancement of patient care. Additionally, memristive devices are increasingly being utilized in the creation of smart implants. Their unique properties allow for adaptive learning and precise control of biological processes, leading to more personalized and responsive treatments. This capability significantly contributes to improving the overall quality of life for patients by providing tailored therapeutic interventions and minimizing the need for invasive procedures.

Moving on to biometrics, RRAM offers promising solutions for various authentication systems. In fingerprint recognition [28], RRAM devices provide higher accuracy and robustness, enabling efficient matching algorithms. By storing and processing vast amounts of data, they contribute to reliable and secure identification. Similarly, memristive devices play a role in retina scanning, aiding in the precise mapping and identification of unique features. Their ability to store and retrieve patterns allows for fast and reliable authentication. Moreover, memristors can enhance voice and speech recognition systems by efficiently processing and storing speech patterns, resulting in improved accuracy and faster response times in voice-controlled applications.

Within the domain of face detection [29], memristors play a critical role in various applications. Memristor-based facial recognition systems benefit from efficient storage and retrieval of facial features, enabling faster identification and matching. This has wide-ranging implications for security systems, access control, and personalized user experiences. Memristive devices also find use in emotion recognition, storing patterns related to emotional responses. This has applications in psychology, market research, and human–computer interaction, facilitating a deeper understanding of human behavior. Furthermore, RRAM enables real-time analysis of video feeds, enhancing surveillance systems. Face detection and tracking algorithms can be significantly accelerated, improving the accuracy and reliability of security systems. Continued research and development in this field will undoubtedly lead to further innovations, bringing us closer to a more efficient and interconnected future. However, RRAM is still under active research and development. Challenges such as endurance, reliability, and scaling need to be addressed before it can reach commercial maturity and compete with established memory technologies. Nevertheless, due to its exciting properties and potential, RRAM holds promise for revolutionizing the memory landscape in the future.

1.3 Transition metal oxides and transition metal dichalcogenides

In this section, we explore the fascinating properties and versatile applications of transition metal oxides (TMOs) and 2D TMDs, as shown in figure 1.8. These materials have gained popularity in electronics and nanotechnology due to their unique characteristics [30–38]. We focus on understanding their atomic and nanoscale behavior by studying their synthesis, structural analysis methods, and examining their electronic and optical properties. TMOs and TMDs find applications in diverse fields such as electronics, energy storage, catalysis, and sensing.

1.3.1 Material growth

There are a variety of methods for growing TMOs and TMDs. Some of the most common methods include CVD and ALD.

1.3.1.1 Chemical vapor deposition

CVD is a widely utilized technique for the growth and fabrication of memristive devices, as discussed in section 1.2.2.3. It involves the deposition of thin films or

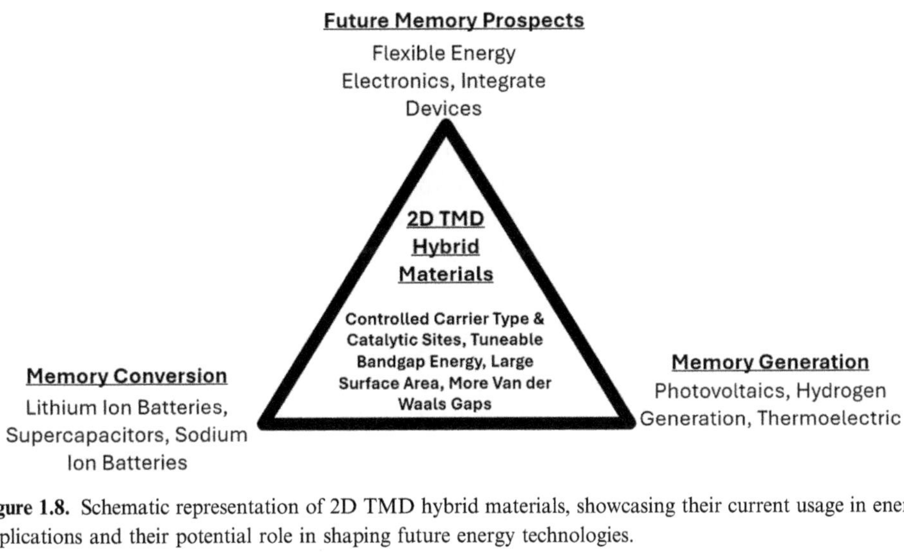

Figure 1.8. Schematic representation of 2D TMD hybrid materials, showcasing their current usage in energy applications and their potential role in shaping future energy technologies.

layers onto a substrate through the chemical reaction of vapor-phase precursor molecules. CVD allows for precise control over film thickness, composition, and crystalline structure. In the context of memristor device growth, CVD plays a critical role in depositing the active materials that exhibit RS behavior. The process begins with the delivery of precursor gases into a reaction chamber. These gases contain the desired elements required for the memristor material. Inside the chamber, the precursor molecules undergo controlled chemical reactions to form a solid film on the substrate surface. The choice of precursor molecules is crucial, and they are selected based on their volatility and ability to react with the substrate surface. Prior to deposition, the substrate is prepared by cleaning and surface treatment to ensure proper adhesion and nucleation of the film [16, 26, 47]. The typical process steps involved in CVD for memristor device growth include precursor delivery, reaction, film formation, and subsequent cooling or annealing processes. These steps are carefully controlled to achieve the desired film properties. The selection of precursor molecules is critical in CVD. It depends on the specific materials required for the memristor device. Common precursors used in CVD for memristive devices include metal–organic compounds, metal halides, and metal carbonyls [48, 49]. The precursor molecules should be volatile enough to be carried into the gas phase and react with the substrate surface. Prior to deposition, the substrate is prepared by cleaning and surface treatment to ensure proper nucleation and adhesion of the deposited film. Substrates with suitable properties, such as high temperature stability and compatibility with the desired film material, are selected. These parameters are optimized to promote the desired chemical reactions and to achieve the desired film characteristics such as composition, thickness, and crystallinity. Different CVD techniques can be employed depending on the specific requirements of the memristor device [48]. Each technique offers advantages in terms of control, scalability, and film quality. After deposition, the films are characterized using various analytical techniques to assess their properties. Techniques such as scanning electron microscopy (SEM), atomic force microscopy (AFM), x-ray diffraction (XRD), and electrical measurements are commonly used to evaluate the film morphology, crystal structure, composition, and RS behavior. In some cases, post-deposition treatments such as annealing or doping may be applied to further enhance the film properties and optimize the RS behavior of memristive devices. CVD is a versatile and widely used technique in the growth and fabrication of memristive devices. It offers precise control over film properties and enables the deposition of high-quality thin films with desirable RS characteristics.

1.3.1.2 Atomic layer deposition

ALD is a precise and controllable thin-film deposition technique that finds extensive applications in the fabrication of memristor RS devices. ALD offers atomic-level control over film thickness and uniformity, making it an ideal method for creating high-performance and reliable memristor devices. In this detailed explanation, we will explore the principles of ALD, its advantages, and its specific utilization in the fabrication of memristor RS devices. ALD operates based on a sequential and self-limiting process. It involves the exposure of a substrate to alternating pulses of gaseous reactants, creating a single atomic layer at a time. This self-limiting nature of ALD enables precise control over film thickness, conformality, and composition, making it well-suited for memristor device fabrication [50]. The ALD process typically consists of several steps. First, the substrate is exposed to a precursor gas, which chemically reacts with the substrate surface, forming a monolayer. The precursor gas is then purged, removing any excess or unreacted species. Next, a second reactant gas is introduced, which reacts with the previously formed monolayer, resulting in the growth of another atomic layer. This process of alternating precursor dosing, reactant exposure, and purging is repeated until the desired film thickness is achieved. One of the primary advantages of ALD in memristor fabrication is its ability to deposit conformal and uniform films on complex three-dimensional structures [51]. This is particularly important for memristors, which often have intricate nanostructures and require precise control over film deposition. ALD can coat high-aspect-ratio structures, such as nanowires or nanopores, ensuring consistent film quality throughout the device [50]. Furthermore, ALD enables the deposition of a wide range of materials with excellent control over stoichiometry and composition [50, 51]. The use of ALD in memristor fabrication has been extensively explored in research and development. For instance, ALD has been employed to deposit high-quality switching layers in RRAM devices. In RRAM, the switching layer undergoes reversible resistance changes, enabling non-volatile memory storage. ALD-deposited switching layers exhibit excellent uniformity, low defect densities, and controlled composition, leading to improved device performance and reliability. Moreover, ALD is valuable in the formation of conductive electrodes in memristor devices. ALD plays a crucial role in the fabrication of memristor RS devices. Its ability to provide atomic-level control over film thickness, conformality, and composition makes it an ideal technique for depositing high-quality switching layers and conductive electrodes [50]. The conformal deposition capability of ALD ensures uniformity in complex device geometries, while its material versatility allows for tailored memristor properties.

1.3.2 Device characterization

In recent years, memristive RS devices have become a subject of significant interest in the world of electronics due to their distinctive electrical behavior and their potential to revolutionize various fields. These devices are based on a special type of electronic component called a memristor, which possesses the remarkable ability to change its resistance in response to the flow of electrical charge. This unique property makes memristors highly valuable for memory and computing applications, as they can 'remember' their resistance state even when the power is turned off. To make the most of memristors and use them in practical ways, it is important to understand how they work. This understanding process is called 'characterization', where we study and analyse how memristors behave under different situations. In this section, we will explore the tools and techniques used to understand memristive RS devices better. By learning these things, we can uncover how memristors really work, find any challenges they might have, and tap into their full potential for new technologies such as advanced memory systems and neuromorphic computing.

Electrical I–V characterization using a probe station—is one of the fundamental techniques used to understand the RS behavior of memristors, as shown in figures 1.9. and 1.10. This technique involves applying a voltage across the device and measuring the resulting current. By sweeping the voltage across a specific range, one can identify the regions associated with different resistive states. *I–V* curves provide valuable insights into the switching dynamics, such as the compliance current, forming voltage, and the stability of the resistive states.

Compliance current in memristive devices is a preset limit on the maximum current allowed during switching from a HRS to an LRS. In an *I–V* curve, this

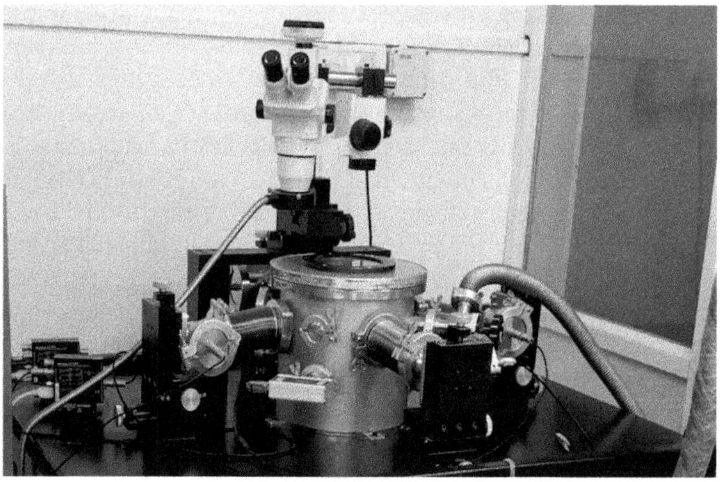

Figure 1.9. Electrical characterization using a probe station.

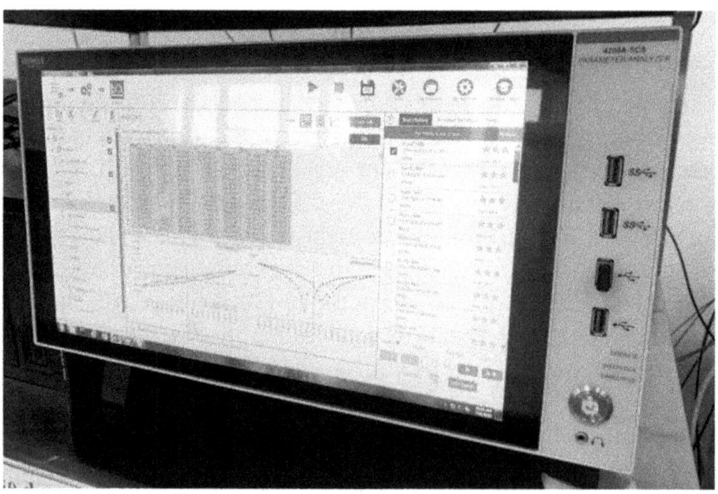

Figure 1.10. Keithley 4200-SCS Semiconductor Parameter Analyzer.

appears as a plateau where the current is capped despite increasing voltage. This limit prevents damage to the device by avoiding excessive current flow, ensuring reliable operation and prolonging the device's lifespan. Properly setting the compliance current is crucial; too low a limit can cause unstable switching, while too high a limit can degrade the device or cause breakdown. Time-dependent characterization techniques focus on studying the dynamic behavior of memristors during RS events. Pulse measurements, commonly known as pulse width modulation (PWM), involve applying short voltage pulses with varying widths and amplitudes to the device. By monitoring the current response during these pulses, critical information such as switching speed, endurance, and retention characteristics can be obtained [52]. Time-dependent characterization techniques are vital for assessing the performance and reliability of memristive devices under different operating conditions.

Conductive atomic force microscopy (C-AFM) is a powerful imaging technique that enables localized electrical characterization of memristive devices. By integrating an electrical probe with AFM, C-AFM allows for simultaneous topographic imaging and electrical measurements at a nanoscale resolution. This technique can provide valuable information about the distribution of resistive states, filament formation, and localized variations in device performance [53].

X-ray photoelectron spectroscopy (XPS) is a surface-sensitive technique that helps analyse the chemical composition and oxidation states of the materials in memristive devices. XPS can determine the presence of different elements, such as oxygen vacancies or metal ions, and provide insights into the device's RS mechanisms. By analysing the surface chemistry, XPS helps in understanding the relationship between the material properties and the device performance.

Transmission electron microscopy (TEM) is an advanced imaging technique that provides detailed information about the morphology of memristive devices. With TEM, it is possible to observe the formation and dissolution of conductive filaments, as well as examine the interfaces between different layers within the device. By visualizing the structural changes during RS events, TEM contributes to a better understanding of the underlying physical mechanisms.

Characterization tools and techniques play a vital role in unraveling the behavior and performance of memristive RS devices. *V–I* characterization, time-dependent techniques, C-AFM, XPS, and TEM are among the key methods used to understand the electrical properties, structural changes, and surface chemistry of memristive devices [54, 55]. By employing a combination of these techniques, researchers and engineers can gain valuable insights into the fundamental processes governing memristor operation, leading to improved device design and optimized performance for a wide range of applications.

1.3.3 Resistive switching in TMOs and 2D TMDs

By studying these materials in-depth, we gain insights into their behavior at the smallest levels and discover new avenues for their use in technology. TMOs are a fascinating class of materials characterized by the bonding of transition metal atoms with oxygen. The recent progress in non-volatile RRAM technology based on various binary metal oxides such as [34] TiO_2 [35], ZnO [36], NiO [37], WO_3 [39–41], CuO_x [42], TaO_x or [43] Ta_2O_5, and HfO_2 is reviewed. Significantly, TiO_2 and ZnO have extensively studied oxides that have been explored in various potential technological applications. This review also reflects that TiO_2 and ZnO possess the maximum number of reports for RRAM applications compared to the other binary metal oxides [34, 38]. One of the remarkable features of TMOs is their diverse and intricate structures, which can take on different arrangements, including octahedral, tetrahedral, and various distorted shapes. These structural variations lead to a broad spectrum of electronic and magnetic properties in TMOs, making them highly versatile and valuable for various applications. Due to their unique electronic structures, TMOs offer tunability, allowing researchers and engineers to fine-tune their properties for specific applications. Additionally, TMOs exhibit robust mechanical strength, making them durable and suitable for applications where material integrity is crucial. Another intriguing aspect of TMOs is their interaction with light, which opens up possibilities for utilizing them in optoelectronic devices and other light-based technologies. Understanding the layered structure of TMOs is of paramount importance as it directly influences their electrical conductivity, chemical reactivity, and interactions with other materials. This knowledge empowers scientists and engineers to harness the full potential of TMOs and design innovative materials and devices. As a result of these remarkable attributes, TMOs find applications in a wide array of fields, including electronics, sensors, catalysis, energy storage, and more [33]. The study of TMOs in memristive device systems has yielded significant insights, particularly in the context of RS-based NVM applications. These materials, known for their unique electronic and structural properties, have been central to the development of advanced memristive devices, contributing to both technological advancements and a deeper understanding of material behavior at the atomic and electronic levels. Singh *et al* [34] synthesized TMOs in device structures such as $TiN/TiO_x/HfO_x/TiN$ and $Ti/ZrO_2/Pt$, demonstrating the potential of these materials in creating stable and efficient memristive devices. These structures highlight the role of TMOs in achieving reliable switching behavior, essential for memory applications. Similarly, Kim *et al* [36] developed TMOs using a $TiN/Hf/HfO_x/TiN$ configuration, which further underscored the importance of precise material engineering in optimizing device performance, particularly in terms of endurance and retention. Govoreanu *et al* [37] introduced a novel TMO configuration using $Al/Ti/Al_2O_3$/s-CNTs, showcasing the versatility of TMOs in different device architectures. This work emphasized the potential of integrating TMOs with other materials such as CNTs to enhance device functionalities. Ahn *et al* [38] continued this exploration with the $TiN/TiO_x/HfO_x/TiN$ structure, reinforcing the significance of TMOs in achieving desirable memristive properties.

Further contributions to the field were made by Kumar *et al* [39], who developed a $Pt/Ta_2O_{5-x}/TaO_{2-x}/Pt$ structure, and Lee *et al* [40], who constructed devices using a $Ta/TaO_x/TiO_2/Ti$ configuration. These studies demonstrated how variations in TMO compositions and layer structures can lead to differences in switching mechanisms, offering insights into the optimization of memristive devices for specific applications. Baek *et al* [41] produced devices with a W/AlO/TaO_x/ZrO_x/Ru structure, illustrating the potential of TMOs in complex multilayered systems. Meanwhile, Kim *et al* [42, 43] synthesized TMOs with a Pt/Al_2O_3/HfO_2/Al_2O_3/TiN/Si structure, contributing to the understanding of how the interplay between different oxide layers can influence device performance, particularly in achieving high ON/OFF ratios and low power consumption. Cheng *et al* [45] added to this body of knowledge with a Ni/GeO/STO/TaN configuration, demonstrating the ongoing evolution of TMO-based devices and their potential in future NVM technologies. Collectively, these studies underscore the transformative potential of TMOs in memristive devices, with each contribution enhancing our understanding of how these materials can be harnessed to meet the stringent performance requirements of RS-based NVMs. As highlighted in table 1.1, the best performances of these TMO-based devices align closely with the technological requirements for future NVMs, suggesting that continued research in this area will be pivotal in driving innovation across various industries.

Table 1.1. Technology requirements for RS-based NVMs versus best performances reported for RS-based NVMs.

Parameter	Technology requirements	TMO based RRAMs		
		Best performances	Device structure	Reference
Operating voltages	< 1 V	0.7 V	TiN/TiO_x/HfO_x/TiN	[34]
		0.8 V	Ti/ZrO_2/Pt	[35]
		0.5 V	TiN/Hf/HfO_x/TiN	[36]
Power consumption	≈ 10 pJ per transition	0.1 pJ per transition	TiN/Hf/HfO_x/TiN	[36]
		0.1–7 pJ per transition	Al/Ti/Al_2O_3/s-CNT	[37]
Switching time	< 10 ns per transition	300 ps	TiN/TiO_x/HfO_x/TiN	[38]
		< 10 ns	TiN/TiO_x/HfO_x/TiN	[34]
		Approximately ns level	TiN/Hf/HfO_x/TiN	[36]
Endurance	> 10^9 cycles	10^{12} cycles	Pt/Ta_2O_{5-x}/TaO_{2-x}/Pt	[39]
		5 × 10^9 cycles	Pt/TaO_x/Pt	[40]
		> 10^{12} cycles	Ta/TaO_x/TiO_2/Ti	[41]
		10^{10} cycles	Pt/TaO_x/Ta	[41]
		10^{11} cycles	W/AlO/TaO_x/ZrO_x/Ru	[42]
Data retention	> 10 years	> 10 years at 85 °C	Pt/Al_2O_3/HfO_2/Al_2O_3/TiN/Si	[43]
		> 10 years at 85 °C	Pt/TaO_x/Pt	[40]
MIM cell size	576 nm^2	5 nm^2	TaN/TiN/Zr/HfO_2/C-AFM tip	[44]
I_{ON}/I_{OFF} ratio	10^6	3 × 10^6	Ni/GeO/STO/TaN	[45]
		2 × 10^6	Pt/Gd_2O_3/Pt	[46]

TMDs are made up of stacked layers of transition metal atoms and chalcogen atoms, such as sulfur or selenium. These layers are held together by weak van der Waals forces, allowing for easy separation into ultrathin sheets only a few atoms thick. These ultrathin TMD sheets have remarkable properties, including strong light interaction, efficient heat conduction, and flexibility. These properties make TMDs suitable for applications such as photodetectors, solar cells, and flexible electronics. Their exceptional properties have opened exciting possibilities for nanoscale devices with exceptional optical, and mechanical characteristics.

Both TMOs and TMDs exhibit a special ability of RS, which makes them excellent candidates for memristor technology. Memristors can change their resistance and retain that change even when the power is turned off. This property is valuable for NVM and neuromorphic computing. The RS in TMOs and TMDs is attributed to the movement of charged defects within the materials, creating or breaking pathways for electricity. Controlling this switching process is crucial for designing efficient memristive devices capable of storing large amounts of information in compact spaces. Moreover, TMOs and TMDs demonstrate compatibility with existing semiconductor fabrication techniques, making their integration into advanced memristor technologies seamless. This compatibility allows for their smooth integration into the advancement of sophisticated memristive systems. As we continue to study and explore these materials, we expect to uncover further exciting insights, and continued research will unlock their full potential and lead to significant advancements in how we store and process information in the next generation of electronic devices. The potential for revolutionizing electronics is immense, and these materials play a crucial role in shaping this exciting field.

Resistive switching, a fascinating phenomenon observed in various materials, has garnered significant attention in the field of electronics. This subsection focuses on two important classes of materials, namely TMOs and 2D TMDs, which exhibit intriguing RS behavior. Researchers and industry players are continuously exploring new materials and device architectures to improve the reliability, endurance, and manufacturability of RRAM technology. Various materials, such as metal oxides and chalcogenides, are being investigated to achieve better RS characteristics and lower switching voltages. TMOs boast a wide range of electronic, magnetic, and structural properties, making them ideal candidates for RS applications. Researchers have proposed various mechanisms for RS in TMOs, such as oxygen vacancy migration, metal cation migration, and filament formation/rupture. To implement TMO-based RS devices, different configurations such as metal–insulator–metal (MIM) and metal–insulator–semiconductor (MIS) are employed. Important performance metrics, including ON/OFF ratio, endurance, retention, and switching speed, are considered when evaluating TMO-based RS for application in NVM, neuromorphic computing, and analog circuits. Their potential for low-power operation and scalability makes TMO-based RS an attractive choice for future electronic devices.

Additionally, TMOs and TMDs offer adjustability in their electronic and optical properties, as well as flexibility, making them highly versatile for memristor technology [47]. Figure 1.11 presents a visual representation of different memristor

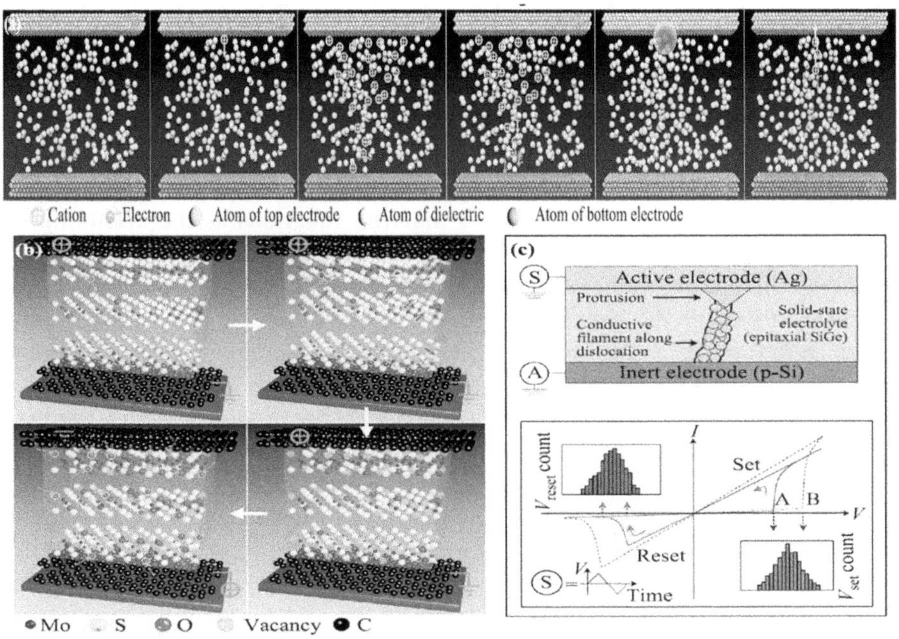

Figure 1.11. (a) The electrochemical metallization mechanism in 2D material based memristors is illustrated through schematic panels, showcasing the SET and RESET processes from left to right. (b) MoS_2-based memristors operate through the valence-change memory mechanism, where the SET and RESET processes are primarily governed by sulfur ion diffusion and migration, exchange between sulfur and oxygen ions, and oxygen ion diffusion and migration. (c) Memristors with a specially designed protrusion exhibit conductive-bridge behavior and display a characteristic *I–V* hysteresis curve. (Reprinted by permission from Springer Nature Customer Service Centre GmbH: Springer Nature, *Frontiers of Physics*, [16], copyright (2021).)

operation mechanisms. In figure 1.11(a), the electrochemical metallization mechanism in 2D material based memristors is illustrated. The schematic panels demonstrate the SET and RESET processes, depicting the electrochemical reactions involved as they progress from left to right. Figure 1.11(b) focuses on MoS_2-based memristors, which operate using the valence-change memory mechanism. The SET and RESET processes in these memristors primarily rely on sulfur ion diffusion and migration, exchange between sulfur and oxygen ions, and the diffusion and migration of oxygen ions [45–47]. These processes play a crucial role in controlling the resistance switching behavior of MoS_2-based memristors. In figure 1.11(c), memristors with engineered highlights exhibit conductive-bridge behavior, where the presence of a specially designed protrusion influences the formation and dissolution of conductive pathways. The resulting *I–V* hysteresis curve demonstrates the characteristic nonlinear relationship between the applied voltage and the resulting current, showcasing the unique electrical properties of memristors with engineered protrusions. Through these graphical representations, figure 1.11 provides valuable insights into the diverse operation mechanisms of memristors [16, 26, 48–57]. Understanding these mechanisms is essential for advancing the development and utilization of memristive devices in various fields, including electronics, computing, and beyond.

Figure 1.12 provides an in-depth characterization of the schematics, devices, and materials used in TMD crossbar structures. Figures 1.12(a) and (b) illustrate the MIM configurations formed by TMD crossbars, presented through schematic diagrams and optical images [58]. These visuals highlight the architecture of TMD crossbar devices, where the TMD material functions as the insulating layer positioned between metal electrodes. Figure 1.12(c) details a novel, lithography-free, and transfer-free sandwich structure employing a monolayer of molybdenum disulfide (MoS_2) directly grown on a gold (Au) foil, with gold electrodes serving as both the top (TE) and bottom (BE) contacts, unless specified otherwise. Figure 1.12(d) shows an optical image of a MoS_2-based, lithography-free device constructed with gold electrodes on a silicon/silicon dioxide (Si/SiO_2) substrate [31, 59]. The active region covered with MoS_2 is marked by a dashed box. Figure 1.12(e) presents a cross-sectional TEM image of this lithography-free device,

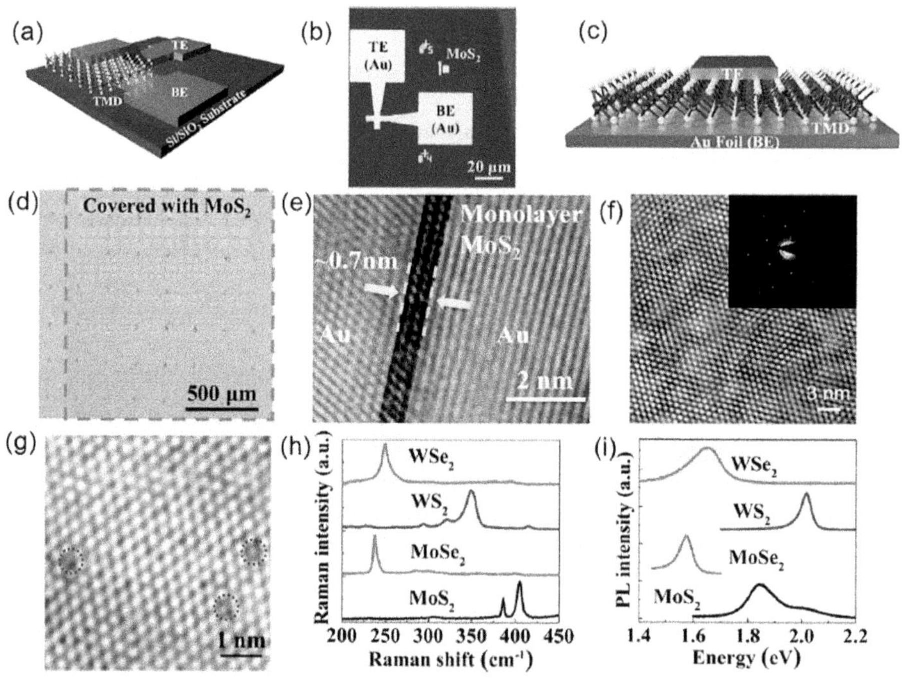

Figure 1.12. (a), (b) MIM structures of TMD crossbar sandwich illustrated through schematics and optical images. (c) Schematic of a lithography-free and transfer-free sandwich using TMD (MoS_2) grown with gold as the electrodes. (d) Optical image of MoS_2 litho-free devices with Au electrodes on a Si/SiO_2 substrate. The area covered with MoS_2 is indicated by the dashed box in panel (d). (e) TEM cross-section image of a litho-free device ($Au/MoS_2/Au$) revealing an atomically sharp and clean monolayer interface. (f) High-resolution TEM image of MoS_2 after being transferred onto a TEM grid. (g) Atomically resolved STM images of monolayer MoS_2 on Au. (h), (i) Raman and PL spectra of MOCVD-grown monolayer MoS_2, $MoSe_2$, WS_2 and WSe_2, used in some of the MIM device studies. (Reproduced with permission from [3]. Copyright 2018 American Chemical Society.)

revealing a clean, atomically sharp interface in the Au/MoS_2/Au structure, which demonstrates the high-quality contact achieved in these devices [60]. The high-resolution TEM image in figure 1.12(f) offers further insight into the atomic structure and uniformity of a MoS_2 monolayer after being transferred onto a TEM grid. Figure 1.12(g) features an atomically resolved scanning tunneling microscopy (STM) image of a MoS_2 monolayer on a gold substrate, confirming its monolayer nature and atomic arrangement. Figures 1.12(h) and (i) display Raman and photoluminescence (PL) spectra of various monolayers, including MoS_2, molybdenum diselenide ($MoSe_2$), tungsten disulfide (WS_2), and tungsten diselenide (WSe_2), synthesized via metal–organic CVD (MOCVD) [61–64].

These spectra serve to validate the material quality and confirm their monolayer properties, which are crucial for MIM device studies. Figure 1.12 presents a schematic overview of 2D TMD hybrid materials, emphasizing their current applications in energy-related fields and their potential to shape future energy technologies, particularly in memristive devices [65]. The unique two-dimensional structure of TMDs, consisting of transition metal atoms intercalated between chalcogen layers, grants them distinctive electronic, optical, and mechanical properties, making them highly attractive for applications in energy storage, catalysis, and photovoltaics [66]. The figure underscores the transformative potential of 2D TMD hybrid materials in advancing energy technologies, with a specific focus on their use in next-generation memristive devices [67]. Memristive devices are renowned for their resistance-dependent behavior and hold promise for advanced computing architectures and neuromorphic computing. Researchers and enthusiasts gain a deeper understanding of the significance of 2D TMD hybrid materials in the realm of energy applications and their far-reaching implications for the future of energy technologies [16]. 2D TMDs are atomically thin semiconductors known for their unique properties, including a direct bandgap and strong spin-orbit coupling [56]. The synthesis of 2D TMDs involves methods such as mechanical exfoliation and CVD [57].

In the realm of RS, 2D TMDs exhibit intriguing behavior driven by mechanisms such as field-driven ion migration, charge trapping, and phase change [58]. Defects and interfaces in 2D TMDs play pivotal roles in governing their RS behavior. To optimize device performance, researchers explore various device configurations, including vertical and lateral structures, while employing strategies such as strain engineering and interface engineering [58]. These efforts have led to potential applications of 2D TMD-based RS in flexible electronics, memristive systems, and neuromorphic computing [31]. The atomically thin nature of 2D TMDs also allows for their integration with other 2D materials, paving the way for novel device architectures. Figure 1.13 illustrates the key operational mechanisms of memristor devices that utilize 2D TMD materials, which are vital in defining their RS behavior. The filament formation schematic in figure 1.13(a) represents the process of conductive filament formation within the 2D TMD material [68]. In this mechanism, the application of an external electric field causes the migration and accumulation of ions (such as oxygen vacancies or metal cations) within the material, forming a localized conductive path (or filament) between the electrodes. This filament connects the top and bottom electrodes, reducing the device's

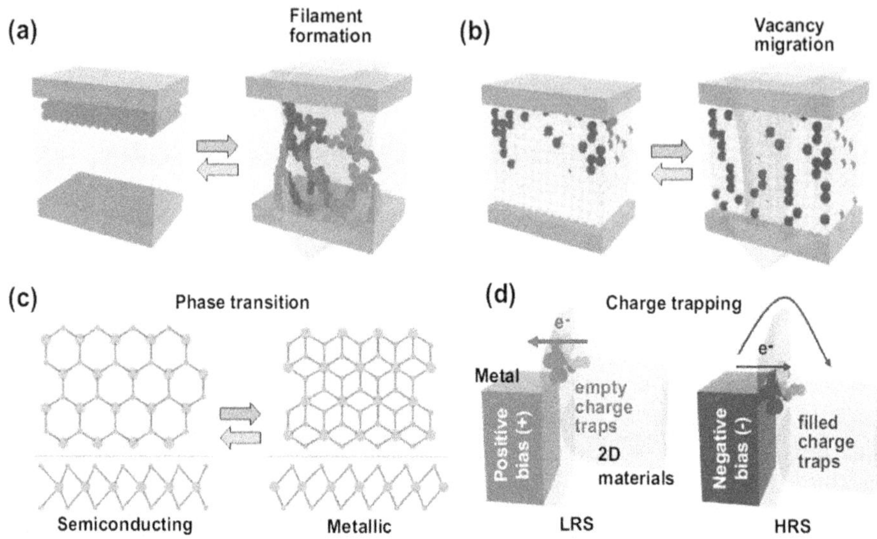

Figure 1.13. The exemplary operational mechanisms of memristor devices utilizing 2D TMD materials, along with corresponding schematic depictions: (a) filament formation, (b) vacancy migration, (c) phase transition, and (d) charge trapping. (Reproduced from [31]. CC BY 4.0.)

resistance and switching it to an LRS. Breaking or dissolving the filament through a reverse voltage returns the device to a HRS [69]. The vacancy migration mechanism in figure 1.13(b) is based on the movement of atomic vacancies, such as sulfur or selenium vacancies, within the 2D TMD material. Under an applied voltage, these vacancies migrate towards one of the electrodes, altering the material's conductivity. The accumulation or depletion of vacancies near the electrode interface modulates the resistance of the device, allowing it to switch between high- and low-resistance states. This migration is reversible, enabling multiple cycles of RS. The phase transition schematic in figure 1.13(c) depicts the phase transition mechanism, where the switching behavior of the memristor relies on a reversible change in the material phase [70]. For instance, the application of an external voltage can induce a transition from an insulating phase to a more conductive metallic phase, thereby altering the resistance state of the device. This mechanism leverages the unique ability of certain 2D TMD materials to undergo phase changes under electrical stimulation, making them suitable for NVM applications. The illustration of charge trapping in figure 1.13(d) shows the charge trapping and detrapping mechanism. Here, RS is achieved through the trapping of charges (such as electrons or holes) at defective sites or within localized energy states in the 2D TMD material. When a voltage is applied, charges are trapped at these sites, leading to a change in the local conductivity and, hence, the overall resistance of the device. Reversing the voltage can release the trapped charges, returning the device to its original resistance state. Figure 1.13 presents an in-depth exploration of the operational mechanisms of memristor devices that leverage 2D TMD materials. Memristors, with their unique resistance-retentive properties, hold tremendous promise in revolutionizing neuromorphic computing and non-volatile memory applications [71].

In summary, figure 1.13 presents four pivotal operational processes through schematic illustrations and accompanying labels, such as filament formation, demonstrating how a conductive filament is either established or dissolved within the 2D TMD material under the influence of an electric field; this process profoundly impacts the resistance behavior of the memristor [5]. For vacancy migration, showcasing the movement of charged vacancies within the 2D TMD material, this schematic highlights how the memristor's resistance undergoes alterations due to changes in material conductivity. The phase transition phenomenon takes place within the 2D TMD material when subjected to an electric field, signifying significant variations in resistance and the device memory capabilities. Charge trapping is the trapping and release of charge carriers within the TMD material; this process intricately contributes to the modulation of memristor resistance and memory functions.

Memristive devices have benefited greatly from the use of diverse materials, each offering unique properties that enhance device performance, reliability, and scalability. For example, the TiN/AlN/graphene (G)/Pd structure utilizes the insulating properties of aluminum nitride (AlN) combined with the high conductivity of graphene, resulting in devices with improved endurance and fast switching speeds, suitable for memory and neuromorphic computing [72–74]. Similarly, the Au/Ti/MoS_2/Ti/Au structure leverages the semiconducting properties of molybdenum disulfide (MoS_2) to enable low-power operation and high switching speeds, making it ideal for flexible electronics [72]. The W/MoS_2/SiO_2/p-Si configuration combines tungsten electrodes with MoS_2 and silicon dioxide (SiO_2) layers, achieving high switching performance with compatibility for integration into existing semiconductor technology, which is promising for non-volatile memory applications [73]. Other notable structures include Cu/MoS_2/Au, which uses copper high conductivity and MoS_2 semiconducting properties to offer reduced fabrication costs and potential for large-scale production in memory devices [74]. The Ag/MoS_2/Pt and Ag/MoS_2/Ag configurations exploit the filament-forming properties of silver and the unique characteristics of MoS_2, resulting in reliable, bidirectional switching suitable for neuromorphic computing [75]. The Ag/WSe_2/Ag and Pd/WS_2/Pt structures utilize two-dimensional materials such as tungsten diselenide (WSe_2) and tungsten disulfide (WS_2), which provide high electron mobility and efficient RS, promising for optoelectronics and low-power applications [76]. Finally, the Ag/ZrO_2/WS_2/Pt device combines zirconium dioxide's high dielectric constant with WS_2 semiconducting properties, enhancing switching performance for applications such as neuromorphic computing and high-density storage [77, 78]. These material combinations in memristive devices demonstrate the potential for advancements across various fields, including memory, artificial intelligence, and flexible electronics, by optimizing the choice of materials for specific performance needs [79].

By deciphering the operational principles depicted in figure 1.13, researchers and industry experts gain a deeper understanding of memristor devices using 2D TMD materials, propelling advancements in electronic components and paving the way for cutting-edge memory technologies. Resistive switching in both TMOs and 2D TMDs holds immense promise for the development of next-generation electronic devices. The distinct properties and switching mechanisms of these materials offer a versatile platform for a wide range of applications. However, further research and exploration are necessary to fully realize the potential of these materials in advanced memristive systems. Figure 1.14(a) presents a schematic of the mechanical exfoliation of MoS_2 using adhesive tape, a key technique for producing 2D materials with controlled thickness, highlighting the precise separation of layers. Figure 1.14(b) illustrates the chemical vapor deposition (CVD) process for MoS_2 synthesis, a widely used method in 2D material fabrication, where a sulfur source reacts with a molybdenum source to deposit MoS_2 on a substrate, thereby demonstrating the growth mechanism. Figure 1.14(c) depicts a vertical MoS_2 memristor schematically, highlighting its unique properties and functionality. Figure 1.14(d) is a schematic illustration of the lateral MoS_2 memristor, showcasing its distinct structure and operation, each with a focus on different aspects related to MoS_2 and memristor technology. Table 1.2 lists the properties of various 2D materials used in memristive neuromorphic circuits.

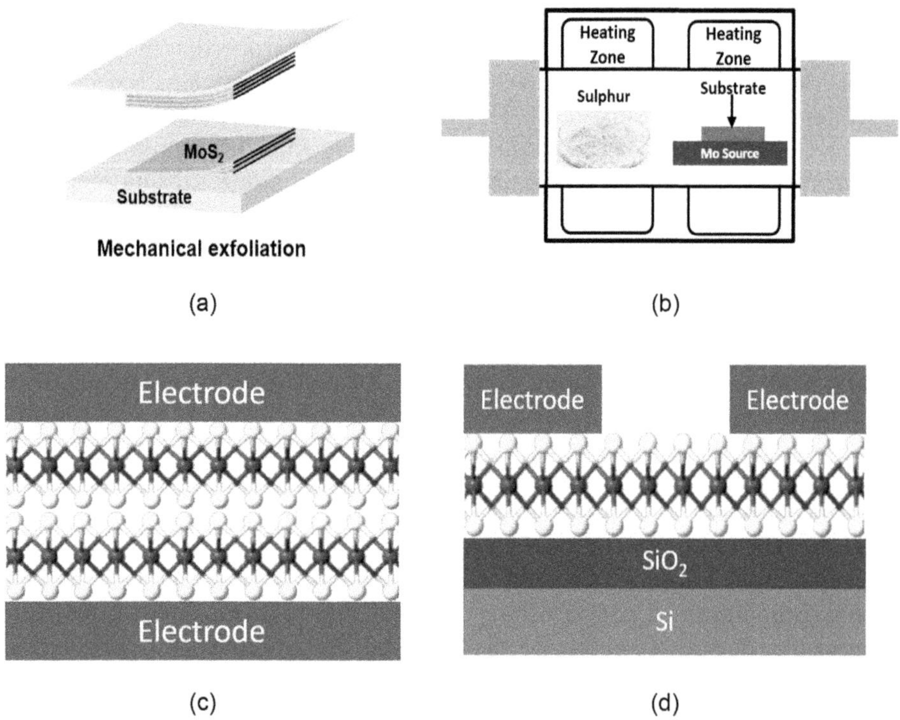

Figure 1.14. (a) The process of mechanically exfoliating MoS_2 with the assistance of tape. (b) The process of CVD, where a sulfur source reacts with a Mo source to deposit MoS_2 on the substrate. (c) The vertical MoS_2 memristor and its properties. (d) The lateral MoS_2 memristor and its properties. (Reprinted by permission from Springer Nature Customer Service Centre GmbH: Springer Nature, Science China Infortmation Sciences, [80], coypright 2023.)

Table 1.2. Different 2D materials used for memristive neuromorphic circuits.

Memristive device	Power consumption		Indicators for spiking neural networks (SNNs)		R_{OFF}/R_{ON}	Retention (s)	RS mechanism	Reference
	Voltage (V)	Energy per spike	PPF (%)	STDP (%)				
Au/Ti/MoS_2/Ti/Au	NA	6.46 pJ	280	270/−38	NA	NA	NA	[72]
W/MoS_2/SiO_2/P-Si	NA	0.1 nJ	130	NA	NA	NA	Interfacial potential barrier	[73]
Cu/MoS_2/Au	0.25/–0.15	NA	NA	20/–50	> 5	1.8×10^4	CM	[74]
Ag/MoS_2/Pt	0.8/–0.6	600 fJ	80	80/–60	$> 10^2$	10^5	CM	[75]
Ag/MoS_2/Ag	0.18/−0.3	4.5 fJ	150	NA	$> 10^7$	10^4	CM	[76]
Ag/WSe_2/Ag	0.7/0.3	NA	NA	NA	$> 10^3$	10^4	Selenium vacancies	[77]
Pd/WS_2/Pt	0.6/−0.2	299.8 fJ	100	90/−90	NA	NA	Sulfur and tungsten vacancies	[78]
Ag/ZrO2/WS_2/Pt	0.16/−0.06	NA	70/−40	45	$> 10^6$	10^4	CM	[79]

1.3.4 TMOs and 2D TMDs: material properties and selection criteria

TMOs are a class of materials that consist of transition metals (elements in the d-block of the periodic table) combined with oxygen. They exhibit a wide range of interesting properties, making them suitable for various applications such as electronics, catalysis, and energy storage [39–43]. TMOs are well-known for their diverse electronic, magnetic, and optical properties. For instance, some TMOs can exhibit metal-to-insulator transitions, where they switch from being conductive to insulating as temperature or other external factors change. This property makes them promising candidates for memristive devices, which are essential components in neuromorphic computing and artificial intelligence applications [45].

2D TMDs are a family of materials that belong to the class of two-dimensional materials, which means they are composed of single or few atomic layers. These materials have gained significant attention in recent years due to their unique electronic, optical, and mechanical properties [46]. One of the fascinating properties of 2D TMDs is the existence of a direct bandgap in their electronic structure, unlike their bulk counterparts. This direct bandgap makes them suitable for optoelectronic devices, such as photodetectors and light-emitting diodes (LEDs). Moreover, 2D TMDs have shown promise in memristive applications. Memristors based on 2D TMDs can provide advantages such as high speed, low energy consumption, and scalability, making them potential candidates for next-generation memory and neuromorphic computing devices [72–79].

1.3.5 Structural and chemical characterization

The structural and chemical characterization of memristive devices plays a crucial role in understanding their properties and performance. In this context, optical and electron microscopy techniques are essential tools for investigating the properties of the materials used in these devices. Here, we will discuss how optical measurements, SEM, and TEM have been employed to study and analyse the MoS_2 thin films used in the fabrication of optical memristor devices.

The first step in the characterization process involves using optical measurements to study the optical properties of MoS_2 thin films. The results from these measurements revealed a strong absorption band in the visible light region. This important finding suggests that MoS_2 thin films could be promising candidates for fabricating optical memristor devices. The ability of MoS_2 to absorb visible light effectively opens up opportunities for utilizing light-induced effects in the operation and functionality of the memristor devices. Further, SEM was employed to investigate the surface morphology of MoS_2 nanosheets. The images obtained through SEM showed that the nanosheets possess a smooth surface with few defects. This surface characteristic is highly advantageous for achieving superior performance in memristor devices. A smooth surface with minimal defects ensures a more uniform and reliable behavior of the device during its operation. It contributes to the stability and endurance of the memristor, making it a more robust and long-lasting component in electronic circuits. The deposited MoS_2 monolayer properties were analysed using several techniques [83], including AFM, Raman spectroscopy, PL, and XPS.

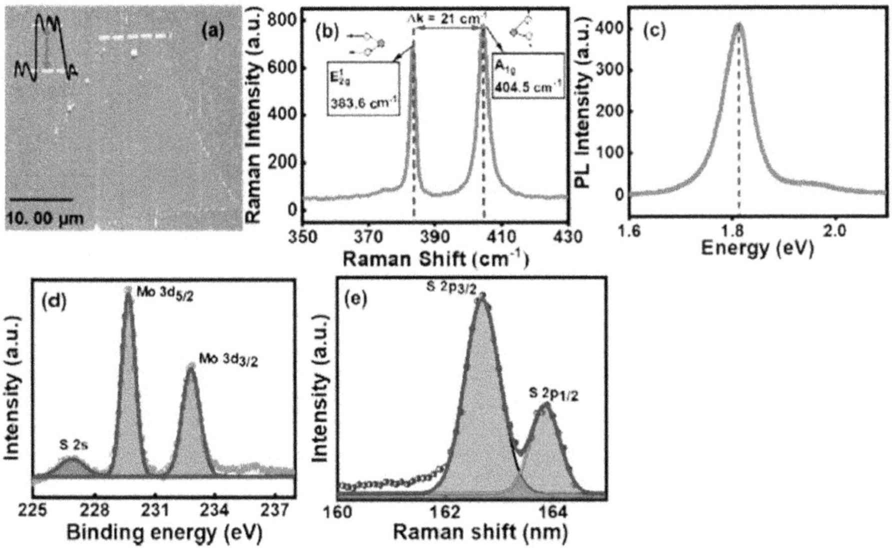

Figure 1.15. (a) AFM, (b) Raman, and (c) PL spectra of the MoS_2 monolayer. XPS spectra of (d) Mo 3d and (e) S 2p [83].

Figure 1.15(a) shows the surface structure and thickness of the MoS_2 monolayer on a SiO_2/Si substrate, indicating a uniform monolayer with a thickness of about 0.7 nm, as confirmed by the depth profile in the inset. The edges of adjacent MoS_2 crystals are depicted. The Raman spectrum in figure 1.15(b) shows distinct peaks at 383.6 cm^{-1} (E_2g, in-plane) and 404.5 cm^{-1} (A_1g, out-of-plane). The 21 cm^{-1} difference between these peaks and their similar intensities confirm the monolayer structure of MoS_2 and match the known literature, indicating a surface exposed along the basal plane. The PL spectrum of the MoS_2 monolayer is shown in figure 1.15(c). XPS analysis was used to determine the electronic structure and crystal phase of the MoS_2, with figures 1.15(d) and (e) displaying the core-level spectra for Mo 3d and S 2p, respectively. The Mo 3d spectrum shows double peaks at 229 eV (Mo $3d_{5/2}$) and 232 eV (Mo $3d_{3/2}$), aligning with known binding energy values and lacking a peak at 236 eV, which indicates no Mo–O interaction. Similarly, the S 2p spectrum shows peaks at 163 eV (S $2p_{3/2}$) and 164 eV (S $2p_{1/2}$), with no higher energy peaks, confirming the sulfur atoms are unoxidized [83]. These XPS findings confirm the formation of the 2H-MoS_2 crystal phase rather than the 1T-MoS_2 phase, as noted in earlier studies. Additionally, figure 1.15(e) shows a strong PL peak around 1.8 eV, verifying the monolayer structure and high crystalline quality of the MoS_2.

Moreover, TEM was used to capture cross-sectional images of the MoS_2 thin films. The TEM images exhibited a uniform thickness of the films and a well-defined interface between the MoS_2 and the substrate. These features are critical for achieving high-quality performance in memristor devices. The uniform thickness ensures consistent electrical properties across the device, avoiding variations that might hinder its functionality. Additionally, a well-defined interface between MoS_2 and the substrate ensures efficient charge transport, which is essential for the RS system to show a reliable and rapid response to external stimuli. The combined use of optical measurements, SEM, and TEM has provided valuable insights into the structural and chemical properties of MoS_2 thin films, which are essential for understanding and optimizing the performance of memristor devices. By gaining a deeper understanding of the material's characteristics, researchers and engineers can enhance the design and fabrication of mutlilayer MoS_2 thin films.

In addition to optical measurements, SEM, and TEM, AFM is another crucial technique utilized for the structural and chemical characterization of memristive devices. AFM is a powerful imaging technique that allows researchers to visualize and measure the surface topography of materials at the nanoscale. By using a sharp probe that scans the surface, AFM generates high-resolution images, providing valuable information about the surface roughness, grain size, and other surface features of the material. In the context of memristive devices based on MoS_2 thin films, AFM can be used to study the nanoscale morphology of the films. It can reveal details about the individual MoS_2 nanosheets, such as their height, lateral dimensions, and surface roughness. This information is crucial for understanding how the nanosheets' physical characteristics influence the RS device's overall performance. Additionally, AFM plays a key role in identifying defects or imperfections on the MoS_2 thin-film surface, which can significantly impact the RS device's electronic properties, such as conductivity, switching behavior, and stability. By providing high-resolution images and quantifying surface features, AFM enables researchers to gain deeper insights into the relationship between material structure and device performance.

1.4 Analytical and physical electro-thermal modeling of nanoscale memristors

Nanoscale memristors have emerged as highly promising devices that hold significant potential in various electronic and computing applications. These cutting-edge components exhibit exceptional electrical characteristics, such as NVM, low power consumption, and synaptic-like behavior. These qualities make them indispensable in the advancement of neuromorphic computing systems and future memory technologies. To fully harness the capabilities of these nanoscale memristors, a comprehensive understanding and accurate modeling of their electro-thermal behavior are essential.

The electro-thermal aspects of these devices play a crucial role in their performance and reliability. In this section, we aim to delve deep into the analytical and physical aspects of electro-thermal modeling, shedding light on the underlying principles that govern the behavior of these nanoscale memristors. Through this exploration, we hope to provide valuable insights and practical knowledge for researchers and engineers working in this exciting field. Moreover, we present an investigation of the nonlinearity and transient behaviors exhibited by memristors. Understanding these dynamic characteristics is vital for designing effective analytical models that can faithfully represent their intricate behavior under various conditions. In addition, we will explore the applications of memristors in systems such as neuromorphic computing and memory devices. Utilizing analytical modeling techniques, we will analyse the performance of these systems to gain a deeper understanding of their efficiency and potential for real-world implementation.

Nanoscale memristors have emerged as a promising candidate for revolutionizing electronic devices and computing architectures due to their unique properties and potential applications in various fields. As electronic devices continue to shrink, conventional modeling approaches face challenges in accurately capturing the behavior of these nanoscale components. Therefore, the development of analytical and physical electro-thermal models specifically tailored for nanoscale memristors has become a critical area of research. The integration of memristors into electronic circuits offers benefits such as non-volatile memory, neuromorphic computing, and energy-efficient computing, among others [81]. However, to fully harness these advantages, a deep understanding of their electrical and thermal characteristics is essential.

The research community has made significant steps in developing accurate models for nanoscale memristors, drawing inspiration from a wide range of disciplines, including solid-state physics, materials science, and electrical engineering. Analytical models based on fundamental principles help in gaining insights into the underlying physics governing memristive behavior [81]. Additionally, physical models leverage advanced simulation techniques, such as finite element analysis and quantum mechanical simulations, to capture intricate electro-thermal phenomena occurring at the nanoscale. We provide a comprehensive review of the state-of-the-art analytical and physical electro-thermal modeling techniques applied to nanoscale memristors by synthesizing and analysing the research findings from various studies. We aim to present a cohesive understanding of the current landscape in this field and identify potential avenues for future research.

1.4.1 Analytical modeling approaches

To gain a better understanding of memristors, one can adopt an analytical model approach, developing a smart model using analytical methods. This model helps researchers to comprehend how memristors behave at different stages of processing. Analytical models are crucial as they provide profound insights into the workings of memristors. Given their significance in brain-inspired computers, a thorough understanding is essential to fully exploit their capabilities in advanced computing. By revealing the essential equations that describe their operations, we achieve a profound grasp of these intriguing components. One distinguishing aspect of our approach lies in its ability to handle the unique features of memristors, such as their adaptability and response to various situations. Incorporating these crucial aspects into an analytical model yields a more realistic understanding of memristors' functionality in real-world scenarios.

The memristance value can be determined by analysing the current passing through the memristor. This implies that when the current flow is interrupted in the

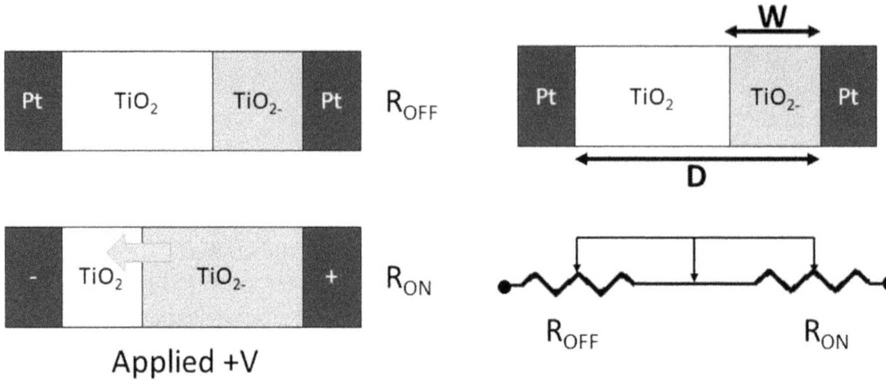

Figure 1.16. Working principle of a memristive device.

memristor, it preserves its memristance value. Subsequently, when the current passes through the memristor again, the memristance value will change from its previously retained value, which was recorded before the interruption occurred [82]. A memristor is analogous to a resistor with memory with the *I–V* curve of the memristor shows the pinched hysteresis loop characteristic. If a bipolar signal that is periodic in nature is applied to a memristor it shows a pinched hysteresis *I–V* characteristic that always crosses the origin. As the frequency of the applied signal increases the pinched hysteresis loop shows a singled valued function and behaves as a linear resistor. When the frequency reaches infinity, the pinched hysteresis loop behaves as a single-valued function which has resemblance to the resistor following Ohm's law. Memristor-based applications require an appropriate model for analysis and simulation of the system. From the literature, we can see that the HP memristor model works on the principle of the drift of oxygen vacancies [82]. In The HP Labs model, positively charged oxygen vacancies are present at one side of the TiO_2 oxide layer, which is sandwiched between the two noble metallic layers, i.e. platinum, as shown in figure 1.16 [82].

1.4.2 Physical electro-thermal modeling approaches

Memristors, the intriguing memory resistors with their unique ability to remember previous resistance states, have become a subject of immense interest due to their diverse applications in cutting-edge technologies. As these devices are increasingly integrated into electronic systems, comprehending their electrical and thermal behavior has become paramount for optimal performance and reliability. This has led to the development of physical electro-thermal modeling approaches that aim to capture the intricate interactions between electrical and thermal phenomena in memristors [83]. In this section, we investigate various models that have been proposed to elucidate the behavior of memristors under different operating conditions. This investigation covers electrical models to describe dynamic behavior and thermal models to understand heat generation and dissipation mechanisms.

Moreover, we explore the coupling of electrical and thermal models to predict the overall behavior of the device accurately. By exploring these physical electro-thermal modeling approaches, we can pave the way for the advancement and deployment of memristor-based technologies in memory storage, neuromorphic computing, and beyond, ushering in a new era of electronics innovation.

Memristive devices, which consist of an MIM multilayer structure with an insulating layer sandwiched between two metal electrodes, operate based on RS mechanisms. These mechanisms lead to either an 'ON' or 'OFF' state in response to external electrical bias. Depending on the oxide thickness, the dominant switching mechanisms can be either interfacial or electroforming. At larger oxide thickness ($\geqslant$50 nm), interfacial or bulk conduction dominates the switching mechanism, while at lower thickness the electroforming process takes over [84]. In the electroforming process, the switching is caused by the formation or rupture of conductive filaments (CFs) between the top and bottom electrodes of the memristive device. Memristive devices offer great potential for the future NVM market due to their high density and cost-effectiveness in a 3D crossbar array configuration. Previous research has focused on various aspects of memristive devices, such as physical electro-thermal modeling of Ta_2O_5 bilayer-based RRAM [85] and physics-based compact numerical models for HfO_2-based RRAM [86]. However, some of these studies had limitations, such as large device dimensions lacking consideration of heating and electric field distribution effects on ionic movement, or assumptions about the independence of resistance in CFs.

The proposed 3D physical electro-thermal model for nanoscale Y_2O_3-based memristive devices with a device size of 10 nm (radius of the top electrode) utilizes a quantitative thermodynamic numerical approach and is implemented in COMSOL, allowing the solution of partial differential equations using the finite element method (FEM) [75]. This model considers heat transfer and electrodynamic equations to accurately simulate the behavior of Y_2O_3-based memristive devices. The researchers worked on fixing the problems that earlier studies had and took into account all the important physical and thermal factors related to tiny memristive devices. This helped them learn much more about how these small devices actually work. As a result, they made significant progress in understanding nanoscale memristive devices. This new found knowledge opens up exciting possibilities for using these devices in advanced memory technologies that can store data even when the power is turned off. This is a route that may lead to potential applications of these devices in future, cutting-edge data storage technologies.

1.4.3 Experimental validation

Memristors are very interesting because they can be used in advanced memory and computing devices. They can switch between two different resistance states (high-resistance and low-resistance) when we apply electricity to them. Memristors have emerged as promising candidates for next-generation NVM and bioinspired neuromorphic computing due to their rapid switching capabilities and compatibility with existing complementary metal oxide semiconductor (CMOS) fabrication processes. The fundamental principle of memristors involves toggling between high-resistance and low-resistance states under external electrical stimuli. To achieve this switching, CFs must form inside the memristor switching layer through an electroforming process, which necessitates a sufficiently large input voltage [87, 88]. However, the dynamics of CF formation strongly influence the memristor switching performance, making the minimization of CF formation energy a critical aspect [89–92].

By layering deposition of Y_2O_3 on a silicon substrate, adding metal electrodes, and testing the device behavior with different voltages, researchers found slight variations in the memristors response, which they linked to specific factors in the fabrication process. The Y_2O_3-based memristor structure can have symmetric or asymmetric top and bottom electrodes. In symmetric combinations, the same metal (Al, Mo, Au, Ag, Pd, Ta, TiN) is used for both the TE and the BE. In asymmetric combinations, active metal Ag is used as the TE, while different metals such as Al, Au, Mo, Pd, Ta, and TiN are used as the BE. The simulated device structure includes a thick SiO_2 insulating layer surrounding the memristor. This layer acts as a heat shield, maintaining a stable temperature during switching operations. The memristor's total thickness is 100 nm, with a 65 nm BE, 5 nm Y_2O_3 switching layer, and 30 nm TE.

The memristor RS process consists of two main stages, 'SET' and 'RESET'. During the SET process, two sub-processes occur, fast shunting of electrodes and the radial growth of CFs. The RESET process also involves two sub-processes, nucleation and growth of the gap due to rupturing of CFs [90, 91]. Researchers used COMSOL Multiphysics and physics-based equations to simulate and model the SET and RESET processes. They considered various physical parameters and their numerical values to better understand the behavior of the memristor during switching [92].

1.5 Conclusion

As we conclude this chapter on the fundamentals of RS, we have explored its foundational concepts, historical developments, advantages, and diverse applications. A detailed analysis of the materials and structures involved, particularly focusing on TMOs and TMDs, has demonstrated their significant role in enabling memristive technologies. In discussing the switching behavior of these materials, we delved into the essential processes of SET and RESET, which are central to the functioning of memristive devices. Using advanced simulation tools such as COMSOL Multiphysics, along with physics-based equations, researchers have been able to model these complex processes, offering deeper insights into the physical mechanisms that govern memristor behavior. This understanding is crucial for optimizing device performance and paving the way for new applications in the future. In the upcoming chapters, we will explore how RS devices are applied in selector-based memristive crossbar technology, addressing both their operational principles and the challenges involved in their design and integration.

Bibliography

[1] Chua L 1971 Memristor—the missing circuit element *IEEE Trans. Circuit Theory* **18** 507–19

[2] Lanza M *et al* 2021 Standards for the characterization of endurance in resistive switching devices *ACS Nano* **15** 17214–31

[3] Ge R *et al* 2018 Atomristor: nonvolatile resistance switching in atomic sheets of transition metal dichalcogenides *Nano Lett.* **18** 434–41

[4] Longnos F *et al* 2013 On the impact of Ag doping on performance and reliability of GeS_2-based conductive bridge memories *Solid State Electron.* **84** 155–9

[5] Ando K, Fujita S, Hayashikoshi M and Fujimori Y 2017 Non-volatile memories *Normally-Off Computing* (Tokyo: Springer)

[6] Min K, Jung D and Kwon Y 2021 Investigation of switching uniformity in resistive memory via finite element simulation of conductive-filament formation *Sci. Rep.* **11** 2447

[7] Sebastian A *et al* 2020 Memory devices and applications for in-memory computing *Nat. Nanotechnol.* **15** 529–44

[8] Markovic D *et al* 2020 Physics for neuromorphic computing *Nat. Rev. Phys.* **2** 499–510

[9] Xiaoyue J, Dong Z, Zhou G, Lai C S, Yan Y and Qi D 2021 Memristive system based image processing technology: a review and perspective *Electronics* **10** 3176

[10] Rose G S, Rajendran J, Manem H, Karri R and Pino R E 2012 Leveraging memristive systems in the construction of digital logic circuits *Proc. IEEE Conf.* **100** 2033–49

[11] Gao Y, Kavehei O, Sarawi S F A, Ranasinghe D C and Abbott D 2016 Read operation performance of large selectorless cross-point array with self-rectifying memristive device *Integration* **54** 56–64

[12] Cagli C, Nardi F and Ielmini D 2009 Modeling of set/reset operations in NiO-based resistive-switching memory devices *IEEE Trans. Electron Devices* **56** 1712–20

[13] Borghetti J *et al* 2010 Memristive' switches enable 'stateful' logic operations via material implication *Nature* **464** 873–6

[14] Sawa A 2008 Resistive switching in transition metal oxides *Mater. Today* **11** 28–36

[15] Yang J J, Zhang M-X, Strachan J P, Miao F, Pickett M D, Kelley R D, Medeiros-Ribeiro G and Williams R S 2010 High switching endurance in TaO_x memristive devices *Appl. Phys. Lett.* **97** 232102

[16] Zhou Z 2022 Emerging of two-dimensional materials in novel memristor *Front. Phys.* **17** 23204

[17] Pershin Y V and Ventra M D 2011 Memory effects in complex materials and nanoscale systems *Adv. Phys.* **2** 145–227

[18] Zrinski I, Minenkov A, Mardare C C, Hassel A W and Mardare A I 2021 Composite memristors by nanoscale modification of Hf/Ta anodic oxides *J. Phys. Chem. Lett.* **12** 8917–23

[19] Jo S H, Chang T, Ebong I, Bhadviya B B, Mazumder P and Lu W 2010 Nanoscale memristor device as synapse in neuromorphic systems *Nano Lett.* **10** 1297–301

[20] Yang J *et al* 2008 Memristive switching mechanism for metal/oxide/metal nanodevices *Nat. Nanotech.* **3** 429–33

[21] Strukov D *et al* 2008 The missing memristor found *Nature* **453** 80–3

[22] Enaganti P K, Kothuru A and Goel S 2022 Laser-induced graphene-based miniaturized, flexible, non-volatile resistive switching memory devices *J. Mater. Res.* **37** 3976–87

[23] Lee J H, Lim D H, Jeong H, Ma H and Shi L 2019 Exploring cycle-to-cycle and device-to-device variation tolerance in MLC storage-based neural *IEEE Trans. Electron Devices* **66** 2172–8

[24] Maheshwari S *et al* 2021 Design flow for hybrid CMOS/memristor systems—part II: circuit schematics and layout *IEEE Trans. Circuits Syst.* I **68** 4876–88

[25] Rana A *et al* 2017 Endurance and cycle-to-cycle uniformity improvement in tri-layered CeO_2/Ti/CeO_2 resistive switching devices by changing top electrode *Mater. Sci. Rep.* **7** 39539

[26] Liu C *et al* 2020 Two-dimensional materials for next-generation computing technologies *Nat. Nanotechnol.* **15** 545–57

[27] Dastanova N, Duisenbay S, Krestinskaya O and James A P 2018 Bit-plane extracted moving-object detection using memristive crossbar-CAM arrays for edge computing image devices *IEEE Access* **6** 18954–66

[28] Nili H *et al* 2018 Hardware-intrinsic security primitives enabled by analogue state and nonlinear conductance variations in integrated memristors *Nat. Electron.* **1** 197–202

[29] Ibrayev T *et al* 2018 On-chip face recognition system design with memristive hierarchical temporal memory *J. Intell. Fuzzy Syst.: Appl. Eng. Technol.* **68** 1393–402

[30] Kourosh K, Jian Z O, Torben D, Arnan M, Takayoshi S and Michael S F 2016 Two dimensional and layered transition metal oxides *Appl. Mater. Today* **5** 73–89

[31] Kwon K C *et al* 2022 Memristive devices based on two-dimensional transition metal chalcogenides for neuromorphic computing *Nano-Micro Lett.* **14** 58

[32] Choudhary N, Islam M A, Kim J H, Ko T J, Schropp A, Hurtado L, Weitzman D, Zhai L and Jung Y 2018 Two-dimensional transition metal dichalcogenide hybrid materials for energy applications *Nano Today* **19** 16–40

[33] Chimene D, Alge D L and Gaharwar A K 2015 Two-dimensional nanomaterials for biomedical applications: emerging trends and future prospects *Adv. Mater.* **27** 7261–84

[34] Singh C and Ray N 2023 Memristors and resistive switching in metal oxides *Optical Properties of Metal Oxide Nanostructures* Progress in Optical Science and Photonics vol 26 *ed V Kumar, I Ayoub, V Sharma and H C Swart (Singapore: Springer)*

[35] Kim S and Park B G 2016 Power and low resistance state dependent bipolar reset-switching transitions in SiN-based resistive random-access memory *Nanoscale Res. Lett.* **11** 360

[36] Govoreanu B *et al* 2011 10×10 nm^2 Hf/HfO_x crossbar resistive RAM with excellent performance, reliability and low-energy operation *2011 Int. Electron Devices Meeting (Washington, DC)* pp 31.6.1–4

[37] Ahn C, Jiang Z, Lee C S, Chen H Y, Liang J, Liyanage L S and Wong H S P 2015 1D selection device using carbon nanotube FETs for high-density cross-point memory arrays *IEEE Trans. Electron Devices* **62** 2197

[38] Patil A R, Dongale T D, Kamat R K and Rajpure K Y 2023 Binary metal oxide-based resistive switching memory devices: a status review *Mater. Today Commun.* **34** 105356

[39] Lee M J *et al* 2011 A fast, high-endurance and scalable non-volatile memory device made from asymmetric Ta_2O_{5-x}/TaO_{2-x} bilayer structures *Nat. Mater.* **10** 625

[40] Wei Z *et al* 2008 True random number generator using current difference based on a fractional stochastic model in 40-nm embedded ReRAM *IEEE Int. Electron Devices Meeting (San Francisco, CA)* pp 4.8.1–4.8.4

[41] Baek I G *et al* 2004 Highly scalable nonvolatile resistive memory using simple binary oxide driven by asymmetric unipolar voltage pulses *IEEE Int. Electron Device Meet. (San Francisco, CA)* pp 587–90

[42] Kim Y B *et al* 2011 Bi-layered RRAM with unlimited endurance and extremely uniform switching *2011 Symp. on VLSI (Kyoto, Japan, 14–16 June)* pp 52–53

[43] Wang L G, Qian X, Cao Y Q, Cao Z Y, Fang G Y, Li A D and Wu D 2015 Excellent resistive switching properties of atomic layer-deposited $Al_2O_3/HfO_2/Al_2O_3$ trilayer structures for non-volatile memory applications *Nano. Res. Lett.* **10** 135
[44] Nagareddy V K, Ott A K, Dou C, Tsvetkova T, Sandulov M, Craciun M F, Ferrari A C and Wright C D unpublished
[45] Cheng C H, Chin A and Yeh F S 2010 Novel ultra-low power RRAM with good endurance and retention *Symp. VLSI Technol. (Honolulu, HI)* pp 85–6
[46] Cao X, Li X M, Gao X D, Yu W D, Liu X J, Zhang Y W, Chen L D and Cheng X H 2009 Realization of forming-free ZnO-based resistive switching memory by controlling film thickness *J. Appl. Phys.* **106** 073723
[47] Shao B B, Liu Z F, Zeng G M, Wang H, Liang Q H, He Q Y, Cheng M, Zhou C Y, Jiang L B and Song B 2020 Two-dimensional transition metal carbide and nitride (MXene) derived quantum dots (QDs): synthesis, properties, applications and prospects *J. Mater. Chem.* A **8** 7508
[48] Villena M A, Hui F, Liang X, Shi Y, Yuan B, Jing X, Zhu K, Chen S and Lanza M 2019 Variability of metal/h-BN/metal memristors grown via chemical vapor deposition on different materials *Microelectron. Reliab.* **102** 113410
[49] Dragoman M, Aldrigo M, Dragoman D, Ian M P, Iordanescu S, Dinescu A, Donato A D and Modreanu M 2021 Multifunctionalities of 2D MoS_2 self-switching diode as memristor and photodetector *Physica* E **126** 114451
[50] Chen H *et al* 2022 Performance optimization of atomic layer deposited HfO_x memristor by annealing with back-end-of-line compatibility *IEEE Electron. Device Lett.* **43** 1141–4
[51] Wang T Y *et al* 2019 Atomic layer deposited $Hf_{0.5}Zr_{0.5}O_2$-based flexible memristor with short/long-term synaptic plasticity *Nanoscale Res. Lett.* **14** 102
[52] Koryazhkina M N *et al* 2022 Resistive state relaxation time in ZrO_2(Y)-based memristive devices under the influence of external noise *Chaos Soliton Fractals* **162** 112459
[53] Filatov D, Kazantseva I, Antonov D, Antonov I, Shenina M, Pavlov D and Gorshkov O 2018 Conductive atomic force microscopy study of the resistive switching in yttria-stabilized zirconia films with Au nanoparticles *Scanning* **2018** 5489596 9
[54] Bejtka K, Milano G, Ricciardi C, Pirri C F and Porro S 2020 TEM nanostructural investigation of Ag-conductive filaments in polycrystalline ZnO-based resistive switching devices *ACS Appl. Mater. Interfaces* **12** 29451–60
[55] Martín G *et al* 2017 Transmission electron microscopy assessment of conductive-filament formation in Ni–HfO_2–Si resistive-switching operational devices *Appl. Phys. Express* **11** 014101
[56] Radisavljevic B *et al* 2011 Single-layer MoS_2 transistors *Nat. Nanotech.* **6** 147–50
[57] Lee C H *et al* 2014 Atomically thin p-n junctions with van der Waals heterointerfaces *Nat. Nanotechnol.* **9** 676–81
[58] Lam C Y K, Zhang Q, Yin B, Huang Y, Wang H, Yang M and Wong S H D 2021 Recent advances in two-dimensional transition metal dichalcogenide nanocomposites biosensors for virus detection before and during COVID-19 outbreak *J. Compos. Sci.* **5** 190
[59] Chakrabarti B, Roy T and Vogel E M 2014 Nonlinear switching with ultralow reset power in graphene–insulator–graphene forming-free resistive memories *IEEE Electron. Device Lett.* **35** 750–2
[60] Yan X B *et al* 2020 Memristors based on multilayer graphene electrodes for implementing a low-power neuromorphic electronic synapse *J. Mater. Chem.* C **8** 4926–33

[61] Liu B, Liu Z W, Chiu I S, Di M F, Wu Y R, Wang J C, Hou T H and Lai C S 2018 Programmable synaptic metaplasticity and below femtojoule spiking energy realized in graphenebased neuromorphic memristor *ACS Appl. Mater. Interfaces* **10** 20237–43
[62] Zhao X L *et al* 2017 Confining cation injection to enhance CBRAM performance by nanopore graphene layer *Small* **13** 1603948
[63] Zhao X L *et al* 2018 Breaking the current-retention dilemma in cation-based resistive switching devices utilizing graphene with controlled defects *Adv. Mater.* **30** 1705193
[64] Liu S *et al* 2016 Eliminating negative-SET behavior by suppressing nanofilament overgrowth in cation-based memory *Adv. Mater* **28** 10623–9
[65] Zhou Z Y *et al* 2020 Designing carbon conductive filament memristor devices for memory and electronic synapse applications *Mater. Horiz.* **7** 1106–14
[66] He C L *et al* 2009 Nonvolatile resistive switching in graphene oxide thin films *Appl. Phys. Lett.* **95** 232101
[67] Jeong H Y *et al* 2010 Graphene oxide thin films for flexible nonvolatile memory applications *Nano Lett.* **10** 381–4386
[68] Nagareddy V K, Barnes M D, Zipoli F, Lai K T, Alexeev A M, Craciun M F and Wright C D 2017 Multilevel ultrafast flexible nanoscale nonvolatile hybrid graphene oxide-titanium oxide memories *ACS Nano* **11** 3010–21
[69] Jaafar A H and Kemp N T 2019 Wavelength dependent light tunable resistive switching graphene oxide nonvolatile memory devices *Carbon* **153** 81–8
[70] Sokolov A S, Ali M, Riaz R, Abbas Y, Ko M J and Choi C H 2019 Silver-adapted diffusive memristor based on organic nitrogen-doped graphene oxide quantum dots (NGOQDs) for artificial biosynapse applications *Adv. Funct. Mater.* **29** 1807504
[71] Yan X B *et al* 2018 Graphene oxide quantum dots based memristors with progressive conduction tuning for artificial synaptic learning *Adv. Funct. Mater.* **28** 1803728
[72] Shen J Q, Zhou B Z, Wang F, Wan Q, Shan X, Li C, Lin X and Zhang K L 2020 Low consumption two-terminal artificial synapse based on transfer-free single-crystal MoS_2 memristor *Nanotechnology* **31** 265202
[73] He H K, Yang R, Zhou W, Huang H M, Xiong J, Gan L, Zhai Y T and Guo X 2018 Photonic potentiation and electric habituation in ultrathin memristive synapses based on monolayer MoS_2 *Small* **14** 1800079
[74] Xu R J *et al* 2019 Vertical MoS_2 double-layer memristor with electrochemical metallization as an atomic-scale synapse with switching thresholds approaching 100 mV *Nano Lett.* **19** 2411–7
[75] Wang K Y *et al* 2020 A pure 2H-MoS_2 nanosheet-based memristor with low power consumption and linear multilevel storage for artificial synapse emulator *Adv. Electron. Mater.* **6** 1901342
[76] Feng X W *et al* 2019 A fully printed flexible MoS_2 memristive artificial synapse with femtojoule switching energy *Adv. Electron. Mater.* **5** 1900740
[77] Li Y *et al* 2019 Aerosol jet printed WSe_2 based RRAM on Kapton suitable for flexible monolithic memory integration *2019 IEEE Int. Conf. on Flexible and Printable Sensors and Systems (FLEPS)* pp 1–3
[78] Yan X B *et al* 2019 Vacancy-induced synaptic behavior in 2D WS_2 nanosheet-based memristor for low-power neuromorphic computing *Small* **15** 1901423
[79] Yan X B *et al* Robust Ag/ZrO_2/WS_2/Pt memristor for neuromorphic computing *ACS Appl. Mater. Interfaces* **11** 48029–38

[80] Tong W and Liu Y 2023 Recent progress of layered memristors based on two-dimensional MoS_2 *Sci. China Inf. Sci.* **66** 160402

[81] Kumar S, Agrawal R, Das M, Jyoti K, Kumar P and Mukherjee S 2021 Analytical model for memristive systems for neuromorphic computation *J. Phys. D: Appl. Phys.* **54** 355101

[82] Prodromakis T, Peh B P, Papavassiliou C and Toumazou C 2011 A versatile memristor model with nonlinear dopant kinetics *IEEE Trans. Electron. Devices* **58** 3099–105

[83] Patel C *et al* 2022 Large and uniform single crystals of MoS_2 monolayers for ppb-Level NO_2 sensing *ACS Appl. Nano Mater.* **5** 9415–26

[84] Das M, Kumar A, Singh R, Htay M T and Mukherjee S 2018 Realization of synaptic learning and memory functions in Y_2O_3 based memristive device fabricated by dual ion beam sputtering *Nanotechnology* **29** 055203

[85] Bocquet M *et al* 2014 Robust compact model for bipolar oxide-based resistive switching memories *IEEE Trans. Elect. Devices* **61** 674–81

[86] Traore B, Blaise P, Vianello E, Perniola L, Salvo B D and Nishi Y 2016 HfO_2-based RRAM: electrode effects, Ti/HfO_2 interface, charge injection, and oxygen (O) defects diffusion through experiment and *ab initio* calculations *IEEE Trans. Elect. Devices* **63** 360–8

[87] Kumar S, Gautam M K, Gill G S and Mukherjee S 2022 3-D physical electro-thermal modeling of nanoscale Y_2O_3 memristors for synaptic application *IEEE Trans. Elect. Devices* **69** 3124–9

[88] Niraula D and Karpov V 2018 Comprehensive numerical modeling of filamentary RRAM devices including voltage ramp-rate and cycle-to cycle variations *J. Appl. Phys.* **124** 174502

[89] Gaba S, Sheridan P, Zhou J, Choi S and Lu W 2013 Stochastic memristive devices for computing and neuromorphic applications *Nanoscale* **5** 5872

[90] Niraula D and Karpov V 2017 Numerical modeling of resistive switching in a RRAM device *Proc. of the 2017 COMSOL Conf.* (Boston, MA: COMSOL) https://www.comsol.com/paper/numerical-modeling-of-resistive-switching-in-a-rram-device-50522

[91] Goodwill J M, Sharma A A, Li D, Bain J A and Skowronski M 2017 Electro-thermal model of threshold switching in TaO_x-based devices *ACS Appl. Mater. Interfaces* **9** 11704–10

[92] Gautam M K, Kumar S, Chaudhary S, Hindoliya L K, Kumbhar D D, Park J H, Htay M T and Mukherjee S 2023 Experimental validation of switching dependence of nanoscale-Y_2O_3 memristor on electrode symmetry via physical electro-thermal modeling *ACS Appl. Electron. Mater.* **5** 3885–93

Chapter 2

Integrated selector-based resistive random-access memory (RRAM) and memristors

2.1 Introduction

A memristive crossbar array (MCA) is a two-dimensional array of resistive random-access memory (RRAM) arranged in a grid, where each RRAM is located at the intersection of a row and a column. Crossbar arrays are thus an arrangement of RRAM organized in a grid-like matrix [1]. Each cell in the array consists of an RRAM positioned at the intersection of horizontal and vertical metal lines. This configuration allows for efficient and compact data storage and processing. The requirement for advanced memory technologies that can keep up with the ever-increasing demands of modern computing have led to the exploration of novel solutions that push the boundaries of conventional memory architectures [2]. One such innovative approach gaining significant attention is the integration of selector-based RRAM. RRAM provide a high-density storage solution by utilizing the intersections of the grid for data storage, which allows for the integration of a large number of memory cells in a small area [3]. This is crucial for applications requiring compact and scalable memory solutions. In this chapter, we explore advanced memory technology by examining the integration of resistive switching capabilities with the unique features of RRAM in selector-based resistive switching systems. Our focus is on the selector memory device, a crucial component in the crossbar array, enabling efficient multibit data storage and retrieval [4]. For example, Zhang *et al* [3, 4] reported the impact of resistive switching element (RSE) parameters on the read performance of a two-terminal one-selector–one-resistor cell [4]. While increasing RHRS improves the RM, too large a value leads to RM degradation when RHRS exceeds an optimal value. The crossbar structure facilitates parallel processing and data access. Since each RRAM cell can be addressed individually, multiple operations can be performed simultaneously, enhancing processing speed and

doi:10.1088/978-0-7503-6169-9ch2

© IOP Publishing Ltd 2025. All rights, including for text and data mining (TDM), artificial intelligence (AI) training, and similar technologies, are reserved.

efficiency. It can achieve low power consumption due to the resistive switching properties, which minimizes the energy required for data storage and retrieval compared to traditional memory technologies [5]. In an integrated selector-based device, the resistive switching system incorporates selectors at each intersection. Selectors are nonlinear devices that help control the memristive elements by allowing current to pass only when a certain threshold voltage is applied. This prevents unintentional changes in the state of the RRAM and mitigates issues such as sneak paths, which are unwanted current paths that can interfere with the proper functioning of the memory array [6]. Common selector devices include diodes, transistors, or more advanced threshold switching devices such as metal–insulator–metal (MIM) structures. The rapid development of the MCA has positioned it as one of the most promising devices for next-generation memory solutions [7–11]. However, the maximum size of the crossbar array is hindered by the cross-talk phenomenon among array cells. This interference leads to a potential misreading of the high-resistance state (HRS) due to the sneak current flowing from neighboring cells with a low-resistance state (LRS). In response to this challenge, Huang *et al* [2] have proposed various solutions aimed at reducing the sneak current by incorporating a selector into the MCA device. One such approach involves the demonstration of a one-diode–one-memristive crossbar structure with different types of rectifying diodes for achieving high-density unipolar MCA integration [12–15]. In a resistive switching device, an integrated selector is used to address each RRAM independently. The selector is typically a transistor or a diode integrated with the RRAM to control access to individual cells. This integration prevents interference between cells and ensures accurate read and write operations by isolating each cell. The crossbar array act as the storage element while the selectors enable precise control over which RRAM is accessed during read and write operations [16–19]. The selector's role is crucial in managing the current flow through the crossbar and preventing unintended interactions between adjacent cells, which is essential for reliable memory operation.

2.2 Selector based resistive switching technology

RRAM can be scaled down to nanometer dimensions, allowing for very high-density memory storage [3]. The crossbar architecture enables the integration of a large number of memory cells in a small area [4, 20–24]. RRAMs retain their state without power, ensuring data are preserved over time. Non-volatility reduces the need for a constant power supply, leading to energy savings [3]. Memristive crossbars can perform computational tasks within the memory array, such as matrix operations, which are essential for machine learning and neural networks [25–30]. For example, Yu *et al* [16] reported that the switching dynamics and electrical behavior of memristive devices resemble those of synapses and neurons, making these devices promising candidates for brain-inspired computing. Parallel processing within the crossbar array can significantly speed up computational tasks. RRAM inside an MCA architecture can mimic synaptic functions, enabling the development of neuromorphic systems that operate similarly to the human brain. The ability to change resistance based on input history makes RRAM suitable for learning algorithms and adaptive systems [35–39]. Selectors are crucial in preventing sneak paths, which are unintended paths that current can take through the crossbar, causing errors. Advances in material science and nanofabrication techniques are continuously improving the performance and reliability of memristive crossbars.

2.2.1 One-selector–one-resistor (1S1R)

Zhang *et al* [4] and Huang *et al* [2] proposed the one-selector–one-resistor (1S1R) configuration, as shown in figure 2.1, consisting of one resistor (R) and one selector (S) in series. This configuration is a memory cell structure commonly used in RRAM crossbar arrays. In this configuration, each memory cell consists of a resistive switching element (R) paired with a selector device (S). The resistor (R) stores data by changing its resistance state (high or low), while the selector (S), typically a diode or a threshold switch, controls the current flow. This pairing helps mitigate sneak-path currents, unintended currents that could flow through unselected cells, by allowing current to pass only when the selector is activated [7]. For example, Chen *et al* [43] reported that the sneak-path current causing cross interference impedes practical applications. The 1S1R configuration supports high-density integration, as it reduces the number of components per cell, and provides a simpler architecture compared to more complex configurations. However, it has limitations in current control and scalability at smaller geometries, making it suitable primarily for certain high-density, low-cost applications.

2.2.1.1 Working principle

The 1S1R configuration in RRAM crossbar arrays is designed to manage memory cells by pairing each resistive switching element (R) with a selector device (S) [3] as discussed by Wang *et al* [8]. The resistor stores data by changing its resistance state, representing binary information with HRS and LRS. The selector, typically a diode or threshold switch, controls current flow, blocking unintended currents, known as sneak-path currents, that can interfere with data accuracy in neighboring cells. During a write operation, a voltage applied across the selected cell changes the resistor's state, with the selector ensuring current flows only through the targeted cell. For reading, a lower voltage activates the selector for the specific cell, allowing the system to detect its resistance state while preventing leakage into unselected cells [9]. This configuration offers advantages in reducing sneak-path currents, supporting high-density integration, and simplifying fabrication by avoiding

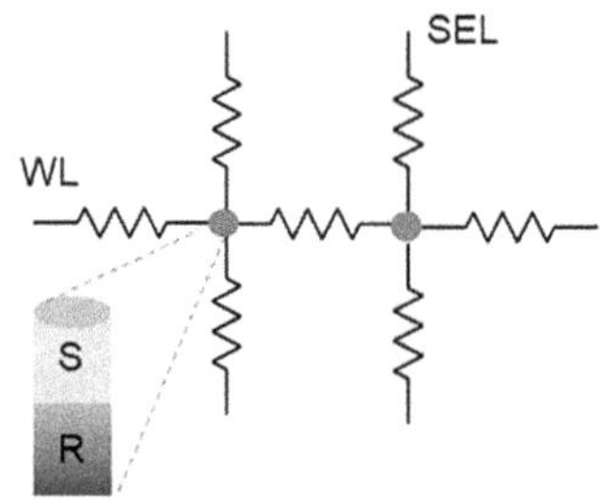

Figure 2.1. Circuit design of the 1S1R configuration.

complex circuitry [10]. However, it faces challenges such as limited current control compared to transistor selectors, scalability issues due to increased leakage at smaller scales, and material endurance concerns from repeated switching cycles [9]. When a voltage is applied to the write line (WL), it activates the corresponding selector (SEL) in that row by providing the necessary gate voltage. The selector then allows current to flow through the connected resistor (R), altering its resistance state to either a high resistance (representing a '0') or a low resistance (representing a '1'). During read operations, the SEL line is also activated to allow current sensing through the selected cell, facilitating accurate data retrieval while preventing interference from adjacent cells [3]. The 1S1R configuration has several key applications, primarily in high-density memory and neuromorphic computing due to its simple structure and effective current management capabilities [5]. For example, Sung *et al* [5] reviewed the applications of memristive crossbars in both machine learning and neuromorphic computing, focusing on the structure of unit cells and the network topology.

2.2.1.2 Non-volatile memory

1S1R is widely used in RRAM as a non-volatile memory (NVM) solution. In RRAM arrays, the 1S1R configuration helps reduce sneak-path currents, ensuring accurate read and write operations. This makes it useful for high-density storage in low-power, high-performance memory applications [6]. The compact and stackable structure of 1S1R enables high storage density, making it a promising alternative to conventional flash memory in applications such as solid-state drives (SSDs) and embedded memory in mobile devices.

2.2.1.3 Neuromorphic computing

1S1R architectures are utilized in neuromorphic systems, where the memory cells can mimic synaptic behavior, with the resistor representing the synaptic weight [8]. For example, Wang *et al* reported a feasible solution for the realization of a protein-based 1S1R array to achieve high-density storage. The 1S1R unit shows characteristics similar to those of synapses in the human brain under impulse excitation and has great potential in simulating the human brain for neuromorphic calculations. For example, Gao *et al* [9] describe the implementation of synaptic learning in the two main types of neural networks, namely the deep neural network (DNN) and the spiking neural network (SNN). Bio-inspired learning, such as the spike-timing dependent plasticity scheme, is shown to enable unsupervised learning processes which are typical of the human brain. By adjusting the resistance, 1S1R arrays can simulate learning and memory functions in artificial neural networks (ANNs), enabling energy-efficient hardware for machine learning applications. This application is particularly valuable for artificial intelligence (AI) edge computing, where low power consumption and high processing speeds are essential [9].

2.2.1.4 In-memory computing

1S1R configurations enable in-memory processing by storing and processing data within the same cell, reducing the need for data transfer between memory and processing units [10]. This approach is beneficial in applications requiring high-speed data processing with minimal latency, such as real-time analytics, signal processing, and Internet of Things (IoT) devices.

2.2.1.5 Image processing and pattern recognition

In applications such as image processing and pattern recognition, the 1S1R structure supports efficient memory access and data handling. For example, Kobayashi *et al* [11] reported how the rise of AI and bio-inspired circuits offers an opportunity for emerging memory technology and shifts the application from pure data storage to storage and computing tasks, and also enlarges the range of required specifications at the device level due to the exponential number of new systems and architectures. High-density crossbar arrays can process large volumes of image data quickly, making them ideal for tasks in medical imaging, object recognition, and remote sensing.

2.2.1.6 Data encryption and security

1S1R-based RRAM is increasingly being explored for hardware security applications, such as physically unclonable functions (PUFs) and encryption keys [12]. The unique resistance patterns in each memory cell provide an inherent randomness, which can be leveraged to create secure, device-specific cryptographic keys.

These applications make 1S1R configurations versatile and valuable for industries that prioritize high-density storage, low-power operation, and data security, including consumer electronics, healthcare, automotive, and IoT systems [8].

2.2.1.7 Advantages and disadvantages of 1S1R

The advantages of 1S1R are as follows.

High-density integration: The 1S1R configuration requires only one resistor and one selector per memory cell, allowing for compact, high-density memory arrays. This structure is ideal for applications where maximizing storage capacity is essential, such as NVM.

Simple structure and fabrication: Compared to more complex memory architectures, 1S1R is relatively simple to fabricate. This simplicity reduces manufacturing complexity and costs, which is beneficial for applications requiring low-cost, scalable memory solutions [2].

Reduced sneak-path currents: The inclusion of a selector device, such as a diode or a threshold switch, helps control sneak-path currents. This is essential in crossbar arrays, where unintended current pathways could lead to data inaccuracies [5]. The selector limits current flow to only the selected cells, improving data reliability.

Low power consumption: Due to the absence of additional transistors, 1S1R cells can operate with lower power compared to transistor-based configurations [8]. This makes the configuration suitable for low-power applications, such as IoT devices and mobile electronics.

Potential for neuromorphic computing: In applications such as neuromorphic computing, 1S1R cells can mimic synaptic functions by adjusting resistance values, enabling energy-efficient, brain-like computing suitable for AI and machine learning at the hardware level [4].

The disadvantages of 1S1R are as follows.

Limited current control: Compared to transistor-based selectors, diode or threshold-switch selectors in 1S1R offer limited control over current flow. This can result in suboptimal write and read precision, particularly in high-performance applications requiring fine current regulation [1].

Scalability challenges at smaller nodes: As device dimensions shrink, the effectiveness of the selector devices in suppressing sneak-path currents decreases. Smaller geometries lead to increased leakage currents and instability, which can limit the scalability of 1S1R arrays for very high-density applications [3].

Data integrity issues from sneak paths: Although the selector reduces sneak-path currents, it may not fully eliminate them, particularly in large arrays with many low-resistance cells. This can compromise data integrity, resulting in potential read/write errors [8].

Lower endurance and reliability: Repeated switching cycles in 1S1R cells can lead to thermal stress and material degradation, particularly in selector devices. This affects the long-term endurance and reliability of the memory cell, which may be problematic in applications requiring frequent data writing [39].

Compatibility and integration challenges: Finding materials for selectors and resistors that are compatible with existing CMOS processes can be challenging. Integrating 1S1R cells with CMOS technology requires careful material selection, which can add to the design complexity and cost [3].

2.2.2 One-diode–one-resistor

Wang *et al* [5] presented the one-diode–one-resistor (1D1R) configuration, with a structure as shown in figure 2.2, consisting of one resistor (R) and one diode (D) [6, 8].

The 1D1R configuration is a memory cell architecture used in resistive RRAM systems. It consists of a single resistor, which acts as the memory element, and a diode, which serves as a selector [3]. This configuration is designed to enhance data integrity and reduce unwanted sneak-path currents in crossbar memory arrays.

2.2.2.1 Working principle

In the 1D1R configuration, the operation begins when a voltage is applied to the WL, activating the diode (D) that allows current to flow in one direction only. This forward biasing of the diode directs the current through the RRAM cell (R), changing its resistance state and effectively writing data into the memory cell [7, 8]. During this process, the bit line (BL) serves to either complete the circuit for the

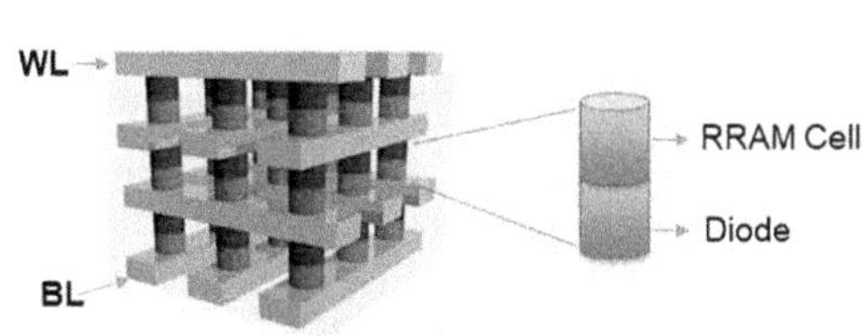

Figure 2.2. Circuit design of 1D1R.

write operation or to sense the current during read operations. When reading data, the WL is activated, and the current flowing through the RRAM cell is measured via the BL, enabling the determination of the cell's resistance state (high or low) [11]. This design ensures that the current flows exclusively through the targeted RRAM cell, thereby minimizing sneak-path currents and enhancing the data integrity, reliability, and performance of memory operations within the crossbar array.

2.2.2.2 Applications of 1D1R

Applications of 1D1R are as follows.

Non-volatile memory: 1D1R configurations are commonly used in NVM applications where data retention without power is required [3] For example, Huang *et al* reported a ZnO-based memory system with a complementary 1D1R structure for possible application in passive crossbar arrays.

Resistive memory arrays: These are particularly suited for high-density resistive memory arrays, enabling compact and efficient data storage solutions [8].

Neuromorphic computing: The 1D1R architecture can be utilized in applications that mimic neural networks for AI and machine learning tasks [11].

2.2.2.3 Advantages and disadvantages of 1D1R

The advantages of 1D1R are as follows.

Reduced sneak-path currents: The diode effectively blocks unwanted currents, enhancing data integrity by preventing interference from adjacent cells [1, 5].

Lower power consumption: Diodes generally consume less power than more complex selectors, making 1D1R designs energy-efficient [9]. For example, Huang *et al* [2] proposed the novel block structures of the logic block, connection block, switch block, and the FPGA architecture based on the 1D2R element. Compared to the conventional 1T2R-based non-volatile field-programmable gate array (NVFPGA), this novel structure could improve the operation speed by 53% with a 40.5% lower operation power. Compared with the conventional 1R-based NVFPGA, the proposed scheme could greatly reduce the write error rate by eight orders with more than 20 times lower write power.

Cost-effective fabrication: The simplicity of the diode in the design reduces fabrication costs compared to more complex selector architectures [17].

Improved reliability: The rectifying properties of the diode help maintain reliable read and write operations, contributing to overall system stability [13].

The disadvantages of 1D1R are as follows.

High off-state leakage: While better than some selectors, diodes can still exhibit significant leakage currents in highly scaled arrays, which can compromise data integrity [10].

Temperature sensitivity: Diodes are susceptible to temperature fluctuations, which can affect their performance and lead to variability in memory operations [19].

Limitations in large arrays: As array sizes increase, the effectiveness of diodes in controlling sneak paths may diminish, leading to reliability issues [7].

Integration challenges: Integrating diodes with advanced CMOS nodes can present challenges due to differences in fabrication processes and material compatibility [21].

2.2.3 One-transistor–one-resistor

Wang *et al* [8] presented the one-transistor–one-resistor (1T1R) configuration involving one resistor (R) and one transistor (T), as shown in figure 2.3. The circuit design of the 1T1R configuration includes an RRAM cell consisting of a TE, a resistive switching layer made of hafnium oxide (HfO_2), and a bottom electrode (BE), combined with a transistor for selective access. In this set-up, the TE receives the drain voltage (V_D), which is applied to induce a change in the resistance state of the HfO2 layer, thereby writing data to the RRAM cell [28].

In this case, the transistor acts as an access device, providing better control over the memristor and enhancing read/write operations [8–10]. The configuration consists of one transistor (T) and one resistive random-access memory (RRAM) cell (R) in a memristive crossbar array. In this architecture, the transistor serves as an access device, providing precise control over the RRAM cell and facilitating efficient read and write operations [10].

2.2.3.1 Working principle

In the 1T1R configuration, when a voltage is applied to the gate (V_G) of the transistor, it turns 'ON', allowing current to flow through the RRAM cell. The drain voltage (V_D) applied to the top electrode of the RRAM cell induces a change in the resistance state of the resistive switching layer, effectively writing data into the memory cell [8]. During a read operation, the gate voltage selectively enables the transistor, while a lower voltage is applied to sense the current flowing through the RRAM cell. This configuration ensures that only the targeted memory cell is accessed, minimizing sneak paths and enhancing data integrity and reliability [9].

2.2.3.2 Data writing

To write data to the RRAM cell, a V_D is applied to the top electrode (TE). This voltage induces a conductive filament to form within the HfO_2 layer, shifting it from a HRS to an LRS [24], as shown in figure 2.3. The transistor (T) must be turned 'ON' by applying a V_G to its gate terminal, allowing current to flow through the RRAM cell during the writing process. The precise control offered by the transistor ensures that only the targeted memory cell is affected, thus minimizing the risk of sneak paths [27].

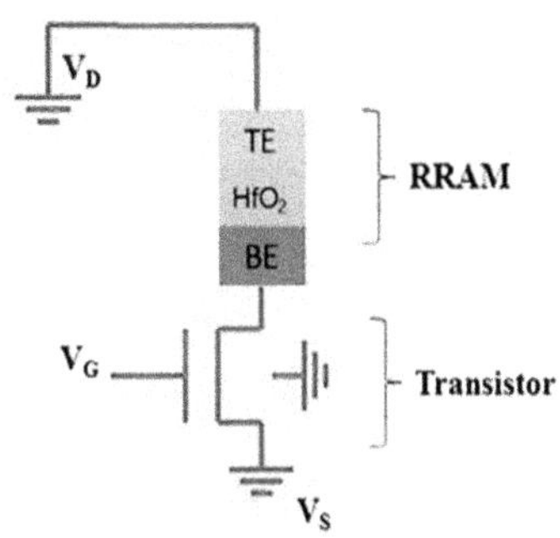

Figure 2.3. Circuit design of 1T1R.

2.2.3.3 Data reading

During the read operation, the V_G is adjusted to activate the transistor, allowing current to pass through the RRAM cell. A lower voltage is applied to the TE to sense the current flow, which corresponds to the resistance state of the HfO_2 layer [8], as shown in figure 2.3. If the resistance is in an LRS, it indicates that the cell is in the 'ON' state, while a HRS suggests the cell is 'OFF'. This capability to read the resistance state accurately ensures reliable data retrieval.

2.2.3.4 Applications of 1T1R

The applications of 1T1R are as follows.

Non-volatile memory: For storing data in computing devices, benefiting from the high density and low power consumption of 1T1R [8].

Neuromorphic computing: To emulate synaptic behavior in artificial neural networks, utilizing the analog resistance states of RRAM cells [30].

Data storage: In embedded systems and memory solutions, providing fast read/write capabilities and high integration density [9].

The advantages of 1T1R are as follows.

Precise control: The transistor provides enhanced current control, allowing for accurate read and write operations [16].

Low leakage currents: The use of a transistor helps reduce leakage, improving stability and reliability in large arrays [26].

Compatibility with CMOS technology: 1T1R configurations can be easily integrated into existing semiconductor fabrication processes [8].

Scalability: The architecture supports scaling to larger memory arrays, making it suitable for high-density applications [13].

The disadvantages of 1T1R are as follows.

Lower memory density: The requirement for a transistor per RRAM cell increases the area footprint, resulting in reduced overall memory density compared to other configurations such as 1S1R or 1D1R [8].

Complex fabrication: The 1T1R configuration involves a more complex and costly fabrication process, requiring additional masking and etching steps [15].

Device scaling challenges: Maintaining performance while scaling down transistors within the crossbar array poses significant hurdles [3]. These characteristics highlight the advantages and limitations of the 1T1R architecture, making it suitable for specific applications while posing challenges in others.

This configuration effectively prevents sneak paths, enhances data integrity, and ensures accurate read and write operations in the crossbar array. For example, Wang *et al* [8] reported the design and optimization of an *n*-bit 1T1R RRAM array designed using TiO_2- and HfO_x-based memristors.

2.2.4 Other configurations

Similarly, other 2D2R, 2.5T1R, 3T1R, 4T2R, and 1T2R1T cell structures are designed on the basis of the primary cell structures and represent more advanced designs within RRAM, as shown in table 2.1 [8]. These configurations enables

Table 2.1. Comparison of various cell structures based on RRAM.

Bit cell	Cell structure	Capacity	Cell area (F^2)	Search energy/bit (fJ)	Reference
2D2R	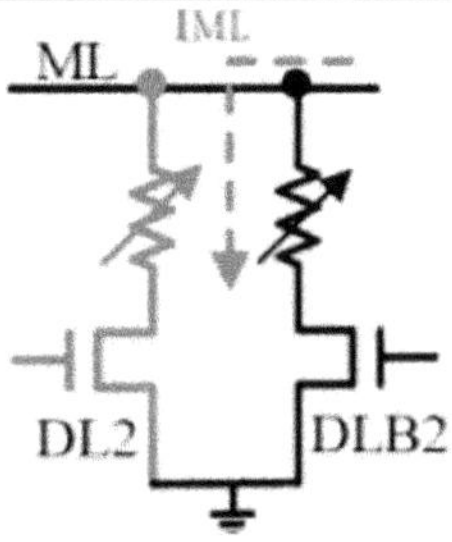	16 kb	16.3	N/A	[27]
2.5T1R	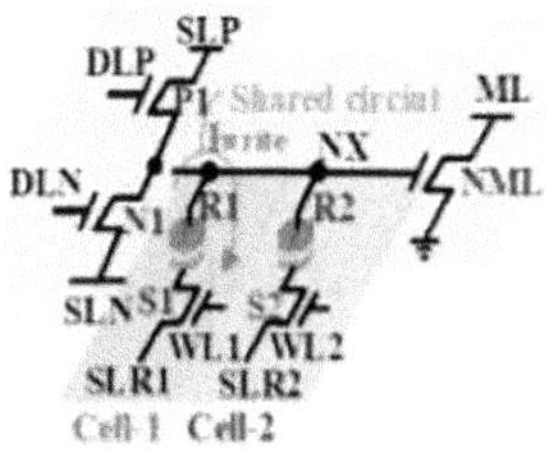	16 kb	138	0.28–0.71	[29]
3T1R	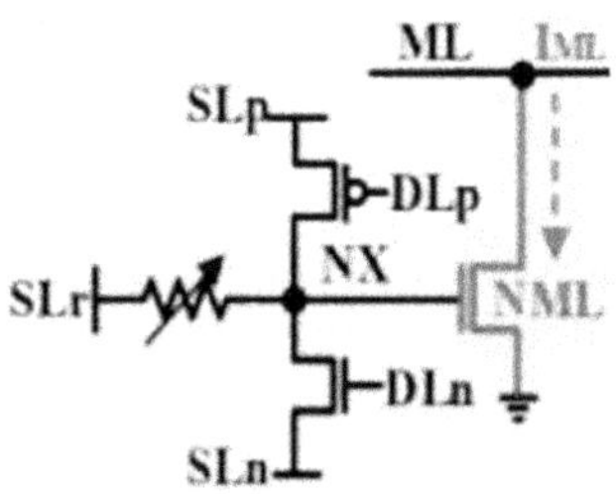	4 kb	193	0.51	[23]
4T2R	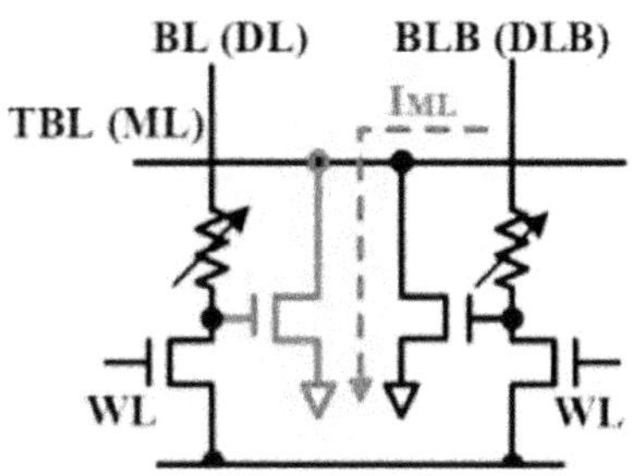	4 kb	299	N/A	[30]
1T2R1T	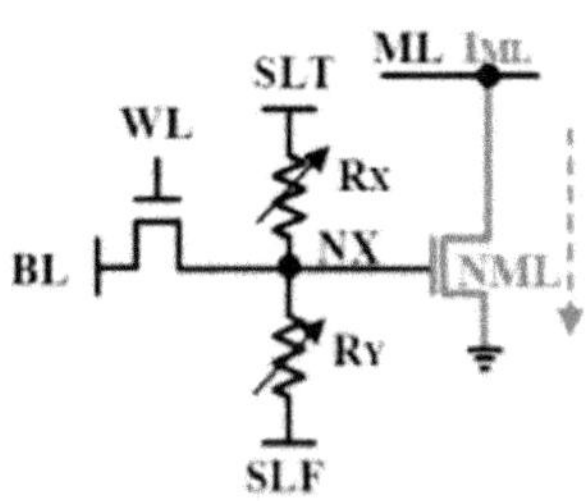	384 b	N/A	N/A	[35]

differential sensing and offer improved control over memory operations, providing several advantages over the 1T1R architecture. Fore example, one of the key innovations in the 2T2R set-up is its ability to perform differential sensing, which enhances read accuracy and noise immunity by allowing for the comparison of resistive states. Additionally, the presence of two transistors provides greater flexibility for complex memory operations, such as multilevel cell (MLC) storage and improved support for in-memory computing [15]. Each architectural advancement brings improvements in current control, selectivity, and scalability but also introduces new challenges related to complexity, fabrication costs, and integration. Researchers continue to explore these designs to overcome existing limitations and enhance their suitability for applications in memory storage, neuromorphic computing, and in-memory processing [19].

2.2.5 Applications of selector devices

Applications of selector devices encompass high-density storage solutions for devices that require substantial NVM, hardware accelerators for AI and machine learning tasks that utilize in-memory computing for efficient data processing, systems designed to emulate neural networks for robotics, sensory processing, and cognitive computing, as well as compact, energy-efficient computing devices for IoT applications, where processing power must be in close proximity to the data source. Selector devices are vital components in MCA based models with memory and computing architectures, as they isolate individual RRAM cells during read and write operations, thus preventing sneak currents and ensuring reliable device functionality. Acting as switches, selector devices regulate the current flow through the RRAM, significantly influencing the overall performance and energy efficiency of RRAM-based systems [13].

2.2.5.1 Requirements for selector devices

The successful implementation of selector devices in conjunction with RRAM hinges on several key principles and requirements. First and foremost, these devices must possess a high level of nonlinearity, featuring a sharp turn-on characteristic [2]. By achieving this, the selector ensures that current primarily flows through the intended RRAM and not through its neighboring devices, thus reducing and/or removing the issue of sneak currents. Moreover, a vital requirement for selector devices is to maintain a low leakage current. High leakage currents could lead to unplanned sneak paths, causing data corruption and increased power consumption [14]. However, by minimizing the leakage current, the selector device allows for minimal interference with neighboring RRAM. Furthermore, the selector device must be designed to be compatible with the specific RRAM technology in deployment. These demands align its manufacturing requirements with those of RRAM and ensure its seamless and effective operation within the same architectural framework [13]. Considering the ongoing pursuit of high-density memory and computing applications, scalability is a crucial attribute for selector devices. They must be capable of downsizing to smaller dimensions and accommodating higher integration densities without sacrificing performance. Additionally, the reliability and endurance of the selector device play essential roles in the overall stability and long-term functionality of RRAM-based systems. As such, the selector must be engineered to withstand a substantial number of switching cycles without suffering degradation. Another critical aspect is the demand for low power consumption in modern memory and computing technologies. The selector device must be optimized to consume minimal power during both read and write operations, contributing to the overall energy efficiency of the system [15].

Selectors are critical components in RRAM-based systems, particularly in crossbar arrays. They act as control devices that regulate the current flow to individual RRAMs, preventing unintended changes in their resistance states. Selector devices are essential for ensuring reliable operation of memristive crossbar memory arrays by mitigating issues such as sneak paths, unwanted current paths that can cause data corruption or errors. Various types of selectors are used, such as diodes, which are the simplest form and allow current to flow in only one direction, thereby preventing reverse currents that could affect neighboring RRAM cells [8]. Transistors offer more advanced control by gating current flow based on external signals. Threshold switching devices, such as MIM structures, have nonlinear current–voltage characteristics; they stay in a high-resistance state until a certain threshold voltage is reached, then switch to a low-resistance state to allow current flow. The working principle of selectors involves a sharp change in resistance at a specific voltage threshold, ensuring that only the intended RRAM cell is activated while others remain unaffected [14]. For example, Deng *et al* [15] reported that the ECM effect determined the switching properties when Cu or Ag electrodes are used. Investigations with conductive tip AFM on Cu/TiO_2/Pt structures proved the filamentary character of switching. This controlled current flow effectively prevents sneak paths, preserving the integrity of the stored data.

2.2.5.2 Important roles played by memristive crossbars

Selectors play a crucial role in preventing sneak paths in dense crossbar arrays. Without selectors, currents could inadvertently flow through unintended paths, leading to erroneous read/write operations. Selectors block these unintended currents, enhancing the reliability and accuracy of memory operations. They also enable the scaling down of memristive crossbars to nanometer dimensions by mitigating cross-talk and interference issues that become more pronounced at smaller scales [31]. With effective selector technology, memristive crossbars can achieve high-density storage, as selectors ensure that memory cells can be packed closely without interfering with each other's operation.

Typically, selectors are integrated in series with each RRAM at each intersection of the crossbar grid, allowing precise control of each memory cell. The materials used for selectors need to be compatible with the RRAM materials to ensure seamless integration and reliable operation [16]. Advanced nanofabrication techniques are employed to create these integrated structures with high precision and consistency.

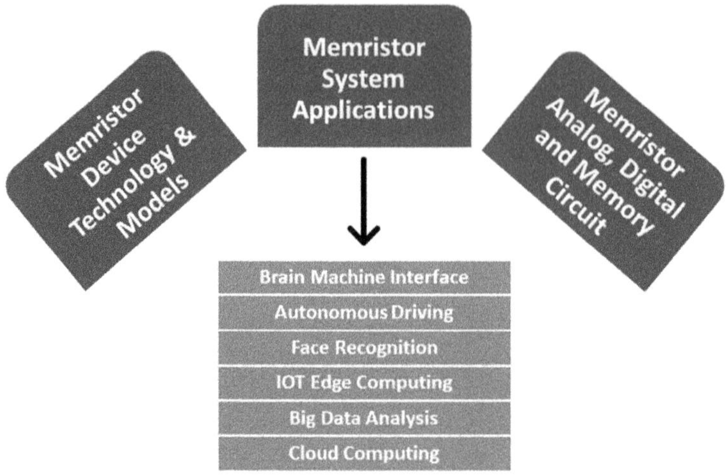

Figure 2.4. Memristive technology-based applications.

RRAM-based digital–analog and memory circuits utilize RRAM in conjunction with other electronic components to perform diverse functions. These include advancements in memristor device technology and models, as well as applications in analog–digital and memory circuits. The broader applications of memristor systems span areas such as brain–machine interfaces, autonomous driving, face recognition, IoT edge computing, big data analysis, and cloud computing, as shown in figure 2.4 and discussed below.

2.2.5.3 Digital–analog converters

Digital–analog converters (DACs) have found a remarkable application of RRAM, wherein these sophisticated devices enable the conversion of digital signals into their corresponding analog representations [17]. One of the most captivating features of RRAM is its unique ability to persistently retain the analog state even when the power supply is disconnected, elevating their significance in specific domains such as audio processing and control systems [13]. This special feature of RRAM allows it to save important analog information. This means that even if the power goes off and comes back on, the RRAM can pick up where it left off without losing any data [24]. This makes them valuable in applications where continuous and reliable data storage is essential. Because of this, DACs that use RRAM provide exceptional benefits in situations where having stable and strong data is extremely important. This in turn, improves the overall efficiency and reliability of various technological uses [16].

2.2.5.4 Analog–digital converters

Analog–digital converters (ADCs) are essential components in many electronic devices and systems as they play a crucial role in converting continuous analog signals, such as sound, temperature, or voltage, into discrete digital data that can be processed and manipulated by digital circuits. Traditionally, ADCs have been implemented using various methods, but RRAM offer a unique and promising alternative. Shen *el al* [20] reported such RRAM devices, with their main characteristics, such as the potentiation/depression response, short-/long-term plasticity (STP/LTP), transition from short-term memory (STM) to long-term memory (LTM), and spike-time-dependent plasticity (STDP), revealing the great potential of RRAM devices in the field of neuromorphic applications. RRAM is a special type of electronic component that can change its resistance based on the amount of charge that has passed through it in the past [17]. This characteristic is known as memristance, and it allows these devices to 'remember' their previous states, similar to how a neuron in the human brain retains its previous activity levels. This ability makes RRAM highly attractive for a variety of applications, including ADCs [21]. In the context of ADCs, RRAM can be utilized to improve the efficiency and accuracy of the analog–digital conversion process. When an analog signal is fed into an ADC, the RRAM can actively adjust its resistance according to the incoming signal characteristics [25]. This dynamic resistance adaptation allows the RRAM to finely tune the conversion process, enabling a more precise mapping of the analog signal to its corresponding digital representation. RRAM-based ADCs provide more reliable and accurate conversions than traditional ADCs, which often suffer from precision limitations, especially with complex signals. It enhances performance, ensuring better continuity and consistency even in challenging signal conditions. Overall, RRAM offer a promising solution for improving ADC performance, making them valuable for electronics and digital signal processing advancements [21].

2.2.5.5 RRAM-based flip-flops

RRAM-based flip-flops offer a transformative approach to traditional digital circuits, potentially replacing transistors in flip-flop circuits [4]. This switch can lead to improved performance and reduced power consumption in sequential logic circuits. RRAM, with its unique resistance-altering property, behaves as a storage element, much like transistors. The integration of RRAM in flip-flop circuits brings several benefits [16]. First, it reduces power requirements, making the electronics more energy-efficient. Second, the RRAM non-volatile behavior enables faster state transitions, enhancing overall system speed. This speed is particularly valuable in real-time data analysis and AI algorithms [21]. Moreover, RRAM-based flip-flops offer the prospect of overcoming traditional transistor limitations, potentially improving data processing efficiency. Integrating memory and computation in a single RRAM-based circuit may mitigate the 'von Neumann bottleneck' [30].

2.2.5.6 Resistive memory cells

Resistive memory cells function as memory cells in digital memory circuits, storing information in their resistance state, making them promising candidates for future-generation memory technologies. These cells have the potential to revolutionize memory storage due to their unique properties. By leveraging the inherent memristive behavior, they offer advantages such as low power consumption, high density, and faster access times compared to traditional memory technologies [8].

For example, Lee *et al* [10] reported the benefits of high yield, robust memory performance at high temperature (200 °C), excellent scalability, and multilevel operation, which are promising for applications in next-generation NVM. Their applications in various fields, including AI, neuromorphic computing, and advanced data storage systems, are being explored actively. As resistive memory continues to advance, it may unlock new possibilities for more efficient and powerful computing devices. Consequently, these innovative memory cells hold significant potential in shaping the landscape of future digital technologies [13].

2.2.5.7 Neuromorphic memory arrays

Within the realm of cutting-edge neuromorphic computing systems, the utilization of RRAM memory arrays assumes a pivotal role in facilitating the representation of synaptic weights between artificial neurons [21]. These revolutionary RRAMs possess a unique attribute, the capacity to dynamically and adaptively alter their resistance, which, in turn, bestows upon them the remarkable ability to partake in the processes of learning and information processing that are inherent in the functionality of complex neural networks [5]. As a result, these RRAM-based memory arrays serve as a foundational cornerstone, empowering the realization of highly efficient and bio-inspired cognitive architectures, propelling the field of neuromorphic computing towards unprecedented advancements in the domain of AI [7]. For example, Wu *et al* [25] reported RRAM is a promising electrical synaptic device for efficient neuromorphic computing. A human face recognition task was demonstrated on a 1 kb 1T1R array using an online training perceptron network. The RRAM device structure and materials stack were optimized to achieve reliable bidirectional analog switching behavior.

2.2.5.8 Programmable logic devices

Programmable logic devices (PLDs), such as field-programmable gate arrays (FPGAs), can integrate RRAM into their design. RRAM plays a crucial role in offering reconfigurable and adaptive digital logic, enabling the creation of highly flexible and efficient digital circuit designs. This integration empowers engineers to achieve enhanced versatility and improved performance in their circuits [19, 21]. By leveraging RRAM within PLDs, the potential for innovative applications and advanced functionalities is unlocked. The combination of PLDs and RRAM opens up new possibilities in various fields, including AI, signal processing, and data encryption. This symbiotic relationship enhances the adaptability and configurability of digital circuits, making them ideal for rapidly evolving technological landscapes [24].

2.2.5.9 Hybrid digital–analog computation

The emergence of hybrid digital–analog computation marks a significant advancement, empowered by the incorporation of RRAM. These remarkable components facilitate the creation of computing systems that combine digital and analog circuits, giving rise to a transformative paradigm in computational technology [29]. The convergence of computational approaches holds the promise of accompanying in a new era of efficiency and innovation. This mixed-mode computation has the potential to enhance efficiency and open up new opportunities in various fields, including control systems and data processing [32].

2.2.5.10 The potential of selector devices

RRAM systems with RRAM device technology have a wide range of applications spanning from memory technologies to neuromorphic computing and reconfigurable electronics [18]. Their unique properties, such as non-volatility and analog behavior, make them promising components for next-generation electronic devices and systems. These applications hold the potential to revolutionize various industries, from computing to energy and beyond [8].

To address these requirements and principles effectively, work on diverse types of selector devices tailored to meet the specific needs of RRAM-based systems is required. Common variants include bipolar junction transistors (BJTs), unipolar resistive switching devices, and various diode types such as Schottky diodes and p–n junction diodes [16]. Through continuous innovation and refinement, these efforts aim to unlock the full potential of RRAM-based technologies for a wide range of applications.

2.3 Sneak path technology

The sneak-path issue in 1S1R configurations in RRAM crossbar arrays arises from unintended current pathways that can compromise data accuracy and memory cell reliability [8]. This challenge occurs because of the inherent structure of crossbar arrays, where each row and column is interconnected. In dense crossbar architectures, if a voltage is applied to a specific cell for a read or write operation, some of the current may 'sneak' through neighboring unselected cells, leading to incorrect or ambiguous data retrieval [27]. This section is a detailed look at the causes, impacts, and solutions for sneak-path currents in 1S1R configurations.

2.3.1 Causes of sneak-path currents

Crossbar array structure: In an RRAM crossbar array, each memory cell is placed at the intersection of a row and column. When a voltage is applied to a specific cell, the current is ideally supposed to flow only through that cell [3]. However, the interconnected nature of rows and columns allows the current to find alternative paths through adjacent cells, especially when they are in an LRS.

Low-resistance state cells: Cells in the LRS act as conductive pathways, allowing current to 'leak' into other areas of the array, even if they are not actively selected [8]. These unintended pathways become problematic in large arrays, where multiple low-resistance cells increase the risk of sneak paths.

Lack of isolation in 1S1R: While 1S1R configurations include a selector device (such as a diode or threshold switch) to help control current, these components provide less isolation than transistor-based selectors [3]. Diode and threshold-switch selectors exhibit nonlinear I–V characteristics, which means they can still permit some current flow under certain conditions, leading to partial suppression of sneak paths rather than complete isolation.

2.3.2 Impacts of sneak-path currents

Reduced data integrity: Sneak-path currents can result in read errors by altering the measured resistance of the targeted cell, making it challenging to distinguish between high and low-resistance states [13]. This issue affects data accuracy, leading to potential read/write errors.

Power consumption: As sneak-path currents flow through unintended pathways, they increase the power required for each operation, which is particularly detrimental in large-scale arrays where multiple sneak paths may exist. Higher power consumption not only limits energy efficiency but also leads to excessive heating, which can accelerate device degradation [8].

Decreased reliability and scalability: Sneak-path currents become more significant as the crossbar array scales down to smaller geometries. With reduced distances and denser arrangements, the likelihood of sneak paths increases, which impacts the overall stability and reliability of the memory device [14]. This scalability limitation is one of the major challenges in adopting 1S1R configurations for high-density applications.

2.3.3 Mitigation techniques for sneak-path currents

Selector device improvements: Using selector devices with higher nonlinearity, such as advanced threshold switches or selector diodes with sharper *I–V* characteristics, can help suppress sneak-path currents more effectively [11]. The ideal selector will exhibit a high resistance in the 'OFF' state and quickly switch to low resistance when activated, providing better isolation for unselected cells.

Adaptive biasing techniques: By carefully managing the voltages applied to unselected rows and columns, it is possible to minimize sneak-path currents. This approach, known as biasing or voltage isolation, adjusts the background voltage levels to reduce the incentive for current to flow through unintended paths [10].

Enhanced circuit design: Adding transistor-based selectors or complementary circuitry can provide better isolation in high-density applications. However, this approach increases complexity, area, and cost, which may offset the simplicity benefits of the 1S1R configuration. Transistor-based selectors, while more complex, offer better control over current pathways, reducing the likelihood of sneak paths in large-scale arrays [12].

The sneak-path issue in 1S1R configurations presents a significant challenge for the reliability and scalability of RRAM crossbar arrays [13]. Although selector devices are integrated to suppress unwanted currents, their effectiveness can be limited by nonlinear behaviors and design constraints, in particular as memory densities increase. Effective mitigation requires a combination of advanced selector devices, improved circuit design, and voltage management techniques. Balancing these factors is crucial to achieving reliable, low-power, and high-density memory solutions that leverage the simplicity of the 1S1R configuration while addressing the challenges posed by sneak-path currents.

2.4 Memristive crossbars

In this section, we explore the amazing possibilities of memristive crossbars and how they can be used in many different ways [12]. Such RRAMs are the focus of interest to transform various areas of technology. The memristive crossbar is a promising NVM technology that has gained considerable attention in recent years. It belongs to the class of RRAMs, which store data by altering their resistance in response to electrical signals. RRAM offers several advantages over traditional memory technologies such as NAND flash and DRAM, including faster read and write speeds, lower power consumption, and potentially higher storage density [19]. The basic principle of RRAM involves the use of a metal–insulator–metal (MIM) structure or a similar configuration; the insulating layer, made of metal oxides or other resistive materials, acts as the storage medium. When a voltage is applied across the electrodes (metal layers), it causes the resistance of the insulating layer to change. This change can be in two states, representing the binary data ('0' or '1'), and it remains stable even when the power is turned off, making it non-volatile. Figure 2.5 illustrates the impact of device nonlinearity on the performance of passive crossbar arrays. In figure 2.5(a), combining a bipolar RRAM with a bidirectional selector produces an overall current–voltage (I–V) characteristic with significantly

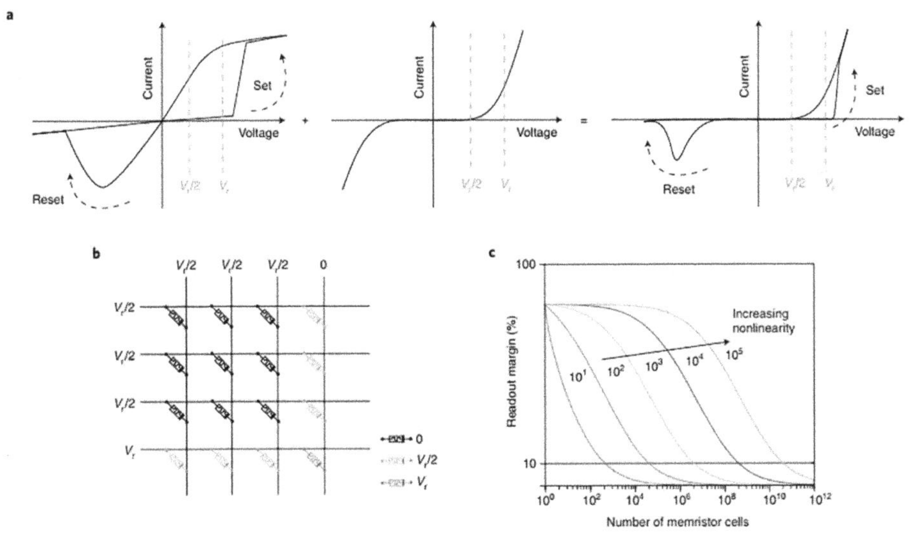

Figure 2.5. Impact of device nonlinearity on the capacity of a passive array. (a) Connecting a bipolar RRAM (left panel I–V) with a bidirectional selector (middle panel I–V) results in a characteristic I–V curve (right panel) with significantly lower current at half read voltage ($V_r/2$) compared to the original RRAM, attributed to the selector's nonlinearity. (b) Schematic of a crossbar array during read operation: the top electrode of the selected cell (blue) is biased at full voltage (V_r) while the bottom electrode is grounded, with all other wires biased at half voltage. This causes half-selected devices to experience half bias, resulting in sneak-path current in the array. (c) Higher nonlinearity, defined as the ratio of current at V_r to current at $V_r/2$, effectively suppresses sneak-path current, allowing for a much larger operational array under the same readout margin (the window between current read at high- and low-resistance states). (Reprinted by permission from Springer Nature Customer Service Center GmbH: (*Nature*), *Nature Materials*, [19], copyright 2019.

reduced current at half the read voltage ($V_r/2$) compared to the original RRAM, due to the selector's nonlinearity. Figure 2.5(b) shows the crossbar array during a read operation, where the selected cell (blue) is biased at full voltage (V_r), while all unselected cells are biased at $V_r/2$. This set-up creates sneak-path currents through half-selected devices, which degrade performance. Figure 2.5(c) highlights the role of high nonlinearity defined as the ratio of current at V_r to $V_r/2$ in suppressing these sneak currents, enabling larger operational arrays while maintaining a reliable readout margin between high- and low-resistance states.

Apart from the factors discussed earlier, resistive crossbars can be categorized into three groups based on their conductance state: binary memristive crossbars, multilevel memristive crossbars, and analog resistive crossbars [3]. A binary resistive crossbar comprises two existing conductance states, HRS and LRS, with the SET process displaying an abrupt change, while the RESET process exhibits a gradual transition. Memristive crossbar devices also have the potential to achieve multiple conductance levels, including continuous analog conductance [19]. The LRS's characteristics depend heavily on the current compliance during the SET operation, denoted as I_{SET}, while the HRS tuning is influenced by the stop voltage during the RESET operation, known as V_{stop}. In the process of adjusting multilevel conductance states, the program-and-verify method is commonly employed [20, 21]. To achieve memristive crossbar multilevel conductance state, two programming approaches have been introduced. First, fine-tuning of LRS is accomplished by carefully controlling the SET compliance current [19] with the results shown in figure 2.5(b), and the second method involves adjusting the HRS by controlling the RESET stop voltage, as illustrated in figure 2.5(c). In this method, a larger V_{stop} results in a larger HRS, although it can lead to overlapping HRS levels. Sun *et al* [5] have explored this method to practically obtain distinct conductance levels [22]. Another emerging approach involves devices exhibiting varying conductance states with linearly changing RESET pulse amplitudes. In addition to adjusting the programming amplitude, changing the duration of applied voltage pulses, either longer or shorter, can alter the device's state more gradually or rapidly [22]. Therefore, varying the width of the voltage pulse is also a practical means of achieving multilevel conductance states [23]. The width of the voltage pulse can be controlled by applying a series of fixed-width voltage pulses as an alternative method.

2.5 Selector device principles and requirements

Memristive devices with their unique property of memristance have gained widespread interest for applications in neuromorphic computing, analog computing, and NVM. However, efficiently accessing and addressing individual cells in a memristive crossbar array poses a challenge. The role of selector devices is to enable or disable the connection between rows and columns in the array, ensuring precise addressing while minimizing interference between adjacent memristive cells [24].

The key principles of selector devices include nonlinearity, low leakage current, and a high ON/OFF ratio. Nonlinearity ensures effective suppression of sneak currents in the crossbar array, and low leakage current helps minimize power dissipation and prevents data loss [8]. A high ON/OFF ratio ensures a clear distinction between the ON-state (connected) and OFF-state (disconnected) of the selector device, leading to reliable operations. A memory cell array is like a grid where information is stored. Each cell in the grid can hold a digital bit '0' and '1' just like a light switch being in the OFF or ON condition [16]. The cells are made using a combination of two electronic parts: a transistor and a resistor. One may assume the transistor as a tiny gatekeeper that controls the flow of electricity to the resistor, which acts like a small memory storage unit. This grid is designed using a special kind of electronic material called RRAM. This RRAM can remember the resistance they had when electricity flowed through them before. This helps in keeping the information saved even when the power is turned off, making it an NVM.

Figure 2.6 presents a memristive crossbar array, a cutting-edge architecture that holds immense potential for the next generation of memory and computing systems. At its core, the array consists of a network of memristive devices positioned at the intersections of horizontal rows, known as WLs, and vertical columns, referred to as BLs [35]. These memory cells can be accessed via programming the WL and BL. WL is like a special control line that allows us to select an entire row of cells. BL is another control line that connects to a specific cell within the chosen row. By using these lines together, one can read information from or write information to a specific cell in the grid, as shown in figure 2.6. This combination of technology and architecture makes it possible to have a memory system that is both efficient and capable of holding a lot of information compactly [26].

In the particular arrangement of figure 2.7, an intriguing addressing scheme is showcased, where only half of the devices in each row and column are selectively activated. This strategic selection offers multiple advantages, such as improved data storage and retrieval efficiency and reduced power consumption [18]. By selecting only half of the devices, the array achieves a delicate balance between functionality and energy efficiency, ensuring optimal performance while minimizing wasted

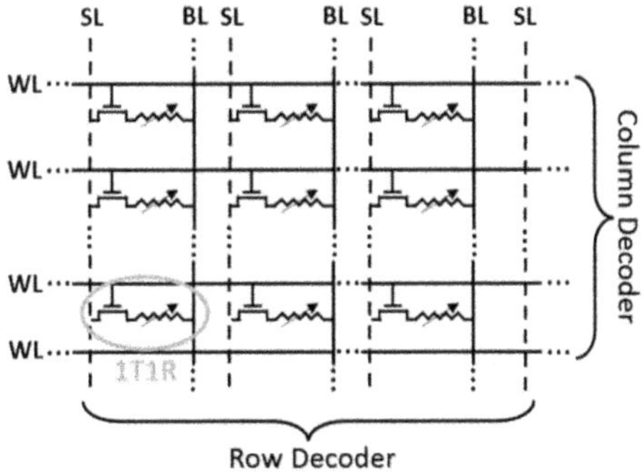

Figure 2.6. Schematic representation of a memory cell array with discrete connected transistors (1T1R) in a memristive crossbar array. The array is organized with WLs and BLs along with a select line (SL) for accessing and controlling individual memory cells within the crossbar structure.

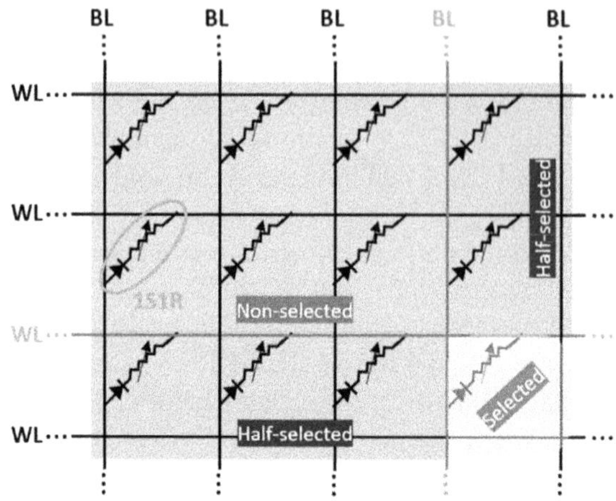

Figure 2.7. One cell selected by activating a specified WL and BL.

power. Crucially, the other half of the devices in both the rows and columns remain in a non-selected state. These non-selected devices are deliberately disconnected from the voltage supply, ensuring they do not consume any power unnecessarily [13]. This feature is essential for maintaining the stability and reliability of the array during various READ and WRITE operations, safeguarding against unintended data corruption or loss. To demonstrate the operation of the array, figure 2.7 further highlights one specific device that is fully selected in both the row and column. In this state, the device is directly connected to the supplied voltage, representing an active memory element ready for read and write operations. This fully selected configuration exemplifies how the array can operate efficiently as an integrated memory and computing unit [24]. To address specific rows and columns in the memristive crossbar array, row decoders, and column decoders are employed, as shown in figure 2.7. The row decoder takes address information as the input and activates the desired row lines, enabling data read and write operations [25]. Similarly, the column decoder decodes column addresses and activates the relevant selector devices, facilitating read and write operations for the selected columns. The effective integration of selector devices, row decoders, and column decoders ensures the reliable and efficient operation of memristive devices in large-scale arrays. This provides a promising platform for future computing and memory applications, contributing to advancements in AI, neuromorphic computing, and other emerging technologies [26]. The MCA showcased in figure 2.7, exemplifies the groundbreaking potential of emerging technologies in the field of computing. Its high-density design, non-volatile storage capabilities, and potential for neuromorphic computing applications make it a prominent candidate for powering advanced AI and machine learning systems [27]. As research in this area continues to progress, memristive crossbar arrays are poised to play a crucial role in shaping the future of computing and revolutionizing the way we process and store information.

2.6 Design and integration challenges

Integrating selector-based RRAM into the fabric of modern computing presents a transformative opportunity with its potential to revolutionize memory and storage paradigms. This technology leverages the intriguing characteristics of resistive switching, offering high speed, low power consumption, and scalability, making it a compelling candidate for next-generation memory solutions [27]. However, this transition is not without its share of complex design and integration challenges, which must be meticulously addressed to unlock the full potential of selector-based RRAM [28]. Central to the operation of selector-based RRAM is the selector device, a pivotal element responsible for isolating and directing current through the memristive crossbar cell. These selector devices exhibit high nonlinearity, essential to ensuring precise cell selection and preventing unwanted current paths. While RRAM cells themselves exploit resistance modulation through metal-ion movement for data storage, the intricate interaction between selectors and cells demands precise control mechanisms to guarantee reliable performance and data retention. In the work frame of design, several critical challenges emerge. The foremost is the need for a high ON/OFF ratio and stability in selector devices to prevent cross-talk and ensure the integrity of data storage.

The variability introduced by manufacturing and process variations is an extensive concern, further complicated by the addition of selector devices, necessitating advanced design strategies to mitigate this. Circuit design for efficient read and write operations must also consider current compliance, preventing device damage during operations [29]. Moreover, the densely packed memory arrays raise the presence of cross-talk and sneak paths, demanding innovative solutions to maintain data integrity. Long-term endurance and data retention in the face of high-write-cycle scenarios presents another remarkable challenge [30]. In terms of putting things together, making sure the new technology fits with the old technologies can be a big challenge. The new memory needs to work smoothly with the existing memory set-up, and this needs careful thought about how that can work together. As the new technology becomes smaller and more advanced, we really need strong methods to fix any mistakes that might happen, so that the data stay reliable. Additionally, because this technology is unique, it is really important to create good ways to test both the individual parts and how they work together in a system, to make sure everything is reliable.

Despite the numerous challenges to address, significant progress has been made in the strategy for developing brain-inspired systems using nanowire networks, as shown in figure 2.8. Researchers are exploring innovative materials to enhance performance and durability, while also designing circuits that enable more efficient and error-free data operations. Advanced computational algorithms are being developed to correct potential errors, and simulations are being conducted to ensure seamless integration of the components. Although selector-based memristive crossbars hold great promise for transforming memory storage and computational processes, they face significant hurdles in performing complex tasks. Realizing their full potential requires creative solutions to overcome intricate design and

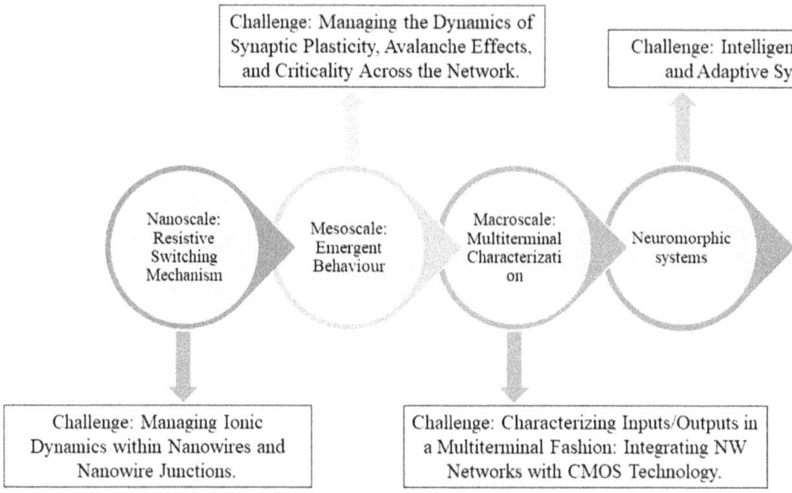

Figure 2.8. Strategy for developing brain-inspired systems utilizing nanowire networks.

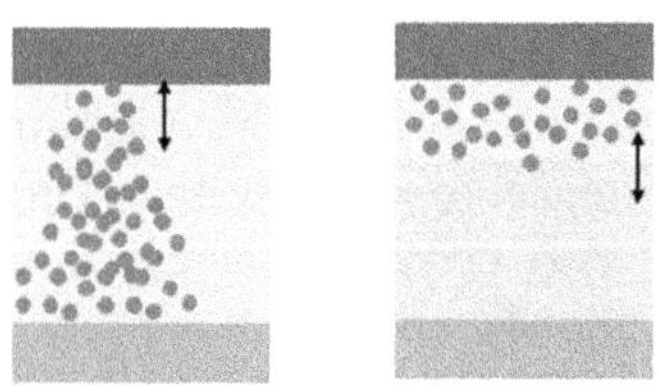

Figure 2.9. Valence change memory-based devices.

compatibility challenges [30]. The resistive crossbar devices relying on oxygen ion migration effects and subsequent valence changes are called valence change memory (VCM). See in figure 2.9 and table 2.2.

2.7 Multibit data storage with a selector-based memristive crossbar

Multibit data storage has emerged as a crucial technology in the modern era, enabling the efficient utilization of memory resources while catering to the ever-increasing demand for higher data storage capacities [8]. In this context, the selector-based resistive crossbar has gained significant attention for its potential to revolutionize the field of NVM systems. The selector-based resistive crossbar presents a novel approach to multibit data storage by leveraging the inherent properties of resistive switching materials [11]. Contrasting traditional binary storage, where each memory cell stores a single bit of information, multibit storage allows a single memory cell to store multiple bits, greatly enhancing memory density and overall efficiency [23, 31]. The key innovation in the selector-based resistive crossbar lies in its use of a selector device that facilitates the reading and writing of multiple resistance states in a single memory cell. This selector, often a diode or transistor, enables precise control over the

Table 2.2. Device performance analysis.

	Filamentary	Interfacial
Single device	Using different materials and scaling down to millimeter sizes for low-voltage operation	Diverse materials, and nanometer-scale scaling, while maintaining high voltage and thick oxide
Array	1T1R and 1S1R. Total capacity up to 1–2 Mb	Up to a few kb, mainly 1R array only
Monolithic CMOS integration	Down to the 2 × technology nodes, and in 3D architectures	Mainly for oxide bilayer
Binary	Good endurance (> 10^6–10^9) and retention (> years)	Endurance and long retention need to be optimized
Analog multilevel memory	Controlling multilevel operations in an array using program/verify algorithms is complex	Less variability but reduced dynamic range and mainly data for single devices
Long-term memory	Retention at high time and for 6–10 years	Single device retention up to years for some material stacks

resistance levels of the memory cell, allowing it to represent multiple bits through distinct resistance values. The storage capacity of a given memory array is dramatically increased, one of the prominent benefits of the selector-based memristive crossbar is its potential to reduce the physical footprint of memory systems. By enabling multibit storage within a single memory cell, the need for a large number of individual cells is diminished, leading to more compact memory designs. This size reduction is especially valuable for mobile devices and other applications with limited physical space [33].

Furthermore, the adoption of multibit storage with a selector-based resistive crossbar can lead to significant energy savings. The ability to store multiple bits in a single cell translates to fewer read and write operations, reducing the overall energy consumption of memory access [3]. However, the realization of efficient selector-based resistive crossbar systems also comes with its own set of challenges. One of the primary obstacles is ensuring the reliability and stability of the resistance states over time. Memory cells must exhibit consistent switching behavior and minimal resistance drift to guarantee accurate and durable multibit storage.

The comprehensive evaluation of selector devices, focusing on their performance when utilizing different types of two-terminal $4F_2$ selector technologies [2]. The notation (NR) indicates instances where specific data is not reported, this information provides valuable insights into the assessment methodology and helps readers understand the context of the findings presented in table 2.2. It plays a crucial role in illustrating the outcomes of the performance assessment, contributing to a deeper understanding of the topic and its implications. Table 2.3 provides a comprehensive evaluation of selector devices based on different two-terminal selector technologies. The term '$4F^2$' typically refers [34] to the size of the memory cell, where F represents

Table 2.3. Performance assessment of selector devices utilizing various two-terminal $4F^2$ selector technologies.

Technology	$Ni/TiO_2/Ni$ [23]	$TaN/SiN_x/$ TaN [35]	MIEC [36]	Ploy *npn* [37]	VO_2 MIT [38]	Epi *npn* [34]
Current density ($mA\ cm^{-2}$)	10^{-4}	0.1	0.15	> 0.02	> 1	> 1
ON/OFF ratio	10^4	150	10^4	500–5000	50	250–4700
Switching speed	NR	< 8.5	NR	NR	< 20 ns	< 10 ns
Technology maturity	Low	Medium	Low	High	Low	High

the feature size. In this context, 'selector devices' are components crucial for the proper functioning of certain types of memory or computing systems.

In addition to reliability, the design and integration of selectors play a crucial role in the overall performance of selector-based resistive crossbars. Selectors must offer low leakage current, a high ON/OFF ratio, and compatibility with the chosen resistive switching material [31]. Developing selectors that meet these criteria is a complex task that requires a deep understanding of both device physics and materials science. The potential applications of selector-based memristive crossbar extend beyond traditional data storage [32]. Due to its high density and energy efficiency, this technology can contribute to the advancement of neuromorphic computing, where memory and processing are closely connected to mimic the human brain's cognitive capabilities. The ability to store multiple analog states in a single cell aligns well with the demands of neural networks and AI algorithms. Multibit data storage using selector-based memristive crossbar holds immense promise for transforming memory systems in various industries. Its ability to efficiently store multiple bits in a single memory cell, coupled with its potential for energy savings and compact designs, positions it as a strong candidate for the future of non-volatile memory technology [33]. While challenges remain, ongoing research and advancements are lighting the way for the practical realization of this innovative approach to data storage.

2.8 Applications and future prospects

The memristive crossbar is an emerging non-volatile memory technology that has shown great promise for various applications in the field of electronics and computing. One specific type of resistive crossbar that has gained attention is the selector-based memristive crossbar, which combines the memory storage capability of resistive crossbar cells with selector devices that control access to these cells. This combination enhances the performance and reliability of resistive crossbar devices, enabling new applications and future prospects. Some of the applications and potential future directions for selector-based memristive crossbar technology are described in the following.

Neuromorphic computing has been revolutionized by the promise of selector-based resistive crossbar technology. Its primary objective is to emulate the intricate computing capabilities inherent in the human brain [33]. This emulation is made possible through a powerful combination of the analog resistance states of memristive crossbar cells and the precise selective addressing provided by selectors. The integration of these elements opens the door to creating artificial synapses within the architecture of neuromorphic systems [34]. These synthetic synapses play a pivotal role in enabling the realization of highly efficient and remarkably low-power neural networks [33, 40]. This innovative approach holds the potential to redefine the model of computational technology, leading us toward a future where machines can mimic the complex and adaptive nature of the human mind. This advancement is anticipated to have a significant impact, effectively bridging the gap between traditional computing and the realm of cognitive computation. As we delve deeper into this fascinating field, the convergence of neuroscience and technology brings us closer to unlocking the full potential of intelligent machines.

The fascinating field of in-memory computing presents a combined effect between data storage and processing, making it an ideal candidate for the benefits of selector-based memristive crossbar device. This innovative technology brings a willing-to-change capability, the ability to directly perform computations within the memory array itself [16]. Figure 2.10 presents the bipolar resistive switching behavior in hexagonal boron nitride (h-BN) memristors, evaluated for neuromorphic computing applications. Figure 2.10(a) shows the *I–V* characteristics of a single memristor across 120 cycles, highlighting stability over repeated switching. Figure 2.10(b) illustrates analog switching between two distinct low-resistance states, while figure 2.10(c) demonstrates stable conductance levels during these analog transitions. Figure 2.10(d) depicts the cumulative distribution of resistance states across 48 memristors over 1500 cycles, indicating device reliability. Figure 2.10(e) and (f) show the distribution of the SET and RESET voltages for 48 and 16 devices, respectively, under varying current compliance. Figure 2.10(g) presents the results from a multilayer perceptron simulation on the MNIST dataset, and figure 2.10(h) provides statistics on device conductance for a 64×64 crossbar array after conductance tuning, showcasing potential for practical implementation in neuromorphic circuits [41].

This innovative approach eliminates the traditional requirement of transferring data to and fro between separate storage and processing units. The effects of this advancement are particularly significant for tasks involving substantial data processing, such as data-intensive operations [8]. The perfect integration of data storage and processing at the memory level has the potential to not only boost the efficiency of existing computational processes but also show the way for entirely new approaches to computing. By reducing data transfer expenses, this integration supports the interest of higher performance and reduced energy consumption, driving us towards more efficient and effective computational methodologies [3]. As we explore deeper into this model, the possibilities for innovation and optimization across various computational domains become increasingly inviting.

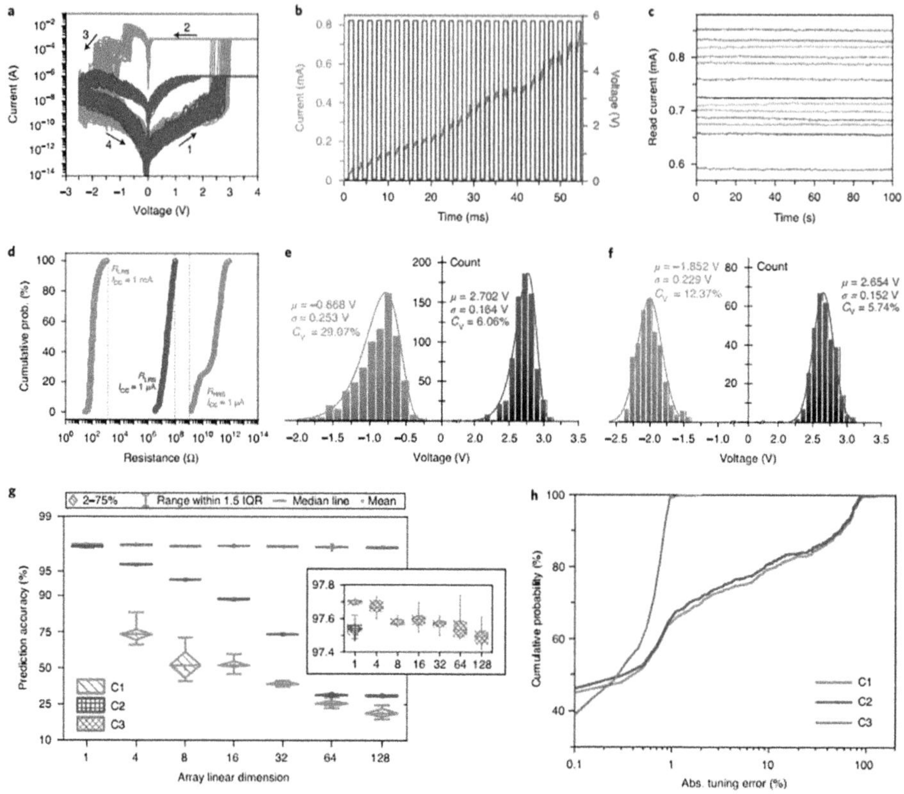

Figure 2.10. Bipolar resistive switching in h-BN memristors for neuromorphic computing. (a) *I–V* characteristics of a single memristor measured during 120 cycles. (b) Analog switching between two low-resistance states demonstrated. (c) Stable conductance states during analog transition. (d) Cumulative distribution of resistance states for 48 memristors over 1500 cycles. (e) Distribution of device SET and RESET voltages for 48 devices. (f) Similar distribution for 16 devices with different current compliance. (g) MNIST dataset simulation results for a multilayer perceptron. (h) Example of device conductance statistics for a 64 × 64 crossbar array circuit after tuning. (Reproduced with permission from [41]. Copyright 2020 Springer Nature.)

High-density storage stands at the threshold of a critical revolution in the advancement of large-density storage, driven by the extraordinary capabilities carried forward by selector-based resistive crossbar devices [3, 8, 13]. Figure 2.11 outlines the instructions for performing erase, write, and read operations on cell m11 using two different biasing methods in memristive arrays. Figure 2.11(a) shows the sequence under the one-half bias scheme, and figure 2.11(b) shows the same operations under the one-third bias scheme. These bias schemes provide different ways of applying voltage to selectively operate on cell m11 while minimizing interference with other cells, illustrating strategies to improve accuracy and reduce unintended cell activation in crossbar architectures [42]. This technology has the inherent power to completely reshape the concept of memory storage, pushing the boundaries of density to unique levels. Its exceptional scalability stands as a key

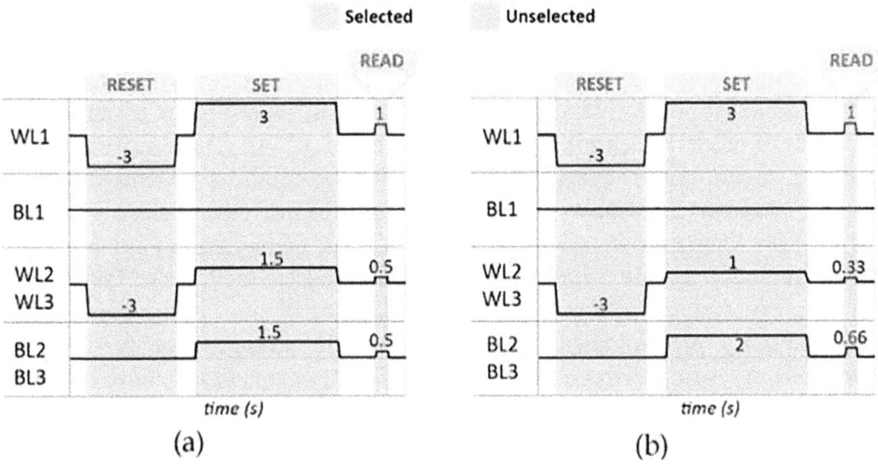

Figure 2.11. Instructions for erasing all cells, writing 1 to cell m11, and reading m11 using both (a) the one-half and (b) the one-third bias schemes. (Reproduced from [44]. CC BY 4.0.)

differentiator, facilitating continuous adaptation to the ever-expanding requirements of data-intensive applications [27]. In addition, the encouragingly low power consumption of the selector-based memristive crossbar makes it an appropriate solution for critical use cases, such as solid-state drives (SSDs) and the dynamic state of in-memory computing. In the sophisticated world of SSDs, where the demand for efficiently storing and swiftly accessing massive datasets is paramount, selector-based MCA emerges as a game-changer [17]. Its ability to manage and manipulate large volumes of data seamlessly, without compromising on energy efficiency, positions it as an ideal innovation in the storage domain. This technology is not just about improving the efficiency of current systems, it is about unlocking doors to entirely novel possibilities, in particular as data-driven applications continue their explosive growth across diverse fields. The incorporation of high-density prowess, adaptability, and energy consciousness in selector-based memristive crossbar is leading to a new era of storage solutions, driving us closer to the realization of highly efficient, scalable, and sustainable data storage architectures [8]. The potential impact on fields ranging from AI to cloud computing is immeasurable, covering the way for a data-centric future where storage limitations cease to delay our limitless objectives [13].

Advanced logic circuits move toward new possibilities as selector devices complement the power of memristive crossbar cells, establishing a path to progressive logic circuit architectures. This remarkable combination introduces circuits that go beyond the limitations of volatility, allowing them to repeatedly retain their states, while also involving reconfigurability as a fundamental characteristic [12]. The implications of this interaction resonate through the domain of field-programmable gate array (FPGA) technology, where the quick, efficient transformation of logic circuits lies at the middle of innovation. These circuits can change and adapt to different computer needs, making them useful in various applications such as controlled computing and AI systems. This evolution in logic circuit design unlocks the potential for more active and intelligent devices, enabling us to navigate the complexities of modern technology with high efficiency [34]. As we move into a time when digital technology is everywhere in our lives, combining selector devices and memristive crossbar cells shows progress, lighting the way to a future where long-lasting, flexible logic circuits empower the next wave of technology advancements.

Hybrid memory systems, integrating a selector-based memristive crossbar into hybrid memory systems, offers the potential to control the unique capabilities of multiple memory technologies. By combining the strengths of NAND flash, DRAM, and the memristive crossbar, these hybrid systems can achieve a balanced combined effect that leads to significant improvements in overall system performance. The result is a perfect equilibrium between speed, data storage density, and non-volatile memory characteristics [16]. In this mix of different memory technologies, selector-based technology helps us to access data quickly and keeps it safe. The speed at which we read and write data in DRAM and NAND flash, the other types of memory, goes well with memristive crossbar's ability to keep data even when the power is turned off. Collectively, these technologies create a memory system, meeting the needs of all kinds of modern computer tasks. This general approach to memory design addresses the limitations of individual memory technologies, such as the volatility of DRAM and the slower write speeds of NAND flash [18]. By strategically integrating these technologies, the hybrid memory system achieves a delicate balance, optimizing the data storage and endurance of the device. The benefits of such a hybrid set-up extend to various domains, from high-performance computing to mobile devices, where the demand for efficient, reliable, and fast memory solutions continues to grow [21]. The combined effect between these technologies paves the way for future advancements in computing, enabling innovative applications that require the perfect blend of speed, capacity, and non-volatility. Hybrid memory systems, which use a combination of selector-based memristive crossbars, NAND flash, and DRAM, are a big improvement in memory technologies [38]. This approach solves problems from each memory type, creating a powerful memory set-up that fits the needs of modern computers and pushes the limits of data storage and processing.

In AI acceleration, the unique and compelling characteristics of the innovative selector-based memristive crossbar memory technology seamlessly combines the benefits of high-density storage with remarkably low-power operation, creating an interesting proposal for various AI model deployment and acceleration scenarios [36]. The continuous integration of the selector-based memristive crossbar into AI architecture delivers a definite rise in energy efficiency, a key concern in modern AI applications [39]. By minimizing energy consumption, this advancement paves the way for sustainable and resource-conscious AI implementations. Selector-based memristive crossbars align with the technical demands of AI with the priority for energy-efficient solutions.

Bibliography

[1] Lee M J *et al* 2011 High-endurance and scalable non-volatile memory device made from asymmetric $Ta_2O_{(5-x)}/TaO_{(2-x)}$ bilayer structures *Nat. Mater.* **10** 625–30

[2] Huang Y *et al* 2012 A new dynamic selector based on the bipolar RRAM for the crossbar array application *IEEE Trans. Electron Devices* **59** 2277–80

[3] Zhang L, Cosemans S, Wouters D J, Groeseneken G, Jurczak M and Govoreanu B 2015 One-selector one-resistor cross-point array with threshold switching selector *IEEE Trans. Electron Devices* **62** 3250–7

[4] Zhang L, Cosemans S, Wouters D J, Groeseneken G, Jurczak M and Govoreanu B 2015 On the optimal ON/OFF resistance ratio for resistive switching element in one-selector one-resistor crosspoint arrays *IEEE Electron Device Lett.* **36** 570–2

[5] Sung C, Lim S and Hwang H 2020 Experimental determination of the tunable threshold voltage characteristics in a $Ag_xTe_{1-x}/Al_2O_3/TiO_2$-based hybrid memory device *IEEE Electron Device Lett.* **41** 713–6

[6] Ji Y *et al* 2013 Flexible and twistable non-volatile memory cell array with all-organic one diode–one resistor architecture *Nat. Commun.* **4** 2707

[7] Khan M U *et al* 2019 Schottky diode based resistive switching device based on ZnO/PEDOT:PSS heterojunction to reduce sneak current problem *J. Mater. Sci. Mater. Electron.* **30** 4607–17

[8] Wang X *et al* 2021 A 4T2R RRAM bit cell for highly parallel ternary content addressable memory *IEEE Trans. Electron Devices* **68** 4933–7

[9] Gao Z, Romero M F and Calle F 2018 Thermal and electrical stability assessment of AlGaN/GaN metal–oxide–semiconductor high-electron mobility transistors (MOS-HEMTs) with HfO_2 gate dielectric *IEEE Trans. Electron Devices* **65** 3142–8

[10] Kumar D, Kalaga P S and Ang D S 2020 Visible light detection and memory capabilities in MgO/HfO_2 bilayer-based transparent structure for photograph sensing *IEEE Trans. Electron Devices* **67** 4274–80

[11] Kobayashi M, Ueyama N, Jang K and Hiramoto T 2018 Experimental demonstration of a nonvolatile SRAM with ferroelectric HfO_2 capacitor for normally off application *IEEE J. Electron Devices Soc.* **6** 280–5

[12] Lin J, Wang S and Liu H 2021 Multi-level switching of Al-doped HfO_2 RRAM with a single voltage amplitude set pulse *Electronics* **10** 731

[13] Wang X Y *et al* 2021 High-density memristor-CMOS ternary logic family *IEEE Trans. Circuits Syst.* I **68** 264–74

[14] Mandapati R *et al* 2013 On pairing of bipolar RRAM memory with NPN selector based on set/reset array power considerations *IEEE Trans. Nanotechnol.* **12** 1178–84

[15] Deng Y *et al* 2013 RRAM crossbar array with cell selection device: a device and circuit interaction study *IEEE Trans. Electron Devices* **60** 719–26

[16] Pisarev A D, Busygin A N, Udovichenko S Y and Maevsky O V 2020 A biomorphic neuroprocessor based on a composite memristor-diode crossbar *Microelectron. J.* **102** 104827

[17] Singh A, Lebdeh M A, Gebregiorgis A, Bishnoi R, Joshi R V and Hamdioui S 2021 SRIF: scalable and reliable integrate and fire circuit ADC for memristor-based CIM architectures *IEEE Trans. Circuits Syst.* I **68** 1917–30

[18] Yang C, Wang X and Zeng Z 2022 Full-circuit implementation of transformer network based on memristor *IEEE Trans. Circuits Syst.* I **69** 1395–407

[19] Xia Q and Yang J J 2019 Memristive crossbar arrays for brain-inspired computing *Nat. Mater.* **18** 309–23

[20] Gopalakrishnan K *et al* 2010 Highly-scalable novel access device based on mixed ionic conduction (MIEC) materials for high density phase change memory (PCM) array *Symp. VLSI Technol. (Honolulu, HI)* pp 205–6

[21] Lee M H, Kao C Y, Yang C L, Chen Y S, Lee H Y, Chen F and Tsai M J 2011 Reliability of ambipolar switching poly-Si diodes for crosspoint memory applications *69th Annu. Device Res. Conf. (Santa Barbara, CA)* pp 89–90

[22] Son M, Lee J, Park J, Shin J, Choi G, Jung S, Lee W, Kim S, Park S and Hwang H 2011 Excellent selector characteristics of nanoscale VO_2 for high-density bipolar ReRAM applications *IEEE Electron. Device Lett.* **32** 1579–81

[23] Christensen D V 2022 Roadmap on neuromorphic computing and engineering *Neuromorph. Comput. Eng.* **2** 022501

[24] Long B, Li Y and Jha R 2012 Switching characteristics of Ru/HfO_2/TiO_{2-x}/Ru RRAM devices for digital and analog nonvolatile memory applications *IEEE Electron. Device Lett.* **33** 706708

[25] Yu S, Wu Y, Jeyasingh R, Kuzum D and Wong H S P 2011 An electronic synapse device based on metal oxide resistive switching memory for neuromorphic computation *IEEE Trans. Electron Devices* **58** 27292737

[26] Bedeschi F, Fackenthal R, Resta C and Donze E M 2009 A bipolar-selected phase change memory featuring multi-level cell storage *IEEE J. Solid State Circ.* **44** 217227

[27] Li B *et al* 2015 RRAM-based analog approximate computing *IEEE Trans. Comput. Des. Integr. Circ. Syst.* **34** 19051917

[28] Jo S H *et al* 2010 Nanoscale memristor device as synapse in neuromorphic systems *Nano Lett.* **10** 12971301

[29] Hansen M *et al* 2018 Unsupervised Hebbian learning experimentally realized with analogue memristive crossbar arrays *Sci. Rep.* **8** 8914

[30] Talati N, Gupta S, Mane P and Kvatinsky S 2016 Logic design within memristive memories using memristor-aided logic (MAGIC) *IEEE Trans. Nanotechnol.* **15** 635–50

[31] Reuben J 2020 Rediscovering majority logic in the post-CMOS era: a perspective from in-memory computing *J. Low Power Electron. Appl.* **10** 28

[32] Gupta V, Kapur S, Saurabh S and Grover A 2020 Resistive random access memory: a review of device challenges *IETE Tech. Rev.* **37** 377–90

[33] Chen A 2016 A review of emerging non-volatile memory (NVM) technologies and applications *Solid State Electron.* **125** 25–38

[34] Xing J, Serb A, Khiat A, Berdan R, Xu H and Prodromakis T 2016 An FPGA-based instrument for en-masse RRAM characterization with ns pulsing resolution *IEEE Trans. Circuits Syst.* I **63** 818–26

[35] Luo Q *et al* 2015 Cu BEOL compatible selector with high selectivity ($>10^7$), extremely low off-current ($\sim$pA) and high endurance ($>10^{10}$) *IEEE Int. Electron Devices Meeting (IEDM) (Washington, DC)* pp 10.4.1–4

[36] Aluguri R and Tseng T Y 2016 Notice of violation of IEEE publication principles: overview of selector devices for 3-D stackable cross point RRAM arrays *IEEE J. Electron. Devices Soc.* **4** 294–306

[37] Ji X, Hao S, Pang K Y, Lim K G and Zhao R 2020 A vacuum gap selector with ultra-low leakage for large-scale neuromorphic network *IEEE Electron. Device Lett.* **41** 505–8

[38] Srinivasan V S S *et al* 2012 Punchthrough-diode-based bipolar RRAM selector by Si epitaxy *IEEE Electron Device Lett.* **33** 1396–8

[39] Huang J J, Tseng Y M, Hsu C W and Hou T H 2011 Bipolar nonlinear Ni/TiO_2/Ni selector for 1S1R crossbar array applications *IEEE Electron Device Lett.* **32** 1427–9

[40] Hardtdegen A, La Torre C, Cüppers F, Menzel S, Waser R and Hoffmann-Eifert S 2018 Improved switching stability and the effect of an internal series resistor in HfO_2/TiO_x bilayer ReRAM cells *IEEE Trans. Electron Devices* **65** 3229–36

[41] Chen S *et al* 2020 Wafer-scale integration of two-dimensional materials in high-density memristive crossbar arrays for artificial neural networks *Nat. Electron.* **3** 638–45

[42] Kim K H, Seo M J and Jang B C 2023 Amorphous ITZO-based selector device for memristor crossbar array *Micromachines* **14** 506

[43] Chen Z *et al* 2024 Assessment of functional performance in self-rectifying passive crossbar arrays utilizing sneak path current *Sci. Rep.* **14** 24682

[44] Darwish M and Pohl L 2024 Insulator metal transition-based selector in crossbar memory arrays *Electron. Mater.* **5** 17–29

Chapter 3

Memristive devices in brain-inspired computing

3.1 Introduction

The convergence of neurobiology and computational science has given rise to brain-inspired computing (BIC), a domain that seeks to replicate cognitive processes in silicon. These special components mimic how our brains work, assisting computers in acquiring and retaining knowledge like human learning and memory. This chapter dives into how these devices are changing the game, making computers smarter and more efficient, just like our brains. Ryu *et al* [1] verified that the recognition rate in the bilayer device (Ti/TiO_2/HfO_2/Si) is significantly more accurate in a neural network model employing the Fashion MNIST dataset [3]. BIC technology emerged in the early 1970s, facilitating a connection between the human brain and computers. It achieves this by translating electrical signals from brain activity into comprehensible information. Zhang *et al* [2] highlighted that the approach is of use in a broad range of applications from neural simulation to intelligent computing and could potentially be used to create a general-purpose computing infrastructure. Consequently, BIC system users thoughts can be understood through the processed data, all without the need for neuromuscular control. BCI systems can potentially discern user intentions by analyzing these brain activity-related electrical signals [3]. This technology holds promises for assisting individuals who suffer from conditions like cerebral palsy and brain stem strokes, which result in neuromuscular impairment. These BCI applications primarily depend on advancements in the current human brain physiological signal detection technology [1–3].

Memristive devices have emerged as a fascinating class of electronic components that hold great promise in the field of brain-inspired computing. They can change their resistance state in response to an applied voltage or current, this property makes them suitable for applications in brain-inspired computing, where they can be used to simulate the synapses of neurons. In the human brain, synapses are the

doi:10.1088/978-0-7503-6169-9ch3

© IOP Publishing Ltd 2025. All rights, including for text and data mining (TDM), artificial intelligence (AI) training, and similar technologies, are reserved.

connections between neurons, they are responsible for transmitting signals from one neuron to another [3]. The strength of a synapse can be changed by the amount of activity that it experiences and that process, known as synaptic plasticity, that is essential for learning and memory. Memristors are a promising technology for implementing synaptic plasticity in neuromorphic systems, these are scalable, efficient, and energy-efficient, making them well-suited for use in large-scale neuromorphic systems. Kim *et al* [4] explained how memristor-based neuromorphic computing can learn, infer, and even create, various artificial neural networks. Additionally, memristors are non-volatile, which means that they can store synaptic information even when the power is turned off, this makes them ideal for use in applications where long-term storage of synaptic information is required.

Deep learning (DL), a cornerstone of contemporary artificial intelligence (AI), has emerged as a transformative technology, drawing inspiration from the architecture and functionality of biological neural networks. These computational models rely on interconnected, parallel-operating units that emulate aspects of brain functionality. The success of DL can be attributed to three key factors: the availability of extensive datasets, exponential growth in computing power, and advancements in algorithmic design. However, the looming limitations posed by the end of Moore's law, which restricts further scaling of traditional CMOS technology, raise concerns about sustaining progress in AI due to potential hardware constraints.

Memristive devices, often hailed as groundbreaking post-CMOS technology, offer promising solutions to these challenges in brain-inspired computing. Their unique characteristics, such as non-volatility, high density, and low energy consumption, position them as ideal candidates for implementing energy-efficient in-memory computing architectures. These architectures can be leveraged to build specialized DL accelerators and spiking neural networks that align closely with the principles of neuromorphic engineering. Unlike conventional von Neumann architecture, which separates memory and computation, memristive systems allow for data storage and processing to occur within the same physical location, dramatically enhancing speed and efficiency. These devices have been identified as pivotal for advancing non-von Neumann paradigms, enabling real-time learning and inference in AI systems.

Furthermore, lessons drawn from biological systems are steering innovations in AI hardware and algorithms. For instance, concepts like reservoir computing, inspired by recurrent neural networks in biology, demonstrate how dynamic memory and temporal pattern recognition can be effectively achieved using memristors. This integration underscores the potential of memristive devices to support the development of neuromorphic and brain-inspired computing systems that emulate the cognitive capabilities of the human brain. Looking ahead, the convergence of memristive technology and tailored algorithmic approaches could catalyze the next wave of breakthroughs in AI, offering a pathway toward more efficient, scalable, and biologically inspired computing solutions. Such advancements are poised to redefine the trajectory of AI, paving the way for truly intelligent, power-efficient systems capable of learning and adapting in real-world environments.

3.2 Overview of memristive devices significance in brain-inspired computing

The ongoing advancements in AI are primarily driven by three factors: the proliferation of massive datasets, continuous improvements in computing power, and innovative algorithmic developments. DL, a subset of machine learning (ML), has particularly benefited from these factors, with graphics processing units (GPUs) emerging as effective co-processors to accelerate the implementation of DL algorithms. The integration of DL with GPU-based systems has led to significant breakthroughs across various AI applications. However, this progress has also triggered an exponential rise in the demand for computational resources, with recent analyses indicating a 300 000-fold increase in computing requirements since 2012. This demand is predicted to double approximately every 3–4 months outpacing the improvements historically achieved through Moore's law, which has provided only a sevenfold increase in the same timeframe.

At the same time, Moore's law has shown signs of slowing significantly, suggesting that further miniaturization of complementary metal-oxide-semiconductor (CMOS) transistors may soon reach its physical and economic limits. This situation necessitates exploring alternative technological roadmaps to achieve scalable and efficient AI solutions. Innovations in hardware architectures, including GPUs, field-programmable gate arrays (FPGAs), and application-specific integrated circuits (ASICs), have significantly contributed to overcoming these limitations. These architectures move beyond the traditional von Neumann model, which separates memory and computing units, a design that creates performance bottlenecks due to energy- and time-intensive data movement.

Memristive devices offer a promising pathway for addressing these challenges by integrating memory and computation into a single unit. Unlike standard digital CMOS components, which struggle to efficiently manage the vast number of continuous weights and synapses required by artificial neural networks (ANNs), memristors provide non-volatility, scalability, and energy-efficient operation. These characteristics make them particularly suited for implementing in-memory computing paradigms, enabling real-time processing with reduced latency and power consumption.

As AI workloads become increasingly complex and data-intensive, the shift from von Neumann architectures toward neuromorphic computing models, inspired by the human brain, could revolutionize the landscape. Memristor-based systems are at the forefront of this transformation, offering the potential for significant gains in computational efficiency, scalability, and integration of learning algorithms tailored to these emerging architectures. Memristive devices can be used to simulate synaptic plasticity in several ways, one of which is to use the device's resistance state to represent the strength of the synapse. When a voltage is applied to the device, its resistance can be changed, this change can be used to represent a change in the strength of the synapse [1]. Another way to use memristive devices in BIC is to use them to create ANNs. Zhang *et al* proposed memristor ANN focused on fully connected neural networks [3]. ANNs are computer models that are inspired by the way the brain works, they are made up of interconnected nodes, each of which represents a neuron, and the strength of the connections between the nodes can be adjusted as the strength of synapses in the brain. A comprehensive review of current brain-inspired learning representations in ANNs was conducted by Schmidgall *et al* [6]. Memristive devices can be used to create ANNs that are more efficient and energy efficient than traditional neural networks because memristive devices can be used to store the weights of the network, which eliminates the need for a separate memory unit. Jeong *et al* [7] reported proposed memristors are good candidates as synaptic devices for weight storage and matrix-vector multiplication required in ANNs. These include variability in device characteristics, scalability to large-scale neural networks, and the need for reliable fabrication techniques to ensure consistent performance [7]. Here is a key concept in neuromorphic computing for synaptic emulation, learning, and adaptation to BIC and its connection to memristors.

Neuromorphic computing: It aims to develop computing systems that can perform tasks inspired by the brain's neural networks. Unlike traditional digital computers that use binary logic gates, neuromorphic systems employ analog circuits to emulate the behavior of neurons and synapses, enabling them to process information more efficiently for certain tasks [2]. The brain is a highly efficient and powerful computing system that can process complex information, recognize patterns, and learn from experience. Kim *et al* [8] ANN simulation shows that the neuromorphic system with the implanted SiN_x/a-Si memristor provides a 91.3% learning accuracy. In neuromorphic computing these are capabilities by building circuits and systems that mimic brain architecture and computational principles.

Memristors and synaptic emulation: A memristor is a two-terminal electronic device whose resistance depends on the history of the applied voltage. This means that the resistance of a memristor can change depending on how much voltage has been applied to it in the past [1]. This property is called memristive switching. Synapses are the connections between neurons in the brain. They are responsible for transmitting signals from one neuron to another. The strength of a synapse can change over time, a phenomenon known as synaptic plasticity [3]. This change in strength can be caused by a variety of factors, such as the frequency of activity between the neurons, the level of calcium ions in the synapse, and the presence of neurotransmitters [7]. Memristors have been proposed as potential candidates for emulating synapses in neuromorphic systems. This is because memristors can also exhibit synaptic plasticity. In particular, memristors can be programmed to change their resistance in a way that mimics the long-term potentiation (LTP) and long-term depression (LTD) of biological synapses. LTP is a long-lasting increase in the strength of a synapse, it is thought to be involved in learning and memory. LTD is a long-lasting decrease in the strength of a synapse, it is thought to be involved in forgetting. Kunwar *et al* [9] provided the Au/Nb:STO device exhibits high stability, low variability, and continuous conductance change during LTP and LTD cycles.

Learning and adaptation: Memristors are non-volatile memory devices that can be used to implement synaptic plasticity, which is the ability of synapses to change their strength in response to experience. This is a key mechanism for learning and adaptation in the brain. One form of synaptic plasticity is spike-timing-dependent plasticity (STDP), which refers to the fact that the strength of a synapse is more likely to increase if a presynaptic neuron fires shortly before a postsynaptic neuron fires and to decrease if the presynaptic neuron fires shortly after a postsynaptic neuron fire STDP were successfully emulated based on the voltage-dependent analog RS characteristics of the Au/Nb:STO devices. Kunwar *et al* [9]. Memristors can be used to implement STDP by measuring the timing of spikes from presynaptic and postsynaptic neurons. If a presynaptic spike occurs shortly before a postsynaptic spike, the resistance of the memristor will increase, this represents an increase in the strength of the synapse [3]. Conversely, if a presynaptic spike occurs shortly after a postsynaptic spike, the resistance of the memristor will decrease, this represents a decrease in the strength of the synapse. Neuromorphic systems are ANNs that are inspired by the structure and function of the brain. Memristors can be used to implement different forms of synaptic plasticity, such as STDP, which is a key mechanism for learning and adaptation in biological neural networks. This allows neuromorphic systems to learn from incoming patterns of signals and adjust their synaptic strengths accordingly. Ryu *et al* evaluate pattern recognition accuracy simulation from Fashion MNIST dataset by using a three-layer neural network and synaptic weight of a Ni/Ta_2O_5/Si device [1]. Memristive devices can be used to create synapses with a wide range of properties, which makes them well-suited for modeling the diversity of synapses in the brain. They can be arranged in networks that can learn and adapt to new information in a similar way to the human brain [5]. Potentially these devices are much faster and more energy-efficient than traditional electronic circuits, which could make them ideal for use in brain-inspired computing systems. At the core of neuromorphic computing lies the goal of replicating the synaptic connections between neurons found in biological brains. Synapses, which are responsible for transmitting signals and enabling learning through synaptic plasticity, play a vital role in information processing. Memristive devices have emerged as promising contenders for mimicking synaptic behavior due to their unique characteristic of adjusting resistance based on applied voltage history. Berdan *et al* demonstrate that single solid-state TiO_2 memristors can exhibit non-associative plasticity phenomena observed in biological synapses [7]. One of the most remarkable features of memristive devices is their capacity to mimic synaptic plasticity, the ability of synapses to strengthen or weaken over time-based on neural activity as shown in table 3.1. This phenomenon closely resembles the learning and adaptation observed in biological neural networks [8–10].

Memristors have several advantages over traditional computing devices, non-volatile in which a resistance state can be retained even when the power is turned off, this makes them ideal for applications that require long term storage of data. Spiking neural networks (SNNs) from CMOS Image sensor (CIS) are ANNs that are designed to mimic the spiking behavior of neurons in the human brain as shown in figure 3.1. Neural network for sight includes artificial photoreceptor and neural

Table 3.1. Memristive synapse with different resistive switching material.

Synapse based on memristive device	Potentiation pluses (*P*)	Depression pulses (*D*)	Repeated *P*/*D* cycles	References
AlO_x/HfO_2	0.9 V/100 μs	−1 V/100 μs	3	[19]
$ZnSnO_y/ZnSnO_x$	0.8 V/500 ns	−1 V/500 ns	5000	[20]
TaO_x/TiO_2	3 V/40 ms	−3 V/10 ms	10	[21]
TaO_x/ZTO	0.80 V/1 μs	−0.9 V/1 μs	790	[23]
HfO_x/TaO_x	0.78 V/1 μs	−0.87 V/1 μs	35	[24]
a-TiO_2/a-TiO_x	4.6 V/5 μs	−2.9 V/180 μs	32	[25]
Ag/ZnO/TiN	0.8/500 μs	−0.6/500 μs	9	[26]
ZnO/TaO_x	0.8/10 μs	− 0.1/10 μs	5130	[15]

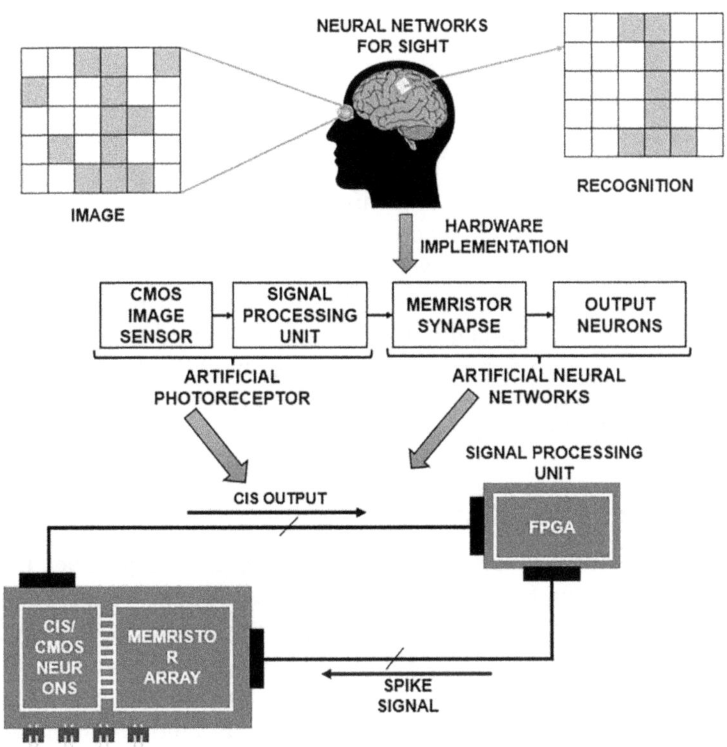

Figure 3.1. Proposed neuromorphic system for visual pattern recognition using memristive devices for brain-inspired computing and perception systems.

network which processing signal through synapse and passed it to output neurons having interface with FPGA and memristive device for computational work. Memristors can be used to create artificial synapses for SNNs, its computing

Table 3.2. Artificial synapses required performance [15]

Parameters	Required value
Dynamic range	>100
Weight precision	>64
Energy consumption	<10 fJ/Spike
Endurance	$>10^9$
Retention	>10 Years

paradigm inspired by the architecture of the human brain [7, 11]. Memristors can be used to create neuromorphic computing systems, which can mimic the learning and memory capabilities of the human brain [12–14]. By using memristors to create artificial synapses within SNNs, we are effectively creating a platform that emulates how our brain processes information with required values of artificial synapses as mentioned in table 3.2. This innovative approach is a testament to the profound impact that memristive devices can have in reshaping the landscape of computational systems to mirror the intricacies of the human brain [9]. As a result, memristors hold the potential to revolutionize brain-inspired computing, opening doors to highly efficient, adaptable, and intelligent systems that rival the capabilities of our minds [4, 15].

ANNs are computing systems that are inspired by the human brain that are made up of many interconnected nodes, each of which can be thought of as a neuron. The nodes in an ANN are arranged in layers, and information flows from the input layer to the output layer through the hidden layers. ANN are capable of learning and performing tasks that are difficult or impossible for traditional computers [16]. Memristive devices are a promising new technology with the potential to revolutionize computing, they are already being used in various applications, and their use is likely to grow in the future [17].

3.3 Diverse memristive device technology

Various memristive/RRAM device technologies are currently under investigation for their applicability in brain-inspired computing. These technologies hold the promise of enabling the development of computing systems that surpass traditional computers in terms of efficiency, scalability, and energy conservation [18]. Resistive random-access memory (RRAM), phase change memristor, oxygen vacancy memristors, and ferroelectric memristors rank prominently among the most promising memristive device technologies for brain inspired computing [19].

Memristor technology is emerging as a promising solution for non-CMOS and beyond-von Neumann computing architectures. Since its introduction in 2008, and with roots tracing back to earlier research under different terminologies, memristors have grown to encompass diverse materials, mechanisms, and computational strategies. These devices have demonstrated potential in applications such as in-memory computing systems, DL accelerators, and neuromorphic computing, showcasing their ability to revolutionize AI hardware.

Memristors, being two-terminal devices with resistance dependent on their historical electrical input, offer high integration density, non-volatile resistance states, rapid switching speeds, and exceptional energy efficiency. These attributes make them ideal for next-generation memory and computing technologies. For instance, resistive random-access memory (ReRAM) and phase-change memory (PCM), two extensively studied memristive device types, exemplify the versatility of this technology. ReRAM devices operate based on redox processes, often involving conductive filaments formed within insulating films, while PCMs rely on phase transitions between amorphous and crystalline states. Both technologies support multiple resistance states, enabling advanced computing capabilities beyond simple binary operations.

ReRAM devices can be classified based on intrinsic or extrinsic switching mechanisms, influenced by material properties or ion diffusion from electrodes. Subtypes such as electrochemical metallization cells (ECMs), valence change memories (VCMs), and thermochemical memories (TCMs) are defined by the driving forces behind their redox processes. Similarly, PCMs use the amplitude and duration of voltage pulses to control phase transitions, facilitating resistance switching critical for computational tasks. Memristors' ability to achieve multiple resistance states is crucial for complex applications, yet benchmarking their performance remains a challenge due to diverse operational parameters. In addition to pure digital memory, memristors hold promise for analog computing tasks, such as in-memory processing, where data movement inefficiencies inherent to von Neumann architectures are eliminated. This capability is particularly valuable for AI workloads, including SNNs and reservoir computing. As memristive technologies evolve, interdisciplinary efforts spanning material science, electrical engineering, and computational neuroscience are driving innovations. These efforts are shaping the future of scalable, energy-efficient, and bio-inspired computing systems, positioning memristors as key enablers of the next technological paradigm shift.

Resistive random-access memory (RRAM): These devices are made of a thin film of semiconductor material, such as silicon oxide or hafnium oxide family oxides [19, 21]. This material has a property called resistive switching, which means that its resistance can change in response to an applied voltage. When a voltage is applied to the device, it can create a conductive path through the material, which changes its resistance state, and a change in resistance can be used to store information [22]. For example, a high resistance state can be used to represent a 1 bit of information, and a low resistance state can be used to represent a 0 bit of information. This allows RRAM devices to be used as memory devices, like the way that transistors are used in traditional computer memory as SET and RESET [23] as shown in figure 3.2. RRAM devices can also be used to implement synaptic plasticity, this means that they can be used to create ANNs that can learn and adapt in a way that is like the way that the brain learns and adapts. RRAM devices are promising new technology for memory and neuromorphic computing that have the potential to be more energy efficient and scalable than traditional memory technologies. They are also more

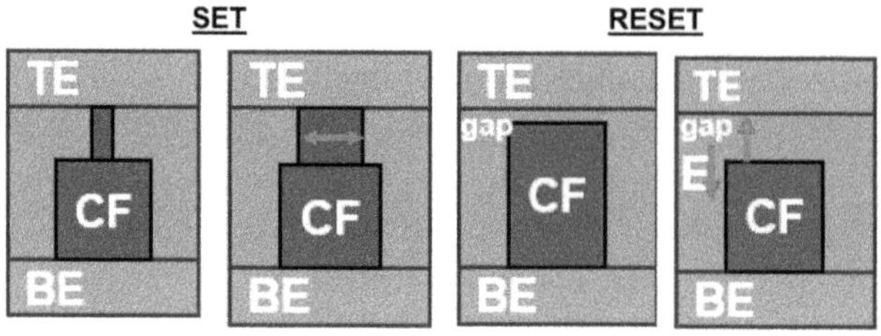

Figure 3.2. The mechanisms of device nonlinearity during the SET and RESET process.

compatible with the way that the brain works, which makes them a good candidate for ANNs [24].

Phase change memristor (PCM): In brain-inspired computing, memristors based on PCM are essential. These components are made of materials that change their crystal structure when exposed to an electric charge [16]. This structural change is important as it allows data to be stored in a way that is similar to how the human brain works. By applying voltage, the configuration of memristors can be changed, which mimics the synaptic behavior of the brain. This modern advancement uses the material's inherent ability to change its state to effectively store data. Like the connections between neurons in the brain, memristors can form and reshape pathways, enabling complex computations [17]. This technological breakthrough is a significant step towards the realization of neuromorphic systems, which seamlessly combine biological principles with computational approaches. The potential of memristors to be efficient and adaptable information storage solutions is made more promising for development and manufacture.

Oxygen vacancy memristors: These are special devices formed from a certain kind of material that has gaps or vacancies where oxygen should be. There are gaps as little spaces within the material, and we can put the gaps in different arrangements, which can represent information that may be a '0' or '1', just like a light switch that can be off or on [16]. So, when we want to keep something in mind, we adjust these gaps using voltage, and their arrangement stores that information. The oxygen vacancies can be moved around by an applied voltage, and this can be used to store information [18]. Scientists have been studying these unique memristors, and it turns out they could be quite useful for making computer memory.

Ferroelectric memristors: These are typically made of materials such as lead zirconate titanate (PZT) and barium titanate ($BaTiO_3$), which have spontaneous electric polarization. The polarization state of a ferroelectric memristor can be switched by applying a voltage that is greater than a certain threshold voltage [6]. This property can be used to store information, as the polarization state of the memristor can represent a binary value, such as '0' or '1'. Ferroelectric memristors have been proposed as a potential building block for BIC systems [19]. This is because they can be used to emulate the behavior of synapses, which are the connections between neurons in the brain. Synapses are responsible for learning and memory, and they can be strengthened or weakened by the passage of electrical signals. They can be used to mimic this behavior as their resistance can be changed by the application of electrical pulses [20], there are several advantages to using ferroelectric memristors in BIC systems. First, they are non-volatile, meaning that they can retain their stored information even when the power is turned off. This is important for BIC systems, as they are often required to operate in real-time. Second, ferroelectric memristors are relatively low-power devices, which is another important consideration for BIC systems [11]. However, there are also some challenges associated with using ferroelectric memristors in BIC systems. One challenge is that these are still relatively new devices, and their performance characteristics are not yet fully understood. Another challenge is that they are often sensitive to environmental factors, such as temperature and humidity [13]. Despite these challenges, ferroelectric memristors are a promising technology for BIC. As research in this area continues, ferroelectric memristors will likely become more widely used in these types of systems.

3.4 Neuromorphic computing and its relationship with brain-inspired concepts

The use of memristive devices in BIC is still in its early stages, but the potential of this technology is very promising. Memristive devices could be used to create computing systems that are more efficient, scalable, and energy-efficient than traditional computers [20, 21]. They could also be used to create more fault-tolerant computing systems that can learn and adapt in a way that is similar to the way that the human brain learns and adapts. The potential applications of memristive devices in BIC are vast and still being explored. This technology has the potential to revolutionize the way we design and build computing systems [22]. Here are some specific examples of how memristive devices could be used in BIC:

Synaptic emulation: Memristive devices are electronic components that can change their resistance state depending on the amount of current that has passed through them. This property makes them a promising candidate for emulating the behavior of synapses in the brain, these are the connections between neurons, and they play a critical role in learning and memory [23]. When a neuron fires, it sends an electrical signal to the synapses that connect it to other neurons. The strength of these signals can be modified by synapses, a process known as synaptic plasticity as shown in figure 3.3(a) as experimentally shown in figure 3.3(b). This plasticity is what allows the brain to learn and adapt. Memristive devices can be used to emulate synaptic plasticity in several ways [24]. One way is to use the memristor's resistance state to represent the strength of the synapse. When a current passes through the memristor, its resistance state can be changed [25]. This can be used to simulate the strengthening or weakening of a synapse. Another way to use memristive devices to emulate synapses is to use their ability to store information. The memristor's resistance state can be used to store the weight of a connection between two neurons, this weight can then be modified as the synapses learn and adapt. In this research area continues, memristors are likely to play an increasingly important role in the development of AI and ML [26]. They have the potential to create new AI systems that are more powerful, efficient, and adaptable than the systems that are currently available [27].

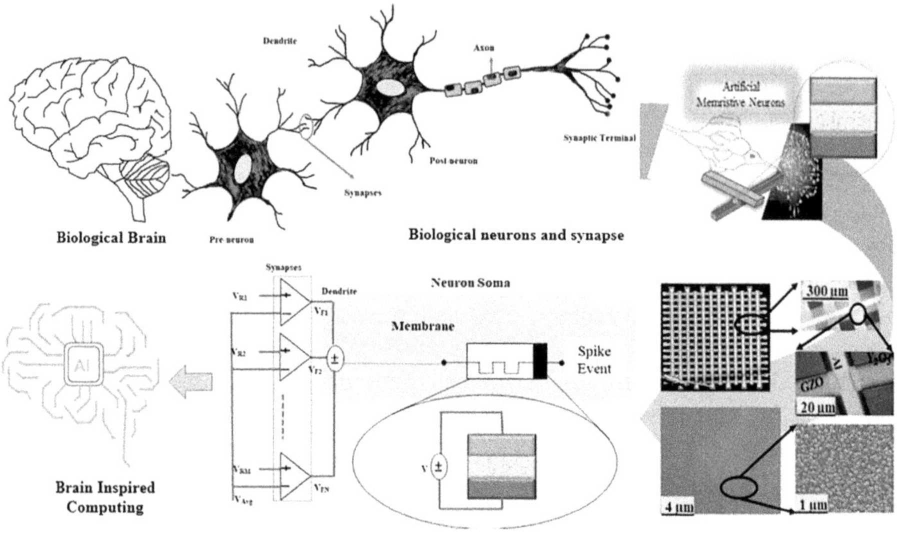

Figure 3.3. (a) Biological synapses based on neural subsystem and (b) electronic synapse.

Neuromorphic computing systems: Memristive components possess the ability to alter their resistance state based on the quantity of current flowing through them. This characteristic renders them a promising contender for constructing neuromorphic computing systems. These systems inspired by the structure and functionality of the brain aim to replicate the highly parallel and low-power computational structure of the human brain. The human brain functions as an immensely parallel computational framework, accomplishing intricate tasks with minimal power consumption [28]. One way of approach to integrate memristive devices into neuromorphic computing systems is via involving their potential for analog computation, in contrast to digital computation, the human brain excels at analog computation due to its enhanced efficiency. Memristors can perform analog computation within neuromorphic systems, potentially yielding significant efficiency enhancements [23]. Furthermore, memristive devices offer the prospect of innovating novel ML algorithms, surpassing the efficiency and potency of conventional algorithms. These advanced algorithms find utility across a wide spectrum of challenges, encompassing tasks like image recognition, natural language processing, and speech recognition. Although memristors remain a relatively nascent technology, they possess the capability to reshape the realm of AI [24]. Synapses emulators serve as connectors between neurons, essential for learning and memory processes. Utilizing memristors, one can encode the connection weight between two neurons permitting subsequent adjustments as synapses learn and acclimate [14].

Fault tolerance: Memristive devices exhibit characteristics of non-volatile memory that respond to electric currents by altering their resistance state. This unique attribute renders them well-suited for distributed information storage, as data can be dispersed across numerous memristive devices. In cases of individual memristive device failure, data truthfulness remains unbroken within the other functioning devices, this deviation from conventional memory components like transistors contribute memristive devices enhanced fault tolerance [24]. For instance, the memristive crossbar array (MCA) is a matrix of memristive devices utilized for data storage and manipulation. If some of the memristors stop working in this setup, the information won't get lost. This is because the information is stored in the connections between the memristors, not in just one of them [25]. Memristive devices are good at handling mistakes, which makes them very promising for jobs like AI, ML, and neuromorphic computing. Memristive devices are great at both things, so if we use them in these tasks, the computers could become much better and work faster. They offer additional advantages that significantly enhance their potential to enhance error handling in computers, their capacity to scale up makes them suitable for building large-scale computers with ease [12]. Furthermore, their low-energy requirements contribute to environmentally friendly computing, and their high-speed operation ensures computers integrated with these devices can perform tasks swiftly and efficiently.

Learning and adaptation: Memristive components represent specialized electrical devices capable of modifying their electrical resistance in response to applied voltage. These components find utility in constructing computer systems endowed with the ability to learn and enhance their performance [16]. To conceptualize this, envision utilizing one such device to retain the strength of a connection between two artificial brain cells. As the brain-inspired system undergoes learning, these connections can be finely tuned using these specialized devices. This process empowers the system to extract insights from its surroundings, progressively elevating its intellectual capabilities [26]. Despite the relatively recent emergence of these components, they possess the potential to revolutionize the fundamental operation of computers. Their transformative influence could extend to the creation of novel forms of intelligent technology, such as learning-enabled robots or computers with heightened comprehension of human interaction.

3.5 Synaptic response of physical nanoscale memristor model

It is a significant area of interest within the realms of nanotechnology and neuromorphic computing. This research delves into the intricate behaviors and characteristics exhibited by nanoscale memristors as they endeavor to replicate synaptic functions observed in the human brain. A memristor, a passive electronic device equipped with two terminals that retain data even when power is cut, demonstrates a unique memory effect [14]. This property allows it to alter its resistance state by applying voltage, smoothly transitioning between two stable states. This intrinsic feature makes memristors highly appealing for integration into neuromorphic computing applications as artificial synapses. Recently, there has been a growing interest in crafting physical nanoscale memristor models, tailored explicitly for synaptic purposes [25–27]. These models strive to capture the fundamental physics dictating memristor behavior at the nanoscale, a critical aspect for comprehending and enhancing their synaptic attributes.

The physical nanoscale memristor models are a promising tool for the development of artificial synapses in neuromorphic computing applications. As technology continues to develop, these models are expected to become more accurate and efficient, making them even more useful for this purpose. Nanoscale memristors are engineered at remarkably small dimensions which make them exceptionally suitable for the development of compact and energy efficient neuromorphic systems [29]. The term 'synaptic response' pertains to the memristor's ability to alter their conductance, essentially representing their synaptic weight, in response to electrical stimuli as shown in figure 3.4. This understanding holds utmost significance in the design of neuromorphic circuits and ANNs allowing for the replication of various synaptic behaviors, including short-term and long-term plasticity, spike-timing-dependent plasticity, and mirroring the plasticity observed in biological synapses [30]. It employs physical models and simulations to search into the intricate distinctions of memristor synaptic responses, considering factors such as material composition, structural design, and electrical properties. This comprehensive approach also considers quantum effects that come into play due to the nanoscale dimensions, including tunneling and quantum-well effects [28]. Advanced materials, such as transition metal oxides and 2D materials, have been instrumental in engineering memristors with desired synaptic properties, showcasing unique electronic characteristics at the nanoscale. Fine-tuning the synaptic response is achieved through adjustments in material composition and device structure. Electrical characterization techniques, like current–voltage measurements and pulse-response analysis, play a pivotal role in elucidating memristor behavior [29].

As the exploration of various nonvolatile memory technologies unfolds, memristors undoubtedly stand out as a leading candidate. Figure 3.5(a) highlights

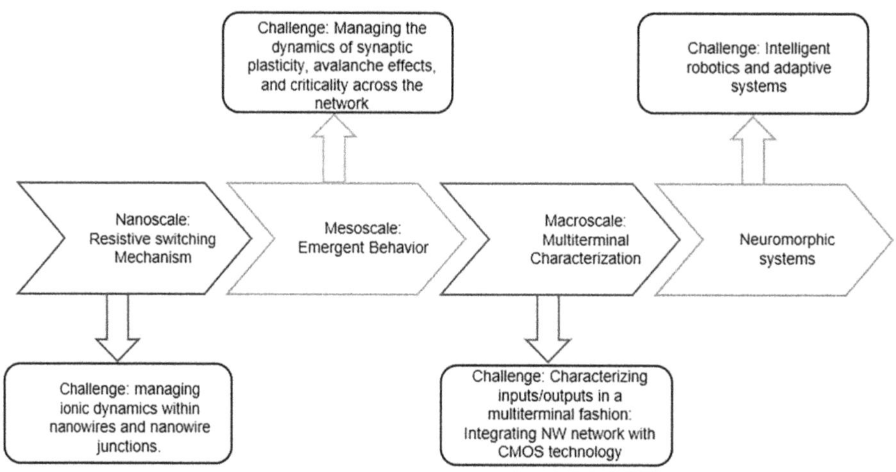

Figure 3.4. Illustration of various possible circuit/device implementations of neurobiological processes. The neuron is mimicked by pulse accumulation and that can be reproduced by the matrix-vector multiplication (MVM) in crosspoint array circuits, while the integration of neurons is mimicked by pulse accumulation mechanisms in PCMs and RRAMs.

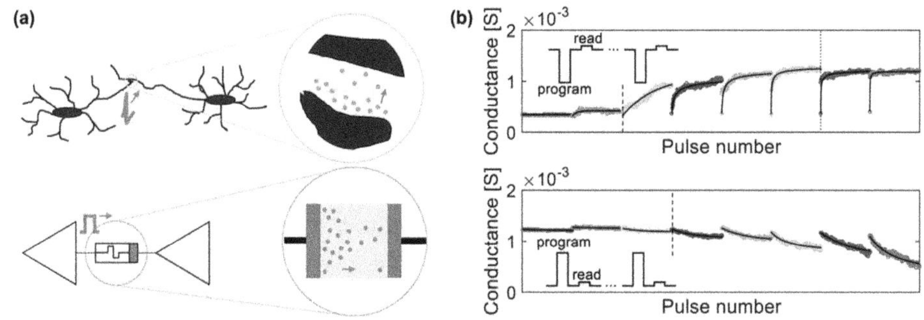

Figure 3.5. (a) Schematic analogy between ionic motion in a biological synapse (e.g. Na^+, Ca^{2+} ions), in between two neurons, and in an RRAM device (e.g. metal or oxygen ions) connecting two electronic neuron units. (b) Examples of conductance series of potentiation (top) and depression (bottom) operations obtained for 300 identical pulses with $\Delta t = 10$ μs. Each colour corresponds to a different series of 300 pulses starting from a similar initial state and operated with increasing absolute potential between 0.55 V (left) and 0.9 V (right) with a step of 50 mV. Reproduced from [8] CC BY 4.0.

the analogy between ionic motion in resistive-switching devices and vesicle motion in biological synapses, emphasizing how both systems modulate signal transmission through mobile species in a junction.

To study this behaviour, trains of identical electrical pulses were applied while the device conductance was read after each pulse. The experiment was repeated for different pulse amplitudes (ΔV) and pulse widths (Δt), always starting from the same initial state. Figure 3.5(b) shows representative conductance trajectories for 300 identical pulses with fixed $\Delta t = 10$ μs and increasing ΔV.

The results reveal three regimes:

- Low ΔV (left of dashed line): No visible conductance chang—pulses are too weak to cause switching.
- Intermediate ΔV (between dashed and dotted lines): Each pulse introduces a small but cumulative change, producing smooth analogue potentiation or depression.
- High ΔV (right of dotted line): The first pulse dominates the response, leading to digital-like switching, where only a few distinct conductance states appear.

These trends, visible in figure 3.5(b), summarize the device's transition from no response → analogue behaviour → abrupt digital switching as the pulse amplitude increases.

3.6 Impact of switching speed on synaptic weight response

The 3-D physical electro-thermal model, as detailed in [31], is rooted in minimizing free energy when voltage is applied, comprehensively considering the influences of the electric field, thermal factors, and the diffusion of oxygen vacancies within the memristor material. The simulation outcomes of this model showcase a consistent pinched hysteresis loop in resistive switching (R_S) response across multiple switching cycles, demonstrating a low coefficient of variability (C_v), signifying robust reproducibility in switching behavior. The model also explores the impact of voltage ramp rate (V_{RR}) on device characteristics, including switching response and synaptic plasticity [32]. Additionally, it sheds light on the effect of oxide layer thickness on switching voltages in nanoscale devices. These physical nanoscale memristor models, by faithfully capturing the fundamental physics of memristor operation, hold great potential for designing and optimizing memristor-based synapses to meet specific requirements. In neural networks, synapses play an indispensable role and memristors present an enticing avenue for replicating their functionality. These passive two-terminal devices exhibit resistance that can dynamically adjust based on the history of the applied voltage, rendering them a vital component in brain-inspired computing. The primary objective of studying the synaptic response of physical nanoscale memristor models is to gain insight into how these devices can effectively mimic the functions of biological synapses [33].

The sequential processing of fetch, decode, and execution of instructions through the classical von Neumann bottleneck of conventional digital computers has resulted in less efficient machines as their ecosystems have grown to be increasingly complex. A synapse is essentially a two-terminal device and bears a striking resemblance to an electrical device termed a memristor. Like a biological synapse, the conductance of a memristor can be incrementally modified by controlling charge or flux through it.

3.7 Memcapacitive devices for synaptic learning in brain-inspired computation

Memcapacitors are a type of electronic device that can store and process information in a similar way to synapses in the brain that are very energy-efficient, which makes them ideal for use in large-scale neuromorphic systems. BIC is a field of computer science that aims to develop new computing systems that are inspired by the structure and function of the human brain [34].

Figure 3.6 illustrates eight distinct non-pinched I–V hysteresis curves, represented as C_xM_y, where 'x' and 'y' are indices denoting the capacitive (C_x) and memristive (M_y) states of the system. This diagram demonstrates how the interaction between

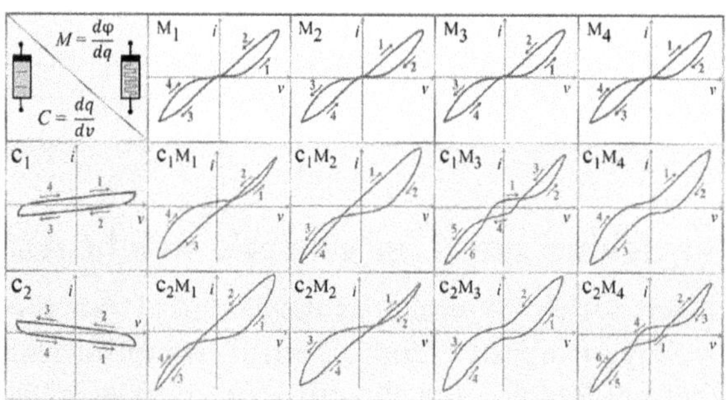

Figure 3.6. Schematic diagram of eight nonpinched I–V hysteresis curves types (C_xM_y; $x = 1, 2$; $y = 1, 2, 3, 4$) duo to the capacitive-coupled memristor effect between the capacitive state (C_x) and the memristive state (M_y). Reprinted with permission from [35]. Copyright (2019) American Chemical Society.

capacitive and memristive elements within the device gives rise to a variety of hysteresis loop shapes. The states C_1 and C_2 represent two different types of capacitive behavior, with C_1 potentially reflecting a simpler, linear capacitive characteristic and C_2 possibly indicating a more complex, nonlinear response. The memristive states M_1 to M_4 correspond to different modes of memristive switching, which can vary in terms of their resistance change behavior, such as the degree of hysteresis or the speed of switching.

The 'non-pinched' nature of the hysteresis curves suggests that, unlike traditional memristive systems that exhibit pinched *I–V* loops (a defining characteristic of memristors at low voltage conditions), the coupled capacitive and memristive elements in this system produce a broader range of voltage–current behavior. This non-pinch phenomenon can be attributed to the interaction between the capacitive storage effect and the memristive switching mechanism. As the voltage is applied, the device alternates between storing charge in the capacitive state (C_x) and undergoing resistance changes in the memristive state (M_y), leading to complex hysteretic loops that deviate from the simple pinched curves typically seen in memristive devices.

Such behavior is critical for applications in areas like neuromorphic computing and advanced memory technologies, where both capacitive and memristive properties are exploited. The ability to control and manipulate these dual states (capacitive and memristive) enables more sophisticated memory and computation mechanisms that combine the benefits of both storage types, potentially leading to devices with greater functionality and efficiency.

Neuromorphic computing is a subfield of brain-inspired computation that focuses on developing ANNs that can learn and adapt like the human brain [11]. The concept of spike encoding and decoding serves as a cornerstone for comprehending synaptic responses in memristors, with electrical pulses mimicking spike events in the brain. Memristor synapses exhibit behaviors like potentiation (increased conductance) and depression (decreased conductance) in response to spike events, like LTP and LTD observed in biological systems processes essential for learning and memory [13].

Figure 3.7 provides a detailed schematic of the transition between capacitive-coupled memristive behavior and the pure memristive effect under varying conditions. The figure is broken into four stages, each representing a different influencing factor that alters the behavior of the memcapacitive device. Figure 3.7(a) represents the standard voltage–current relationship for the system before any external factors are applied. In this initial state, the device demonstrates the baseline behavior of both the capacitive and memristive components, with the resulting *I–V* curve likely reflecting a combination of these effects, which are responsible for the unique properties of memcapacitive systems. The curve at this stage would typically show a standard hysteretic loop, where the memristive behavior may still dominate in certain regions, depending on the device's configuration and voltage range. As seen in figure 3.7(b), when a larger voltage is applied, the device's behavior transitions due to increased capacitive coupling. The hysteresis loop may expand or shift as the voltage exceeds the initial threshold, prompting the memristor to exhibit stronger resistance switching.

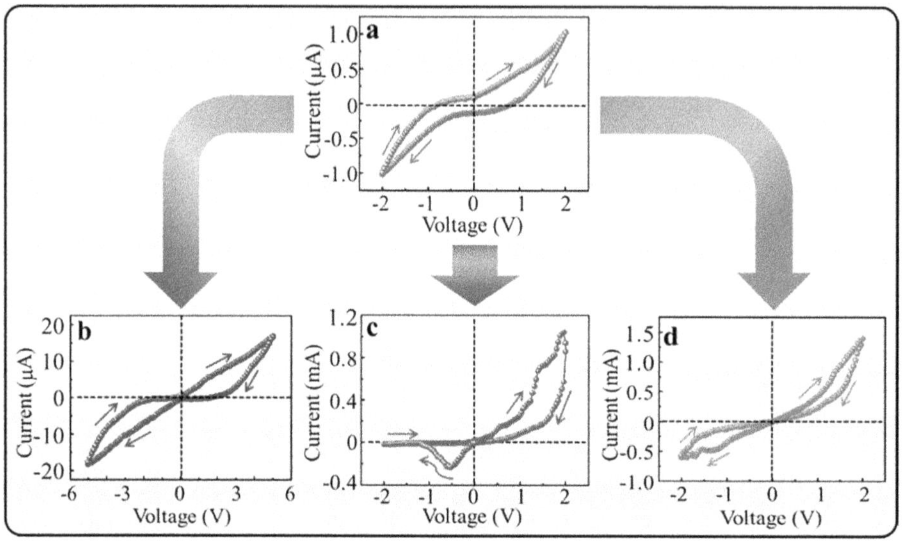

Figure 3.7. Transition between the capacitive-coupled memristive and pure memristive effect. (a) Initial $I-V$ curve. (b) Applying larger voltage. (c) Adding moisture. (d) Increasing temperature. Reprinted with permission from [35]. Copyright (2019) American Chemical Society.

In this stage, the memristive element is likely undergoing more significant changes in its resistance, thus influencing the overall current–voltage relationship. This behavior reflects the nonlinear switching characteristic of memristors, and the system may move further into a more pronounced memristive regime, where the capacitive effects are less prominent. As seen in figure 3.7(c), the introduction of moisture into the device impacts the internal resistance and charge dynamics. Moisture can alter the ionic conductivity within the memristor material, which can influence both the capacitive and memristive properties. As moisture increases the ionic mobility, the memristor may exhibit more pronounced hysteresis due to the enhanced charge transport characteristics. This modification could also influence the transition between the capacitive-coupled and pure memristive effects, either enhancing or diminishing the capacitive coupling, depending on the material and environmental conditions. In figure 3.7(d), the final factor, temperature increase, further modifies the memcapacitive device's behavior by affecting both the capacitive and memristive components. Typically, higher temperatures increase the mobility of charge carriers and can lead to faster switching speeds in memristive devices. As the temperature rises, the resistance of the memristor may decrease, and the overall device performance could shift towards pure memristive behavior, reducing the influence of capacitive effects. This shift could cause the system to exhibit more traditional memristive characteristics, with a more typical pinched $I–V$ loop or altered hysteresis behavior, depending on the temperature range.

Together these four conditions applied voltage, moisture, and temperature demonstrate the complex interactions that govern the transition between capacitive-coupled memristive behavior and the pure memristive effect. The study of these transitions is crucial for understanding and controlling memcapacitive devices, especially in applications that require precise manipulation of both capacitive and resistive properties, such as in neuromorphic computing and memory technologies. Incorporating memristor-based synapses into ANNs facilitates weight updates, enabling efficient ML algorithms to adapt and learn from data. Moreover, the non-volatile nature of memristors, allowing them to retain their state even when power is disconnected, positions them as promising candidates for non-volatile memory and neuromorphic applications. The careful characterization of the synaptic response, considering different input patterns and conductance changes over time, further refines the applicability of memristors in ANNs [23]. It also explores integration possibilities with other nanoscale devices, such as transistors and resistive RAM, to create holistic neuromorphic circuits primed for edge computing and IoT applications due to their exceptional energy efficiency. Despite the promise of memristor technology, challenges like device variability, endurance, and scalability remain crucial points of research, material science advancements and innovative fabrication techniques are continuously addressing these obstacles [26].

Figure 3.8 outlines the physical mechanisms that govern the behavior of memcapacitive devices under various conditions, specifically focusing on the capacitive-coupled memristive effects and their modifications under larger voltage and moisture influence. This figure consists of three parts, each illustrating how different factors affect the *I–V* curve and the underlying memcapacitive behavior. Figure 3.8(a) illustrates the interplay between the capacitive and memristive effects. The capacitive-coupled memristive mechanism occurs when the device exhibits both capacitance and resistance properties. This coupling leads to hysteretic behavior in the *I–V* curve, where the current response is not only dependent on the applied voltage but also influenced by the device's previous states. In this region, both the capacitive and memristive properties work together, and the device shows a combination of resistive switching and charge accumulation, which results in a unique nonlinear *I–V* response. This mechanism is key to the memcapacitive devices' functionality, as it allows for more efficient energy storage and computation. As seen in figure 3.8(b), when a larger voltage is applied, the device exhibits a pinched *I–V* curve, a characteristic feature of memristive systems. This pinched behavior occurs because the voltage applied to the device causes significant resistance switching, and the device transitions between different resistance states (high resistance state to low resistance state). As the voltage increases, the system's memristive effect dominates, leading to the characteristic 'pinch' in the *I–V* curve. This is a hallmark of memristive devices and represents the transition to a more purely memristive behavior, where the capacitive effects play a less prominent role. In the case of figure 3.8(c), moisture is introduced to the memcapacitive device, influencing its electrical properties. Moisture increases the ionic conductivity within the device, which can alter the resistance switching behavior and result in the formation of a pinched *I–V* curve. This change occurs because moisture affects the ion migration and charge distribution within the material, thus modifying both the capacitive and memristive effects. The pinched *I–V* curve observed in this condition demonstrates

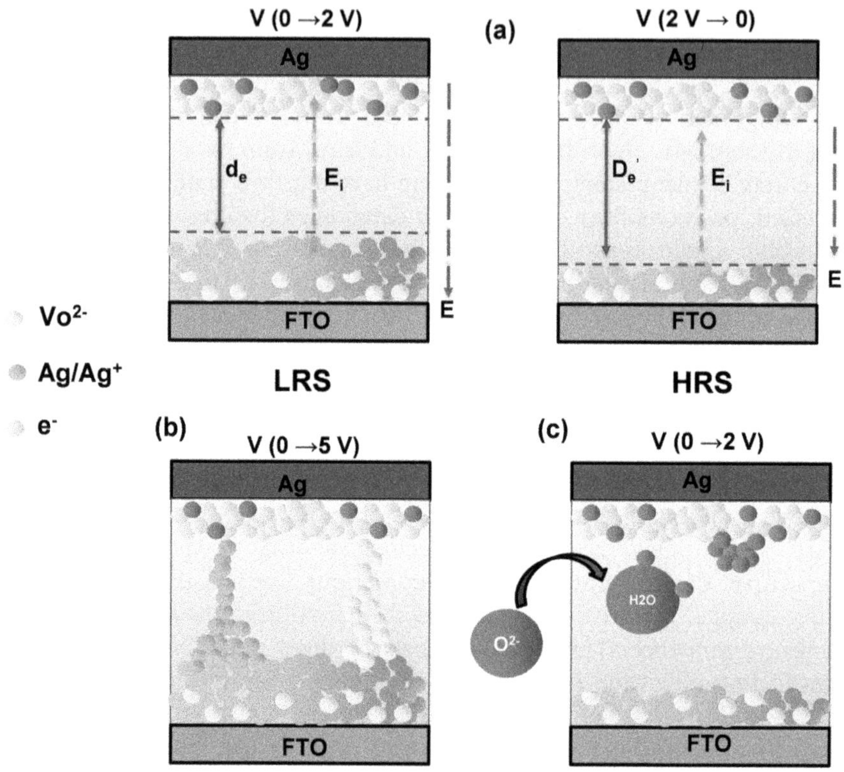

Figure 3.8. Schematic diagram of physical mechanism. (a) Capacitive-coupled memristive mechanism. (b) Mechanism of pinched *I–V* under larger voltage. (c) Mechanism of moisture induced a pinched *I–V* curve.

how external environmental factors, such as humidity, can modify the electrical behavior of memcapacitive devices, which is crucial for their real-world application and reliability.

Figure 3.8 demonstrates the physical mechanisms behind the capacitive-coupled memristive effects and how they are influenced by factors like applied voltage and moisture. These mechanisms provide critical insight into the functionality of memcapacitive devices, which are important for next-generation memory and computational systems. Understanding these transitions helps in developing more efficient memcapacitive technologies for use in diverse applications, such as neuromorphic computing and energy-efficient memory systems.

In parallel, modeling synaptic responses aids in predicting the influence of device variations on neural network performance. The way synapses respond in memristors is not straightforward, and this complexity can be helpful for certain tasks in neural networks, making learning and information processing more effective. Memcapacitive devices have the potential to revolutionize the field of BIC by making it possible to develop neuromorphic systems that are more efficient, powerful, and adaptable than ever before [32].

3.8 Benefits and challenges of using memristive devices for learning

Memristive devices, a class of electronic components that can store and process information in a manner similar to synapses in the human brain, have gained significant attention in the field of education and learning technology [27]. These devices offer a range of benefits and present several challenges when incorporated into the learning process. Benefits from memristive device can be explained as:

- **Neuromorphic learning:** It is a specialized area of research that aims to develop computing systems and hardware architectures inspired by the structure and functioning of the human brain. This field seeks to replicate the brain's ability to process information in a highly efficient and adaptive manner, which is quite different from traditional von Neumann computing architectures [16]. The statement suggests that memristive devices are particularly well-suited for neuromorphic computing. This suitability stems from their unique characteristics, including the ability to mimic the synaptic behavior found in biological neural networks [18]. Synapses are connections between neurons in the brain that strengthen or weaken over time based on the patterns of electrical signals passing through them. Memristive devices can emulate this behavior, making them valuable components for building ANNs. These are computational models inspired by the structure and function of biological neural networks. ANNs consist of interconnected nodes, or 'neurons,' which process and transmit information through weighted connections [25]. These networks are used in ML and DL to recognize patterns, make predictions, and perform various tasks. The statement suggests that memristive devices can play a crucial role in crafting ANNs for neuromorphic computing. These ANNs would not only replicate the brain's structure but also its ability to adapt and learn from data. This adaptability is a key advantage, as it allows ANNs to improve their performance over time and become more efficient at the tasks they are trained for. Furthermore, the statement highlights that the use of memristive devices in ANNs can lead to significant improvements in ML algorithms employed in educational applications [29]. Educational applications encompass a wide range of uses, from personalized learning platforms to intelligent tutoring systems. The efficiency gains mentioned in the statement can be attributed to the memristive device's ability to better model the brain's learning and adaptation processes. Traditional ML algorithms often require extensive data processing and training, but ANNs built with memristive devices can potentially reduce the amount of data needed for training and make learning more flexible and efficient.
- **Energy efficiency:** Memristive devices present a remarkable advantage in terms of their energy efficiency, this advantage becomes particularly evident when we compare them to traditional electronic components. Unlike conventional components, memristive devices demand only minimal power to operate effectively [30]. This attribute makes them exceptionally suitable for various applications where energy conservation is of paramount importance. One of the most notable applications of memristive devices benefiting

from their energy efficiency is their deployment in portable devices. Portable gadgets, including smartphones, tablets, and wearable technology, rely heavily on conserving energy to ensure extended battery life. Memristive devices can significantly contribute to prolonging the battery life of these devices due to their low power consumption. Furthermore, memristive devices find their niche in settings characterized by limited power resources [4]. One such example is classrooms in less developed areas, where access to a stable and abundant power supply may be a challenge. In such environments, the ability of memristive devices to function efficiently with minimal power input is particularly advantageous. They can support educational technology solutions, such as laptops, tablets, or digital learning platforms, without straining the available power resources [6]. By harnessing the energy efficiency of memristive devices, educational institutions in less developed regions can bridge the digital divide and provide students with access to modern technology without the burden of high energy costs. This not only facilitates learning but also contributes to a more sustainable and environmentally friendly approach to education. Their ability to operate effectively with minimal power consumption is not only beneficial for extending battery life but also for enabling access to modern technology in resource-limited educational environments, ultimately fostering more inclusive and sustainable learning opportunities [12].

- **Low latency:** It is a crucial attribute of memristive devices and plays a pivotal role in transforming the landscape of educational applications [21]. Memristive devices exhibit the remarkable capability to process information with exceedingly low latency, ushering in a new era of real-time feedback and interaction in the realm of education. This inherent characteristic holds immense promise, as it has the potential to revolutionize how learners engage with educational content and acquire knowledge. In the context of educational applications, low latency refers to the minimal delay between an input stimulus and the corresponding output or response generated by the memristive device [16]. This swift processing time ensures that interactions between learners and educational systems occur in near real time, creating an environment where feedback is immediate and seamless. Moreover, the low latency of memristive devices contributes to the provision of instantaneous responses to learners as per specified applications.
- **Parallel processing:** Memristive devices facilitate parallel processing through their unique resistive switching mechanism, enabling multiple bits of data to be manipulated concurrently. These devices are often organized into crossbar arrays, forming grids where individual memristors represent data bits and can be individually addressed [32]. This parallel architecture allows for simultaneous operations on data, making memristive devices highly efficient for tasks like matrix operations, which are essential in fields ranging from ML to scientific simulations. Additionally, memristive devices offer the advantages of low power consumption and adaptability, as they can be configured for various computational tasks. In essence, memristive devices represent a

promising avenue for next generation computing systems, offering a powerful tool for parallel processing in a variety of applications, including education, scientific research, and AI [24].

- **Non-volatile memory:** Memristive devices serve as advantageous components in non-volatile memory systems due to their distinctive operational characteristics. Unlike traditional non-volatile memory technologies, which rely on charge storage and are subject to wear and degradation over time, memristive devices store data by altering their resistance state, a process that is inherently non-volatile. This means that data retention is robust, with no need for periodic refresh cycles, and the devices are highly durable [25]. Furthermore, memristive non-volatile memory offers fast write and read speeds, making it suitable for a wide range of applications, from storage in consumer electronics to high-performance computing systems. The energy efficiency and scalability of memristive non-volatile memory make it an attractive candidate for future memory technologies, promising improved reliability and performance in comparison to conventional options [27].

We are currently grappling with several challenges when it comes to implementing memristive devices in the context of educational applications, as mentioned below:

- **Technology maturity:** Memristive devices, while holding immense promise, also present certain disadvantages in terms of technology maturity. One significant drawback lies in their relatively recent emergence and ongoing development. Unlike well-established technologies such as semiconductor-based memory, memristive devices are still in the early stages of maturity. This means that their manufacturing processes may not be as refined or cost-effective, leading to higher production costs and potential reliability issues [30]. Additionally, because they are not yet widely adopted, there is a scarcity of standardized protocols and industry-wide support, limiting their seamless integration into existing ecosystems. As a result, the lack of technological maturity in memristive devices can pose challenges in terms of widespread adoption and dependable long-term performance, making them less accessible and dependable compared to more established memory technologies [17].
- **Device variability:** It represents a significant disadvantage of memristive devices that exhibit notable variations in their electrical characteristics from one unit to another, even within the same production batch [5]. This inherent variability can lead to inconsistent performance and reliability, posing challenges for their widespread adoption in various applications. Manufacturers struggle to achieve uniformity in device behavior, which can hinder the development of robust and predictable systems [13]. In applications where precise and consistent performance is essential, such as high-performance computing and critical control systems, this variability in memristive devices can introduce uncertainties and reliability concerns, making them less desirable than other, more stable semiconductor-based alternatives [24]. Addressing and minimizing device variability remains a crucial challenge in advancing the practical use of memristive technology.

- **Programming and control:** Memristive devices present a notable disadvantage in the realm of programming and control. Unlike traditional computing elements that follow well-established protocols and standardized architectures, memristive devices are relatively novel, and there is a lack of mature programming paradigms and control mechanisms tailored to their unique characteristics [8]. This deficiency complicates the development of software and hardware ecosystems that can fully leverage memristive technology. Furthermore, the fine-tuning of memristive devices for specific applications requires intricate control schemes, often necessitating specialized knowledge and expertise. This complexity can result in challenges related to compatibility, reliability, and the efficient utilization of memristive devices, hindering their seamless integration into existing computing systems and impeding their widespread adoption [12]. As a result, the current limitations in programming and control represent a significant drawback in realizing the full potential of memristive devices in various technological domains.
- **Scalability:** It emerges as a notable disadvantage of memristive devices. While these devices offer exciting prospects in terms of compactness and energy efficiency, their scalability for large-scale applications remains a challenge. As we seek to harness the potential of memristive technology in advanced computing systems, the need arises for consistent and cost-effective fabrication of vast arrays of memristive devices [17]. Achieving uniformity and reliability at scale becomes increasingly difficult, potentially leading to inconsistencies in performance and device behavior. Additionally, the integration of memristive devices into existing technology infrastructure necessitates the development of new fabrication processes, control systems, and interface standards, all of which can be resource-intensive and time consuming [34]. These scalability issues may impede the widespread adoption of memristive technology in scenarios where seamless expansion and integration are crucial, limiting its applicability and competitiveness in certain domains.
- **Integration:** Integration presents a notable disadvantage in the context of memristive devices. While these devices offer groundbreaking capabilities, seamlessly incorporating them into existing technological ecosystems can be a formidable challenge [21]. The unique electrical characteristics and operational paradigms of memristive technology often require substantial modifications and adaptations to hardware, software, and infrastructure. Achieving compatibility with established computing systems and educational platforms may demand significant development efforts, including the creation of specialized drivers, control mechanisms, and interface standards [27]. Additionally, integrating memristive devices often entails addressing issues related to device variability, which can further complicate their incorporation into larger systems. This complexity in integration can lead to increased costs, time constraints, and potential disruptions in educational environments, and limiting their widespread adoption [15].
- **Summary:** Memristive devices offer significant benefits for learning applications, including enhanced learning capabilities, energy efficiency, scalability, and improved speed and performance. However, their adoption faces several

challenges, such as fabrication complexities, variability issues, integration difficulties, and the need for algorithmic adaptation [27]. Addressing these challenges through continued research and development will be crucial for realizing the full potential of memristive devices in learning applications.

Bibliography

[1] Ryu J H and Kim S 2020 Artificial synaptic characteristics of TiO_2/HfO_2 memristor with self-rectifying switching for brain-inspired computing *Chaos Solitons Fractals* **140** 110236

[2] Zhang W, Ma S, Ji X, Liu X, Cong Y and Shi L 2024 The development of general-purpose brain-inspired computing *Nat. Electron.* **7** 954–65

[3] Zhang T, Yang K, Xu X, Cai Y, Yang Y and Huang R 2019 Memristive devices and networks for brain-inspired computing *Phys. Status Solidi (RRL)* **13** 1900029

[4] Kim S J, Kim S and Jang H W 2021 Competing memristors for brain-inspired computing *iScience* **24** 101889

[5] Zhang Y *et al* 2020 Brain-inspired computing with memristors: Challenges in devices, circuits, and systems *Appl. Phys. Rev.* **7** 011308

[6] Schmidgall S, Ziaei R, Achterberg J, Kirsch L, Hajiseyedrazi S P and Eshraghian J 2024 Brain-inspired learning in artificial neural networks: A review *APL Mach. Learn.* **2** 021501

[7] Jeong H and Shi L 2018 Memristor devices for neural networks *J. Phys. D: Appl. Phys.* **52** 023003

[8] Kim K *et al* 2020 Enhanced analog synaptic behavior of SiNx/a-Si bilayer memristors through Ge implantation *NPG Asia Mater.* **12** 77

[9] Kunwar S *et al* 2023 An interface-type memristive device for artificial synapse and neuromorphic computing *Adv. Intell. Syst.* **5** 2300035

[10] Xu Q, Chen S, Geng H, Yuan B, Yu B, Wu F and Huang Z 2020 Fault tolerance in memristive crossbar-based neuromorphic computing systems *Integration* **70** 70–9

[11] Querlioz D, Dollfus P, Bichler O and Gamrat C 2011 Learning with memristive devices: How should we model their behavior? *IEEE/ACM Int. Symp. on Nanoscale Architectures (San Diego, CA, USA)* 150–6 *2011*

[12] Secco J, Corinto F and Sebastian A 2018 Flux–charge memristor model for phase change memory *IEEE Trans. Circuits Syst. Express Briefs* **65** 111–4

[13] Lim D H *et al* 2021 Spontaneous sparse learning for PCM-based memristor neural networks *Nat. Commun.* **12** 319

[14] Majumdar S, Tan H, Qin Q H and Dijken S V 2019 Energy-efficient organic ferroelectric tunnel junction memristors for neuromorphic computing *Adv. Electron. Mater.* **5** 1800795

[15] Kumar D, Keong L B, Atab N E and Tseng T Y 2022 Enhanced synaptic features of ZnO/TaO_x bilayer invisible memristor for brain-inspired computing *IEEE Electron Device Lett.* **43** 2093–6

[16] Zhou E, Fang L, Liu R and Tang Z 2017 An improved memristor model for brain-inspired computing *Chin. Phys. B* **26** 118502

[17] Mehonic A and Kenyon A J 2022 Brain-inspired computing needs a master plan *Nature* **604** 255–60

[18] Ji X, Dong Z, Lai C S and Qi D 2022 A brain-inspired in-memory computing system for neuronal communication via memristive circuits *IEEE Commun. Mag.* **60** 100–6

[19] Woo J, Moon K, Song J, Lee S, Kwak M, Park J and Hwang H 2016 Improved synaptic behavior under identical pulses using AlO_x/HfO_2 bilayer RRAM array for neuromorphic systems *IEEE Electron Device Lett.* **37** 994–7

[20] Kumar D, Saleem A, Keong L B, Singh A, Wang Y H and Tseng T Y 2022 $ZnSnO_y/ZnSnO_x$ bilayer transparent memristive synaptic device for neuromorphic computing *IEEE Electron Device Lett.* **43** 1211–4

[21] Wang I T, Chang C C, Chiu L W, Chou T and Hou T H 2016 3D $Ta/TaO_x/TiO_2/Ti$ synaptic array and linearity tuning of weight update for hardware neural network applications *Nanotechnology* **27** 365204

[22] Hsu C L, Saleem A, Singh A, Kumar D and Tseng T Y 2021 Enhanced linearity in CBRAM synapse by post oxide deposition annealing for neuromorphic computing applications *IEEE Trans. Electron Devices* **68** 1296–301

[23] Kumar D, Shrivastava S, Saleem A, Singh A, Lee H, Wang Y H and Tseng T Y 2022 Highly efficient invisible TaO_x/ZTO bilayer memristor for neuromorphic computing and image sensing *ACS Appl. Electron. Mater.* **4** 2180–90

[24] Saleem Kumar A D, Singh A, Rajasekaran S and Tseng T Y 2022 Oxygen vacancy transition in HfO_x-based flexible, robust, and synaptic Bi-layer memristor for neuromorphic and wearable applications *Adv. Mater. Technol.* **7** Art. no. 2101208

[25] Choi S H, Park S O, Seo S and Choi S 2022 Reliable multilevel memristive neuromorphic devices based on amorphous matrix via quasi-1D filament confinement and buffer layer *Sci. Adv.* **8** eabj7866

[26] Park J, Ryu H and Kim S 2021 Nonideal resistive and synaptic characteristics in Ag/ZnO/TiN device for neuromorphic system *Sci. Rep.* **11** 16601

[27] Merkel C *et al* 2016 Neuromemristive systems: boosting efficiency through brain-inspired computing *Computer* **49** 56–64

[28] Zhou Z *et al* 2019 Synapse behavior characterization and physical mechanism of a TiN/SiO_x/p-Si tunneling memristor device *J. Mater. Chem. C* **7** 1561–7

[29] Kumar S, Gautam M K, Gill G S and Mukherjee S 2022 3-D physical electro-thermal modeling of nanoscale Y_2O_3 memristors for synaptic application *IEEE Trans. Electron Devices* **69** 3124–9

[30] Su J *et al* 2022 Integration of resonant band with asymmetry in ferroelectric tunnel junctions' *npj Comput. Mater.* **8** 54

[31] Hu X, Feng G, Duan S and Liu L 2015 Multilayer RTD-memristor-based cellular neural networks for color image processing *Neurocomputing* **162** 150–62

[32] Jo S H, Chang T, Ebong I, Bhadviay B B, Mazumder P and Lu W 2010 Nanoscale memristor device as synapse in neuromorphic systems *Nano Lett.* **10** 1297–301

[33] Wu W *et al* 2018 A methodology to improve linearity of analog RRAM for neuromorphic computing *2018 IEEE Symp. on VLSI Technology (Honolulu, USA)* 103–4

[34] Chu M *et al* 2015 Neuromorphic hardware system for visual pattern recognition with memristor array and CMOS neuron *IEEE Trans. Ind. Electron.* **62** 2410–9

[35] Sun B *et al* 2019 A unified capacitive-coupled memristive model for the nonpinched current–voltage hysteresis loop *Nano Lett.* **19** 6461–5

IOP Publishing

Resistive Switching Systems for In-Memory Computation and Artificial Intelligence

Shaibal Mukherjee

Chapter 4

Memristive devices as computational memory

4.1 Introduction and brief overview of memristive devices

In the ongoing pursuit of advancing computing technologies and harnessing the power of artificial intelligence (AI), researchers and engineers are tirelessly working to develop innovative methods for improving the efficiency and performance of memory devices [1]. Among these efforts, memristive devices have emerged as a promising solution for computational memory, marking a significant departure from traditional memory architectures and opening a new era of transformative possibilities [2].

Memristive devices represent a unique class of non-volatile resistive switching technologies that have captivated the scientific community, largely due to their remarkable and distinctive properties. These innovative breakthroughs hold the promise of transforming the foundation of computing systems, offering a compelling vision of a future where memory devices break away from traditional models and adopt entirely new operational principles.

This chapter begins by highlighting the evolving nature of computer programs and applications, in particular, emphasizing the impact of technologies such as big data and the Internet of Things (IoT). In this fast-paced environment, there is a growing demand for improved performance in areas such as storage capacity, energy efficiency, and computational power, as shown by Lebdeh *et al* [6]. Figure 4.1 introduces a variety of deep learning (DL) neural network algorithms, including deep neural networks (DNNs) and convolutional neural networks (CNNs), underscoring the diversity of algorithms developed to meet these increasing demands. The focus then shifts to the advancements in memristive devices for synaptic applications within DL algorithms, as described by Wang *et al* [20]. Key improvements include linear memristive device reading, handling both positive and negative weights using differential pairs, and the adaptation of vector matrix multiplication and accumulation

doi:10.1088/978-0-7503-6169-9ch4 © IOP Publishing Ltd 2025. All rights, including for text and data mining (TDM), artificial intelligence (AI) training, and similar technologies, are reserved.

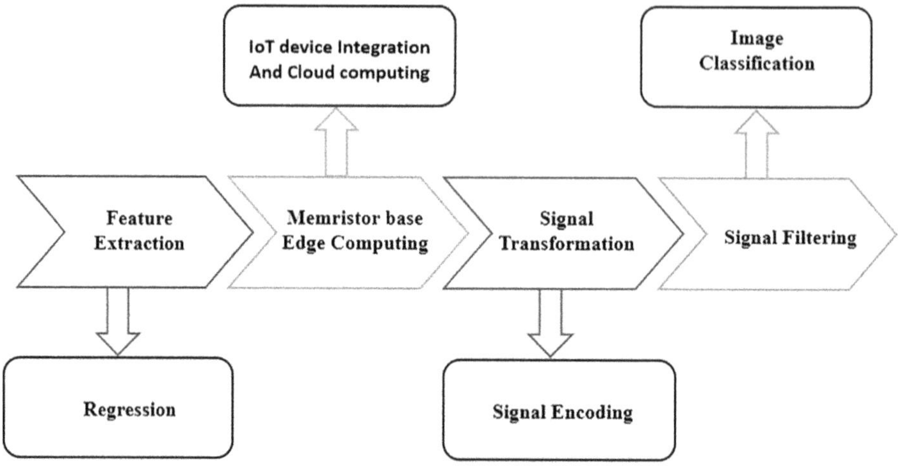

Figure 4.1. Visual representation showcasing common applications of memristors in signal processing, including the pivotal role played by the memristor array in edge computing, and various signal processing techniques that can be executed through the utilization of memristor arrays.

(VMMA) to 2D and 3D memristive arrays. Additionally, linear conductance updates are achieved through identical pulses, enhancing the performance of these devices. Figure 4.1 also explores the integration of various memristive devices such as resistive random-access memory (RRAM), phase-change memory (PCM), spin torque transfer random-access memory (STT-RAM), and ferroelectric random-access memory (FeRAM). This section demonstrates how a memristive neuromorphic computing system can be integrated into a single chip, highlighting the potential for combining different technologies in one platform. Furthermore, the distinctive properties of memristive devices in emerging algorithms, including their relevance in spike-timing-dependent plasticity (STDP), dendrite filtering, and their stochastic behavior, are discussed. This section also examines various architectures, including spiking neural networks (SNNs), reservoir computing, Hopfield neural networks (NNs), cellular NNs, and p-bits, which can effectively leverage the capabilities of memristive devices. Despite these advancements, current architectural and device technologies face challenges in keeping up with the dynamic and fast-changing landscape of computing. To address these challenges, researchers are exploring innovative architectures, such as computation-in-memory (CIM), as discussed by Ali *et al* [4], which leverages memristive devices. Memristive circuits, capable of performing both logical and arithmetic operations within non-volatile memory, are central to enabling these new architectures. As shown in figure 4.2, memristive devices represent the fourth fundamental circuit element by establishing a relationship between flux and charge, as shown by Prodromakis *et al* [2]. The significance of memristive devices in computational memory cannot be overstated. These devices have the potential to revolutionize various aspects of computing, in particular in neuromorphic and non-volatile memory applications. Memristance, a key electrical property, connects charge flow and resistance, making memristive devices uniquely suited for information

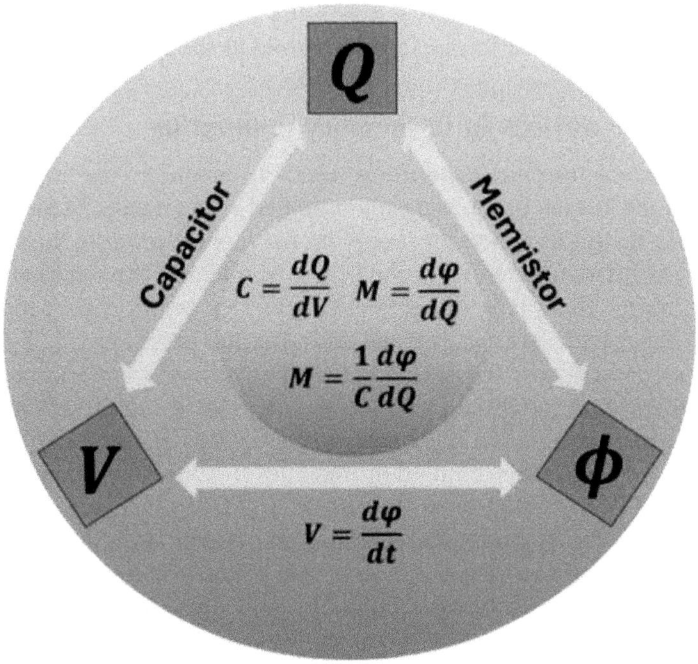

Figure 4.2. Fourth fundamental circuit element.

storage and processing. Unlike traditional resistors, which have fixed resistance, memristors can 'remember' the history of applied voltage or current, making them highly attractive for advanced memory applications.

Memristive devices offer several advantages over traditional memory technologies. One notable feature is their ability to enable parallel processing, allowing data storage and computation to occur in the same location. This reduces data transfer and latency, significantly speeding up memory-intensive tasks, making them ideal for applications where performance is critical. Additionally, their analog computing capabilities are particularly valuable in neuromorphic systems, where tasks such as pattern recognition, learning, and decision-making require precision and efficiency. Memristive devices are also energy-efficient, consuming less power than conventional memory technologies, which makes them an excellent choice for in-memory computing (IMC) and energy-conscious systems. By integrating computation and memory, they contribute to reduced energy consumption, aligning with the growing emphasis on energy-efficient computing, as shown by Zhao *et al* [8]. Moreover, memristive devices are highly adaptable, and are capable of adjusting their resistance levels in response to changing inputs or conditions. This adaptability is especially useful in neuromorphic systems, where learning and adaptation are vital. In conclusion, memristive devices bring significant advantages, including parallel processing, analog computing, low power consumption, and adaptability. These features make them invaluable in computational memory and applicable across a wide range of use cases, from high-speed data processing to energy-efficient computing systems. They represent a promising alternative to traditional memory technologies and are poised to play a critical role in the future of computing.

4.2 Memristive devices in in-memory computing

The field of neuromorphic computing seeks to emulate the architecture and functioning of the human brain using silicon-based components. Memristive devices play a pivotal role in this context by enabling the replication of biological synapses, the connections between neurons in the brain. Mimicking the synaptic behavior of the human brain, memristive devices facilitate the creation of artificial neural networks (ANNs) with spiking neurons and synaptic plasticity [3]. This approach holds immense promise for the development of energy-efficient and highly parallel neuromorphic systems, potentially revolutionizing AI and cognitive computing. One of the most remarkable features of memristive devices is their ability to emulate synaptic behavior and this emulation includes phenomena such as long-term potentiation (LTP) and long-term depression (LTD), which are fundamental to the learning and memory processes in biological systems [4].

Figure 4.3 presents two distinct designs for a binary multiply-accumulate cell (MAC), each utilizing a different technology and approach. The first design by Wang *et al,* shown in figure 4.3(a), employs traditional CMOS technology, renowned for its low power consumption and compatibility with conventional manufacturing processes, in which 'X' and the memristor are considered as inputs to a NAND gate which activates a multiplexer with another given input with the inverse of the amplifier. In contrast, the second design, figure 4.3(b), integrates memristive technology, utilizing memristors to harness potential benefits for neuromorphic computing and memory-based processing, as shown by Zhao *et al* [8], in which the memristor is connected with two inverse connections of a NOT gate for nullifying the effect of fluctuations. The resulting output is then passed through another NOT gate, functioning similarly to a MOS device, whose behavior is influenced by the input signal (P_{in}) and the enabled power (P_{en}) applied at the gate terminal. This configuration also provides a zoomed-in representation of a memristive-based cell, offering a visual approximation of its physical dimensions.

Each option presents trade-offs in performance, power efficiency, and technological implementation, allowing decision-makers to select the most appropriate design based on specific application needs. Whether the priority is computational

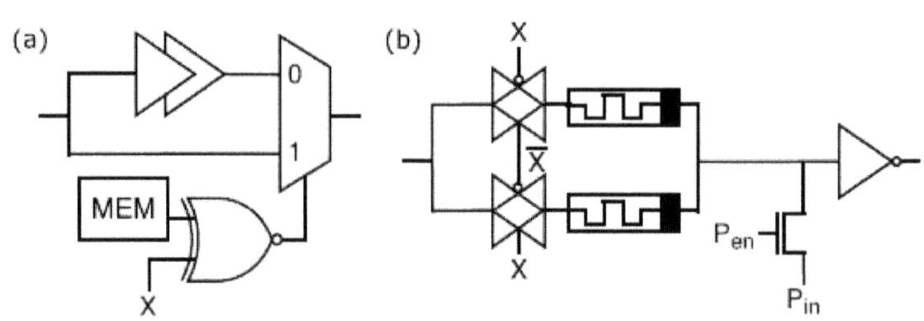

Figure 4.3. Binary MAC cell options using (a) CMOS technology and (b) memristive technology.

efficiency, memory-intensive tasks, or power limitations, these options offer flexibility. Memristive devices, in particular, can emulate synaptic processes, enabling the development of ANNs that can learn and adapt to patterns, as described by Li *et al* [15]. This ability to mimic biological functions is a key reason for the growing integration of memristive devices into computational memory systems. Memristive devices are non-volatile, meaning they can retain data without continuous power supply, offering significant advantages for both memory storage and processing. Moreover, they are highly energy-efficient, requiring very little power for read and write operations. This energy-saving feature is crucial for creating low-power, high-performance computing systems, where reducing power consumption is a top priority.

As computer science continues to advance rapidly and the volume of big data grows exponentially, traditional computing architectures, particularly the von Neumann architecture, face significant challenges. These challenges arise from the inherent separation between the processing units (CPU) and memory units (RAM), which necessitates frequent data transfers between them. This division results in high communication costs and latency, which limits the overall efficiency of the system, particularly when dealing with large datasets and complex tasks. In this context, the memristive IMC paradigm has emerged as a promising alternative to address these issues, as discussed by Li *et al* [27].

Memristive devices, which integrate memory and processing within the same unit, enable IMC, thus eliminating the need for data transfer between separate memory and processing components. This integration can significantly reduce both energy consumption and latency, enhancing computational efficiency, particularly in data-intensive tasks. Memristive in-memory computing has been identified as a key solution for next-generation computing systems, particularly in fields such as AI and machine learning (ML), where vast amounts of data must be processed quickly and efficiently.

IMC is an innovative computing paradigm that performs computations directly within the memory, eliminating the need to transfer data to a separate processing unit. This approach can significantly reduce latency and energy consumption by avoiding the constant movement of data between the memory and the processor. Memristive devices are highly promising for IMC as they can simultaneously store and compute data due to their unique electrical properties, which allow them to alter their resistance when voltage is applied [5]. The significance of IMC using memristive devices lies in its ability to enable a new generation of high-performance, energy-efficient computing systems [6]. IMC can accelerate a wide range of applications, including ML, AI, and scientific computing [7]. Computation within a memory-based architecture, often referred to as IMC, is a cutting-edge model that leverages the inherent properties of memristive devices to perform both storage and computation in a single hardware unit. This model differs from traditional computing, where data are continuously transferred between storage and processing units, leading to substantial energy and time costs. Memristive devices, with their non-volatile memory and the ability to change resistance analogously, have become key players in developing memory-based architectures, with the potential to transform computational methods [8]. The memristive devices used in memory-based computing can be broadly categorized into various types, each serving different purposes. Analog memristors offer a continuous range of resistance states, making them ideal for applications such as neuromorphic computing, analog signal processing, and in-memory ML. In contrast, digital memristors have discrete resistance states and function similarly to traditional digital memory elements, with the added benefit of faster read and write operations due to their memristive nature [9].

Memristor arrays, consisting of multiple memristive devices arranged in a grid structure, are versatile and capable of performing various computational tasks such as matrix-vector multiplication, pattern recognition, and content-addressable memory. These arrays excel at parallel processing, which accelerates certain algorithms and applications. Crossbar arrays, a specific type of memristor array, are densely packed and commonly used for analog and digital signal processing, offering compact, energy-efficient hardware for in-memory computing. Hybrid memory–CPU systems combine memristive devices with traditional CPUs or GPUs to create systems that exploit the advantages of memristive memory for tasks such as data storage while using conventional processors for complex computations. This approach strikes a balance between performance and energy efficiency [10]. In-memory accelerators are specialized hardware units incorporating memristive devices to accelerate specific computations, such as sparse matrix operations, database queries, and bioinformatics tasks, significantly enhancing application performance [11]. The use of memristive devices in memory-based architectures presents numerous advantages, including reduced energy consumption, lower latency, and the potential for exponential growth in computational capabilities. As research in this area advances, it promises to meet the rising demand for energy-efficient, high-performance computing solutions, ushering in a new era where memory is at the core of computing.

The acceleration of memristive IMC primarily stems from the highly parallel execution of matrix-vector multiplication (MVM) operations enabled by memristor crossbar arrays. MVM, a fundamental mathematical operation, is central to various applications, including digital signal processing, ML, and equation solving. In traditional processors such as CPUs and GPUs, MVM is executed using MAC units, which involve multipliers, adders, and registers. These units require repeated data fetching, registering updates, and processing cycles, making the operations time-consuming and resource-intensive, especially for large-scale matrices. In contrast, the memristor crossbar array provides a fully connected topology that allows for simultaneous execution of MVM. In this approach, input vectors are encoded as time-serial voltage signals, while the matrix values are represented by the memristors' conductance. The output vector is directly derived from the current signals using Ohm's law and Kirchhoff's current law, achieving MVM operations with $O(1)$ time complexity, irrespective of matrix size. This high efficiency positions memristive IMC as a transformative solution for accelerating computational tasks requiring MVM.

Despite these advantages, the analog nature of memristive IMC introduces accuracy limitations influenced by hardware constraints. Quantization errors arise from the limited number of memristor conductance states and intrinsic device variability. Furthermore, peripheral circuits, particularly digital-to-analog converters (DACs) and analog-to-digital converters (ADCs), also constrain precision. High-precision ADCs, crucial for accurate MVM results, are often impractical due to substantial hardware overheads, especially in cases involving large-scale data accumulation.

Memristive IMC has been experimentally demonstrated across diverse domains, such as neural networks, scientific computing, and other AI-driven applications. These applications, however, impose varying requirements on computational accuracy and hardware solutions. For example, scientific computing demands ultra-high precision, as small errors can cascade into significant inaccuracies, necessitating robust compensation strategies. In contrast, neural network inference tolerates lower precision, focusing on overall data patterns rather than exact numerical outputs. This flexibility categorizes such tasks as 'soft' applications, reducing hardware design complexity.

4.3 The importance of in-memory computing

Additionally, other non-volatile memory (NVM) technologies, such as flash, phase-change memory (PCM), ferroelectric field-effect transistors (FeFETs), and magnetic random-access memory (MRAM), have been explored for IMC. These technologies offer unique advantages and are tailored to meet specific application requirements. Nonetheless, the inherent parallelism and efficiency of memristive IMC continue to make it a compelling choice for advancing computational paradigms in data-intensive domains.

4.3.1 Addressing the von Neumann bottleneck

IMC is a computing paradigm that revolutionizes traditional data processing by moving computation tasks directly into memory, as depicted in Prodromakis *et al* [2]. Unlike conventional architecture where data travel continuously between the processor and memory, IMC integrates computation within memory units to achieve faster processing, lower energy consumption, and improved efficiency. This paradigm has garnered significant attention due to the growing demands of data-intensive applications such as AI, ML, and big data analytics. Traditional computers operate on the von Neumann architecture, where the separation between memory and processing units leads to frequent data transfers. This results in latency, increased power consumption, and limited bandwidth. IMC eliminates this bottleneck by enabling data to be processed where it is stored, significantly reducing communication overhead and accelerating computational tasks.

4.3.2 Energy efficiency

Modern computing workloads, particularly those involving AI and big data, are notorious for their high energy demands, largely driven by the frequent movement of data between memory and processing units. IMC addresses this challenge by minimizing data movement, which is a major contributor to energy consumption in traditional architectures. By performing computations directly within the memory, IMC significantly reduces energy usage, making it an ideal solution for energy-intensive tasks. This efficiency is particularly critical for applications deployed in resource-constrained environments, such as edge devices and IoT nodes, where power availability is often limited. With its ability to combine high performance and energy efficiency, IMC is poised to enable the deployment of advanced computing capabilities in a wide range of low-power, real-time applications, from smart sensors to autonomous systems.

4.3.3 Acceleration of AI and ML workloads

AI models, particularly DNNs, rely heavily on massive MVMs, which are computationally intensive and resource-demanding. The inherently parallel architecture of IMC is particularly suited for executing these operations efficiently, as demonstrated by Dou *et al* [9]. Memristor-based IMC takes this efficiency a step further by enabling analog computations directly within memory arrays, bypassing the need for traditional data transfers between memory and processing units. This integration not only accelerates MVMs but also significantly reduces energy consumption, making it highly advantageous for rapid training and inference in neural networks. By performing computations at the data's location, memristor-based IMC enhances performance and scalability, positioning it as a transformative solution for the computational demands of modern AI applications.

4.3.4 Real-time data processing

IMC facilitates real-time analytics by processing data directly within the memory, eliminating the need to transfer data to a CPU or GPU for computation, as highlighted by Li *et al* [15]. This on-the-fly processing capability significantly reduces latency, making IMC essential for applications that require immediate responses. For instance, in autonomous vehicles, IMC ensures rapid decision-making by analysing sensor data in real time, enhancing safety and performance. In financial trading systems, it supports ultra-low-latency processing of market data, enabling timely and accurate execution of trades. Similarly, in healthcare monitoring, IMC enables continuous and immediate analysis of patient data, providing critical insights for timely medical interventions. By addressing the latency challenges inherent in traditional architectures, IMC plays a pivotal role in advancing real-time, high-stakes applications.

4.3.5 Scalability for big data applications

With data volumes growing exponentially, traditional computing architectures are increasingly challenged to manage the load efficiently. The frequent movement of large datasets between memory and processing units in conventional systems creates bottlenecks in performance, energy consumption, and scalability. In contrast, IMC offers a scalable solution by integrating computation directly within the storage hardware. This design eliminates the need for extensive data transfers, enabling systems to process massive datasets efficiently. By performing computations where the data reside, IMC can handle petabytes of data while maintaining high performance, making it a powerful approach for data-intensive applications such as big data analytics, AI, and scientific simulations. This seamless integration of computation and storage positions IMC as a critical enabler for managing the growing demands of modern data-driven technologies.

4.3.6 Support for diverse applications

IMC has emerged as a transformative technology with applications across a variety of fields. In AI and ML, IMC accelerates training and inference tasks for neural networks and other models by performing matrix-vector multiplications directly within the memory. This drastically reduces computational time and energy consumption, making it an ideal solution for both cloud-based and edge AI applications. IMC also plays a pivotal role in scientific computing, where high-precision calculations are essential for simulations and research in areas such as weather modeling, molecular dynamics, and astrophysics. By eliminating data transfer bottlenecks, IMC enhances the performance and efficiency of these complex computations. In edge computing, IMC enables low-power, high-speed processing for IoT and embedded systems, facilitating real-time analysis of sensor data, autonomous vehicles, and smart devices while addressing the constraints of energy efficiency and latency. Additionally, IMC offers significant advantages in digital signal processing (DSP), supporting real-time applications in communication and media systems, such as audio and video compression, image recognition, and wireless communication. By addressing the demands of diverse domains, IMC demonstrates its versatility and potential to drive innovation across AI, scientific research, edge computing, and DSP applications.

4.3.7 Enhanced data security

IMC systems significantly enhance data security by minimizing the need for data transfer between memory and processing units, thereby reducing the exposure of sensitive information to external threats. Unlike traditional computing architectures, where data frequently traverse multiple pathways and interfaces—each presenting potential vulnerabilities—IMC processes data directly within the memory hardware. This streamlined approach inherently limits opportunities for interception or tampering, making it a robust choice for security-critical applications.

This capability is particularly crucial in fields such as financial systems, healthcare, and defense, where data integrity and confidentiality are paramount. For instance, in financial systems, IMC can protect sensitive transactional data from breaches during computation, ensuring secure processing of banking operations. In healthcare, it safeguards patient records and medical data, preserving privacy while supporting real-time diagnostics and treatment decisions. In defense, IMC's secure architecture provides a foundation for processing classified information, bolstering the integrity of military communications and decision-making systems.

By embedding security directly into the hardware design, IMC not only enhances computational efficiency but also aligns with the growing demand for secure, reliable, and privacy-focused computing solutions.

4.3.8 Reduction in hardware complexity

IMC systems offer a transformative approach to computation by integrating processing and memory within compact units, effectively reducing the complexity and size of traditional computing systems. This compact design is particularly advantageous for portable devices and embedded systems where space and power resources are limited. By eliminating the need for frequent data movement between separate processing and memory units, IMC systems also enhance energy efficiency, making them ideal for resource-constrained applications.

4.3.9 Challenges and future potential

Despite their promise, IMC systems face several challenges that must be addressed prior to their widespread adoption. One major hurdle is the development of robust and reliable memory technologies, such as memristors, resistive RAM (RRAM), and PCM. These emerging technologies are still under refinement to achieve the performance, stability, and scalability required for practical deployment. Additionally, the analog nature of computations in IMC systems introduces inherent imprecision, which can be a limiting factor for tasks demanding high numerical accuracy, such as scientific simulations or financial modeling. Transitioning from traditional von Neumann architectures to IMC also presents significant challenges in system integration, as it requires the redesign of software and algorithms to fully leverage the benefits of this novel computing paradigm.

Despite these challenges, the future of IMC is highly promising. With the rise of the Artificial Intelligence of Things (AIoT), IMC is poised to become a foundational technology, enabling highly efficient and adaptive systems that seamlessly integrate with the interconnected devices of the modern world. By addressing current limitations, IMC has the potential to drive innovation across domains such as real-time AI, edge computing, and next-generation IoT applications.

IMC represents a paradigm shift in computing technology, addressing critical bottlenecks of traditional architectures while offering significant improvements in performance, energy efficiency, and scalability. As AI, IoT, and big data continue to grow, IMC's role in enabling faster and more efficient data processing will become increasingly vital, driving innovation across multiple industries.

4.4 Multilevel conductance state programming

Memristive devices are emerging as promising candidates for non-volatile memory and neuromorphic computing applications due to their unique properties, including the ability to change their resistance (or conductance) based on the history of applied voltage/current. The concept of multilevel current/conductance programming in memristive devices is an important aspect of their potential as computational memory elements. Memristive devices can exhibit a variety of conductance states, each corresponding to a distinct level of resistance [9–13]. By controlling these states, it becomes feasible to store and process multiple bits of information within a single device, ultimately enabling the realization of multilevel data storage. Multilevel programming refers to the ability to store more than just two resistance states. Memristive devices can exist in multiple intermediate resistance states between the high-resistance state (HRS) and low-resistance state (LRS). By carefully controlling the voltage or current applied during programming, it is possible to create and stabilize these intermediate states [10, 11]. The ability to achieve multiple resistance states allows memristive devices to be used as analog memory elements. This is particularly important for neuromorphic computing and artificial neural networks, where synaptic weights are often represented as analog values. The architecture considered for this application, illustrated in figure 4.4, consists of a traditional processor, primary DRAM memory, an innovative data-centric CIM core, and external memory. Both the main memory and CIM core retrieve data from the external memory, with the CIM core offering direct access from the processor and an expanded address space [12]. To simplify memory coherence, the CIM core is loaded with external data, such as databases, through a one-time initialization process.

These intermediate resistance states can represent the strength of a synaptic connection, enabling fine-grained analog computations. In neuromorphic computing, one key function of memristive devices is to emulate synaptic plasticity [11]. Multilevel programming allows these devices to mimic the strengthening or weakening of synapses in biological neurons, making them suitable for implementing various learning algorithms, such as STDP [12, 13]. Memristive devices are

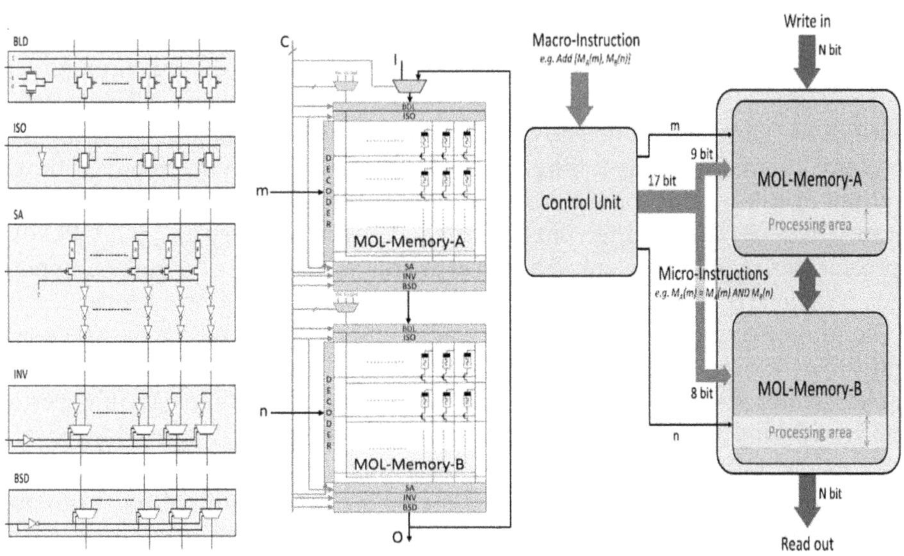

Figure 4.4. Computational memory architecture.

known for their energy-efficient operation. Their ability to store multiple resistance states can enable efficient representation of analog values and potentially lead to lower power consumption in neuromorphic systems compared to traditional digital implementations [13].

Here are some illustrative instances showcasing the versatile use of multilevel current/conductance state programming in memristive devices for the realization of intricate synaptic plasticity mechanisms. STDP is a synaptic plasticity paradigm that reinforces synapses when the presynaptic neuron fires before the postsynaptic neuron and weakens them when the firing order is reversed. Memristive devices can emulate STDP by precisely timing the programming pulses to coincide with spike events at the pre- and postsynaptic neurons. LTP represents synaptic strengthening in response to high-frequency stimulation. Memristive devices can replicate LTP by repeatedly applying programmed pulses, mimicking the effect of high-frequency neural activity. LTD, conversely, reflects synaptic weakening due to low-frequency stimulation [14]. In memristive devices, LTD can be achieved by sustaining the application of a programmed pulse over an extended duration. By harnessing these and other synaptic plasticity mechanisms, memristive devices facilitate the creation of neuromorphic computing systems capable of learning and adapting to their surroundings. This technological leap opens the door to a new era of intelligent machines proficient in tasks such as image recognition, natural language processing, and machine translation.

Programming the conductance state at multiple levels entails configuring the device to one of several potential conductance levels to signify diverse data values. Multilevel conductance state programming in memory computing using memristive devices is an innovative concept that fuses memristor technology with memory computing, resulting in memory systems that are both more efficient and versatile. This concept entails the capacity to adjust the resistance of memristive devices to several distinct levels. While traditional binary memory devices such as flash memory have only two states ('0' or '1'), memristors can exhibit multiple conductance states, enabling them to store multiple bits of data in a single cell, as described by Yang *et al* [14]. The process of multilevel conductance state programming entails precisely fine-tuning these resistance levels to represent a broader spectrum of values. IMC, a computing paradigm that processes data directly within memory, reduces the need for data transfers between memory and the CPU. This approach can significantly enhance the efficiency and speed of specific computing tasks, particularly those involving large datasets and complex operations.

The programming state in memory computing of multilevel conductance using memristive devices offers several key advantages and versatile applications. It enables greater memory density through the storage of multiple data bits per cell, thereby reducing the physical space required for memory systems. Moreover, it enhances processing speed as memory computing conducts operations directly in memory, reducing data transfer times. These devices are prioritized for their energy efficiency, making them crucial for power saving computing. Additionally, their ability to store multiple data levels in a single cell enables analog processing, which is particularly valuable in fields such as neuromorphic computing. With applications spanning artificial intelligence, data analytics, and emerging technologies such as quantum computing, memristive devices present a promising future. However, it is essential to acknowledge that memristor technology is still evolving and has not yet achieved widespread commercial adoption, with ongoing research addressing technical challenges to make it a practical and scalable solution.

The memristor overwrites logic (MOL) memory architecture, as depicted in figure 4.4, has the capability to execute a wide array of operations, encompassing both logical computations and storage functions [9]. For each operation in the list, a set of suitable commands is simultaneously dispatched to the constituent blocks that compose the architecture, and each of these operations is executed within a single computational step. In this operation, 2 bit vectors, MA(m) and MB(n), situated at specific addresses m and n, corresponding to MOL-memory-A and MOL-memory-B, respectively, are involved [15]. In this instance, MOL-memory-A is configured in read mode enabling it to access and read the bit-vector MA(m), which subsequently undergoes a bit-wise inversion via the INV block; the 1 bit shifter remains inactive. Concurrently, MOL-memory-B is set to overwrite mode, facilitating a MOL-AND operation with the vector MB(n). The outcome of this bit-wise logical operation replaces the previous vector MB(n), and this entire process transpires within a single computational step [19], as shown in figure 4.4.

Multilevel conductance state programming in memristive devices is an intriguing domain with the potential to revolutionize non-volatile memory, neuromorphic computing, and analog computing. As this technology matures, it is poised to play a central role in the evolution of the next-generation information processing systems. Researchers and engineers are diligently working to enhance programming methods and tackle the challenges associated with memristive devices, paving the way for exciting advancements in the realms of computing and memory technologies. Memristive devices possess unique attributes that render them suitable for diverse applications, including multilevel data storage and NN emulation. Within the context of memristive devices, conductance state programming pertains to the capability of configuring and manipulating the device's resistance levels in terms of conductance for the purpose of storing and processing data in a non-volatile manner [8]. The programming of memristive devices involves the application of specific voltage or current pulses to induce changes in conductance states. Various programming techniques are employed to attain multilevel conductance state programming. Achieving dependable and precise programming of multilevel conductance states in memristive devices presents challenges that necessitate addressing factors such as device variability, endurance, and sneak paths [9].

ANNs are modeled after the biological NNs found in the human brain, capable of adaptively executing complex tasks through their interconnected structure. These networks have been instrumental in driving major advancements in ML, significantly impacting applications such as natural language processing, image classification, and object detection. However, despite their impressive representation capabilities, ANNs face limitations due to the large volume of parameters and computational procedures required, which significantly increase both data storage and movement needs. This becomes especially problematic in resource-constrained environments, such as edge computing and the IoT, where computational power is limited.

To address these challenges, using memristor arrays to accelerate ANNs has emerged as a promising solution. Memristive neural networks, which exploit the unique properties of memristors for both memory and computation, can help alleviate the bottlenecks associated with traditional ANN hardware implementations, as discussed by Ernoult *et al* [21]. Memristive devices offer advantages such as low power consumption and efficient data storage, making them well-suited for edge devices. These networks operate in two major phases: inference and training. Inference involves the use of a pre-trained model to make predictions, while training adjusts the network parameters based on data input. A variety of hardware implementations have been proposed to support these phases, with a particular emphasis on inference applications. Furthermore, different approaches to training memristive neural networks have been explored, and these methods are integral to optimizing the performance of ANNs in practical applications.

In recent years, the remarkable potential of memristive devices has gained significant attention, primarily for their potential to revolutionize computational memory systems. These devices exhibit unique characteristics that position them as promising candidates for advancing memory and storage technologies [19–22]. Their capacity to offer higher storage density compared to current memory technologies holds great promise, especially in the context of data-driven applications such as big data analytics [20–26]. Particularly intriguing is its ability to emulate synaptic behavior akin to biological neurons, which could profoundly impact the future of computational memory systems [15]. This burgeoning interest has sparked the field of neuromorphic computing, with the use of memristive devices potentially leading to the development of ANNs that are inherently capable of learning and adapting, thereby driving progress in ML, robotics, and cognitive computing.

The potential impact of memristive devices on future computational memory systems

To understand the potential of memristive devices in future computational memory systems, it is important to first examine their device-level architecture and programming principles. Figure 4.5(a) shows a microscope image of a 4 × 4 dual-polarity element (DPE) array, and figure 4.5(b) shows the electrical connections and circuit schematic for programming a specific cell, labeled as (3, 2), within the array. In the microscope image, labels identify the primary components: the bottom electrode (BE), top electrode (TE), gate electrode (GE), and ground (GND), which form the DPE structure to enable selective programming and reading for each cell. The circuit schematic shows how rows and columns are defined in the array, with columns assigned to GE and TE, and rows to BE. The polarity of the memristor is essential for the operations. During a SET operation, a positive voltage is applied to TE, while for RESET, a positive voltage is applied to BE. This polarity management facilitates precise control over the resistance state, enabling data storage or erasure [26]. To program a cell, voltage is selectively applied to either TE or BE, with GE used to activate and access the specific cell. Arrows indicate the bidirectional nature of the current flow, meaning current can move in either

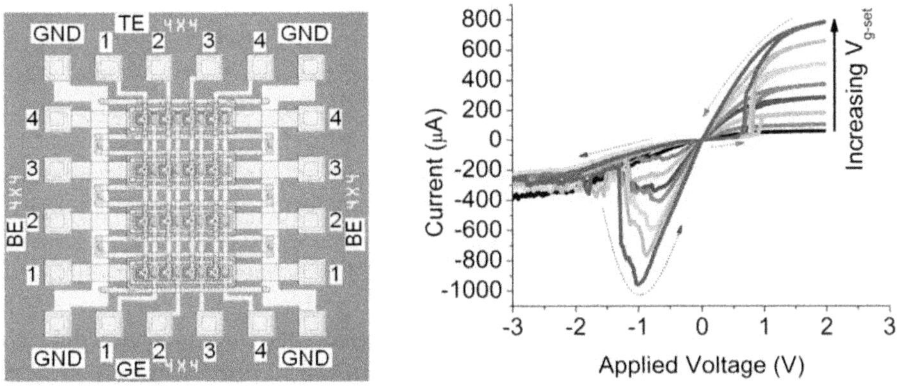

Figure 4.5. (a) Microscope image of the 4 × 4 DPE array with labels corresponding to the bottom electrode (BE), top electrode (TE), gate electrode (GE), and bulk or ground connections (GNDs). (b) Electrical connections for programming cell (3, 2) of the DPE. A circuit schematic representation of the DPE, where the columns are given by GE and TE, and rows by BE. The polarity of the memristor is such that for the SET operation a positive voltage is applied to TE, while for RESET, a positive voltage is applied to BE. A voltage is applied to either TE or BE, while GE is used to select and program the cell. The arrows represent the bidirectionality of the current flow; while reading, the current is read through either row or column. (Reproduced from [26]. Copyright IOP Publishing Ltd. CC BY 3.0.)

direction depending on the operation. During reading, the current is measured from either the row (BE) or column (TE or GE), which provides a readout of the resistance state for data retrieval from the targeted cell.

The adaptability of memristive devices makes them seamlessly integrable into a wide range of memory hierarchies, spanning from embedded systems to high-performance computing platforms. Their scalability renders them a versatile choice for a diverse array of applications, ranging from smartphones to supercomputers [21]. Furthermore, memristors hold the potential to significantly enhance storage density compared to current memory technologies, a highly coveted feature in contemporary data-centric applications such as big data analytics and cloud computing [22]. Figure 4.5 offers a comprehensive view of spiking neural networks integrating memristive and memcapacitive devices. They encompass a wide range of visual insights, from an on-chip memristive neural network to a single 1T1R cell, employing materials such as palladium, hafnium dioxide, and tantalum in their integrated memristors. The micrographs provide structural analyses, showcasing both memristive and capacitive neural networks, while specific images reveal volatile capacitive switching neuro-transistors, neurons, and synapses utilizing silver-based memristors with integrated capacitors [23]. Additionally, the high-resolution transmission electron micrographs offer detailed insights into the intricate composition and architecture of these critical components, including the thickness of silver electrodes in electrochemical metallization cells. Collectively, these visual explanations light on the complex and innovative technology underpinning spiking neural networks [24].

Integrating spiking neural networks with memristive and memcapacitive devices presents an intriguing application training networks for tasks such as alphabet writing. These memristive neural networks replicate the synaptic plasticity observed in biological counterparts, facilitating learning and adaptation. When applied to alphabet writing, these networks can recognize and generate handwritten characters by adjusting synaptic weights based on examples [25, 26]. Memristors play a crucial role in ensuring efficient, low-power learning, making them advantageous for tasks such as alphabet writing across various domains. In the realm of electronic devices, memristors possess transformative potential for computational memory systems. Their non-volatile nature, coupled with superior speed and energy efficiency compared to traditional memory devices, holds the promise of novel high-speed, non-volatile storage solutions, thereby enhancing data center performance and reliability. Moreover, memristors drive the development of neuromorphic computers, ideal for AI and ML applications, drawing inspiration from the structural and functional aspects of the human brain.

4.5 Applications of memristive crossbar arrays

At the forefront of the current paradigm shift stands the remarkable memristive crossbar array, a sophisticated and versatile technology with applications spanning multiple domains. In this section, we embark on an exploration of the realm of memristive crossbar arrays, revealing their pivotal role in shaping the landscape of computer memory. Memristive crossbar array devices can change their resistance based on the history of applied voltage, effectively remembering the amount of charge that has passed through them. This ability to remember previous electrical states makes memristors an ideal candidate for non-volatile memory applications [3]. A significant transformation is currently taking place within the dynamic convergence of computer science and electronics. This metamorphosis is challenging conventional methods of data management and storage within our computing systems. The applications of memristive IMC can be broadly classified into two main categories: soft computing and hard computing. These categories correspond to different computational needs and, consequently, require different hardware solutions and computational accuracies. Applications of memristive crossbar array in computational memory, specifically neuromorphic computing, IMC, edge detection, ML accelerators, and security and cryptography, are described in detail.

4.5.1 Soft computing

This category encompasses applications that tolerate uncertain and imprecise results, making them ideal for fields such as machine learning, ANNs, and other AI-driven tasks. Memristive devices are particularly well-suited for such tasks because their ability to perform computations in-memory allows for parallel processing, which is critical for training deep learning models and neural networks, as described by Mannocci *et al* [17]. In soft computing, approximation and tolerance to errors are often acceptable, which allows memristive devices to perform efficiently while saving energy and processing time. Memristors' inherent ability to store information in their resistance states lends them well to simulating synaptic behaviors in neuromorphic computing, a key area within soft computing. Soft computing involves tasks that can be executed with lower computational accuracy and can tolerate uncertain or imprecise outcomes. One of the most prominent domains within soft computing is ML, which focuses on developing models based on the inherent relationships within data. ML algorithms aim to perform tasks such as classification, clustering, or regression by learning from these data patterns. A key characteristic of an effective ML algorithm is its ability to generalize well, meaning that it should prioritize overall accuracy while being able to handle noisy or imperfect data, which ultimately reduces the demand for high computational precision.

Given its compatibility with soft computing, memristive IMC has significantly advanced hardware implementations of ML algorithms. In this context, memristive ANNs are particularly notable, as they enable both inference and training processes with enhanced efficiency, as described by Ernoult *et al* [21]. Additionally, memristive arrays are being used to address challenges such as the curse of dimensionality in non-ANN ML tasks. These devices, with their inherent stochastic properties, also open new possibilities for specific ML applications where randomness can be leveraged to improve performance or efficiency.

4.5.2 Hard computing

In contrast, hard computing requires more precise, deterministic results. This category includes applications in scientific computing, digital image processing, and signal processing, where exact numerical values are crucial for the task at hand. Memristive in-memory computing can still be beneficial here, particularly in specialized applications where the task can be parallelized, and the speed of computation is prioritized over extreme precision. For example, in digital image processing, memristive circuits can perform pixel-level operations directly in memory, reducing the need for time-consuming data transfers and enabling real-time image enhancement or feature extraction.

4.5.3 Neuromorphic computing

Memristive crossbar arrays are a promising new technology for neuromorphic computing, which is a type of computing inspired by the human brain [2]. These arrays can mimic the intricate synaptic connections between neurons making them ideal for energy-efficient and highly parallel processing tasks such as pattern recognition, ML, and AI [1]. In a traditional von Neumann computer, data must be constantly moved between the CPU and memory, which can be a major bottleneck. Memristive crossbar arrays, on the other hand, can perform computations in-memory, eliminating this bottleneck [5]. This makes them much more efficient for tasks that require a lot of matrix multiplication, such as NNs. Memristive crossbar arrays are still under development, but they have the potential to revolutionize the way computation is done. They could be used to create new types of artificial intelligence hardware that are more powerful and energy-efficient than anything we have today.

4.5.4 In-memory computing

Memristive crossbar arrays provide the crucial foundation for IMC, a revolutionary paradigm that redefines the way we process data. This groundbreaking innovation empowers us to perform computations right at the point where data reside, eliminating the need for constant data transfers between storage and processing units. The implications of this technology are profound, with significant advances in computational speed and energy efficiency poised to transform various industries [16]. By obviating the latency associated with data movement, IMC promises to redefine the landscape of database management, enabling real time data analysis and decision-making [23]. The advantages of memristive crossbar arrays extend to fields such as image processing, where the instantaneous retrieval and manipulation of large image datasets become not just possible but highly efficient [24]. The benefits extend beyond data analytics, which, as a cornerstone of the modern information age, can greatly benefit from in-memory computing's ability to perform complex calculations on large datasets without delay.

4.5.5 Edge detection

With the continued rise of IoT devices, the role of edge computing has seen a notable increase in importance. Memristive crossbar arrays stand out as exceptionally compatible with edge computing applications, primarily due to their minimal power requirements, compact form factor, and their capability to perform localized data processing [17]. These attributes uniquely position them to effectively manage a range of tasks, including the analysis of sensor data, the operation of autonomous vehicles, and the advancement of smart city systems. Memristive crossbar arrays align perfectly with this demand. Their energy-efficient nature ensures that they can operate effectively in resource-constrained environments. Their compact size makes them ideal for integration into IoT devices and sensors, where space is often limited. One of their standout features is the ability to perform localized data processing, reducing the need for extensive data transmission to central servers [21]. This capability is invaluable for real-time decision-making in applications such as autonomous vehicles, where split-second responses are critical. Moreover, in scenarios such as smart city systems, the capacity for localized data processing enhances the efficiency of the network.

4.5.6 Machine learning accelerators

ML models, particularly deep learning architectures such as convolutional neural networks (CNNs) and recurrent neural networks (RNNs), are computationally intensive, requiring vast amounts of data and significant computational resources for operations such as MVM, a core component of NN computations [2]. Traditional systems face challenges in handling these demands due to high computational power requirements, energy inefficiency from frequent data transfers between memory and processors (known as the 'memory wall'), and latency caused by sequential processing. Memristive crossbar arrays address these limitations by directly performing MVM within the memory, leveraging their ability to store weights as conductance levels in memristors and perform computations in a highly parallel manner. When voltage signals representing input data are applied to the rows of the array, the conductance states of the memristors determine the resulting current along the columns, enabling MVM to be completed in a single step across the entire array. This hardware-level parallelism drastically reduces computational time while minimizing energy consumption by eliminating the need for extensive data movement [13]. Additionally, memristive arrays support rapid updates to weights during training, as conductance states can be adjusted *in situ*, leading to faster training cycles for neural networks. Their compact design and scalability make them ideal for deployment in resource-constrained edge devices such as IoT sensors and mobile platforms, enabling real-time decision-making in applications such as autonomous vehicles, smart devices, and medical diagnostics [3]. By lowering the computational and energy barriers, memristive crossbar arrays not only accelerate training and inference times but also make complex ML models more accessible and sustainable. Their potential to integrate into neuromorphic computing and advanced training techniques, such as in-memory stochastic gradient descent, positions them as a transformative technology for future AI applications, enabling faster, more efficient, and environmentally friendly machine learning across diverse domains

4.5.7 Security and cryptography

Memristive crossbar arrays possess unique characteristics that make them highly valuable in the fields of cryptography and security. One of their key advantages is the ability to execute logic operations directly within the array, allowing for efficient processing without the need for external processors. This capability can be leveraged for tasks such as encryption and decryption, where the memristors' conductance states can be used to store and manipulate cryptographic keys. Furthermore, memristive arrays offer inherent non-volatility, meaning that the encryption keys and sensitive information stored within the arrays are preserved even during power outages, providing an additional layer of security [4]. This makes them ideal for safeguarding encryption keys, ensuring that unauthorized access is minimized. Additionally, memristive arrays can play a crucial role in identity verification and secure communication. By using their programmable resistance states to generate unique patterns for authentication processes, they can enhance systems for identity confirmation, making it more difficult for attackers to replicate or steal credentials. In secure communication, memristive arrays can be utilized for real-time encryption and decryption, further strengthening data confidentiality. By integrating these arrays into security systems, they bolster data integrity, protect sensitive information, and provide a more resilient infrastructure for secure communication and identity verification.

4.6 Writing a random alphabet through training using memristive crossbar arrays

The captivating realm of memristive crossbar architecture is a fascinating area of exploration, primarily within neuromorphic computing and resistive memory technologies. In this architecture, memristors are intricately arranged in a crossbar pattern, offering a versatile array of applications [13]. Notably, one significant application involves generating randomized sequences of alphabetical characters. The deliberate configuration of memristors into a crossbar structure creates a complex grid, enabling simultaneous data processing and efficient memory storage. Its pivotal contribution to advancing emerging technologies, particularly in neuromorphic computing, is of utmost importance [27].

Kumar *et al* [28] show that yttrium oxide (Y_2O_3) is a promising material for developing neuromorphic computing devices. These devices mimic the human brain's structure and function, offering potential for energy-efficient and high-performance computing. Kumar *et al* had successfully implemented the writing capability of a fabricated Y_2O_3-based memristor crossbar array (MCA), as shown in figure 4.6. From a larger 30 × 25 array, they randomly selected an 8 × 8 section for testing. Initially, all devices in the MCA were switched to the 'ON' state by applying a constant input voltage of +1.3 V, which produced a current range of 15–24 μA. To write specific alphabet patterns, the input voltage for the chosen devices was further increased to +2.1 V, resulting in a higher current range of 35–45 μA. Using this method, they successfully demonstrated the writing of multiple alphabet patterns

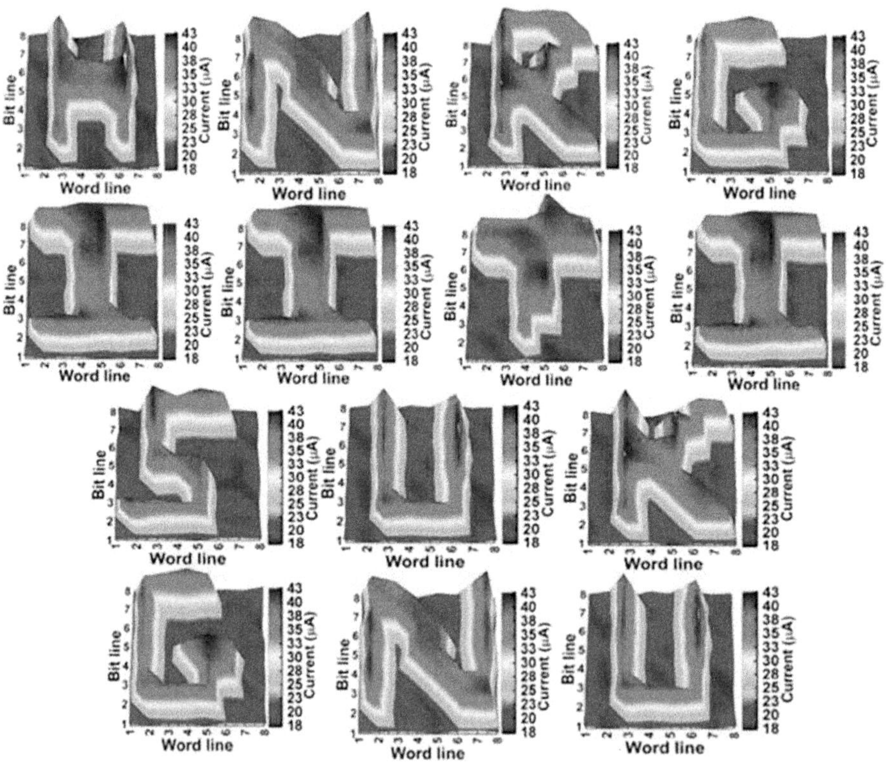

Figure 4.6. (8 × 8) memristive crossbar array electric pulse writing for a random alphabet. (Reproduced with permission from [28]. Copyright 2023 IEEE.)

such as 'HNRG', 'IITI', 'SUK', and 'GNU'. These experiments confirmed the robustness and reliability of the Y_2O_3 MCA for pattern-writing applications.

The use of memristive crossbar arrays in AI and ML has revolutionized hardware-based computational tasks, particularly in the context of data-driven applications. Writing random alphabets involves employing memristive crossbar arrays to train models capable of generating, recognizing, and manipulating alphabetic data [5]. This process leverages the high-density, parallel processing capabilities of memristor technology, integrating it with ML algorithms for efficient and precise operation.

4.6.1 The role of memristive crossbar arrays in training

4.6.1.1 Structure and functionality

Memristive crossbar arrays are composed of a grid-like structure where memristors are positioned at the intersections of horizontal and vertical conductive lines. Each memristor functions as a programmable resistor, capable of storing information by exhibiting different levels of electrical conductance [6].

These arrays excel in performing MVM operations natively within the hardware. When input signals (such as voltage vectors) are applied along one set of lines (e.g. rows), the output signals (e.g. current vectors) are generated along the other set of lines (e.g. columns) as a result of the memristors' conductance states. This operation is:

Highly efficient: MVM, a core computation in machine learning and signal processing, is executed in a single step, leveraging the inherent physical properties of the memristive array.

Parallel: The structure processes multiple data elements simultaneously, enabling high-speed computation.

Energy-saving: By performing computations in-memory, memristive arrays reduce the need for frequent data transfer between memory and processors, significantly lowering energy consumption.

These features make memristive crossbar arrays a promising technology for data-intensive applications, such as neural network acceleration, real-time image processing, and edge AI devices.

4.6.1.2 Training mechanism

During the training phase, memristive crossbar arrays function as hardware implementations of NNs [7], with the conductance of individual memristors representing the weights of the network. The training process involves the following steps:

1. **Input encoding and propagation**:

   Input signals: Inputs to the neural network, such as feature vectors, are encoded as voltage signals. These signals are applied to the horizontal lines (rows) of the crossbar array [8].

   Output currents: As the input voltages propagate through the array, the memristors' conductance states determine the resulting currents along the vertical lines (columns). These currents correspond to the weighted sums of the inputs, effectively performing the MVM inherent to neural network computations.

2. **Feedback and weight adjustment**:
   Error calculation: The output currents are compared to the desired target outputs, and the error (difference between the computed and expected results) is calculated [9].
   Gradient descent: Using algorithms such as gradient descent, the error is backpropagated through the network to determine the adjustments needed for each memristor's conductance.
   Conductance update: Voltage pulses of specific magnitudes and durations are applied to the memristors to fine-tune their conductance levels. This adjustment continues iteratively, reducing the error and improving the accuracy of the model over time.
3. **In-hardware learning advantages**:
   Parallel updates: The inherent parallelism of the crossbar array allows for simultaneous updates across multiple weights, speeding up the training process [10].
   Energy efficiency: By performing computations directly in-memory, memristive arrays eliminate the need for extensive data movement, reducing power consumption.
   Analog precision: Memristors offer fine-grained control over conductance states, enabling precise weight representation and adjustments.

This training process allows memristive crossbar arrays to efficiently learn and adapt, making them well-suited for tasks such as image recognition, natural language processing, and real-time decision-making in AI systems.

4.6.2 Writing random alphabets

4.6.2.1 Task definition

To generate random alphabets, the memristive crossbar arrays must be trained to understand and reproduce the patterns of letter formation [11]. This involves several key steps:

1. **Mapping input signals to output signals**:
   Input signals: These typically consist of feature vectors representing the structural attributes of letters. For example, features may include the shape, stroke width, and curvature of each letter. These vectors are encoded into voltage pulses or currents that serve as inputs to the memristive array [12].
   Output signals: The memristive array generates output signals corresponding to specific alphabet patterns. These signals are decoded into pixel grids or vector shapes that visually represent the letters.
2. **Training the array**:
   Datasets: The training process often leverages datasets containing handwritten or typographic alphabets. Examples include widely used datasets such as EMNIST (Extended MNIST for letters) or custom collections of stylized fonts and scripts [13].

Supervised learning: Input–output pairs from the dataset are used to teach the array how specific input features map to corresponding letter patterns. The conductance states of the memristors are adjusted iteratively through a learning algorithm, such as gradient descent or Hebbian learning, until the system reliably reproduces letter patterns.

Learning nuances: The system learns nuances such as variations in handwriting, font styles, and distortions, allowing it to produce realistic and diverse alphabet patterns during inference.

3. **Generating random alphabets**:

   Once trained, the array can be used to generate random alphabets by introducing stochastic variations into the input feature vectors or directly leveraging the inherent randomness of memristors [14]:

   Feature perturbation: Slight modifications or randomization of input feature vectors can produce new variations of alphabets while maintaining recognizable letterforms.

   Exploiting stochastic behavior: Memristors naturally exhibit variability due to their physical properties. This randomness can be harnessed to introduce subtle differences in the generated patterns, making each letter unique.

   Style control: Additional input parameters can be used to control the style (e.g. bold, italic, or ornamental) or randomness of the generated alphabets, enabling tailored outputs for specific applications.

4. **Applications:**

   Artistic and design fields: For creating unique fonts or decorative alphabets in graphic design.

   Personalization: Customizing handwriting or font styles in digital documents.

   Game development: Generating stylized text or glyphs for dynamic content creation.

This approach highlights the potential of memristive crossbar arrays in bridging hardware efficiency with creative applications.

4.6.2.2 Procedure

This process leverages the unique properties of memristors, such as non-volatility and analog tunability, to create an efficient and compact system for alphabet recognition or generation tasks.

1. **Data preprocessing**: The initial step involves preparing the input data, which consists of alphabets, for compatibility with the memristive array. Each alphabet is encoded into a numerical format suitable for processing [15]. This numerical representation can take various forms:
   - *Binary encoding*: Each alphabet is represented as a binary sequence, where individual bits signify specific features or patterns. For example, 'A' might correspond to '01000001' in ASCII encoding.
   - *Analog signals*: Alternatively, the alphabet can be mapped to continuous analog voltage levels, where each unique voltage corresponds to a specific alphabet.

These encoded inputs are then formatted into electrical signals, such as voltage pulses, which can be applied to the input terminals of the memristive array. This ensures the data are in a form the hardware system can process effectively.

2. **Model training**: Training the system involves configuring the conductance states of the memristors within the array to learn the patterns associated with different alphabets. This is typically achieved through supervised learning, where labeled examples (input–output pairs) guide the training process [16].
   - *Conductance adjustment*: Each memristor's conductance is modulated by applying carefully calibrated voltage pulses. These adjustments encode the relationship between the input signals (numerical representations of alphabets) and the desired outputs.
   - *Weight encoding*: In this context, the conductance of a memristor acts as a synaptic weight in a neural network. Higher or lower conductance values represent stronger or weaker connections, respectively, contributing to the network's ability to differentiate between input patterns.
   - *Learning algorithm*: Gradient-descent-like algorithms may be employed to iteratively update the conductance values until the array correctly associates each input alphabet with its corresponding output. Feedback mechanisms evaluate performance and guide conductance adjustments during training.
3. **Evaluation**: After training, the system is tested with novel inputs to evaluate its ability to recognize or generate alphabets accurately [17].
   - *Recognition process*: New input signals, encoded in the same numerical format as during training, are applied to the array. The trained memristive conductance states process these inputs, generating outputs that correspond to the recognized alphabet.
   - *Information encoding*: The final conductance states of the memristors serve as a physical embodiment of the learned information. These states effectively store the relationships between input patterns and outputs, enabling the system to recall and apply this knowledge during evaluation.
   - *Performance metrics*: Accuracy, precision, recall, and latency are some of the metrics used to assess the system's performance. The robustness of the array's conductance states under varying conditions is also evaluated to ensure reliability.

4.6.2.3 Challenges

1. **Noise and variability**:

   Memristors, like many nanoscale devices, exhibit device-level variability due to factors such as fabrication inconsistencies, material imperfections, and operational fluctuations [18]. This variability can lead to:

   Unreliable conductance states: Slight variations in the programmed conductance of individual memristors may result in inaccuracies when processing input signals.

Cumulative errors: In large crossbar arrays, small errors at the device level can compound, causing significant deviations in output signals.
External noise: Environmental factors, such as thermal noise or electrical interference, can further distort the signals, impacting the accuracy of the system.

To mitigate these challenges, advanced error-correction algorithms, robust training protocols, and adaptive compensation techniques can be employed. Regular recalibration of the memristor states may also be necessary to maintain system performance.

2. **Quantization errors**:

Memristors typically have a finite number of stable conductance states, which limits their ability to represent continuous values with high precision. This quantity introduces errors [19], particularly when the system requires fine-grained adjustments for:

Weight updates: During training, the resolution of conductance changes might be insufficient to capture small gradients, leading to suboptimal learning outcomes.
Signal representation: Limited states can reduce the fidelity of input and output signal encoding, impacting the model's ability to differentiate between similar inputs.

To address quantization issues, researchers employ techniques such as:

Dynamic range optimization: Maximizing the usable conductance range to enhance precision.
Stochastic programming: Introducing randomness to simulate intermediate states and improve effective resolution.
Hybrid approaches: Combining memristive arrays with digital processors to offload precision-sensitive tasks.

4.6.2.4 Applications

1. **Optical character recognition (OCR)**:

Memristive arrays can play a transformative role in enhancing OCR systems by providing faster and more efficient character recognition capabilities [20].

Training on random alphabets: The arrays are trained using a diverse set of randomly generated alphabets, enabling them to learn generalized features that improve recognition accuracy across various fonts, styles, and languages.

Parallel processing: The inherent parallelism of memristive crossbar arrays allows for simultaneous processing of multiple input patterns, significantly speeding up the OCR process.

Energy efficiency: Compared to traditional digital processors, memristive arrays consume less power, making them ideal for real-time OCR tasks in portable and embedded systems.

Applications include document digitization, license plate recognition, and automated text extraction from images or videos. The ability to recognize characters efficiently in noisy or low-quality images is another advantage.

2. **Creative content generation**:

   Memristive systems can also be used for generating stylized or randomized alphabets, opening up new possibilities in artistic and design domains [22].

   Leveraging stochastic properties: The natural variability and stochastic behavior of memristors can be harnessed to produce unique and randomized variations of alphabets. This can be particularly useful for generating creative content such as:

   Custom fonts: Designing new typography styles for graphic design and branding.

   Artistic patterns: Creating visually appealing alphabet-based art.

   Randomized outputs: Producing unpredictable letterforms for use in games, logos, or visual effects.

   The combination of memristive technology with generative algorithms can provide a compact and energy-efficient solution for creative content generation.

3. **Edge AI in IoT devices**:

   Memristive arrays are highly suited for integration into low-power IoT devices due to their lightweight and energy-efficient characteristics [23]. These systems can perform on-device alphabet recognition for tasks such as:

   Voice-to-text conversion: Translating spoken words into written alphabets.

   Smart sensors: Recognizing and processing alphanumeric data locally without relying on cloud computing.

Researchers exploit the capabilities of memristive crossbar architecture to create unpredictable sequences of alphabetic characters, a task with far-reaching implications. These sequences find utility in diverse fields such as cryptography, secure communication, and the generation of random data for scientific simulations [4, 24]. The process itself entails the application of carefully modulated voltage or current signals to the memristors within the crossbar array. This controlled input elicits stochastic variations in the resistive states of the memristors, culminating in the spontaneous selection of alphabetic characters. It is essential to underscore that this approach constitutes a unique and hardware-based methodology for generating random sequences. In the scope of this study, training denotes the method employed to set up memristive crossbar arrays to produce patterns or character sequences as shown in figure 4.6 [28]. This training process involves fine-tuning the voltage or current waveforms applied to the memristors, adjusting their initial resistive states, or employing algorithms that steer the randomization process toward a predefined objective. The capacity to train these arrays unlocks opportunities for the creation of customized random sequences, thereby enabling tailoring to specific applications.

4.6.3 Prospects and challenges

Integration with advanced AI models: The combination of memristive crossbars with advanced deep learning models holds the potential to expand their application to more intricate and diverse writing systems. This includes the capability to handle cursive handwriting, symbolic alphabets, and even hieroglyphic or logographic scripts. By leveraging the unique strengths of memristive crossbars, such as IMC and parallel data processing, these systems can effectively manage the increased complexity of such writing styles. Deep learning architectures such as RNNs or transformer-based models, integrated with memristive crossbars, could enhance real-time learning and adaptation, paving the way for broader linguistic and cultural applications [25].

Improved hardware reliability: As memristive crossbars become more prevalent, ensuring hardware reliability is critical for consistent performance. This involves developing robust fabrication techniques to minimize device-level variability and ensure uniform behavior across large arrays. Additionally, incorporating error-correction mechanisms can address potential faults in memristor operation, enhancing overall system stability [26]. Techniques such as redundancy in memristive arrays or adaptive learning algorithms could compensate for variations and errors, making the technology more reliable for practical applications.

Broader deployment: With advancements in scalability and cost reduction, memristive crossbars could see widespread adoption across various fields. In education, they could power interactive learning tools that teach writing and language skills through dynamic feedback and adaptation [27]. Assistive devices, such as those for individuals with disabilities, could benefit from real-time handwriting recognition and content generation capabilities. Furthermore, content generation systems, such as automated translation or creative writing tools, could utilize memristive-based hardware for efficient processing and output.

Training memristive crossbar arrays to write random alphabets demonstrates the synergy between emerging hardware technologies and AI methodologies. The ability to perform rapid, parallel processing within the memory units themselves eliminates traditional data transfer bottlenecks, significantly enhancing computational efficiency. Although challenges such as hardware reliability and integration with diverse AI models remain, the potential of memristive crossbars to revolutionize fields requiring high-speed, adaptive processing makes them a cornerstone for innovation in AI-driven applications [28]. As research progresses, this integration will likely unlock unprecedented possibilities across education, accessibility, and creative content generation.

Bibliography

[1] Yu J, Nguyen H A D, Xie L, Taouil M and Hamdioui S 2018 Memristive devices for computation-in-memory *Design, Automation & Test in Europe Conf. & Exhibition (DATE) (Dresden, Germany)* pp 1646–51

[2] Prodromakis T and Toumazou C 2010 A review on memristive devices and applications *17th IEEE Int. Conf. on Electronics, Circuits and Systems* pp 934–7

[3] Hamdioui S *et al* 2019 Applications of computation-in-memory architectures based on memristive devices *Design, Automation & Test in Europe Conf. & Exhibition (DATE)* pp 486–91

[4] Ali K A *et al* 2020 Memristive computational memory using memristor overwrite logic (MOL) *IEEE Trans. VLSI Syst.* **28** 2370–82

[5] Siemon A, Wouters D, Hamdioui S and Menzel S 2019 Memristive device modeling and circuit design exploration for computation-in-memory *IEEE Int. Symp. on Circuits and Systems (ISCAS)* pp 1–5

[6] Lebdeh M A, Reinsalu U, Nguyen H A D, Wong S and Hamdioui S 2019 Memristive device based circuits for computation-in-memory architectures *IEEE Int. Symp. on Circuits and Systems (ISCAS)* pp 1–5

[7] Freye F, Lou J, Bengel C, Menzel S, Wiefels S and Gemmeke T 2022 Memristive devices for time domain compute-in-memory *IEEE J. Explor. Solid-State Comput. Devices Circuits* **8** 119–27

[8] Zhao H *et al* 2022 Memristor-based signal processing for edge computing *Tsinghua Sci. Technol.* **27** 455–71

[9] Dou C *et al* 2017 Challenges of emerging memory and memristor based circuits: nonvolatile logics, IoT security, deep learning and neuromorphic computing *IEEE 12th Int. Conf. on ASIC (ASICON)* pp 140–3

[10] Zidan M A, Strachan J P and Lu W D 2018 The future of electronics based on memristive systems *Nat. Electron.* **1** 22–9

[11] Zidan M A *et al* 2017 Memristive computing devices and applications *J. Electroceram.* **39** 4–20

[12] Yang X, Adeyemo A, Bala A and Jabir A 2016 Novel memristive logic architectures *2016 26th Int. Workshop on Power and Timing Modeling, Optimization and Simulation (PATMOS) (Bremen, Germany)* pp 196–9

[13] Serb A, Khiat A and Prodromakis T 2018 Seamlessly fused digital-analogue reconfigurable computing using memristors *Nat. Commun.* **9** 2170

[14] Yang X, Adeyemo A, Bala A and Jabir A 2019 Novel techniques for memristive multifunction logic design *Integration* **65** 219–30

[15] Li C *et al* 2018 Analogue signal and image processing with large memristor crossbars *Nat. Electron.* **1** 52–9

[16] Lin P *et al* 2020 Three-dimensional memristor circuits as complex neural networks *Nat. Electron.* **3** 225–32

[17] Mannocci P, Pedretti G, Giannone E, Melacarne E, Sun Z and Ielmini D 2021 A universal, analog, in-memory computing primitive for linear algebra using memristors *IEEE Trans. Circuits Syst. I* **68** 4889–99

[18] Nguyen H A D, Yu J, Xie L, Taouil M, Hamdioui S and Fey D 2017 Memristive devices for computing: beyond CMOS and beyond von Neumann *2017 IFIP/IEEE Int. Conf. on Very Large Scale Integration (VLSI-SoC) (Abu Dhabi, United Arab Emirates)* pp 1–10

[19] Yu J, Lebdeh M A, Nguyen H A D, Taouil M and Hamdioui S 2020 The power of computation-in-memory based on memristive devices *2020 25th Asia and South Pacific Design Automation Conf. (ASP-DAC) (Beijing, China)* pp 385–92

[20] Wang W *et al* 2022 A memristive deep belief neural network based on silicon synapses *Nat. Electron.* **5** 870–80

[21] Ernoult M, Grollier J and Querlioz D 2019 Using memristors for robust local learning of hardware restricted Boltzmann machines *Sci. Rep.* **9** 1851

[22] Nandakumar S R, Le Gallo M, Boybat I, Rajendran B, Sebastian A and Eleftheriou E 2018 Mixed-precision architecture based on computational memory for training deep neural networks *2018 IEEE Int. Symp. on Circuits and Systems (ISCAS) (Florence, Italy)* pp 1–5

[23] Xia Q and Yang J J 2019 Memristive crossbar arrays for brain-inspired computing *Nat. Mater.* **18** 309–23

[24] Yeo I, Chu M, Gi S -G, Hwang H and Lee B -G 2019 Stuck-at-fault tolerant schemes for memristor crossbar array-based neural networks *IEEE Trans. Electron Devices* **66** 2937–45

[25] Wang C *et al* 2021 Scalable massively parallel computing using continuous-time data representation in nanoscale crossbar array *Nat. Nanotechnol.* **16** 1079–85

[26] Grafals E J M, Divila N, Ge N, Williams R S and Strachan J P 2016 Repeatable, accurate, and high-speed Ti level programming of memristor 1T1R arrays for power efficient analog computing applications *Nanotechnology* **27** 365202

[27] Li H *et al* 2021 Memristive crossbar arrays for storage and computing applications *Adv. Intell. Syst.* **3** 1–26

[28] Kumar S, Kumbhar D D, Park J H, Kamat R K, Dongale T D and Mukherjee S 2023 Y_2O_3-based crossbar array for analog and neuromorphic computation *IEEE Trans. Electron Devices* **70** 473–7

IOP Publishing

Shaibal Mukherjee

Chapter 5

Memristor-based in-memory logic operation and applications

5.1 Introduction

The advent of memristor technology has catalyzed transformative advancements in the domain of very large-scale integration (VLSI). With their unique attributes, including nanometer-scale dimensions and non-volatile memory, memristors have garnered substantial attention as a revolutionary component in modern electronics [1]. Their nanoscale size facilitates innovative circuit design approaches, enabling the development of logic blocks that transcend conventional architectures. Simultaneously, their non-volatile nature introduces possibilities for creating advanced computational models, integrating memory and processing functionalities into a unified platform.

In the evolving landscape of electronic systems and computing paradigms, the pursuit of efficient and high-performing solutions has spurred interest in emerging technologies [2]. Among these, memristors are pivotal in redefining traditional methodologies for memory and logic. Specifically, memristor-based in-memory logic (IML) exemplifies a transformative approach by merging storage and computational tasks within a single device. This dual-purpose functionality significantly optimizes data processing efficiency and energy consumption while reducing the latency associated with traditional memory-transfer architectures [3].

Memristors, short for 'memory resistors', possess the unique ability to store and process information simultaneously, bridging the historical division between memory and computation [4]. Their integration into contemporary computing architecture, particularly in the realm of in-memory computing (IMC), has garnered substantial research focus. This paradigm shift has the potential to drastically enhance the efficiency, speed, and scalability of electronic devices, making memristor-based systems an exciting frontier in technological exploration [5].

doi:10.1088/978-0-7503-6169-9ch5 © IOP Publishing Ltd 2025. All rights, including for text and data mining (TDM), artificial intelligence (AI) training, and similar technologies, are reserved.

Current investigations into memristor-based IML delve into core principles such as resistive switching mechanisms, material innovations, and architectural designs that align with modern computational demands. These studies underscore the potential of memristor technologies to redefine the foundations of electronic computing, with applications ranging from artificial intelligence (AI), and neuromorphic systems, to energy-efficient data processing [6]. Despite their immense promise, challenges such as device variability, endurance, and integration at large-scale remain critical areas for further exploration. Addressing these challenges will be instrumental in realizing the full potential of memristor-based technologies, setting the stage for a profound transformation in the computing domain [7].

5.2 Introduction to memristor-based in-memory logic

The relentless demand for performance optimization and energy efficiency in modern computing has catalyzed the exploration of innovative paradigms, with IMC emerging as a transformative approach to overcome the limitations of traditional von Neumann architectures [1, 6]. This section focuses on the integration of analog and digital processing capabilities within memory arrays, leveraging the unique properties of memristive devices for efficient logic operations.

5.2.1 Memristive devices: principles and characteristics

Memristors, as resistive switching devices, offer a range of properties that make them highly advantageous for modern computing and memory applications. One of their most notable characteristics is non-volatility, which allows them to retain their resistance states even when the power supply is turned off [1]. This capability makes memristors highly efficient for long-term data storage and reduces the need for constant power to maintain stored information, as required by traditional volatile memory technologies such as DRAM [2].

Another significant advantage of memristors is their low power consumption, which stems from their ability to switch resistance states using minimal energy. This makes them an ideal choice for energy-constrained systems, such as portable devices, Internet of Things (IoT) nodes, and edge computing platforms, where power efficiency is a critical design requirement [3]. Additionally, memristors contribute to the development of energy-efficient neural networks and machine learning models, where frequent updates to weights require low-energy write operations.

Memristors also support high density, enabling the creation of compact memory arrays that maximize storage capacity within a small physical footprint. This high packing density is crucial for modern applications that require large-scale storage and computation capabilities in a constrained space, such as advanced mobile devices, embedded systems, and data centers [4]. By leveraging the scalability of memristor arrays, designers can achieve greater integration and miniaturization of hardware without sacrificing performance.

These properties—non-volatility, low power consumption, and high density—not only make memristors a promising technology for next-generation memory but also position them as a cornerstone for emerging applications such as neuromorphic computing, IMC, and high-performance AI systems. Their ability to bridge the gap between storage and processing further underscores their transformative potential in the evolution of modern computing architectures [5].

These properties make memristors suitable candidates for implementing IMC. Traditional architecture faces challenges, such as the memory bottleneck, caused by the separation of processing and memory units, resulting in significant data transfer overheads [6]. Memristors address these issues by merging data storage and computation capabilities, paving the way for high-performance and energy-efficient systems [3, 7].

5.2.2 Analog processing

Memristive devices play a pivotal role in enabling analog computations directly within memory arrays, eliminating the need for separate processing units and reducing data transfer bottlenecks. This capability is particularly beneficial for tasks that rely on high-throughput, energy-efficient computations.

One of the key operations supported by memristive devices is vector-matrix multiplication (VMM), which is fundamental to machine learning tasks, including training and inference in neural networks. Memristive arrays can perform VMM in a highly parallel manner by encoding weights as conductance values and applying input vectors as voltage signals [1]. The resulting output currents correspond to the computed results, enabling efficient and rapid execution of these computationally intensive tasks.

Another critical operation facilitated by memristive devices is convolution, which is integral to image processing and convolutional neural networks (CNNs). By leveraging their ability to perform analog computations, memristive arrays can handle the repeated and localized multiplications required in convolution operations directly within the hardware, significantly accelerating processing times while reducing power consumption [2].

These capabilities make memristive devices a cornerstone for advancing analog computing, offering a scalable and energy-efficient solution for applications such as real-time AI, computer vision, and edge computing [3]. By seamlessly integrating computation and memory, they provide a pathway to overcoming the limitations of traditional digital architecture.

Analog in-memory processing reduces data movement and achieves greater energy efficiency compared to digital systems. For instance, neural network computations benefit from the multistate storage capability of memristors, which emulate synaptic weights in neuromorphic systems [4].

5.2.3 Digital processing

Memristors are not only effective for analog computations but also excel in digital computations, utilizing their discrete resistive states to perform Boolean logic operations, such as AND, OR, and XOR. By harnessing the ability of memristors to switch between distinct resistance states, these operations can be executed directly within the memory array. This eliminates the need for data to be transferred to separate processing units, a common bottleneck in traditional computing architectures. As a result, memristors enable faster computation and reduce energy consumption, as the data remain localized within the memory, reducing both the latency and power loss associated with data movement [2].

For example, performing AND or OR operations in a memristive array involves applying voltage signals that alter the memristors' conductance states, where different resistive levels represent binary values (0 or 1) [3]. The results of these operations can be directly read out from the memory array, without the need for time-consuming and power-hungry data transfers to central processors. This integration of logic and memory operations enhances computational speed and energy efficiency, making memristors well-suited for tasks that require fast and low-power digital computation, such as in embedded systems, IoT devices, and real-time signal processing applications.

By combining both analog and digital processing capabilities, memristive devices offer a versatile and efficient computing model that addresses the growing demand for high-speed, low-power systems in modern applications [4].

5.2.4 In-memory logic

The unified paradigm IML represents a paradigm shift, combining memory and computation in a single unit using the inherent properties of memristors [5–7]. These two-terminal devices enable logic functions and data storage, all within a non-volatile framework.

The *I–V* characteristics of memristors, as illustrated in figure 5.1, reveal their ability to modulate resistance under varying voltage inputs, which forms the basis of their role in logic circuit applications [8]. These unique properties enable the construction of logic circuits where computation and data storage occur within the same framework, reducing reliance on separate processing and memory units.

The integration of memristor-based logic circuits within memory arrays introduces significant advancements in computational efficiency [3]. Memristors can be

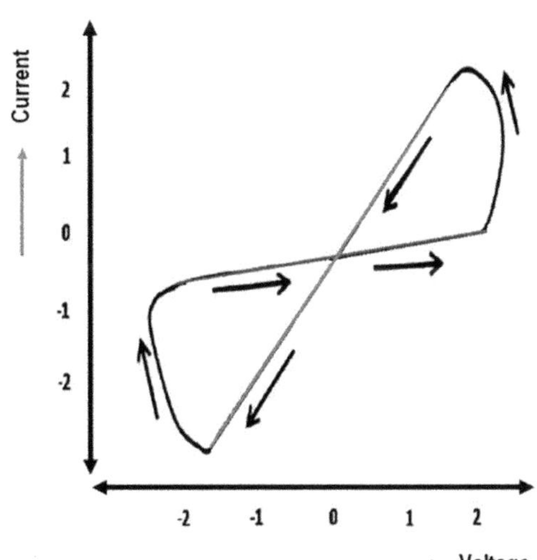

Figure 5.1. *I–V* curve of a generic memristor model with a sinusoidal input voltage.

configured to perform both analog and digital logic operations, making them versatile components for modern computational tasks. In digital circuits, memristors can implement Boolean logic functions such as AND, OR, NAND, and XOR, leveraging their discrete resistive states. These logic operations, carried out directly in-memory, eliminate the need for data movement between traditional processing and storage units, improving speed and reducing power consumption.

5.2.4.1 Advantages of memristor-based logic circuits

Speed and efficiency: Memristors enable faster computation by performing logic operations directly within the device, significantly reducing delays typically caused by the need to transfer data between memory and processing units in traditional computing systems [5]. This direct integration of logic and memory allows for much quicker execution of tasks, improving overall system performance.

Energy efficiency: By integrating processing within the memory, memristor-based logic circuits offer substantial energy savings compared to conventional architectures. The reduction in data movement between separate components, combined with the low power consumption of memristors themselves, leads to lower overall energy usage [1]. This is especially critical for energy-constrained systems, such as those used in IoT, edge computing, and mobile devices.

Scalability: The nanoscale size of memristors makes them well-suited for high-density logic circuits [2]. Their compact form allows for the development of smaller, more efficient systems, capable of supporting large-scale integration without compromising performance. This scalability is essential for the creation of next-generation computing systems, which require both increased computational power and smaller physical footprints.

5.2.4.2 Potential impact and challenges

The integration of memristors into logic circuits presents exciting opportunities, particularly in fields such as neuromorphic computing, AI, and advanced data processing systems. Memristors' ability to mimic synaptic behavior in neural networks, positions them as a key component for AI hardware, while their energy efficiency and speed make them ideal for large-scale data processing tasks [3]. However, there are several challenges that must be addressed to fully realize their potential.

Device variability: Ensuring uniform behavior across large-scale memristor arrays is critical for reliable performance. Variations in the characteristics of individual memristors could impact the accuracy and consistency of computations, posing a significant challenge in scaling up these devices for practical applications [4].

Endurance: Memristors must be durable enough to withstand repeated switching operations without significant degradation in performance. Improving the endurance of memristors is essential for their long-term reliability, particularly in applications involving frequent write cycles [5].

Integration: The seamless integration of memristor-based logic circuits into existing system architecture remains a challenge. Issues such as sneak paths causing unwanted current flow through unintended paths in crossbar arrays must be resolved to ensure that these systems operate efficiently and correctly [6].

Overcoming these challenges can be achieved by optimizing memristor designs and circuit configurations. As these technical issues are addressed, memristor-based logic circuits are expected to become a transformative technology, reshaping traditional computing architectures and enabling systems with enhanced speed, energy efficiency, and scalability [7].

In traditional von Neumann architecture, the separation of memory and processing units creates inefficiencies that hinder overall system performance [4]. The 'von Neumann bottleneck' refers to the time and energy spent transferring data between the central processing unit (CPU) and memory, leading to significant delays and increased power consumption. As modern applications become increasingly data-intensive, these inefficiencies become more pronounced, with higher speeds and lower energy consumption being critical demands [5]. Furthermore, the CPU's sequential processing nature, where one instruction is processed at a time, further restricts system throughput and scalability, making it difficult to handle the computational demands of complex tasks such as big data analysis and real-time AI applications.

Addressing limitations with IML: The IML architecture offers a promising solution to these challenges by integrating computation directly within the memory system [2]. This eliminates the need for constant data transfer between separate memory and processing units, thereby addressing the bottleneck inherent in traditional von Neumann designs. Memristors, which can store resistance states non-volatilely and perform computations, serve as the foundational technology for IML. By combining memory and logic functions into a single unit, memristors enable efficient parallel processing, drastically reducing the time and energy required for data handling.

In an IML architecture, operations such as VMMs or logic operations can be executed directly in-memory, where the data reside, avoiding the need for time-consuming data transfers to external processors [3, 5]. This integration leads to both faster computation speeds and lower power consumption, making IML ideal for high-performance applications such as AI, ML, and edge computing. By overcoming the limitations of the von Neumann bottleneck and enabling more scalable, efficient architecture, IML represents a significant step forward in the evolution of computing systems.

5.2.5 Logic gates within IML

Memristors offer a significant advantage in IML architectures by enabling the execution of logic operations such as AND, OR, and NOT directly within the memory. This ability to perform Boolean functions in-memory reduces the need for data movement between processing units and memory, leading to a substantial reduction in both time and energy consumption [3]. By eliminating the traditional bottleneck of transferring data to external processors, memristor-based IML systems can operate more efficiently and at higher speeds.

Since computations take place directly where the data are stored, memristor-based IML enhances parallel processing capabilities. This parallelism is critical for high-performance tasks that require the simultaneous handling of large volumes of data, such as neural network inference and real-time data analytics [1]. In neural networks, for example, operations such as matrix-vector multiplications and convolutions can be performed within memory, dramatically speeding up the processing of large datasets. In real-time analytics, memristors allow for immediate processing of incoming data streams, facilitating faster decision-making in applications such as autonomous systems and financial trading.

As the computations are performed in a parallel, in-memory fashion, the system can handle multiple operations simultaneously, making it an ideal solution for data-intensive applications [2]. This architecture not only boosts performance but also improves energy efficiency, offering a powerful alternative to traditional von Neumann systems for modern computational needs.

5.2.5.1 Key advantages of memristor-based IML

Non-volatile nature: Memristors have the unique ability to retain their resistance states even in the absence of power, making them non-volatile. This feature significantly reduces energy costs associated with maintaining data in-memory, as there is no need for constant power to refresh or preserve the data. Additionally, this non-volatility enables faster system startups, as data are immediately available when the system is powered on, eliminating the need to reload information from slower storage devices [4].

Increased efficiency: Memristors' ability to execute computations directly within the memory array eliminates the need for frequent data transfers between memory and processing units. This reduction in data movement minimizes latency and energy consumption, as the data remain in place for processing. The direct in-memory computation not only speeds up operations but also contributes to overall energy efficiency, which is especially beneficial for resource-constrained environments such as edge computing, IoT devices, and embedded systems [5].

Compact integration: Memristors are well-suited for dense memory arrays due to their small size and scalable nature. These arrays allow for high computational throughput while occupying a compact physical footprint. This compactness is particularly advantageous in modern computing systems, where space and power are limited. Memristor-based architectures can integrate large amounts of memory and processing power within a small area, enabling the development of high-performance, space-efficient devices and systems for applications such as mobile technology, IoT, and high-performance computing [6].

By leveraging these advantages of non-volatility, increased efficiency, and compact integration, memristor-based systems can significantly improve the performance, energy efficiency, and scalability of computing architectures, providing a promising alternative to traditional memory and processing technologies [7].

5.2.5.2 Transformative impact

Memristor-based IML represents a transformative advancement in computing architecture by combining logic and memory functionalities within a single device [2]. By addressing the limitations of the von Neumann model, IML holds the promise of delivering scalable, energy-efficient, and high-performance systems tailored to meet the demands of modern computational workloads [3]. This shift is particularly relevant in fields such as AI, ML, and neuromorphic computing, where data processing efficiency is paramount [6].

Memristive switches, as analysed by researchers such as Wang *et al* [4], offer transformative potential in modern computing architectures. These devices enable in-memory processing for both analog and digital operations, as illustrated in figure 5.2. The analog capabilities of memristive crossbar arrays are critical for parallel tasks such as VMMs, while their digital functionality allows logic operations to occur directly within the memory [5]. This dual in-memory processing reduces data movement and latency, significantly improving computational efficiency and making them ideal for advanced data-intensive applications. Memristors' ability to retain resistance states even in the absence of power facilitates persistent state computing, enhancing system reliability and enabling energy-efficient paradigms such as persistent neural networks and rapid system boot-ups [6, 7].

Traditional von Neumann architectures, with their inherent data transfer bottlenecks between the CPU and memory, face significant limitations in time and energy efficiency. Memristor-based IML overcomes these issues by integrating computation and storage within the memory unit. As highlighted by Lin *et al* [7], this innovation minimizes data movement and accelerates parallel processing, enabling simultaneous execution of multiple computations. Logic gates such as AND, OR, and NOT, implemented directly within memristive arrays, offer an edge over sequential processing systems by enabling compact and energy-efficient computing.

The limitations of CMOS technology, particularly in terms of spatial efficiency and power consumption, have driven significant interest in nanodevices such as memristors. Studies by Zhang *et al* [5] have demonstrated that memristor-based

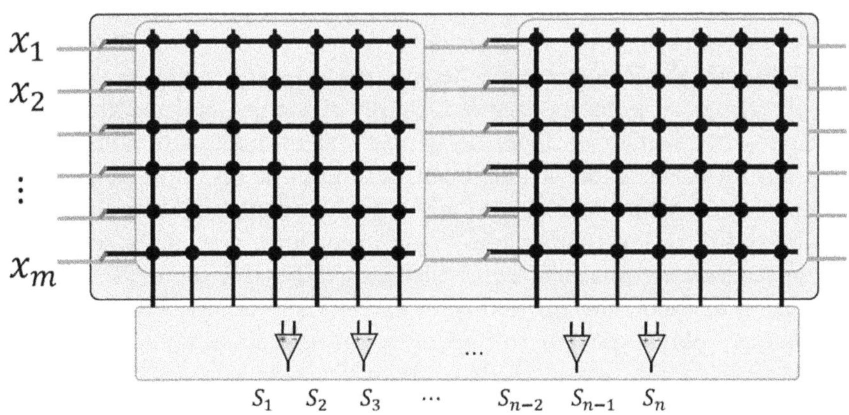

Figure 5.2. Analog and digital processing in-memory functionality.

combinational logic circuits, such as adders, subtractors, and decoders, show over 90% reduction in power consumption compared to traditional CMOS technology. Additionally, their reduced component count improves spatial efficiency, paving the way for the implementation of complex logic circuitry on a microscale. Tools such as MATLAB, Simulink, and Cadence Virtuoso are widely employed to design, implement, and evaluate these circuits, underscoring their practicality and scalability [6].

A hybrid approach integrating analog and digital processing in-memory using memristive devices is another promising direction. This method is particularly relevant to neuromorphic computing, where analog processing emulates synaptic behavior, while digital functions handle more complex computations [8]. As noted by Lee *et al* [9], this synergy holds significant potential but is challenged by issues such as device variability, reliability, and scalability. Ongoing research is exploring solutions to these challenges, offering a roadmap for the development of robust and scalable memristor-based systems for next-generation computing.

5.3 Types of in-memory logic memristive system

IML memristive system-based devices can be organized in a crossbar array configuration. In this set-up, memristors are positioned at each intersection of rows and columns, allowing for parallel processing and storage of information. The conductance state of each memristor can be dynamically changed to represent different weights, making it suitable for neural network-based applications. Memristors exhibit analog behavior, allowing them to represent a range of conductance values rather than just binary states. This analog property is advantageous for tasks such as analog computing, where the continuous nature of data is better suited for certain applications [10]. Memristive devices operate based on resistive switching mechanisms, where the resistance state of the device changes in response to applied voltage or current. Understanding and optimizing these switching mechanisms are crucial for the reliability and performance of IML systems. A memristor's ability to change resistance based on applied voltage enables them to act as both memory elements and logic gates [11].

In the domain of IML memristive systems, a diverse range of devices harness the distinctive characteristics of memristors to optimize computation and memory processes. Specifically, due to the inherent benefits of memristive devices, these types of devices excel in terms of speed, energy efficiency, and the ability to store data in a non-volatile manner. IML memristive systems make up a notable category that includes memristors for various functionalities; one prominent example is the utilization of memristors in logic gates [6]. These adaptable components possess the capability to execute fundamental logic operations, essentially serving as the foundational elements for logic gates such as AND, OR, and NOT gates [12]. Memristors, with their inherent ability to dynamically adjust resistance based on applied voltage, play a pivotal role in these gates, facilitating swift and energy-efficient logic computations. Utilizing crossbar arrays composed of memristive devices as versatile structures for in-memory computing, these arrays enable parallel processing and efficient data storage by encoding information in the resistive state of memristors. The crossbar architecture seamlessly integrates memory and processing functions [7]. Memristors are integral to neuromorphic computing, mimicking the synaptic plasticity observed in biological systems. In-memory neuromorphic circuits leverage memristors to emulate the learning and adaptation capabilities of the human brain, making them well-suited for AI and ML tasks [7]. Specialized in-memory computing units leverage memristors to conduct computations directly within the memory storage, eliminating the need for data transfer between separate memory and processing units [13]. These cells can be designed with integrated logic capabilities, enabling them to perform both memory storage and basic logic operations. This integration streamlines the complete architecture, thereby improving the computational efficiency of memory cells. Programmable logic arrays (PLAs) based on memristive devices offer reconfigurable logic functions [8]. These PLAs can be dynamically adjusted to meet specific computational requirements, providing flexibility in designing customized logic circuits.

In the field of digital electronics, complex computations are simplified through the use of fundamental logic gates. These essential building blocks form the core of digital circuits, each performing specific functions that drive the dynamic interaction of binary digits. This discussion delves into the circuits of these critical logic gates. Figure 5.3 illustrates the implemented circuits for different types of gates. Operating on a single input, the NOT gate (or inverter), a foundational component in digital electronics, produces an output that is the logical inverse of the input—high becomes low and low becomes high, as shown in figure 5.3(a). This ability to negate binary signals is essential to digital logic [8]. Moving on to the AND gate, which plays a vital role in digital circuit design, it requires multiple inputs to generate a high output, but only when all inputs are high, as shown in figure 5.3(b). This reflects a logical conjunction, where the truth of all inputs is necessary for a positive result.

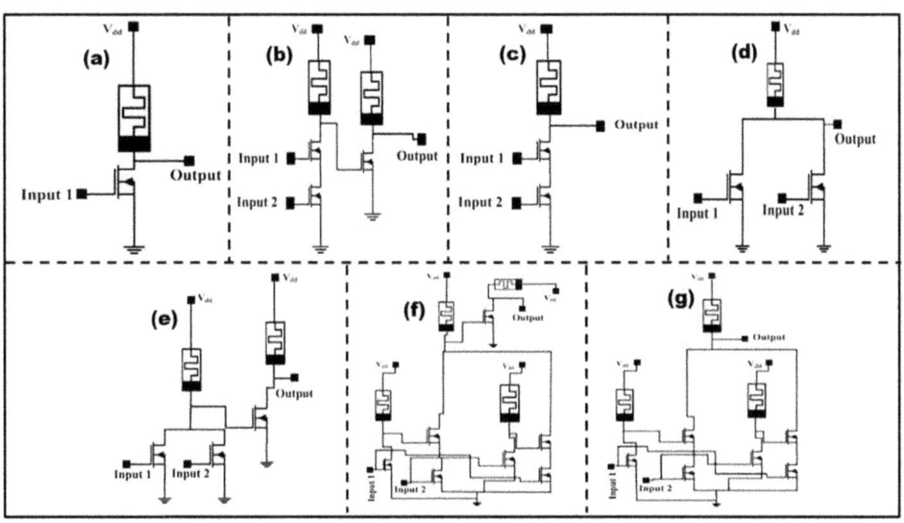

Figure 5.3. Implemented circuits for (a) NOT gate, (b) AND gate, (c) NAND gate, (d) NOR gate, (e) OR gate, (f) XOR gate, and (g) XNOR gate. (Reproduced with permission from [8]. Copyright 2024 IEEE.)

The AND gate's circuit embodies co-operation, activating only when all signals align. The NAND gate, a combination of negation and conjunction, as shown in figure 5.3(c), adds versatility to digital logic by inverting the output of the AND gate. It only produces a low output when all inputs are high [9]. This synthesis of functions makes the NAND gate a powerful tool for a wide range of logical operations.

The NOR gate operates based on inclusive disjunction, as shown in figure 5.3(d), where the output is low only when all inputs are high. This logic reflects scenarios where negation and inclusivity intersect, making the NOR gate invaluable in specific digital decision-making tasks. The OR gate, as shown in figure 5.3(e), which operates on the principle of inclusive disjunction, produces a high output when either or both inputs are high [10]. This reflects the logic of choice and diversity in decision-making. Meanwhile, the XOR gate operates on exclusive disjunction, as shown in figure 5.3(f), providing a high output only when the inputs differ. It introduces sophistication into digital decision-making by handling distinct choices. The XNOR gate complements this by outputting a high signal when both inputs are the same, as shown in figure 5.3(g), whether high or low, thus representing logical equivalence [11]. In the realm of memristive systems, material implication logic (IMPLY) stands as a fundamental and straightforward approach, using a single memristor to implement basic logic gates such as AND, OR, and NOT. The core principle is the memristor's ability to adjust its resistance based on input voltages, forming the foundation for logic operations in memristive systems. Material converse logic (C-IMPLY) shares similarities with IMPLY but uses reversed input polarities [9, 10]. This modification expands the range of logic operations, enhancing the capabilities of memristive systems.

Memristor-aided logic (MAGIC) adopts a more sophisticated approach, employing two memristors and a resistor to construct logic gates. This set-up increases flexibility, allowing for the implementation of multi-level logic and more complex structures. The inclusion of additional components in MAGIC provides adaptability across various computing tasks. Threshold logic, leveraging the threshold-switching behavior inherent in memristors, is particularly effective for applications such as neural networks and pattern recognition, advancing computational models inspired by biological systems [12]. Memristive crossbar arrays (MCAs), dense arrangements of memristors, are designed for matrix operations and neural network acceleration, as shown in figure 5.4. This architecture enhances parallel processing capabilities, making it well-suited for large-scale data manipulation. The design of crossbar arrays optimizes memristors for matrix-based computations. Additionally, hybrid CMOS/memristor circuits represent a fusion of memristors with conventional CMOS technology. This integration enables the execution of more complex logic functions by combining the strengths of both technologies. The hybrid approach leverages the speed and efficiency of memristors while maintaining compatibility with established CMOS-based systems [13].

The advantages of IML memristive systems are manifold. These systems significantly reduce data movement and energy consumption, addressing key challenges in contemporary computing. They also improve processing speed and

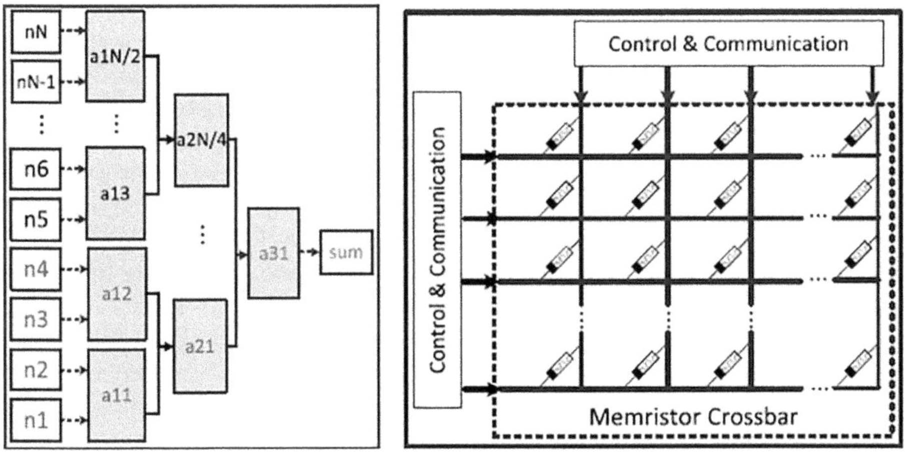

Figure 5.4. Parallel addition of eight input architecture.

parallelism, making them a promising solution for high-performance computing architectures. Furthermore, IML memristive systems simplify hardware architecture, streamlining computational processes. Potential applications include neuromorphic computing and AI, where memristors' unique properties can be harnessed for brain-inspired models. Despite these advantages, challenges such as variability in memristor characteristics, endurance limitations, and reliability concerns remain, requiring further research to fully unlock the potential of memristive systems [14].

Ongoing research continues to explore innovative applications and enhancements in IML memristive systems. Key areas of focus include the development of more sophisticated algorithms and architectures that maximize memristor capabilities, and the optimization of IML systems for specific computational tasks [16]. Scalability is another critical area, particularly in large-scale parallel processing. This involves integrating memristive devices with complex systems to meet the growing demands of computation, which is crucial for applications such as big data analytics that require parallel processing of vast amounts of information [17, 18]. Additionally, hybrid systems that combine memristive devices with emerging technologies such as quantum computing or advanced semiconductor technologies offer promising avenues for creating more versatile and powerful computing architectures. IML memristive systems hold great potential for overcoming the limitations of traditional computing and enabling new paradigms. Research is ongoing to address current challenges and move these systems closer to practical implementation.

5.4 Logic operations using analytical modeling

The von Neumann architecture, the cornerstone of most computer systems, separates memory and processing units, resulting in substantial inefficiencies and energy expenditure due to data transfer requirements [11, 12, 19]. This limitation has prompted the development of large-scale parallel processing hardware such as GPUs and specialized systems to address the memory bottleneck [13]. While the modern digital electronics and mainstream computing lies in metal oxide semiconductor field-effect transistors (MOSFETs) and CMOS technology, their design is not optimized for the intense data processing demands of emerging computational paradigms [14].

Memristors, classified as nanoelectronics devices, possess the unique capability to retain their resistive state. This distinctive feature renders them particularly well-suited for application in neuromorphic computing, a field dedicated to crafting computers that emulate the structure and functionality of the human brain [15]. A significant challenge in neuromorphic computing involves devising effective and dependable methods for executing logic operations. Conventional logic gates, including AND gates, OR gates, and NOT gates, typically rely on transistors for implementation [16]. Nevertheless, transistors are often characterized by larger area and high-power consumption, making them less than ideal for integration into neuromorphic applications. Memristors offer a promising solution by potentially overcoming these limitations and providing a more efficient and reliable means of performing logic operations [17]. Leveraging the memristor's capacity to recall its resistive state enables the creation of logic gates that are not only smaller and faster but also more energy-efficient compared to their traditional transistor-based counterparts. Here, analytical modeling works as an essential tool not only for understanding and refining logic operations in digital electronics but also for gaining deeper insight into the behavior of memristive devices and circuits. The development of such analytical models facilitates the evaluation of memristive logic gate performance and the identification of potential design challenges [18]. They manipulate logical relationships using mathematical expressions by applying concepts from Boolean algebra [19]. Truth tables provide a structured representation facilitating thorough examination of logic circuits. At the gate level, they allow modeling of mathematical depiction with individual logic gates, allowing for predictions based on input conditions [20]. Timing analysis becomes crucial for predicting circuit behavior over time, ensuring proper synchronization. Furthermore, fault analysis models aid in foreseeing and addressing potential errors in logic circuits, thereby enhancing robustness [21]. The realm of analytical modeling extends to sequential logic, where mathematical approaches shed light on the intricacies of memory elements and state transitions. Engineers acquire a systematic and mathematical foundation for designing, analysing, and optimizing logic operations in digital systems through the utilization of various analytical models proposed for memristive logic gates.

Table 5.1 provides a comparative analysis of CMOS and hybrid memristor circuits, focusing on two critical performance metrics: power consumption and propagation delay. These metrics are evaluated for various logic operations, including NAND, NOR, XOR, MUX, and encoder circuits [13].

Power consumption:

CMOS circuits: The power consumption of CMOS circuits varies widely, ranging from 3.288 to 24.37 mW, with more complex logic operations such as NAND and NOR leading to significant increases in power usage [6]. This makes CMOS circuits less energy-efficient, particularly in high-complexity tasks.

Hybrid memristor circuits: In contrast, hybrid memristor circuits exhibit much lower power consumption. Their power consumption ranges from 0.6 to 1.93 μW, demonstrating a clear advantage in terms of energy efficiency [15]. This

Table 5.1. Comparative analysis between CMOS and hybrid memristor.

	CMOS		Hybrid memristor	
Circuit	Power	Propagation delay	Power	Propagation delay
NAND	3.288 μW	315.62 ps	0.6 μW	223.4 ps
NOR	3.43 μW	393.63 ps	0.8 μW	330 ps
XOR	5.72 μW	440 ps	1.32 μW	400.4 ps
MUX	20.8 mW	437.4 ps	1.5 μW	405.3 ps
ENCODER	24.37 mW	201.3 ps	1.93 μW	170.3 ps

is particularly evident in basic logic functions, where hybrid memristor circuits consume far less energy than CMOS circuits.

Propagation delay:

CMOS circuits: The propagation delay for CMOS circuits tends to be higher across various logic gates [8]. For example, the NAND gate in CMOS has a delay of 315.62 ps, while more complex circuits such as MUX and Encoder experience delays between 437.4 ps and 440 ps.

Hybrid memristor circuits: Hybrid memristor circuits generally outperform CMOS in terms of propagation delay, demonstrating faster data processing capabilities [9]. For example, the NAND gate in hybrid memristor circuits has a delay of only 223.4 ps, which is significantly lower than its CMOS counterpart. Similarly, the MUX and encoder circuits in hybrid memristor circuits have delays ranging from 170.3 to 400.4 ps, indicating consistently faster performance.

Key observations:

Power efficiency: Hybrid memristor circuits consistently show lower power consumption across all the logic operations evaluated. With power consumption values ranging from 0.6 to 1.93 μW, they offer a significant energy advantage over CMOS circuits, in particular as the complexity of the logic gate increases [9].

Speed and performance: In terms of propagation delay, hybrid memristor circuits also demonstrate superior performance [11]. The shorter delays in these circuits allow them to execute logic operations faster than CMOS circuits. For instance, even for more complex operations such as MUX and encoder, hybrid memristor circuits maintain shorter delays compared to CMOS.

Overall comparison: The hybrid memristor circuits offer substantial improvements over CMOS circuits in both power efficiency and speed [7]. Their lower power consumption and reduced propagation delay make them a promising alternative for high-performance, energy-efficient computing systems, where both energy savings and speed are crucial.

Hybrid memristor circuits outshine CMOS circuits in terms of both power efficiency and speed, making them highly attractive for applications in energy-constrained, high-performance computing environments [11]. These improvements are especially significant in circuits that require fast data processing and minimal energy consumption, such as those used in emerging technologies such as AI and IoT.

5.5 Applications for data-intensive and highly parallel systems

Memristive devices, which integrate memory and logic operations within a single unit, hold immense potential for data-intensive and highly parallel systems (DIHPSs). By processing data directly within memory through memristive logic, these systems can bypass the traditional von Neumann bottleneck, significantly improving performance and energy efficiency for tasks such as real-time big data analytics and machine learning inference. The analog nature of memristors and their ability to mimic biological synapses make them ideal for developing brain-like computing architectures, enabling cognitive computing, pattern recognition, and advanced data processing. Memristive devices can also be used as accelerators within conventional architectures to tackle computationally intensive tasks [5–9]. For instance, memristor-based neural networks could control nanoscale robots for targeted drug delivery or other medical interventions. Additionally, memristors might play a role in quantum computing architectures, helping to address memory and control challenges. Memristor-based neuromorphic systems could enable robots and autonomous vehicles to learn and adapt in real-time, enhancing their object recognition capabilities. The memristive crossbar array framework includes various devices that alter resistance through different physical mechanisms. Recently, they have been proposed for integration with hybrid memristive systems and CMOS logic, combining the nanoscale benefits of memristors with the reliability and signal restoration features of CMOS. Resistance in memristors is adjusted by applying voltage and current in specific directions, which allows the design of digital logic blocks that support operations such as AND, OR, NAND, NOR, MUX, and DECODER [11]. Within the VLSI industry, testing is critical, and tools such as the output response analyser play a key role in functional and formal verification, supporting modes such as exhaustive testing and gate-level testing. Memristive systems present a highly promising technology for data-intensive and parallel computing applications, offering significant advantages over traditional semiconductor technologies. One notable advantage is their ability to operate at extremely low voltages, leading to considerable reductions in power consumption. Their high-speed operation makes them ideal for real-time processing applications [21]. These systems are also scalable to extremely high densities, making them suitable for tasks requiring extensive data storage and processing capabilities. Beyond these core attributes, memristive systems are pivotal in accelerating the training and inference processes of artificial intelligence models [22]. Moreover, they are integral to the development of high-performance computers that can solve complex problems and create high-density, low-power data storage systems, as shown in table 5.2.

Table 5.2. Device technology.

Technology	FinFET	Memristor
Feature size	22 nm	5 nm
Frequency	3.3 GHz	5.0 GHz
Delay	14 ps	200 ps
Dynamic energy	0.002 45 fJ	1 fJ
Static energy	0.012 97 fJ	Zero leakage
Area	0.248 μm^2	0.0001 μm^2

Memristive systems are essential for building neuromorphic computers that closely emulate the structure and functionality of the human brain, distinguishing them from traditional computing models [23–28].

Table 5.2 compares the performance characteristics of FinFET and memristor devices, offering insights into how each technology performs across a variety of key technological metrics. Below is a more detailed explanation of each parameter:

1. **Feature size**:

   The FinFET device has a feature size of 22 nm, which refers to the smallest possible dimension of the transistor elements on the chip. This size is a widely adopted standard in modern semiconductor manufacturing, as it strikes a balance between miniaturization and performance. The 22 nm feature size allows for a dense packing of transistors, enabling efficient performance in high-speed applications while maintaining the necessary power efficiency [14]. It is commonly used in advanced processors and high-performance computing systems due to its ability to deliver robust processing power while managing heat dissipation and energy consumption effectively. This feature size is key to scaling down devices, supporting faster speeds and higher performance, which are essential for tasks in AI, data processing, and more.

   In contrast, the memristor device has a feature size of 5 nm, which is significantly smaller than that of traditional FinFET devices. This ultra-small size enables a higher level of miniaturization, making memristors highly compact [3]. The reduced feature size allows for much denser integration of memristive elements within a given area, which is particularly beneficial for applications that require high scalability and efficient use of space, such as memory systems. With a smaller footprint, memristors can pack a greater number of memory elements into the same physical space, offering advantages in terms of storage capacity and integration density. This makes memristors especially valuable in high-density memory architectures and other systems that require extensive, space-efficient computation and storage, enabling the development of more powerful and compact computing devices.

2. **Frequency**:

   The FinFET device operates at a frequency of 3.3 GHz, which is a standard operating speed for modern high-performance processors. This frequency allows FinFET-based processors to efficiently manage a wide range of computational tasks, including those in computing systems such as personal computers, servers, and high-performance workstations. The 3.3 GHz frequency is optimal for many conventional tasks such as running operating systems, handling multimedia processing, and executing complex algorithms for scientific computing or machine learning [2]. In essence, this frequency supports the demands of general-purpose computing by providing a balance of speed and power consumption, allowing for versatile use in a variety of applications. It is a reliable choice for systems requiring strong single-core performance, where processing power per cycle is crucial.

On the other hand, the memristor operates at a higher frequency of 5.0 GHz, which offers several key advantages in specific application domains. This elevated frequency allows memristors to perform operations faster, which is particularly useful in tasks requiring real-time data processing or high-performance computing. In such scenarios, the ability to process data quickly and with minimal delay is essential, such as in real-time analytics, high-frequency trading, or interactive applications where low latency is crucial for user experience or system performance [8].

The higher frequency of 5.0 GHz in memristors also benefits applications that rely on memory systems. Memristors, as non-volatile memory devices, can store and process information simultaneously, allowing for faster retrieval and manipulation of data in memory-centric tasks [5]. This speed is essential in systems such as neuromorphic computing, which mimics the brain's architecture and requires fast, efficient processing of large amounts of information with minimal energy consumption.

Moreover, memristors' higher operating frequency can contribute to parallel processing capabilities, which are vital in high-performance tasks such as ML and AI [19]. With the ability to perform multiple operations concurrently, memristors can accelerate training and inference processes for deep neural networks, making them well-suited for AI applications that require significant computational power but with faster response times.

FinFETs are highly efficient for general-purpose computing tasks, and their 3.3 GHz frequency is generally adequate for most conventional applications [21]. Memristors, with their 5.0 GHz frequency, offer superior speed, which is especially beneficial for specialized tasks such as real-time data processing, memory-intensive operations, and neuromorphic computing, where faster computation and reduced latency are key advantages.

3. **Delay**:

The FinFET device has an exceptionally low delay of 14 ps (picoseconds), which represents the time it takes for a signal to propagate through the circuit. This ultra-low delay is crucial for high-performance computing systems where fast data processing and minimal latency are key requirements [13]. For example, in applications such as real-time data processing, high-frequency trading, or high-performance computing (HPC), the 14 ps delay ensures that the processor can handle large volumes of data quickly with minimal delay, enabling seamless execution of complex tasks. This makes FinFET an ideal choice for systems that prioritize speed and efficiency, particularly in environments that require fast response times and high throughput.

In contrast, the memristor device exhibits a much higher delay of 200 ps, which is significantly slower than that of the FinFET. While this delay is still suitable for many applications, it may become a limiting factor for tasks that demand extremely low latency, such as high-speed processing and data-intensive operations. However, the higher delay of memristors may be less of an issue for applications where speed is less critical, such as in low-power systems, non-volatile memory storage, or certain embedded systems that do not require real-time processing [17]. For these types of use cases, the memristor's delay can be acceptable, as its non-volatile nature, low power consumption, and high-density storage capabilities often outweigh the drawbacks of a longer propagation delay.

Despite the higher delay, memristors offer other advantages, such as low power consumption and compact integration, making them suitable for memory-centric tasks and energy-efficient applications. However, for applications where speed and low latency are paramount, such as high-frequency computing or real-time data processing, the 14 ps delay of FinFETs would likely provide a better performance advantage over memristors with a 200 ps delay.

4. **Dynamic energy**:

The dynamic energy consumption of a device refers to the amount of energy used during dynamic operations such as switching or processing, which are crucial for the device's performance [8].

For FinFETs, the dynamic energy consumption is 0.002 45 femtajoules (fJ). This low value indicates that FinFETs are highly energy-efficient when performing dynamic operations, which is essential for performance-demanding applications such as high-speed computing, real-time data processing, and complex computations. FinFETs are designed for high performance with minimal energy expenditure, making them ideal for tasks that require fast data processing with lower power requirements [9]. This makes FinFETs particularly suitable for devices that prioritize low energy consumption without compromising speed and performance.

In contrast, memristors have a higher dynamic energy consumption of 1 fJ, which is significantly higher than that of FinFETs. This suggests that each switching event or processing task in a memristor consumes more energy compared to FinFETs, which may be seen as a drawback in terms of power efficiency [11]. However, memristors come with several advantages that could justify this higher energy consumption. For instance, memristors offer non-volatility, meaning they can retain data without requiring power, and are also capable of performing parallel computation directly within memory arrays. These features make memristors highly suitable for applications that involve memory-intensive tasks and require energy-efficient storage solutions.

Moreover, the higher dynamic energy consumption in memristors could be acceptable in systems that prioritize energy storage or processing within a single device, where the ability to store information and perform computations on the fly may outweigh the concern for lower dynamic energy consumption [5]. For example, in neuromorphic computing, where the efficiency of mimicking brain-like processing is crucial, memristors' energy consumption may be outweighed by their ability to handle computations and memory tasks together, enabling high-density, low-latency systems.

FinFETs are optimal for energy-efficient, high-speed operations, while memristors, with their higher dynamic energy consumption, shine in applications where the integration of memory and processing tasks, along with non-volatility, is more important than minimizing dynamic energy.

5. **Static energy**:

The static energy consumption of a device refers to the amount of energy it consumes when it is idle or not performing any active processing or switching operations. This energy is crucial to consider, particularly for devices intended for low-power applications where minimizing idle power consumption is important.

For FinFET devices, the static energy consumption is 0.012 97 fJ. This is the amount of energy that FinFETs consume even when they are idle, or in a non-switching state. This energy consumption is typical for traditional CMOS-based devices, which require continuous power to retain their data state, even when not actively processing information [7]. This constant power consumption during idle periods contributes to the overall energy usage of FinFETs, making them less suitable for applications that need to minimize idle power consumption.

On the other hand, memristors offer a significant advantage with zero leakage in terms of static energy. This means that when a memristor is not actively in use, it consumes no power. This ability to retain its state without drawing energy while idle is one of the defining characteristics of memristors. Since memristors are non-volatile, they do not need power to maintain their data, unlike conventional devices that rely on continuous power to preserve information [9]. This feature is particularly advantageous in low-power applications where energy efficiency is critical, such as in embedded systems and IoT devices. Memristors' ability to conserve power during idle times allows them to function efficiently in environments where power availability is limited or energy consumption needs to be minimized.

FinFET devices have a fixed static energy consumption, typical of traditional transistor-based systems, while memristors excel in static energy efficiency, making them ideal for applications where low idle power consumption is essential [1]. This is especially useful for memory-centric systems or low-power computing, where non-volatility and zero leakage can significantly reduce energy demands.

6. **Area**:

The area of a device refers to the physical space it occupies on a chip, which directly impacts the overall size and density of components in a system. The FinFET device occupies an area of 0.248 μm^2 per transistor.

This represents the physical space required to implement each FinFET on a chip. While this is relatively compact compared to older transistor designs, it is still significantly larger than that of memristors. The larger footprint of FinFETs reduces the overall density of transistors that can be placed on a chip, which can limit the miniaturization of the chip and the integration of more devices in smaller spaces. As a result, the size of FinFET devices may be a limiting factor in applications that require dense integration of components [2]. In contrast, memristors have a much smaller footprint, occupying only 0.0001 μm^2 per device. This incredibly compact size makes memristors highly space-efficient, allowing for a much higher density of devices on a chip. This feature is particularly valuable for memory applications where large storage capacities are required in compact spaces. The small area of memristors enables the creation of highly dense memory arrays, which helps in minimizing the overall size of systems. Memristors' ability to reduce the physical size of systems while maintaining high memory density is a significant advantage, in particular for low-power memory systems and IoT devices, where space and power are often limited [3].

7. **Comparative analysis**:

   Memristors stand out in terms of their small feature size and zero leakage power, making them highly suitable for low-power, high-density memory systems. Their small footprint allows for more memory elements to be packed into the same area, enabling compact integration for applications that require large storage capacities in minimal space [4]. FinFETs, while more space-consuming, excel in dynamic energy efficiency and speed, making them better suited for high-performance computing tasks. Their larger area requirement reflects the higher processing power they can deliver, especially for tasks that demand fast data processing and low latency [5].

   In conclusion, memristors offer significant advantages in terms of space efficiency, static energy, and the ability to integrate high-density memory systems. However, their higher dynamic energy consumption and delay may limit their application in high-speed, performance-critical systems. On the other hand, FinFETs are well-suited for high-performance computing tasks, offering fast speeds, low latency, and energy-efficient dynamic operations, but at the cost of larger area per device [6]. Therefore, memristors are ideal for applications where low power and compact design are prioritized, while FinFETs remain the preferred choice for high-speed processors and other performance-demanding systems.

   Memristive systems hold immense promise in accelerating various machine learning algorithms, which are used across a wide array of applications, such as image recognition, natural language processing, and speech recognition. These systems can also significantly enhance scientific computing applications, including climate modeling and molecular simulations [7]. The transformative potential of memristive systems lies in their ability to reshape the way data are stored, processed, and computed, which is particularly beneficial for data-intensive and highly parallel systems. By leveraging memristive devices, it becomes possible to construct computing systems that not only excel in power efficiency but also scalability, outpacing traditional architectures in performance.

In these systems, memristors offer a combination of features such as non-volatility, parallel computation, and density, which make them well-suited for next-generation computing tasks [8]. These features enable the acceleration of data-heavy tasks, particularly in neural network training and inference, making them a valuable tool for both AI/ML applications and scientific simulations.

However, despite their promising benefits, several challenges remain for their widespread adoption. One of the primary obstacles is the development of reliable, scalable memristive materials with consistent electrical properties. These materials are critical for ensuring the stability and efficiency of memristive systems across a wide range of applications. In addition to material challenges, there is a need for the design of efficient and reliable memristive devices that can be integrated into large-scale systems. This involves overcoming hurdles in both fabrication and system integration to ensure that memristive devices can operate seamlessly in complex computing environments [9]. Furthermore, novel system architectures must be developed to fully exploit the unique advantages of memristive systems, particularly in terms of memory and processing efficiency. Addressing these challenges will be crucial for enabling the widespread adoption of memristive systems and unlocking their potential in reshaping modern computing paradigms.

The memristor exhibits a distinctive current–voltage curve referred to as a pinched hysteresis loop. In simpler terms, the high resistance state (HRS) occurs when a positive voltage increase leads to only a slight increase in current; the state resembles a narrow pathway, impeding the flow of a significant current. On the other hand, the LRS occurs when a slightly higher voltage causes a rapid increase in current. When transitioning from the LRS, decreasing positive voltage gradually reduces the current until it reaches zero at zero voltage [28]. Conversely, decreasing negative voltage gradually reduces the current until it reaches the HRS. A critical feature of the curve is the 'pinched' section where voltage and current intersect at zero, which is essential for resistive switching. The resistance direction is determined by the flow of current, if it enters a marked point, the resistance decreases, and if it exits, the resistance increases [29]. Memristors are integrated into logic circuits such as AND gates, aligning their voltage states with standard logic, such as CMOS logic. The various resistance states correspond to 0s and 1s in logic operations. The memristor's capacity to switch between high and low resistance states based on applied voltage makes it a crucial component in logic gates, facilitating the creation of electronic circuits for computation and information processing.

5.6 Comparison with CMOS-based logic

In the comparison between memristive-based logic and CMOS-based logic, the adoption of memristive crossbar arrays introduces a revolutionary shift in how logic operations and data processing are conducted. Memristors, which are two-terminal non-volatile memory devices, exhibit a distinct ability to change their resistance based on the applied voltage and to retain that resistance state even after power is removed [10]. This non-volatile nature makes them different from conventional CMOS devices, which require a continuous power supply to maintain state and perform operations.

A memristive crossbar array is a configuration in which memristors are arranged in a grid-like structure, where each intersection of rows and columns forms a memristive element. This arrangement enables the execution of logic operations directly within the memory, using the memristors' ability to modulate their resistance values. These arrays are capable of performing complex logic functions such as AND, OR, XOR, and NOT, and even multiplications and convolutions without needing to transfer data between separate processing and memory units, as is the case in traditional von Neumann architectures [11].

Memristive devices leverage analog resistance modulation, meaning they do not just switch between two discrete states (like traditional binary logic) but can take on a range of resistance levels depending on the voltage applied to them. This capability leads to continuous or multi-level logic states, which provides enhanced flexibility in computation [12]. For instance, AND and OR logic gates can be directly implemented by adjusting the resistance of memristors in a crossbar array, reducing the need for complex digital circuit elements and thus saving space and reducing power consumption.

A significant advantage of using memristive devices in crossbar arrays is the elimination of data movement between memory and processor units. Traditional computing architectures, such as those based on CMOS technology, suffer from the von Neumann bottleneck, where frequent data transfers between memory and processing units lead to inefficiencies in both time and energy consumption. By integrating logic operations directly within the memory (as is done in memristive crossbar arrays), the need for data transfer is minimized, enabling faster computations with significantly lower power consumption [13]. This is especially important for data-intensive tasks such as image recognition, ML, and real-time analytics, where computational efficiency and speed are paramount.

Moreover, memristive systems can exploit parallelism inherently. In CMOS logic, operations are sequential, with data being processed step-by-step. Memristive crossbar arrays, however, can perform multiple operations simultaneously, increasing throughput and reducing the time needed for complex computational tasks. This parallelism is particularly advantageous for applications that require massive data processing in parallel, such as AI, neural networks, and scientific simulations [14].

One of the standout properties of memristive devices is their non-volatility. Unlike traditional volatile memory systems, such as DRAM, which lose their data once the power is turned off, memristors retain their state without continuous power.

This trait makes memristive systems highly suited for low-power and energy-efficient applications. This non-volatility is particularly valuable in systems where data integrity must be preserved without the need for constant power supply, such as edge computing devices and IoT applications [15].

Furthermore, memristive devices can be fabricated at extremely small scales, with feature sizes in the nanoscale range, enabling high-density memory arrays. This small footprint allows memristive systems to be integrated into compact spaces, supporting the development of highly scalable systems [16]. Such scalability is critical for handling large-scale applications, particularly in environments where space and power consumption are limited, such as mobile devices and wearable technologies.

In the realm of neuromorphic computing, which aims to mimic the brain's architecture for computing, memristive devices are especially valuable. Their ability to emulate synaptic behavior, where the resistance of memristors changes based on usage, allows them to simulate the learning and adaptation processes in artificial neural networks. This capability enables memristive systems to naturally support adaptive learning algorithms, pattern recognition, and other core aspects of AI without the need for complex, energy-hungry processors [17]. This makes memristive-based logic systems a compelling alternative for applications in AI, deep learning, and machine learning.

While CMOS-based logic has been the dominant technology for decades, its inherent limitations in energy efficiency, scalability, and data transfer become increasingly apparent as computational demands rise. CMOS circuits consume significant amounts of energy due to the constant movement of data between memory and processors, and they are becoming less efficient as the size of transistors approaches physical limits [18].

Memristive-based logic, on the other hand, offers significant advantages in these areas. Memristive devices consume far less power, particularly in non-volatile states, and their analog resistance modulation offers new ways to compute that traditional digital circuits cannot achieve [19]. This could lead to breakthroughs in low-power, high-performance computing.

Despite the promising advantages of memristive-based systems, several challenges remain before they can be widely adopted. Some of these include:

- **Device variability**: Memristors may exhibit variability in their behavior across different devices and even within the same device over time, which can impact the reliability of computations [20].
- **Endurance**: The number of times a memristive device can reliably change its resistance before degrading is still a significant concern [21].
- **Integration**: Seamlessly integrating memristive devices into existing system architectures, particularly those based on CMOS, presents technical challenges, such as ensuring compatibility and avoiding issues such as sneak paths [22].

Ongoing research is focused on improving the reliability, endurance, and scalability of memristive devices while developing architectures that can leverage the unique properties of these devices for practical computing applications [23].

Memristive-based logic and memristive crossbar arrays represent a highly promising alternative to traditional CMOS-based logic systems. With their ability to perform logic operations within memory, reduce power consumption, and offer parallelism, memristive systems could revolutionize computing, particularly for data-intensive, low-power, and high-density memory applications [24]. While there are still challenges to overcome in terms of device reliability and integration with existing systems, the continued development of memristive technologies offers a glimpse into the future of high-performance computing that is more energy-efficient and scalable than what is currently achievable with CMOS.

The organized arrangement of memristors into a crossbar array establishes a versatile and reconfigurable computing platform. The parallel processing capabilities inherent in the crossbar structure enable simultaneous operations on multiple data points, facilitating the execution of complex computational tasks with high connectivity. Configuring memristors as resistive switches within the crossbar array allows for the creation of logic gates and memory elements with reconfigurable capabilities, as shown in figures 5.4 and 5.5 [31]. Figure 5.5 demonstrates the design and applications of an $N \times N$ unipolar memristive crossbar array for Hamming distance calculation and encryption/decryption. Figure 5.5(a) shows the schematic of the crossbar array, with devices along the selected diagonal (highlighted in red) performing parallel XOR operations to compute the Hamming distance. Figure 5.5 (b) provides an optical micrograph of a 16×16 array (scale bar: 40 μm), showcasing the physical layout. Figure 5.5(c) illustrates the read current of diagonal devices after an initialization step, where all diagonal devices were set to high resistance states. In figure 5.5(d), the readout '1101101010000101' indicates a Hamming distance of 8, validating the array's computation. Figure 5.5(e)–(j) presents current readings for the encryption and decryption of the letters 'P', 'K', and 'U'. Each encryption–decryption sequence highlights the array's versatile in-memory processing capabilities for both logic and secure data operations [25].

The inherent low power consumption of memristive devices, along with their non-volatile memory properties, positions them as an ideal solution for energy-efficient computing. This energy efficiency is particularly evident in memristive crossbar arrays, which are fundamental to IMC. These arrays minimize the need for data movement by enabling computations directly within the memory array, which not only saves time but also drastically reduces energy consumption [28]. By performing computations within the memory, the need for frequent data transfer to external processing units is eliminated, enhancing both speed and energy efficiency.

Memristive devices are also making significant strides in neuromorphic computing, where their ability to emulate synaptic behavior mirrors the functionality of biological neurons. This makes them highly suitable for adaptive learning algorithms, which are key to AI and ML applications [28]. These properties enable memristive systems to provide high computational power while maintaining energy efficiency, especially for tasks requiring parallel processing and real-time adaptation.

Despite these advantages, there are challenges, such as device variability, which can affect the reliability and uniformity of memristive behavior across large-scale arrays. However, ongoing research is focused on addressing these issues by refining

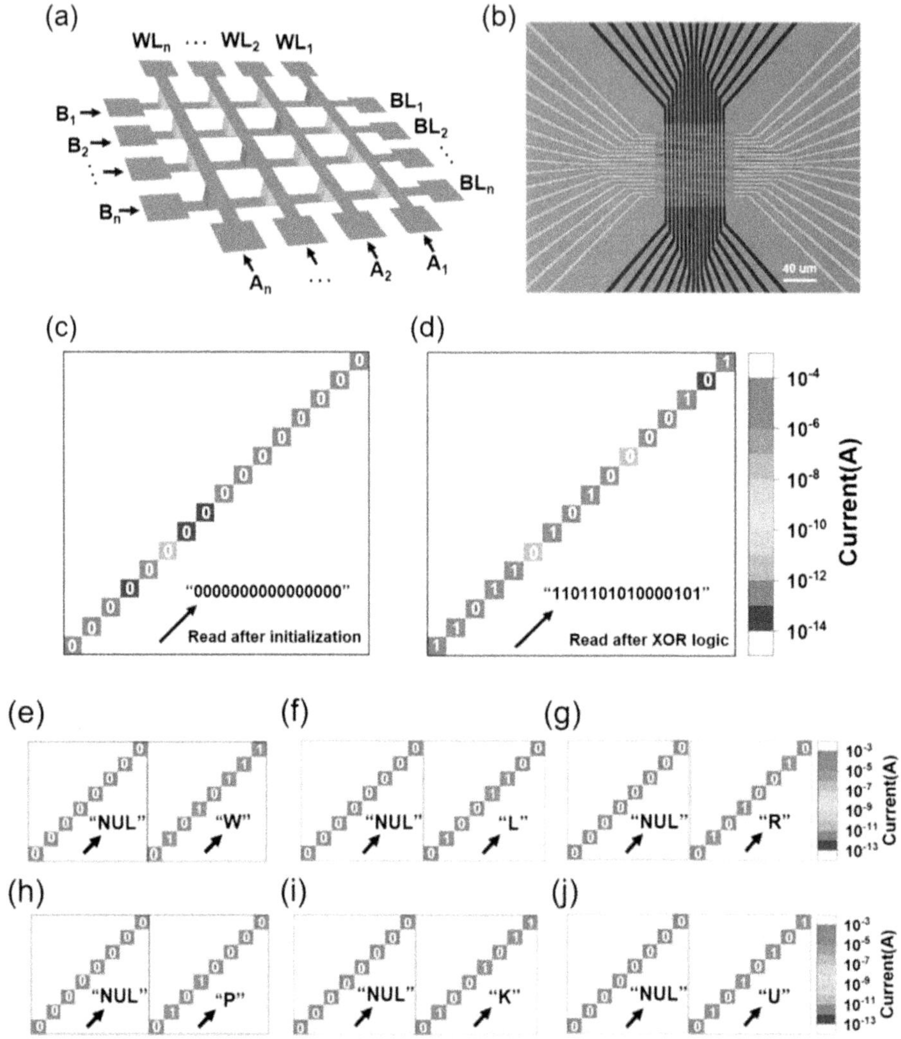

Figure 5.5. (a) Schematic of an $N \times N$ unipolar crossbar array for calculating Hamming distance. The devices located along the selected diagonal, marked in red, can be used for parallel XOR logic operations. (b) Optical micrograph of a 16 × 16 unipolar memristive array. Scale bar: 40 μm. (c) The read current of diagonal devices after the initialization step, where all devices on the selected diagonal were set to the HRS. (d) The read current of diagonal devices after the Hamming distance calculation, resulting in the correct output '1101101010000101', which indicates a Hamming distance of 8. (e)–(j) The read current of diagonal devices after the initialization step (left part) and logic operation (right part) for (e) encryption of 'P', (f) encryption of 'K', (g) encryption of 'U', (h) decryption of 'P', (i) decryption of 'K', and (j) decryption of 'U'. (Reproduced with permission from [33]. Copyright 2019 John Wiley and Sons.)

device designs and exploring new computing paradigms [29]. As the technology matures, it holds the potential to revolutionize how we design and implement logic operations in comparison to traditional CMOS technology.

In the realm of logic design, memristive devices introduce new possibilities, leveraging non-volatility and analog resistance modulation. This contrasts with conventional CMOS technology, which relies on binary states and is reaching its physical limitations in terms of scalability and power efficiency [30]. Memristive-based logic operations provide a promising alternative by offering both energy savings and high-density integration. Factors such as speed, power consumption, and area efficiency need to be considered when evaluating memristive-based logic, as they provide a nuanced understanding of where this technology excels and where it faces challenges.

The energy efficiency of memristive devices is driven by their ability to preserve states without power and perform analog computations remains a central factor in their potential to surpass traditional technologies [31]. Looking ahead, the integration of memristive-based logic with CMOS technology is particularly promising. This combination can lead to the development of more compact circuits with reduced silicon area usage, which enhances circuit design efficiency.

As traditional CMOS technology struggles to meet the growing demands for higher computational power, memristive devices stand out as a potential solution, particularly because they can retain data without the need for continuous power supply [32]. This feature, combined with their ability to perform analog operations directly in-memory, positions memristive systems as a key enabler of the future of computing.

Finally, as the world moves toward more energy-efficient and scalable computing solutions, the integration of nanoscale memristors with CMOS technology appears to offer a compelling alternative. It addresses the limitations of silicon-based systems while providing an opportunity to explore new computing architectures [33]. This will not only address current challenges but will also shape the future of computing, fostering the development of technologies that prioritize energy efficiency, scalability, and seamless integration with existing systems.

Bibliography

[1] Papandroulidakis G, Vourkas I, Abusleme A, Sirakoulis G C and Rubio A 2017 Crossbar-based memristive logic-in-memory architecture *IEEE Trans. Nano.* **16** 491–501

[2] Zhang C *et al* 2023 Logic-in-memory approach realizing memristor-based multiplexers *IEEE Trans. Electron Devices* **70** 6341–6

[3] Liu Y *et al* 2023 Cellular automata imbedded memristor-based recirculated logic in-memory computing *Nat. Commun.* **14** 2695

[4] Borghetti J *et al* 2010 Memristive switches enable stateful logic operations via material implication *Nature* **464** 873–6

[5] Ghodke S S *et al* 2023 Combinational logic circuits based on a power- and area-efficient memristor with low variability *J. Comput. Electron.* **23** 131–41

[6] Ben Hur R and Kvatinsky S 2016 Memristive memory processing unit (MPU) controller for in-memory processing *2016 IEEE Int. Conf. on the Science of Electrical Engineering (ICSEE)* pp 1–5

[7] Reuben J *et al* 2017 Memristive logic: a framework for evaluation and comparison *Int. Symp. on Power and Timing Modeling, Optimization and Simulation (PATMOS)* pp 1–8

[8] Nawaria M *et al* 2023 Memristor-inspired digital logic circuits and comparison with 90-/180-nm CMOS technologies *IEEE Trans. Elect. Dev.* **71** 301–7

[9] Kvatinsky S, Satat G, Wald N, Friedman E G, Kolodny A and Weiser U C 2014 Memristor-based material implication (IMPLY) logic: design principles and methodologies *IEEE Trans. VLSI Syst.* **22** 2054–66

[10] Raghuvanshi A and Perkowski M 2014 Logic synthesis and a generalized notation for memristor-realized material implication gates *IEEE/ACM Int. Conf. on Computer Aided Design (ICCAD)* pp 470–7

[11] Neumann J V 1993 First draft of a report on the EDVAC *IEEE Ann. Hist. Comput.* **15** 27–75

[12] Zidan M A, Strachan J P and Lu W D 2018 The future of electronics based on memristive systems *Nat. Electron.* **1** 22–9

[13] Jouppi N P *et al* 2017 In-data centre performance analysis of a tensor processing unit *Proc. of the 44th Annul Int. Symp. on Computer Architecture (ISCA)* pp 1–12

[14] Nikonov D E and Young I A 2013 Overview of beyond-CMOS devices and a uniform methodology for their benchmarking *Proc. IEEE* **101** 2498–533

[15] Gili X, Barcelo S, Bota S A and Segura J 2012 Analytical modeling of single event transients propagation in combinational logic gates *IEEE Trans. Nucl. Sci.* **59** 971–9

[16] Jooq M K Q, Mir A, Mirzakuchaki S and Farmani A 2018 Semi-analytical modeling of high performance nano-scale complementary logic gates utilizing ballistic carbon nanotube transistors *Physica* E **104** 286–96

[17] Mahapatra S, Vaish V, Wasshuber C, Banerjee K and Ionescu A M 2004 Analytical modeling of single electron transistors for hybrid CMOS-SET analog IC design *IEEE Trans. Electron Devices* **51** 1772–82

[18] Vassiliadis P, Marcel P and Rizzi S 2019 Beyond roll-up's and drill-down's: an intentional analytics model to reinvent OLAP *Inf. Syst.* **85** 68–91

[19] Linn E, Siemon A, Waser R and Menzel S 2014 Applicability of well-established memristive models for simulations of resistive switching devices *IEEE Trans. Circuits. Syst. I: Regul. Pap.* **61** 2402–10

[20] Maan A K, Jayadevi D A and James A P 2017 A survey of memristive threshold logic circuits *IEEE Trans. Neu. Netw. Learn. Syst.* **28** 1734–46

[21] Haron A, Yu J, Nane R, Taouil M, Hamdioui S and Bertels K 2016 Parallel matrix multiplication on memristor-based computation-in-memory architecture *Int. Conf. on High Perf. Comp. and Sim. (HPCS)* pp 759–66

[22] Cai F *et al* 2019 A fully integrated reprogrammable memristor–CMOS system for efficient multiply–accumulate operations *Nat. Electron.* **2** 290–9

[23] Nguyen H A D, Xie L, Taouil M, Nane R, Hamdioui S and Bertels K 2017 On the implementation of computation-in-memory parallel adder *IEEE Trans VLSI Syst.* **25** 2206–19

[24] Hoppe B, Neuendorf G, Landsiedel D S and Specks W 1990 Optimization of high-speed CMOS logic circuits with analytical models for signal delay, chip area, and dynamic power dissipation *IEEE Trans. Comput.-Aided Des. Integr. Circuits Syst.* **9** 236–47

[25] Bolton M L, Siminiceanu R I and Bass E J 2011 A systematic approach to model checking human–automation interaction using task analytic models *IEEE Tran. Syst. Man Cybern.—A Syst. Hum.* **41** 961–76

[26] Liu G *et al* 2021 Design of memristor-based combinational logic circuits *Circuits Syst. Signal Process.* **40** 5825–46

[27] Reddy K O, Gracin D, Ravi V and Durai S A 2019 Design of combinational logic circuits using memristor and CMOS logic *Int. J. Innov. Technol. Explor. Eng.* **8** 2278–3075

[28] Haron A, Yu J, Nane R, Taouil M, Hamdioui S and Bertels K 2016 Parallel matrix multiplication on memristor-based computation-in-memory architecture *Int. Conf. on High Performance Computing and Simulation (HPCS)* pp 759–66

[29] Yakopcic C, Alom M Z and Taha T M 2017 Extremely parallel memristor crossbar architecture for convolutional neural network implementation *2017 Int. Joint Conf. on Neural Networks (IJCNN) (Anchorage, AK, USA)* pp 1696–703

[30] Ou Q F, Xiong B S, Yu L, Wen J, Wang L and Tong Y 2020 In-memory logic operations and neuromorphic computing in non-volatile random access memory *Materials* **13** 3532

[31] Liu Z C and Wang L 2020 Applications of phase change materials in electrical regime from conventional storage memory to novel neuromorphic computing *IEEE Access* **8** 76471–99

[32] Du N, Schmidt H and Polian I 2021 Low-power emerging memristive designs towards secure hardware systems for applications in internet of things *Nano Mater. Sci.* **3** 186–204

[33] Xu L *et al* 2019 Memristor-based efficient in-memory logic for cryptologic and arithmetic applications *Adv. Mat. Tech.* **4** 1900212

IOP Publishing

Resistive Switching Systems for In-Memory Computation and Artificial Intelligence

Shaibal Mukherjee

Chapter 6

Vector multiplications using memristive devices

6.1 Introduction to vector matrix multiplication in MCA

Modern deep learning architectures, as emphasized by research groups such as Liu *et al* [1] and Zhao *et al* [2], depend heavily on vector-matrix multiplications (VMMs), which serve as the foundational computational operation for each layer in deep neural networks (DNNs). Within these VMMs, non-linear activation functions, such as rectified linear units (ReLUs) or sigmoid functions, play a critical role. While the connectivity between layers may vary in state-of-the-art models, the core components of VMMs combined with non-linearities remain consistent. Consequently, the optimization of machine learning algorithms on specialized hardware is intricately linked to the efficient execution of VMMs.

As highlighted by Wang *et al* [3], the rapid evolution of smart computing and data analytics has exposed the limitations of conventional computer architectures. The von Neumann bottleneck, resulting from the separation of processing and memory units, significantly hinders computational efficiency. This bottleneck becomes especially pronounced as computational tasks, such as vector multiplications, demand higher throughput. Moreover, the performance gains driven by Moore's law, historically achieved through transistor scaling, are diminishing due to escalating costs and physical constraints. In this landscape, the computational requirements of a data-driven world have outpaced the capabilities of traditional systems, particularly for operations central to deep learning models. Zhou *et al* [4] suggests that alternative architectures, such as in-memory computing and memristive systems, hold potential to address these challenges, enabling efficient execution of DNNs and other data-centric applications.

To address these challenges, memristive devices, in particular memristive crossbars, offer a promising solution that merges memory and processing capabilities, allowing for in-memory vector multiplications [2]. This integration represents a

doi:10.1088/978-0-7503-6169-9ch6

© IOP Publishing Ltd 2025. All rights, including for text and data mining (TDM), artificial intelligence (AI) training, and similar technologies, are reserved.

fundamental shift in computing, redefining conventional boundaries and presenting exciting possibilities for the future [3].

The adoption of memristive systems has emerged as a transformative approach to address the escalating demands of data-intensive applications. A key aspect of this transformation is the use of VMM, a critical operation in numerous mathematical and computational tasks, within memristive frameworks [1, 3]. Traditional computing architectures, following the von Neumann model, are increasingly strained in addressing the demands of data-intensive tasks, as highlighted by various research groups such as Wang *et al* [3] and Liu *et al* [4]. The fundamental limitation, known as the von Neumann bottleneck, stems from the separation of memory and processing units. This bottleneck forces frequent energy-intensive data transfers between these units, which significantly reduces the efficiency and scalability of essential operations such as VMM, a cornerstone for many modern applications.

Memristive devices, studied extensively by groups such as Yao *et al* [5] and Xia *et al* [6], present a transformative approach to overcoming this bottleneck. By enabling in-memory computation, memristive architectures integrate data storage and processing within the same hardware framework. These devices exploit resistive modulation properties to bypass the inefficiencies of conventional systems. This integration not only minimizes data shuttling but also drastically enhances computational efficiency, as demonstrated by several experiments. Consequently, memristive architectures are emerging as a promising alternative to traditional systems, paving the way for more efficient and scalable solutions to tackle the growing complexity of data-centric computing tasks.

Memristive crossbars, a fundamental component of these systems, facilitate the simultaneous storage and computation of information within the same structure, eliminating the need for data transfer between separate units [6]. This allows VMM to be performed directly within the data store, leading to significant enhancements in efficiency and reduced latency. The integration of VMM in memristive systems brings numerous benefits, such as increased computational speed, lower power consumption, and the elimination of the limitations posed by the traditional separation of processing and memory [7]. These advancements unlock new opportunities for applications in artificial intelligence, machine learning, and other data-intensive fields, marking a significant milestone in the evolution of computational technologies.

Memristive devices are emerging as promising candidates for next-generation computing architecture, particularly in the area of VMM. Their unique features, including analog memory, in-memory computing, and high parallelism, make them well-suited for computationally intensive tasks [8]. Memristors, a relatively recent class of electronic devices, exhibit a property called memristance, which is a form of memory where the resistance of the device is influenced by its historical current or voltage. This allows the resistance to be 'programmed' through specific electrical signals, and the device retains this programmed value even after power is removed. Unlike traditional VMM implementations that rely on von Neumann architectures, where data storage is separated from processing in the central processing unit (CPU), memristive devices introduce an innovative approach by enabling in-memory computing. These devices can be arranged in crossbar arrays, with each intersection representing a memristor [9]. In this configuration, vectors and matrices can be mapped directly onto the crossbar, allowing VMM operations to be performed directly within the memory. This in-memory computation approach effectively eliminates the need for data transfer between memory and the CPU, addressing the von Neumann bottleneck. This paradigm shift significantly enhances computational speed and efficiency, making memristive devices a promising solution for the demands of modern computing architectures.

Memristor-based VMM has been introduced, demonstrating significant power savings compared to conventional CMOS-based VMMs, with reductions ranging from 50% to 85% [4–8]. These implementations typically employ a simple virtual ground approach due to its ease of implementation. This study aims to identify VMM architectures that surpass the virtual ground solution in terms of power efficiency and to explore the trade-offs associated with these alternatives. Specifically, the impact of stochastic errors in different VMM implementations is analysed for digit classification tasks using the MNIST and CIFAR-10 datasets, representing simple and challenging classification tasks, respectively [9, 10].

Figure 6.1 shows a decision tree for selecting the optimal VMM architecture based on specific application requirements, providing a visual representation of how different conditions influence the choice of architecture. Figure 6.1 starts with a schematic illustrating various factors such as sparse input, low throughput, and the presence of a noisy amplifier, which impact the performance and efficiency of VMM systems. These factors then guide the decision-making process, leading to different architectural options: spiking architectures (suitable for low input activity but with slower speed), virtual ground-based approaches (simple and commonly used but less power efficient), and termination resistor-based architectures (offering improved power efficiency and maintaining processing speed without the impact of a noisy amplifier). Each branch highlights the scenarios under which the corresponding VMM architecture is most advantageous. The results indicate that the optimal VMM architecture depends on the specific application requirements, and these findings provide guidance in selecting the appropriate VMM for different scenarios. For instance, spiking architectures save up to 99.9% power when input activity is only 1%, but they tend to be significantly slower. On the other hand, termination

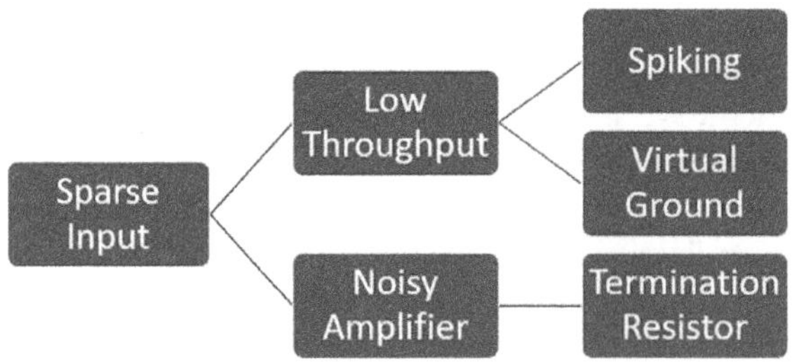

Figure 6.1. The outcomes of this study form the basis for a decision tree outlining the preferred VMM architecture for applications sparse input, low throughput noisy amplifier spiking virtual ground and termination resistor.

resistor-based VMM architectures, without noisy amplifiers, consume 75% less power compared to virtual ground approaches while maintaining comparable processing speed. Previous research has largely focused on determining the required precision of the weight matrix for neuromorphic applications, typically concluding that a 4 bit resolution is sufficient. However, there has been limited exploration into the required accuracy of the VMM itself. This study seeks to address that gap by evaluating the precision needs of VMM implementations for both straightforward and complex tasks, utilizing the MNIST and CIFAR-10 datasets, respectively [11].

6.1.1 Hardware acceleration for vector matrix operations

The design of hardware accelerators leveraging memristive crossbars has been a subject of significant research, particularly by groups such as Zhang *et al* [12] and Liu *et al* [9]. This approach focuses on efficient computation of dot products between input vectors and weight matrices, which are fundamental operations in neural networks. By exploiting the inherent parallelism offered by memristive devices, researchers aim to achieve substantial speed-ups in VMM compared to the traditional von Neumann architecture. Memristors' non-volatile properties play a critical role in reducing data transfer overhead. By retaining intermediate computation results directly within the crossbar structure, the frequent exchange of data between memory and processing units—a major bottleneck in traditional systems—is significantly minimized, as noted by Liu *et al* [9] and Zhao *et al* [12]. This advantage is particularly beneficial in scenarios involving large-scale computations, such as those encountered in artificial neural networks (ANNs).

A conventional VMM design employing memristive crossbars often integrates a virtual ground module, which ensures accurate computations by maintaining the ground voltage in each column. However, as highlighted by Zhang *et al* [11], this architecture may lead to increased power consumption due to the additional current required for stabilizing the virtual ground. To mitigate this, an advanced VMM design has been developed with a focus on reducing power consumption. This optimization is particularly effective when paired with spiking neural network (SNN) models, as demonstrated by Huang *et al*, enabling the hardware to process neural signals more efficiently.

The introduction of memristive crossbar arrays into neuromorphic computing has furthered the potential for power-efficient accelerators. These advancements address the limitations of energy-intensive compute clusters, thereby broadening the applicability of large neural algorithms in real-world scenarios. For example, figure 6.2(a) schematically illustrates the proposed storage system with the near-storage in-memory computing architecture and its implementation based on memristor arrays. The system contains multiple storage banks and in-memory computing banks to compress and decompress the image data. To validate the functionality of the storage system, a two-layer convolutional autoencoder (CAE) within the architecture was implemented (figure 6.2(b)). The network consists of a single convolution layer in the encoder and a single transpose convolution layer in the decoder, which perform input image compression and stored data decompression, respectively.

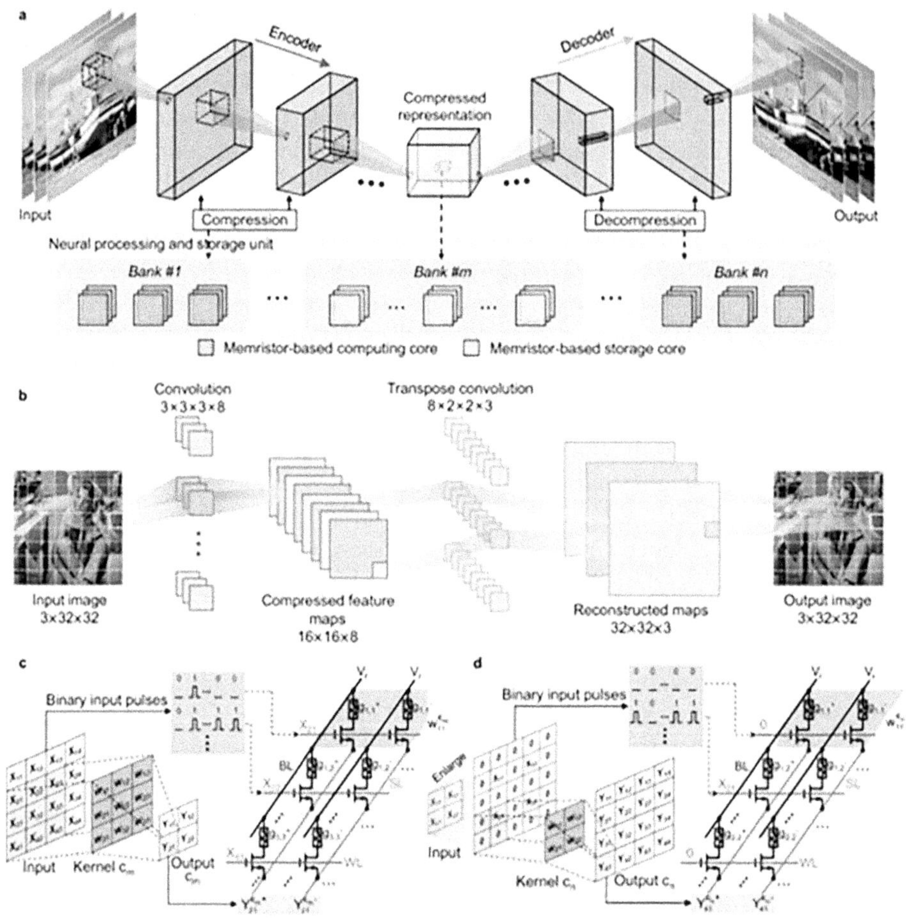

Figure 6.2. (a) Schematic illustration of the proposed near-storage in-memory processing system implemented with memristor-based cores. The upper part shows a multi-layer image compression network. The compression and decompression processes are generally structurally symmetric to ensure that the resolution of the reconstructed image is consistent with that of the input. Once the network completes training, it can be used for any input to acquire a compressed representation. The lower part shows the implementation of the system with memristor-based cores. The green and yellow squares represent the computing and storage cores, respectively. The computing banks and storage banks are located in the neural processing and storage unit. (b) A constructed two-layer convolutional autoencoder (CAE) network that contains eight kernels in convolution layer for compression and three kernels in transpose convolution layer for decompression. Implementation of (c), convolution and (d), transpose convolution with memristor arrays. The blue, red, and yellow rectangles represent the selected elements of the input, kernel weight, and output, respectively. Through the time-division input of the image and multiply-accumulate operation of the source line (SL) output, the pixel value of the output feature map can be obtained. During the entire computing process, a constant read voltage (V_r) is applied to all bit lines (BLs), and the SLs are grounded. Kernel c_m and c_n represent the mth convolution kernel and nth transpose convolution kernel, respectively. Outputs c_m and c_n correspond to the feature maps output by the mth convolution kernel and nth transpose convolution kernel, respectively. Reproduced from [13] CC BY 4.0.

A high-resolution test image is first partitioned into sub-images of the same size as those used in training, and these sub-images are sequentially fed into the network. Figures 6.2(c) and 6.2(d) schematically illustrate the convolution and transpose convolution processes, along with their corresponding operations in the memristor array. In these diagrams, the blue square denotes a sliding input window, which moves across the input to reduce or expand image dimensionality. To enable multi-bit inputs in the memristor array, we employed a bit-slicing encoding scheme. In this approach, the input is converted into a series of binary voltage pulses, flattened, and sequentially applied to the word lines (WLs) of the memristor array using time division. Each signed kernel weight is mapped onto a pair of memristors with differential conductance for weight representation. Multi-bit weights are further decomposed into memristor pairs, each corresponding to a different bit and associated with a weight coefficient (k^{n}), where k is determined by the available conductance levels and n indicates the bit position. The output Y is then obtained by multiplying the source line (SL) output by the respective weight coefficient.

Research by Tang *et al* [14] underscores how memristive crossbars align with the needs of neuromorphic architecture, enabling real-time computations with reduced energy demands. This integration of advanced hardware elements not only enhances the efficiency of neural network operations but also contributes to the broader field of hardware-accelerated machine learning.

In SNNs, neurons communicate using spikes, with information typically encoded in the frequency or timing of these spikes. This biologically inspired mechanism mirrors how neurons in the brain process information, making SNNs a promising model for energy-efficient and event-driven computations. Among various learning mechanisms for SNNs, spike-timing-dependent plasticity (STDP) stands out as it aligns closely with experimental data from neuroscience [5]. STDP adjusts synaptic weights based on the relative timing of pre- and post-synaptic spikes, fostering adaptive and dynamic learning.

However, the application of STDP is often limited to relatively simple architectures, such as networks with a single layer of excitatory neurons and a single layer of inhibitory neurons [8]. While these networks can model certain biological processes, they fall short in performance when compared to deep ANNs, which excel in complex tasks such as image classification and speech recognition.

Deep ANNs, powered by sophisticated architectures and algorithms, consistently outperform SNNs in accuracy for many benchmark tasks. However, this superior performance comes at a cost: deep ANNs require substantial computational power and energy, particularly when running on conventional von Neumann architectures. This demand for power and time underscores a key challenge in the field: how to combine the energy efficiency and event-driven nature of SNNs with the representational power of deep learning models [14].

Emerging solutions focus on hardware acceleration using neuromorphic hardware or memristive devices, which can implement SNNs more efficiently, potentially bridging the gap between biological plausibility and computational efficacy [15]. These approaches aim to leverage the sparse and asynchronous nature of spike-based communication, reducing energy consumption and increasing computational efficiency while striving to match the task performance of deep ANNs.

Figure 6.3 illustrates the architecture of VMM systems that utilize memristive devices at all crossbar junctions. These memristive devices serve as resistive memory elements, enabling efficient implementation of VMM operations. To ensure proper functionality, a differential amplifier is integrated between each output measurement node and the corresponding bias measurement node. The differential amplifier plays a critical role in amplifying output signals to compensate for resistive losses or noise and measuring the difference between the output signal and the bias voltage to maintain operational accuracy. Additionally, the gain of the differential amplifier is specifically designed to meet the architectural requirements, ensuring compatibility and optimal performance. This set-up is essential for realizing fully functional memristive crossbar-based computational systems, emphasizing their potential for energy-efficient and scalable computational architectures [1].

The investigated VMM architectures integrate memristive devices at all crossbar junctions, where these junctions represent points of intersection or connections forming a grid-like structure in the architecture. Memristive devices characterized by resistive switching with memory are positioned at these junctions [16]. To fully implement these VMMs with memristive devices, specific measures are required, including the incorporation of a differential amplifier between each output measurement and the bias measurement. This amplifier enhances the difference between two input voltages, implying distinct processing for the output from memristive devices and the bias measurement. While the basic VMM functions effectively, it consumes more power due to the virtual ground module handling extra current to maintain

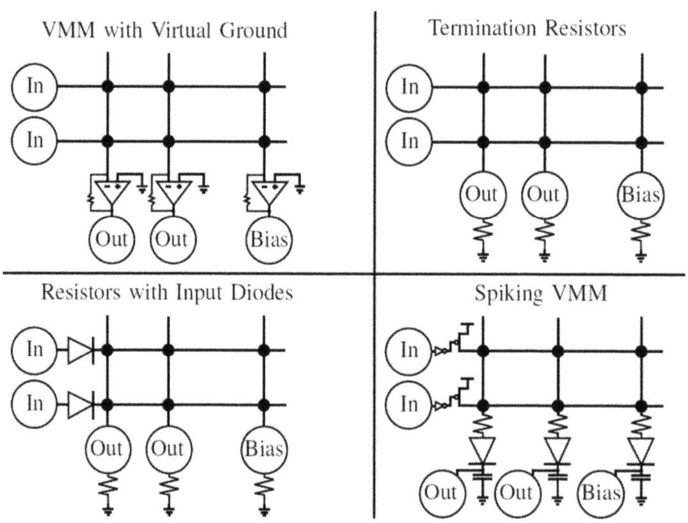

Figure 6.3. The examined VMM architectures feature memristive devices at all crossbar junctions. To fully implement these VMMs, it is essential to incorporate a differential amplifier between each output measurement and the bias measurement, incorporating an architecture specific gain [1].

ground voltage in each column [17]. To design a more power efficient VMM, particularly for a spiking model, various VMM designs that eliminate the need for virtual ground are explored. The capabilities of these alternative designs are compared to the original virtual ground set-up in terms of both accuracy and power consumption. The fundamental of VMM, which incorporates a memristive crossbar and a virtual ground module, proves effective but entails potentially significant additional power consumption. This is attributed to the extra current that the virtual ground module must draw to maintain ground voltage in each column. To develop a VMM with reduced power consumption, focusing particularly on a spiking model, we need to explore and assess alternative VMM architectures that eliminate the necessity for a virtual ground [18]. Examining the capabilities of these architectures and comparing their accuracy and power efficiency to the original virtual ground implementation is essential.

The depiction in figure 6.4(a) highlights critical challenges in traditional memory operations, particularly the inability to execute row and column operations simultaneously in memory crossbars. This limitation stems from the structure's inability to isolate currents from different operations, resulting in interference that degrades system efficiency. The inherent coupling of these currents represents a significant barrier to achieving high-throughput, reliable memory operations.

In contrast, figure 6.4(b) showcases FELIX. In the context of VMM with memristors, FELIX typically stands for field-effect transistor and memristor integrated crossbar. This architecture combines memristors with field-effect transistors (FETs) to enhance the functionality of the crossbar array. The integration of FETs with memristive devices enables better control over individual memristor states, reduces sneak path currents, and improves overall circuit stability and performance. An innovative solution designed to mitigate these issues. FELIX employs transistors integrated with a specialized memory crossbar to ensure that currents corresponding to distinct operations remain separate, thereby eliminating interference. This architecture exemplifies a breakthrough approach, enabling efficient and interference-free execution of memory tasks.

However, the advanced design of FELIX introduces trade-offs. One notable challenge is the overhead associated with increasing the number of memory partitions. While a higher number of partitions enhances operational parallelism, it

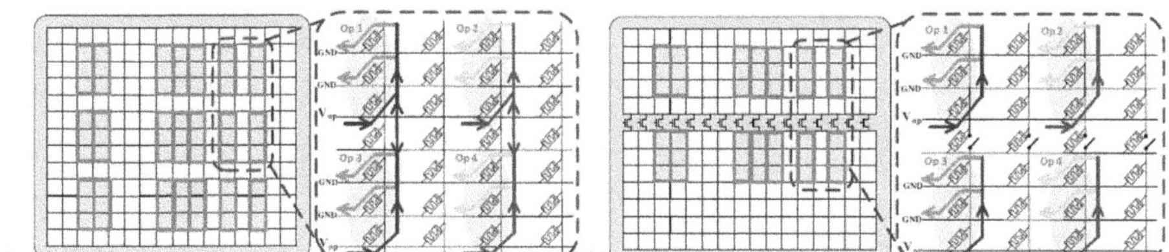

Figure 6.4. (a) Memory constraints hinder simultaneous row and column operations; the crossbar structure fails to differentiate currents for various operations. (b) FELIX utilizes transistors and a memory crossbar, ensuring non-interference of currents for different four operations. (Reproduced with permission from [10]. Copyright 2019 IEEE.)

simultaneously reduces memory utilization efficiency. This occurs because each partition requires dedicated processing elements and additional devices to perform logic operations and store intermediate states. Consequently, as the number of partitions grows, so does the demand for these exclusive resources, leading to a linear increase in hardware requirements.

These processing elements, crucial for executing FELIX's unique logic operations, cannot be repurposed for other tasks, such as logic storage, which adds further constraints to resource utilization. Despite these overheads, FELIX's architecture represents a significant stride toward addressing traditional memory limitations, offering a viable pathway for high-efficiency computing systems tailored for advanced applications such as AI and ML.

Increasing the number of processing elements within a memory structure impacts its size and functionality in multiple ways. First, as the number of processing elements grows, the memory available for storage decreases proportionally. This reduction occurs because more hardware resources are allocated to logic processing rather than data storage. Second, the addition of partitions within the memory necessitates a greater number of transistors to isolate the bit lines effectively. This segmentation results in increased area overhead due to the added components.

Figures 6.4(a) and (b) effectively illustrate these trade-offs by showcasing variations in memory utilization and area overhead for a 1024 × 64 memory block as the number of partitions increases. While higher partitions enhance operational independence and parallelism, they also lead to reduced memory efficiency and increased design complexity.

The innovative design implemented by FELIX targets energy-efficient and high-speed logic operations within in-memory computing systems. By incorporating single-cycle operations directly into the crossbar memory, the architecture supports a wide array of low-latency functionalities. Furthermore, FELIX boosts in-memory parallelism through block switches that enable bit lines to be segmented, facilitating independent parallel operations. This method enhances the versatility of in-memory systems and reduces latency significantly.

The evaluation of FELIX's efficacy highlights its groundbreaking contributions to hardware acceleration. When compared to GPUs, FELIX demonstrates an average speed up of 128.8 times and achieves an extraordinary 5589.3 times reduction in energy consumption across various applications. These results underscore the transformative potential of FELIX in advancing the efficiency of VMM tasks using memristive devices. The model not only addresses conventional challenges but also provides a robust foundation for high-performance neuromorphic computing and beyond.

6.1.2 In-memory computing

In recent times, the field of computing has experienced a paradigm shift towards innovative architectures designed to overcome the limitations inherent in the traditional von Neumann architecture. Among these emerging technologies, memristive crossbars have become a central focus, garnering significant interest for their ability to potentially transform in-memory computing. This investigates the fundamental principles, applications, and advantages of memristive crossbars as robust engines for in-memory computing. Conventional computing architectures confront issues such as memory bottlenecks, elevated power consumption, and constrained scalability. In-memory computing, a disruptive approach, seeks to tackle these challenges by simultaneously processing and storing data in the same location [11]. Memristive crossbars, harnessing the distinctive properties of memristors, present themselves as promising contenders for implementing efficient in-memory computing systems. Memristive crossbars utilize arrays of memristors arranged in a crossbar configuration, establishing a dense and scalable architecture. This section offers an overview of the underlying principles of memristors and their integration into crossbar arrays [20]. A comprehension of the operational principles of memristive crossbars is pivotal to unlocking their potential in in-memory computing. This section delves into how memristors facilitate analog resistance changes based on applied voltage, enabling the storage and processing of information directly within the crossbar structure.

Figure 6.5(a) displays a detailed micrograph depicting the magnetic random-access memory (MRAM) crossbar array, offering a visual representation of the physical structure and arrangement of memory cells within the array. The layout demonstrates a 64 × 64 MRAM crossbar array in 28 nm CMOS technology, emphasizing the integration of the array with peripheral circuitry, leading to a compact and efficient memory array, as depicted in figure 6.5(b). The strategic placement of the MRAM crossbar array within the broader architecture is illustrated in figure 6.5(c). Positioned between the top write/read electronics and bottom time-to-digital converter (TDC) readout electronics, it highlights the role of the crossbar array in the data processing flow [12]. The illustration delves into the structure of an individual bit-cell within the array, covering an area of 0.933 μm^2. Each bit-cell comprises two FET switches and two magnetic tunnel junctions (MTJs) connected in series to form columns. The description further explains that the FET gates are driven by voltage IN (either V_H (1) or V_L (−1)), storing weight W (either R_H (1) or R_L (−1)). It emphasizes the contribution of resistances R_H and R_L to the overall FET switch resistance, as depicted in figure 6.5(d). Figure 6.5(e) illustrates four configurations of a bit-cell, showcasing different combinations of IN and W values ({−1, −1}, {−1, 1}, {1, −1}, {1, 1}). The corresponding bit-cell output resistances (R_H (1) or R_L (−1)) for each configuration are highlighted, offering insights into the electrical characteristics of the array. This comprehensive overview covers the physical appearance, layout, placement in the architecture, and the detailed composition and configurations of individual bit-cells, underscoring the significance of each element in advancing memory technology [12].

Memristive crossbars exhibit exceptional characteristics that make them well-suited for in-memory computing applications. One key advantage lies in their non-volatile nature, meaning that the resistance states persist even when power is turned off. This property ensures data retention without the need for constant power supply, contributing to energy efficiency and data integrity [14, 15]. Furthermore, the analog resistance changes in memristive crossbars enable the implementation of

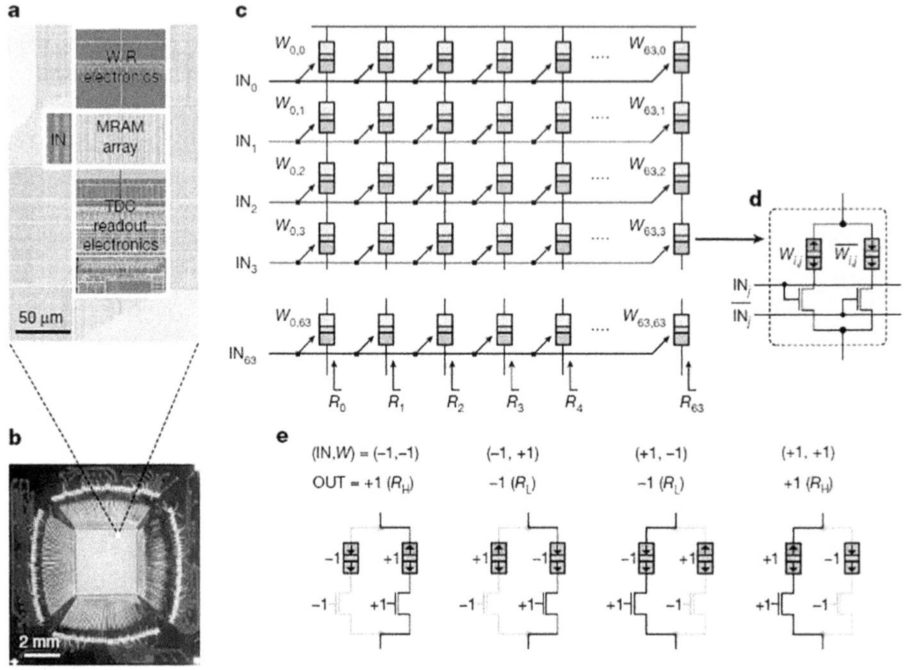

Figure 6.5. (a) MRAM crossbar array micrograph. (b) Layout of the depicted 64 × 64 MRAM crossbar array integrated with peripheral circuitry in 28 nm CMOS technology. (c) The crossbar array is positioned between write/read electronics at the top and TDC readout electronics at the bottom. (d) Each bit-cell in the array, covering an area of 0.933 μm^2, comprises two FET switches and two MTJs, connected in series to form columns. The gates of the left and right FETs are driven by voltage IN (either V_H (1) or V_L (−1)), and their complementary signals. The left and right MJT–FET paths store weight W (either R_H (1) or R_L (−1)). The resistances, R_H and R_L, add to the FET switch resistance. Four configurations of a bit-cell for {−1, −1}, {−1, 1}, {1, −1}, and {1, 1} IN and W combinations are shown in (e), with corresponding bit-cell output resistance (R_H (1) or R_L (−1)). Each column in the crossbar array has a total resistance R, the sum of all bit-cell output resistances, serving as the column's output. (Reproduced with permission from [12]. Copyright 2022 Springer Nature.)

neuromorphic computing paradigms. Inspired by the architecture of the human brain, these crossbars can mimic synaptic weights, fostering the development of artificial intelligence systems that excel in tasks such as pattern recognition and cognitive computing. The scalability of memristive crossbars is another pivotal aspect, as demands for computing power continue to grow and its ability to seamlessly scale up the number of memristors within a crossbar array becomes crucial [16]. This scalability feature positions memristive crossbars as versatile components capable of adapting to the evolving requirements of diverse computing applications. Applications of memristive crossbars have shown promise in various fields, including but not limited to image and signal processing, associative memory, and optimization problems. Their ability to perform computations directly within the memory unit reduces data movement, mitigating the bottlenecks associated with traditional architectures. As research and development in memristive crossbars progress, it is essential to address challenges related to device variability, endurance, and manufacturability [17]. Overcoming these hurdles will contribute to the widespread adoption of memristive crossbars and solidify their position as powerful engines for in-memory computing, paving the way for a new era of computing architectures.

6.2 The power of in-memory computing

In-memory computing, integrated with memristive devices for VMM, represents a groundbreaking approach to addressing computational bottlenecks in traditional architectures. Memristors are non-volatile resistive elements that store and process data by modulating their resistance states, enabling both memory and computation within the same physical space. This capability significantly reduces the need for data transfer between separate memory and processing units, a primary limitation of conventional von Neumann architectures.

The parallel processing capability of memristive devices allows for direct VMM operations within the memory array, streamlining computations and reducing latency. By minimizing data movement, these systems achieve notable improvements in both speed and energy efficiency. This makes memristive in-memory computing (mIMC) particularly advantageous for energy-sensitive applications such as edge computing and IoT devices, where low power consumption and compact processing are crucial.

The integration of memristive devices shifts the paradigm from processor-centric to memory-centric architectures, aligning with principles of neuromorphic computing. These systems mimic biological brain functions by processing data at the location of its storage, eliminating the overhead associated with traditional computation. For instance, addressing challenges such as sparse matrix-vector multiplication (SpMV) where computational inefficiencies arise from mapping zero elements memristive-based systems propose innovative solutions. Figure 6.6 exemplifies these advancements, showcasing the implementation of spin-transfer torque magnetic random-access memories (SRMs) for high-efficiency sparse computations.

These developments highlight the transformative potential of mIMC, offering scalable, energy-efficient solutions for modern computational challenges while paving the way for advancements in neuromorphic and data-centric architecture. SpM is a core computational task in scientific computing, playing a critical role in areas such as solving PDEs, machine learning, and large-scale simulations. It involves the multiplication of a sparse matrix—a matrix with a high proportion of zero elements—with a vector. While the computational focus is on the nonzero elements, traditional methods must still allocate resources for the zero elements, leading to inefficiencies. These inefficiencies arise because zero elements, although computationally irrelevant, consume energy and hardware resources when mapped onto physical memory structures.

Existing mIMC architectures, which aim to integrate processing and memory functions, face substantial limitations in handling SpMV tasks. When these architectures process tasks such as 2D PDEs, the activated memory devices far exceed the number of nonzero matrix elements. For example, the devices activated

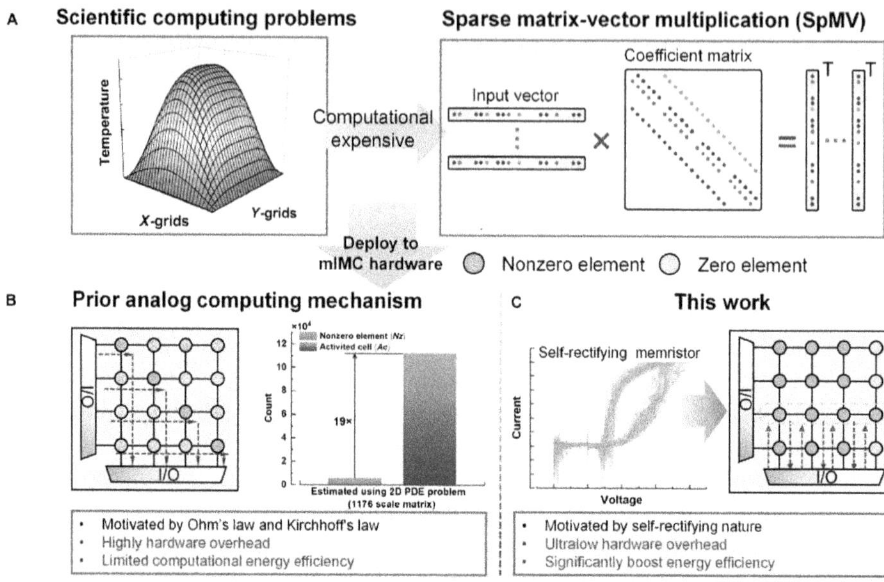

Figure 6.6. The rationale for this research is as follows: (a) In contemporary scientific computing problems, the primary computationally intensive operation is the massive SpMV. (b) When executing scientific computing tasks on previous mIMC hardware, there is a significant decline in performance efficiency in terms of area and energy. This is primarily due to the unavoidable need to map zero elements. For instance, the activated devices assigned to process 2D PDEs are 19 times more numerous than the matrix's nonzero elements. (c) Developing a high-efficiency in-memory sparse computation system by leveraging the corrective properties of SRMs. (Reproduced with permission from [18]. Copyright 2023 The Authors, some rights reserved; exclusive licensee American Association for the Advancement of Science. No claim to original U.S. Government Works. Distributed under a Creative Commons Attribution NonCommercial License 4.0 (CC BY-NC).

to perform computations may be 19 times more numerous than the actual nonzero elements in the matrix. This mismatch results in significant energy consumption and increased area overhead, as physical hardware must allocate space for unproductive zero elements. These constraints reduce the overall efficiency of mIMC systems, limiting their practicality for large-scale or energy-sensitive applications.

To overcome these challenges, researchers propose leveraging SRM to enhance the efficiency of SpMV computations. SRM technology introduces selective activation, focusing computational resources exclusively on nonzero elements. By avoiding unnecessary processing of zeros, this approach significantly reduces energy consumption and enhances memory utilization. Moreover, SRM facilitates parallelism, allowing simultaneous computations to be conducted with minimal overhead. This capability addresses the scalability issues of earlier mIMC systems, enabling the design to handle larger datasets efficiently.

The proposed SRM-based system offers a transformative solution to the inherent inefficiencies of sparse computation. By minimizing area overhead and energy usage, it achieves a balance between performance and scalability. This advancement is particularly impactful for applications requiring high computational efficiency, such as neuromorphic computing and edge-based processing, where energy constraints are a primary concern. The innovation in SRM-based mIMC architecture exemplifies the potential of memory technologies to reshape computational paradigms, addressing the growing demands of modern data-centric tasks.

Figure 6.6 explores the rationale for using advanced techniques in mIMC to enhance performance in scientific computing tasks that involve SpMV, a key operation in many computationally intensive applications. It consists of several parts, each explaining different aspects of the challenges and potential solutions. Figure 6.6(a) shows that, in contemporary scientific computing, one of the most computationally expensive tasks is SpMV. SpMV is a fundamental operation in many areas, including solving PDEs, machine learning models, and simulations of physical systems. The challenge in SpMV arises because it typically involves large matrices, where most of the elements are zero (sparse matrices). Despite these matrices being sparse, the operation still requires substantial computational resources, as it involves accessing and processing each nonzero element efficiently. The computational burden is particularly high because the operation must handle large matrices, making it an ideal candidate for optimization using in-memory computation techniques. Figure 6.6(b) shows the performance decline in mIMC hardware. Previous attempts to implement SpMV on mIMC hardware experienced significant performance degradation. mIMC systems are designed to perform computations directly within memory arrays, such as memristors or static random-access memory (SRAM)-based systems, reducing the need for data movement between the processor and memory, which can be a bottleneck in traditional computing systems. However, in earlier mIMC architectures, the efficiency of sparse computations was limited due to the difficulty in handling sparse matrices. The main issue is the need to map zero elements in the sparse matrix to memory locations, even though these elements do not contribute to the computation. This process leads to an increase in the number of active devices, which in turn consumes more area and energy, undermining the power efficiency of the system. For example, when solving 2D PDEs, the number of activated devices required to process the matrix is much higher than the number of nonzero elements in the matrix, leading to an inefficiency. Specifically, the number of active devices can be 19 times greater than the actual number of nonzero matrix elements, resulting in wasted resources and reduced performance. Figure 6.6(c) shows high-efficiency in-memory sparse computation using SRMs. To address the inefficiency described in part (b), this panel proposes the development of a more efficient in-memory computation system that leverages the unique properties of SRMs. SRMs are a type of non-volatile memory technology that offers high-speed data access and low power consumption, making them ideal for high-performance computing applications. SRMs can store and process data within the memory itself, minimizing the need for data transfers between memory and processors. By utilizing SRMs, it is possible to significantly improve the efficiency of sparse computations. The key advantage of SRMs lies in their ability to perform computations with minimal energy consumption and reduced area requirements, particularly in sparse matrix operations. It suggests that by correcting for the inefficiencies associated with mapping zero elements and leveraging the unique properties of SRMs, a high-efficiency in-memory sparse computation system can be developed. This system could potentially revolutionize scientific computing tasks that rely heavily on sparse matrix operations, offering substantial gains in both energy efficiency and processing speed. The reference to the work of [18] highlights previous research on the use of SRMs in such systems, further supporting the feasibility of this approach.

The challenges and potential solutions for optimizing sparse matrix computations in scientific computing tasks revolve around reducing inefficiencies caused by zero-element mappings, improving data locality, and enhancing both energy efficiency and processing speed in in-memory computation systems. This discussion shows that while SpMV is a key operation, previous mIMC hardware systems suffer from inefficiencies due to the need to map zero elements in sparse matrices, resulting in wasted area and energy. The proposed solution involves using SRMs to develop a high-efficiency in-memory sparse computation system that can overcome these limitations by leveraging the corrective properties of SRMs. This approach promises significant improvements in computational efficiency, energy consumption, and overall system performance for scientific computing applications.

The resistance distribution of the fabricated memristive cells is evaluated using a random-access methodology across 128 cells, each featuring four bit lines (BLs), with a 100% yield rate achieved using a half-biasing scheme. This evaluation distinguishes between the low resistance state (LRS) and the high resistance state (HRS), with the LRS showing an average resistance of 26 GΩ and the HRS showing 33.4 TΩ. The variation in resistance for the LRS is 37.3%, while for the HRS it is 52.9%. The self-rectifying behavior of the device is confirmed by applying a half-read voltage to the selected cells, which shows that LRS cells exhibit a significantly high resistance of approximately 100 TΩ. For half-selected LRS cells, the resistance variation reaches 52.5%.

The fabrication process of these cells demonstrates a high yield rate of over 98%, and the cells maintain stable switching performance even after 12 months of manufacturing. The device's endurance is impressive, exceeding 10^6 cycles, with a memory window of approximately 10^2. Additionally, the switching power consumption is notably low, with only 2.4 aJ required for the SET process and 7.9 aJ for the RESET process. These power consumptions are comparable to the best ultra-low-power devices reported in the field. Due to the device's stability and large dynamic range in direct current (DC) operation, these cells are utilized in further computing demonstrations based on DC *I–V* operation, showcasing their potential for efficient, long-term, and low-power applications. This combination of low resistance variation, stable performance, and low power consumption positions these memristive devices as ideal candidates for applications in next-generation memory and computational systems.

6.3 Optimizing vector matrix multiplications

Memristive devices have garnered significant attention as a transformative technology that extends beyond the capabilities of traditional silicon-based systems, offering unique advantages for advancing computational architectures. These devices, with their ability to both store and process information simultaneously, present new possibilities for enhancing VMMs, which are fundamental to a wide range of computational tasks, including machine learning, signal processing, and scientific simulations. By exploiting memristive devices in vector multiplication, substantial gains can be realized in terms of energy efficiency, processing speed, and overall computational performance [20, 21].

Classified as non-volatile resistive switching devices, memristive devices can modify their resistance based on the voltage history, a key feature that enables them to store and retain data effectively. This memristance property makes them well-suited for applications in neuromorphic computing and other emerging computing paradigms, where energy-efficient and parallel processing capabilities are critical. The application of memristive devices in vector multiplications holds the potential to significantly reduce energy consumption while increasing computation speed, ultimately offering a path to more efficient, scalable, and powerful computing systems [19–23].

This synergy between memristive devices and vector multiplications highlights their transformative potential, emphasizing the need for further exploration and optimization in computational architectures to fully realize the benefits of memristive technology.

6.3.1 In-memory computing

Traditional von Neumann architectures are hindered by the bottleneck created by the continuous data transfer between the processor and memory. This limitation results in slower and more energy-consuming computations. In contrast, memristive devices support in-memory computing, enabling vector multiplication directly within the memory itself. This eliminates the need for frequent data movement between the processor and memory, significantly improving both speed and energy efficiency in computations [22].

One of the key advantages of memristive devices is their ability to perform both computation and data storage within the same unit. This allows for parallel processing, where multiple elements of two vectors can be multiplied simultaneously, drastically reducing the time required for the operation. By exploiting this parallelism and the in-memory processing capability, memristive devices offer a powerful solution for accelerating VMM, a core operation in numerous machine learning and computational tasks [22, 23].

This architecture not only enhances performance but also provides energy efficiency by reducing the number of data transfers, which is a significant advantage for applications in edge computing, neuromorphic systems, and other performance-critical domains. The in-memory processing feature of memristive devices presents a fundamental shift in how computational tasks are approached, offering a pathway toward more efficient and scalable computing solutions.

6.3.2 Adaptive learning with energy efficiency

Memristive devices offer significant advantages over traditional computing elements, particularly in terms of power consumption and computational efficiency.

These devices consume less power, making them ideal for energy-sensitive applications such as battery-powered devices and edge computing. The low power consumption combined with their ability to adapt their resistance values based on input stimuli makes them particularly promising for tasks such as vector multiplications. This adaptive property, akin to synaptic plasticity in biological systems, allows memristive devices to improve and optimize vector multiplication algorithms over time, further enhancing energy efficiency and computation speed [22, 23].

Memristive devices also excel in handling sparse matrix operations, which are common in scientific computing and machine learning. Sparse matrices, which contain a large number of zero elements, are prevalent in many real-world problems. By optimizing vector multiplications specifically for sparse matrices, memristive devices can significantly improve both speed and memory utilization, offering a more efficient solution compared to traditional architectures [5].

In the context of combinatorial optimization, memristive devices can play a role in solving nondeterministic polynomial time-hard problems such as the traveling salesman problem, knapsack problem, and various scheduling tasks. These problems are typically tackled using heuristic algorithms such as simulated annealing, which, while effective, suffers from slow convergence [7]. The proposal to reformulate simulated annealing within the Boltzmann machine framework aims to overcome this limitation by utilizing massively parallel computational models. However, despite the potential advantages of Boltzmann machines, their full implementation is hindered by challenges such as slow all-to-all communication and scalability issues [11].

Recent research is addressing these limitations by integrating memristive devices into the Boltzmann machine architecture, potentially offering high-performance solutions for combinatorial optimization problems. However, for memristive devices to become widely adopted in vector multiplication and other complex computational tasks, challenges such as device variability, precision, and scalability must be overcome. Ongoing advancements in memristive device technologies aim to optimize these parameters, enabling their integration into mainstream computing systems for a wide range of applications in machine learning, optimization, and scientific computing [24].

6.3.3 Rules of vector matrix multiplication

VMM is an essential operation in linear algebra, and its execution using memristive devices brings forward several distinctive aspects. Memristors are resistive devices that store and process information by varying their resistance based on the voltage applied, making them unique for tasks in neuromorphic computing and unconventional computing paradigms [2]. Unlike traditional digital systems, where the weights in neural networks are static, memristors function as dynamic resistors, allowing the network to adapt based on the data it processes.

The parallelism inherent in memristive devices allows them to efficiently execute VMM, particularly when rows of memristors are aligned to represent a matrix and columns serve as the input vector. By applying a voltage across specific pairs, currents flow in ways that mirror the VMM process at the core of neural networks

[7]. The beauty of this approach lies in its analog nature; currents flow smoothly through the system, consuming less power than their digital counterparts while performing computations in real-time.

However, the analog nature of memristors requires careful calibration to account for potential shifts in conductance over time [5]. These shifts, although subtle, can impact the accuracy of computations and thus maintaining precise operations requires ongoing adjustments. Despite these challenges, memristors offer significant advantages due to their ability to mimic the non-linear behavior of biological synapses. This capability enables the construction of neuromorphic networks that replicate the brain's rhythm, offering a powerful new paradigm in learning and computational efficiency.

Moreover, memristors can support sparse connectivity, where neurons form selective connections rather than fully interconnected ones, similar to the brain's efficient architecture [3]. This reduces the complexity of the network and provides opportunities for adaptive learning. Memristors can adjust their conductance in response to incoming data, enabling dynamic learning that evolves over time. This flexibility makes memristive devices more than just static weights in a neural network—they are dynamic elements that transform the learning process itself.

In essence, memristive devices represent a step forward in computational efficiency, adaptability, and the development of neuromorphic systems. They unlock the potential for real-time processing with low power consumption, closely mimicking the natural processes of the brain, and paving the way for more efficient and powerful neural computing systems [14, 25]

6.3.4 Memristive crossbar-based VMM operations

Memristive crossbars and VMM operations are integral components of neuromorphic computing, a branch of AI dedicated to replicating the structural intricacies of the human brain. At the heart of this endeavor are memristors, two-terminal memory devices characterized by voltage dependent resistance. Within neuromorphic systems, the formation of crossbars, achieved by the intersection of rows and columns of memristive devices, establishes the foundational hardware for implementing synaptic weights in neural networks. This configuration enables efficient parallel processing and energy-efficient computations. The suitability of memristive crossbars for vector matrix operations is attributed to their inherent parallel processing capabilities. This design allows multiple computations to occur simultaneously, mirroring the parallelism observed in biological brains [23, 24]. This parallel process significantly enhances the overall efficiency of neuromorphic computing systems, potentially surpassing the power efficiency of traditional von Neumann architectures.

In the context of neural networks, synaptic weights denote the strength of connections between neurons. Memristive crossbars play a pivotal role in efficiently storing and updating these weights, with the resistance of each memristive device in the crossbar corresponding to the strength of the synaptic connection. This correspondence facilitates the implementation of vector matrix operations for neural network computations [11]. The amalgamation of memristive crossbars and vector matrix operations yields several advantages, including heightened energy efficiency, faster processing speeds, and the potential for scalability in large-scale neural network implementations. The integration of these components is crucial for advancing neuromorphic computing, promising more brain-like systems with enhanced capabilities and increased efficiency in artificial intelligence and machine learning [20].

The integration of memristive crossbars and VMM operations forms the main point of advanced computational paradigms, particularly within the realm of neuromorphic computing, a specialized branch of artificial intelligence dedicated to emulating the intricate structural nuances of the human brain. At the core of this technological pursuit are memristors, two sophisticated terminal memory devices renowned for their voltage dependent resistance [18]. Within the framework of neuromorphic systems, the strategic arrangement of crossbars comes to fruition by intersecting rows and columns of memristive devices. This deliberate configuration serves for realizing synaptic weights in neural networks, facilitating a seamless integration of hardware and computational processes. The resulting structure not only enables efficient parallel processing but also lays the foundation for energy-efficient computations, positioning it as a formidable alternative to traditional von Neumann architectures. The inherent parallel processing capabilities of memristive crossbars contribute to their suitability for VMM operations, allowing multiple computations [24]. This design closely mimics the parallelism observed in biological brains, signifying a pivotal step towards achieving computational efficiency in the context of neuromorphic computing systems. The potential surpassing of power efficiency benchmarks set by conventional von Neumann architectures underscores the transformative impact of memristive crossbars in this domain [16].

6.4 Memristive matrix revolution: transforming VMM

VMM is central to numerous computational tasks, such as in machine learning, computer graphics, and scientific computing. Traditional computing architectures, however, face limitations related to energy consumption, processing speed, and scalability when performing VMM. This is where memristive technology offers a transformative solution. Memristors are non-volatile devices capable of retaining resistance values based on the history of charge applied to them [25]. This unique memory-like property makes memristors ideal candidates for in-memory computing, where both data storage and computation occur in the same location, eliminating the need for costly data transfers between memory and processing units.

The so-called memristive matrix revolution is a paradigm shift wherein memristors replace traditional memory and processing units, organizing themselves into arrays. Each memristor in the array represents a matrix element, with the resistance levels corresponding to matrix values. When vector elements are applied as voltages, the resulting currents through the memristors represent the vector-matrix product [26]. This parallel approach to computation can significantly reduce time for VMM, in particular when working with large matrices. Not only does this accelerate computations, but it also cuts down on energy consumption due to the elimination of inter-unit data movement, a key bottleneck in conventional computing.

Memristive arrays also scale efficiently. Adding more memristive devices can extend the system's capacity, allowing it to process massive datasets more effectively. Moreover, the analog nature of memristors aligns with how neurons function in the brain, enabling biomimetic architectures that could revolutionize neuromorphic computing. While the potential of memristive VMM is clear, several challenges remain [27]. These include device variability (which could lead to inaccuracies), limited precision compared to conventional electronics, and the difficulty of integrating memristive arrays with current computing systems.

Despite these challenges, the ongoing research into memristive VMM continues to gain momentum. Addressing issues such as variability and precision, and improving integration, are key to advancing the use of memristive devices in practical applications. If successful, this technology could greatly enhance fields such as deep learning, image processing, and scientific simulations [28]. Additionally, the integration of memristive VMM may complement other emerging technologies, such as neuromorphic and optical computing, in further transforming computational paradigms [25–28].

6.5 Applications of vector matrix multiplications

VMM serves as the backbone for a wide range of applications that require efficient processing of large datasets, real-time computations, and solving complex problems. Its significance spans from fundamental mathematical operations to cutting-edge applications in AI, graphics, simulations, signal processing, optimization, and control systems [15]. The shift toward memristive devices for performing VMM holds the potential to revolutionize these domains by offering enhanced energy efficiency, faster computations, and scalable architectures, described in more detail below.

Machine learning and artificial intelligence

In machine learning, VMM is an essential operation in neural network computations [6]. It is used in both forward propagation and backpropagation processes, where it helps compute the weighted sums of inputs in each layer of the network. The weights of these connections between neurons are represented as matrices, and the inputs are vectors, making VMM a key operation [9]. Efficient VMM algorithms enable faster training and inference in deep learning models, particularly in convolutional neural networks (CNNs) and recurrent neural networks (RNNs), where massive matrix operations are performed at each step of the learning process. By leveraging highly optimized hardware for VMM, systems can significantly reduce the time and energy required for model training [24, 25].

Computer graphics

In computer graphics, VMM is used extensively for geometric transformations of 2D and 3D objects. The transformation matrices, such as those for rotation, scaling, and translation, are multiplied by vectors representing object coordinates to map them from one space to another (e.g. from object space to world space). VMM enables the manipulation of vertices, making it essential for rendering 3D scenes, camera perspective transformations, and applying lighting models [16]. The real-time computation of these transformations is crucial for rendering dynamic scenes in gaming, simulations, and virtual reality [25].

Scientific computing and simulations

VMM plays a critical role in scientific simulations, particularly in solving systems of linear equations and PDEs. These equations often arise in physics, engineering, and computational biology when modeling complex phenomena such as fluid dynamics, heat transfer, and electromagnetic fields. The matrix operations performed during the discretization process of PDEs rely on efficient VMM implementations. These systems of equations, often sparse and large-scale, require high-performance computing (HPC) systems to handle them effectively, with VMM operations acting as the core computational element [26].

Signal processing

VMM is also crucial in signal processing, where it is used in tasks such as digital filtering, where input signal vectors are multiplied by filter matrices to produce output signals. For example, in image processing, VMM operations are employed to apply filters for edge detection, smoothing, or noise reduction. Audio processing, communications, and speech recognition also rely on efficient VMM operations to process and analyse signals in real time. The ability to compute VMM operations with low latency and high accuracy is important for applications in real-time digital signal processing (DSP) systems [24].

Optimization problems

In optimization problems, VMM is used in evaluating constraints and objective functions, particularly in linear programming (LP). For problems such as support vector machines (SVMs) in machine learning, where data points are projected into higher-dimensional spaces to find optimal hyperplanes, VMM helps evaluate the decision boundary. Combinatorial optimization tasks such as the traveling salesman problem and knapsack problems also require VMM for efficient evaluation of cost functions and decision-making under constraints. The ability to perform VMM rapidly allows optimization algorithms to scale better for large datasets [25, 27].

Control systems

In control systems, particularly in the context of robotics, aerospace, and automotive industries, VMM is used in state-space models to describe the dynamics of a system. The system's state, which is represented as a vector, is updated using a system matrix. The control inputs and the state are multiplied to compute the next state of the system, helping predict how the system will behave over time. This is crucial for tasks such as trajectory planning, stability analysis, and real-time control of robotic movements. VMM operations enable the fast computation required in these systems for high-frequency feedback loops [26].

Computer graphics

In computer graphics, VMM is integral to the manipulation of three-dimensional objects through transformations such as translation, rotation, and scaling. Transformation matrices are used to adjust the position, orientation, and size of objects in a 3D space. By multiplying these transformation matrices with the coordinate vectors of the 3D objects, VMM operations allow for accurate positioning within a virtual environment, enabling realistic animations and rendering in games, simulations, and virtual reality [11]. These transformations are crucial in creating dynamic environments and interactions between objects, making VMM a core computational task in computer graphics.

Electrical engineering

In electrical engineering, matrices are commonly used to represent systems of linear equations, particularly in the analysis of electric circuits. VMM becomes essential in solving these systems, facilitating the analysis of complex circuits and the design of electrical components. By using matrix-based methods, engineers can efficiently solve currents and voltages in large, interconnected networks of resistors, capacitors, and inductors [20]. This application is pivotal in optimizing circuit design and ensuring stability and performance in electrical systems.

Physics and mechanical engineering

In physics and mechanical engineering, matrices serve as effective tools to model various mechanical systems, such as those involving springs, masses, and dampers. When forces are applied to these systems, VMM is used to calculate the resulting motion or deformation by multiplying a force vector with a matrix that represents the system's properties. This is particularly useful in simulating and analysing mechanical behaviors in structures, vehicles, and machinery. The ability to solve these systems efficiently through VMM contributes to the design and optimization of mechanical systems across a wide range of industries [19].

6.5.1 Machine learning

In the context of neural networks, the VMM operation is a crucial component of both the training and inference phases. During training, the network adjusts the weights of connections between neurons to learn and adapt to input data. This process is heavily reliant on VMM, as input vectors (representing data) are multiplied by weight matrices (representing learned parameters) to compute the outputs [18]. These outputs are then processed through activation functions, which influence the learning process. The efficiency of these operations directly impacts the network's ability to learn from data and make accurate predictions.

In the inference phase, once the network is trained, VMM is used to propagate signals through the layers of the network, helping generate the final outputs based on the learned weights. This computationally intensive operation is central to neural network functionality, enabling the network to recognize patterns and make decisions [12].

The integration of memristive devices in neural networks offers a transformative approach to VMM. Memristors, known for their ability to store information through resistance changes, simulate synaptic behavior in biological systems. This makes them an ideal candidate for improving the efficiency of VMM in neural networks [16]. Memristive devices, being non-volatile, can retain information even after power is turned off, which contributes to energy efficiency. Additionally, their ability to perform in-memory computations where data processing and storage occur simultaneously significantly reduces the need for data transfer, offering a more power-efficient alternative to conventional computing systems. This capability is particularly advantageous for deep learning and other neural network-based tasks, such as pattern recognition and decision-making, which require large-scale computation [19].

In machine learning, linear regression, which aims to find the best-fitting line among a set of data points, can be framed as a VMM operation. The coefficients of the linear equation are determined by multiplying the input data (as a vector) with the weight matrix, making VMM a key operation in this optimization process [15]. By utilizing memristive devices, this operation could be accelerated, providing faster and more efficient solutions to regression problems, which are fundamental in various machine learning applications.

Figure 6.7(a) illustrates the application of in-memory computing using memristive crossbar arrays to classify MNIST handwritten digits through a two-layer perceptron neural network. The network architecture includes an input layer with 784 terminals, corresponding to the 28×28 pixel resolution of MNIST images, followed by a hidden layer of 128 neurons and an output layer with 10 neurons representing the digits 0 through 9. The matrix multiplications required for the forward propagation of this neural network are implemented directly on 64×64 memristive crossbar arrays [13].

To handle the input-to-hidden layer connection, which involves a weight matrix of size 784×128, the array's limited size necessitates partitioning the weights across 26 sequential updates. Each update maps a portion of the weight matrix onto the crossbar array for computation. Similarly, the hidden-to-output layer connection, involving a smaller 128×10 weight matrix, is implemented through two updates. In the crossbar arrays, the sections actively used for weight mapping and computation during each update are visually highlighted in orange, while the unused regions are shown in gray [7].

Figure 6.7(b) shows that the network was tested on 10 000 MNIST images, achieving a classification accuracy of $93.23 \pm 0.05\%$, which is slightly lower than the software-based baseline of 95.24% due to hardware non-idealities. Detailed results are provided for each digit, with classification accuracy comparisons between software simulations (red bars) and hardware measurements (blue bars).

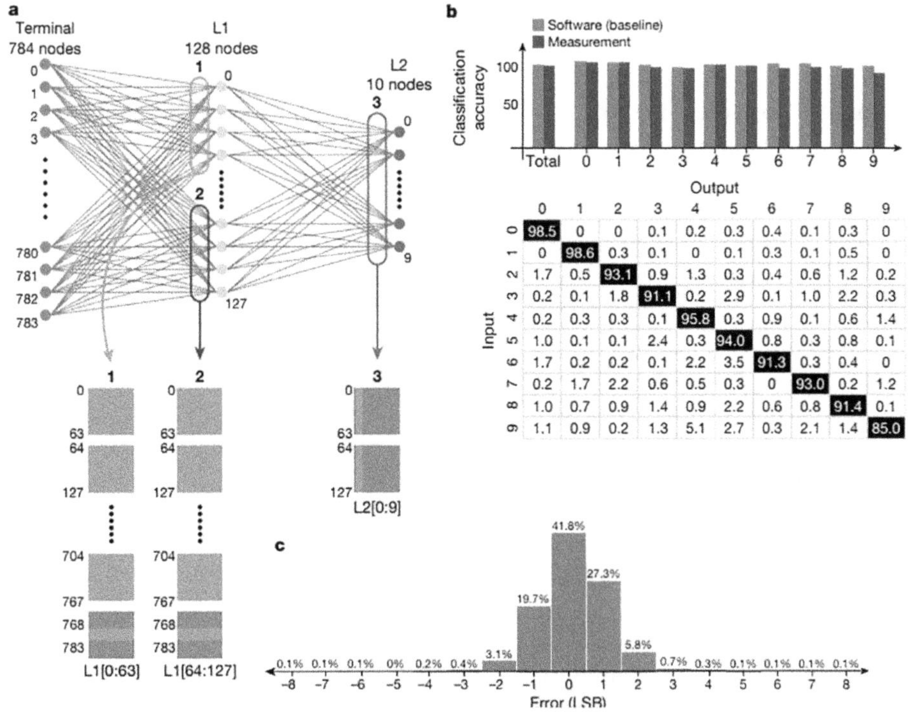

Figure 6.7. In-memory computing for MNIST digit classification using a two-layer perceptron. (a) The network processes 28 × 28 pixel images with 784 inputs, 128 hidden neurons, and 10 output neurons. Memristive crossbar arrays handle matrix multiplications via 28 weight updates, utilizing only portions of the arrays during computation. (b) Classification of 10 000 MNIST images achieved 93.23 ± 0.05% accuracy (baseline: 95.24%). Top: comparison of accuracy between software (red) and hardware (blue). Bottom: distribution of correct (black) and incorrect classifications per digit. (c) Error analysis from 404 million dot products highlights in-memory computing's performance in signal processing tasks. (Reproduced with permission from [12]. Copyright 2022 Springer Nature.)

Additionally, the figure includes a distribution of output predictions for each input digit, showing the percentage of correctly classified outputs (in black) and misclassifications across other digits [6].

An error analysis of the 404 million dot products computed during this task highlights the influence of device-level factors such as variability, noise, and finite precision on overall performance. These findings underscore both the challenges and potential of using memristive devices in crossbar architectures for neural network inference, as shown in figure 6.7(c). The approach demonstrates significant efficiency gains in signal processing tasks, leveraging the crossbar's inherent parallelism and compact architecture, making it a promising candidate for energy-efficient and scalable machine learning applications.

6.5.2 Signal processing

In the context of utilizing memristive devices for VMM in DSP applications, the integration of these devices brings substantial improvements to core DSP operations, particularly filtering. Filtering in DSP typically involves convolving input signals with filter matrices, which is a computationally intensive process. Memristive devices, with their ability to store and process information in-memory, offer a transformative advantage by enabling efficient parallel computation within the memory array itself. This eliminates the need for separate memory and processing units, significantly enhancing speed and reducing energy consumption [18].

Memristive devices are non-volatile resistive devices, meaning they retain information even when power is off. This characteristic enables them to handle tasks such as convolution and other filtering operations more efficiently than conventional digital systems. Moreover, memristors offer low power consumption, which is particularly beneficial in DSP applications where energy efficiency is critical, particularly in portable or edge computing devices [21]. The high integration density of memristive devices allows for more compact and scalable designs, further enhancing the performance of DSP systems.

Additionally, the potential for neuromorphic computing paradigms inspired by the brain's architecture becomes more feasible with memristive devices in VMM [9]. This allows DSP systems to handle more complex signal processing tasks with greater adaptability, such as learning-based filtering or real-time adjustments based on input signals. Such applications could enhance traditional DSP tasks, including noise reduction, frequency analysis, and signal enhancement.

Figure 6.8 illustrates a power-efficient face detection system designed for always-on sensing applications in edge devices, such as smart cameras or portable devices, where continuous operation is essential but power consumption must be minimized. In these applications, face authentication is used to verify a specific individual's identity by analysing fine-grained facial features. However, performing face authentication continuously for every object that enters the field of view would lead to excessive power consumption due to the high computational cost of processing detailed facial features [12]. To avoid this, the system first implements a two-step approach that separates face detection from face authentication, significantly reducing the overall power usage.

In the first stage, figure 6.8(a), face detection is performed, which merely identifies whether a face is present in the scene. This step is less computationally demanding because it does not involve recognizing specific individuals, only detecting the presence of a face. By implementing this low-power detection step continuously, the system ensures minimal power consumption when the device is idle. If no face is detected, the system stays in a low-power state [14]. However, once a face is detected, the system proceeds to the second stage: face authentication, which is more computationally intensive but necessary to identify the specific individual. The step in figure 6.8(b) is only activated when required, ensuring that the power-hungry authentication process is carried out only after the initial face detection has been completed. This strategy of selectively activating high-power processes based on face detection reduces the overall energy consumption, making it ideal for always-on edge devices.

The system described in figure 6.8(c) uses a ten-layer neural network architecture similar to VGG (a well-known deep learning model). Specifically, the seventh layer

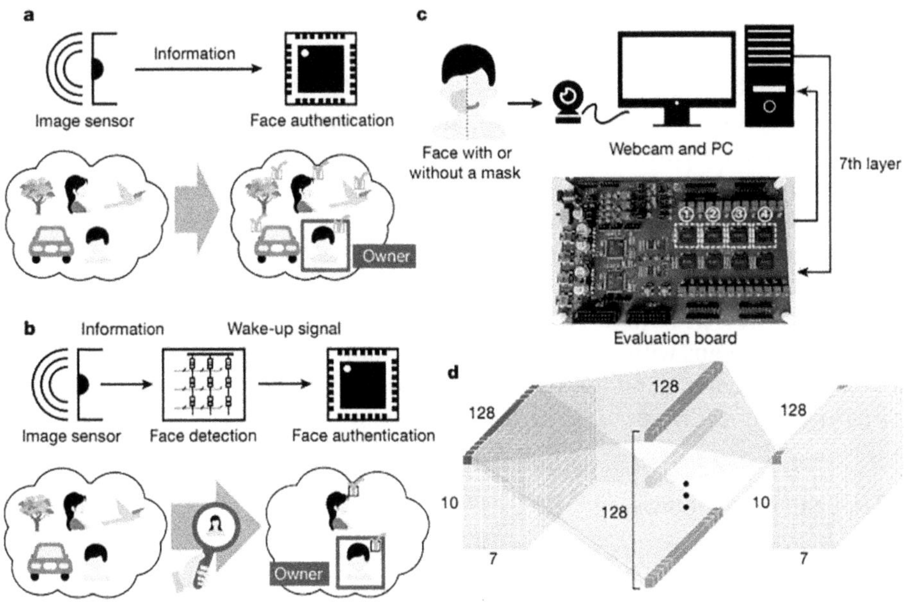

Figure 6.8. Efficient face detection for always-on edge devices. (a), (b) Always-on cameras are designed to enable face authentication, which identifies specific individuals by analysing fine facial details. However, continuously performing face authentication on all objects in the scene requires intensive computation and leads to high power consumption (a). Instead, face detection—determining the mere presence of a face, regardless of identity—requires significantly less computational power (b). This approach allows for power-efficient operation, as the more energy-intensive face authentication is only activated once a face has been detected. (c), (d) A face detection experiment was conducted using a ten-layer VGG-like neural network, with the seventh layer implemented on four parallel MRAM crossbar array chips (c). The system achieved a face detection accuracy of 93.4% when tested on 2 000 scenes with maskless faces and 500 scenes with masked faces. By integrating this four-chip architecture with a camera, the system successfully performed real-time face detection, demonstrating its potential for power-efficient operation in edge device applications. (Reproduced with permission from [12]. Copyright 2022 Springer Nature.)

of the network is implemented using four magnetoresistive random-access memory (MrRAM) crossbar array chips in parallel. MrRAM is a type of non-volatile memory that offers fast data processing and low power consumption, making it an ideal choice for hardware accelerators in edge devices [15]. The parallel implementation of these chips in the seventh layer helps to efficiently process the face detection task while minimizing power usage.

In figure 6.8(d) the face detection accuracy of this system was evaluated using 2 000 scenes with maskless faces and 500 scenes with masked faces. The system achieved an accuracy rate of 93.4%, demonstrating its reliability in recognizing faces even under varying conditions, such as with masks [16]. This high accuracy is crucial for real-world applications, where faces may not always be clearly visible or may be partially obscured. Furthermore, the system was integrated with a camera, enabling real-time face detection and making it suitable for practical deployment in edge devices. The real-time capability further emphasizes the system's potential for use in applications that require continuous monitoring, such as security systems or personalized devices.

This approach enhances energy efficiency in edge devices by first detecting the presence of faces using a low-power method, then activating computationally expensive face authentication only when necessary. The use of MRAM crossbar arrays and the implementation of a VGG-like neural network allow for both accurate face detection and efficient power consumption, making the system well-suited for always-on applications in energy-constrained environments. The integration of memristive devices into VMM for DSP not only enhances computational efficiency but also opens new possibilities for advanced, resource-efficient signal processing [11]. This innovation aligns with current trends in neuromorphic computing and low-power technologies, offering a promising pathway for the future of signal processing in various applications, from audio processing to communications.

6.5.3 Quantum mechanics

Within the domain of quantum mechanics, the evolution of quantum states is intricately illustrated through matrices. Employing VMM in this context provides a sophisticated means to articulate the dynamic transformation of quantum states over time, using the language of mathematical representations. In the realm of quantum mechanics, the quantum states of particles are described by mathematical entities known as state vectors. These state vectors can be represented as matrices, and the evolution of these quantum states is fundamentally captured through matrix operations [30, 31]. By applying VMM, the complex interplay of quantum systems and their evolution can be elegantly expressed mathematically. In essence, VMM serves as a powerful tool for describing the dynamic changes in quantum states as they progress through time [31]. This mathematical framework not only enables a rigorous representation of quantum phenomena but also facilitates a deeper understanding of the intricate relationships governing the behavior of quantum systems. Consequently, the utilization of VMM in the quantum mechanics domain enhances our ability to model and analyse the evolution of quantum states with precision and clarity.

Bibliography

[1] Woods W and Teuscher C 2017 Approximate vector matrix multiplication implementations for neuromorphic applications using memristive crossbars *IEEE/ACM Int. Symp. on Nanoscale Architectures (NANOARCH)* pp 103–8

[2] Nourazar M, Rashtchi V, Azarpeyvand A and Merrikh-Bayat F 2018 Code acceleration using memristor-based approximate matrix multiplier: application to convolutional neural networks *IEEE Trans. Very Large Scale Integr. VLSI Syst.* **26** 2684–95

[3] Nili H *et al* 2018 Hardware-intrinsic security primitives enabled by analogue state and nonlinear conductance variations in integrated memristors *Nat. Electron.* **1** 197–202

[4] Truong S N and Min K-S 2014 New memristor-based crossbar array architecture with 50% area reduction and 48% power saving for matrix-vector multiplication of analog neuromorphic computing *JSTS: J. Semicond. Technol. Sci.* **14** 356–63

[5] Li B, Shan Y, Hu M, Wang Y, Chen Y and Yang H 2013 Memristor based approximate computation *Int. Symp. on Low Power Electronics and Design (ISLPED)* pp 242–7
[6] Xia L, Gu P, Li B, Tang T, Yin X, Huangfu W, Yu S, Cao Y, Wang Y and Yang H 2016 Technological exploration of RRAM crossbar array for matrix-vector multiplication *J. Comput. Sci. Technol.* **31** 3–19
[7] Hu M, Williams R S, Strachan J P, Li Z, Grafals E M, Davila N, Graves C, Lam S, Ge N and Yang J J 2016 Dot-product engine for neuromorphic computing *Proc. of the 53rd Annual Design Automation Conf. on-DAC'16* pp 1–6
[8] Hu M, Strachan J P, Li Z, Stanley R and Williams 2016 Dot-product engine as computing memory to accelerate machine learning algorithms *17th Int. Symp. on Quality Electronic Design (ISQED)* pp 374–9
[9] Wijesinghe P, Ankit A, Sengupta A and Roy K 2018 An all-memristor deep spiking neural computing system: a step toward realizing the low-power stochastic brain *IEEE Trans. Emerg. Top. Comput. Intell.* **2** 345–58
[10] Gupta S, Imani M and Rosing T 2018 FELIX: fast and energy-efficient logic in memory *IEEE/ACM Int. Conf. on Computer-Aided Design (ICCAD) (San Diego, CA, USA)* pp 1–7
[11] Xia Q and Yang J J 2019 Memristive crossbar arrays for brain-inspired computing *Nat. Mater.* **18** 309–23
[12] Jung S *et al* 2022 A crossbar array of magnetoresistive memory devices for in-memory computing *Nature* **601** 211–6
[13] Feng S, Zhang Y, Zhou Z, Huang P, Liu L, Liu X and Kang J 2024 Memristor-based storage system with convolutional autoencoder-based image compression network *Nat. Commun.* **15** 1132
[14] Hamdioui S *et al* 2019 Applications of computation-in-memory architectures based on memristive devices *Design, Automation & Test in Europe Conf. & Exhibition (DATE) (Florence, Italy)* pp 486–91
[15] Gharpinde R, Thangkhiew P L, Datta K and Sengupta I 2018 A scalable in-memory logic synthesis approach using memristor crossbar *IEEE Trans. Very Large Scale Integr. VLSI Syst.* **26** 355–66
[16] Petropoulos A, Boybat I, Le Gallo M, Eleftheriou E, Sebastian A and Antonakopoulos T 2020 Accurate emulation of memristive crossbar arrays for in-memory computing *IEEE Int. Symp. on Circuits and Systems (ISCAS) (Seville, Spain)* pp 1–5
[17] Buchel J *et al* 2023 Programming weights to analog in-memory computing cores by direct minimization of the matrix-vector multiplication error *IEEE J. Emerg. Sel. Top. Curcuits Syst.* **13** 1052–61
[18] Li J *et al* 2023 Sparse matrix multiplication in a record-low power self-rectifying memristor array for scientific computing *Sci. Adv.* **9** eadf7474
[19] Liu S, Wang Y, Fardad M and Varshney P K 2018 A memristor-based optimization framework for artificial intelligence applications *IEEE Circuits Syst. Mag.* **18** 29–44
[20] Lammie C, Eshraghian J K, Lu W D and Azghadi M R 2021 Memristive stochastic computing for deep learning parameter optimization *IEEE Trans. Circuits Syst. Express Briefs* **68** 1650–4
[21] Cui J and Qiu Q 2016 Towards memristor based accelerator for sparse matrix vector multiplication *IEEE Int. Symp. on Circuits and Systems (ISCAS) (Montreal)* pp 121–4

[22] Bojnordi M N and Ipek E 2016 Memristive Boltzmann machine: a hardware accelerator for combinatorial optimization and deep learning *IEEE Int. Symp. on High Performance Computer Architecture (HPCA)* pp 1–13
[23] Sun Z and Huang R 2021 Time complexity of in-memory matrix-vector multiplication *IEEE Trans. Circuits Syst. Express Briefs* **68** 2785–9
[24] Li C *et al* 2018 Large memristor crossbars for analog computing *IEEE Int. Symp. on Circuits and Systems (ISCAS) (Florence, Italy)* pp 1–4
[25] Li J *et al* 2023 A memristive neural network based matrix equation solver with high versatility and high energy efficiency *Sci. China Inf. Sci.* **66** 122402
[26] Yu J, Nguyen H A D, Xie L, Taouil M and Hamdioui S 2018 Memristive devices for computation-in-memory *Design, Automation & Test in Europe Conf. & Exhibition (DATE) (Dresden, Germany)* pp 1646–51
[27] Ma W, Zidan M A and Lu W D 2018 Neuromorphic computing with memristive devices *Sci. China Inf. Sci.* **61** 060422
[28] Bao H *et al* 2022 Toward memristive in-memory computing: principles and applications *Front. Optoelectron.* **15** 23
[29] Liu H, Sun S, Liu J, Li Q, Diao J and Li Z 2021 Binary memristive synapse based vector neural network architecture and its application *IEEE Trans. Circuits Syst. Express Briefs* **68** 772–6
[30] Fyrigos I A, Ntinas V, Sirakoulis G C, Dimitrakis P and Karafyllidis I 2019 Memristor hardware accelerator of quantum computations *26th IEEE Int. Conf. on Electronics, Circuits and Systems (ICECS) (Genoa, Italy)* pp 799–802
[31] Karafyllidis I G, Sirakoulis G C and Dimitrakis P 2019 Memristive quantum computing simulator *IEEE Trans. Nanotechnol.* **18** 1015–22
[32] Fyrigos I A *et al* 2022 Memristor crossbar arrays performing quantum algorithms *IEEE Trans. Circuits Syst.* I **69** 552–63

IOP Publishing

Resistive Switching Systems for In-Memory Computation and Artificial Intelligence

Shaibal Mukherjee

Chapter 7

Stochasticity in memristive systems

7.1 Introduction

Memristors, initially conceptualized by Chua in 1971, became a physical reality through groundbreaking research by HP Laboratories in 2008. These devices play a vital role in linking magnetic flux and charge, with conductance at a specified voltage serving as a key parameter in determining their inherent stability. However, fluctuations in device resistance pose a significant challenge to their efficiency in deterministic memory applications [1, 2]. Understanding the origin of these stochastic variations is essential for uncovering the fundamental mechanisms governing memristive behavior and exploring strategies for effective modulation to enhance device performance.

Stochasticity is particularly pronounced in memristive devices where switching occurs via the migration of metal ions within an insulating matrix. Existing models describing memristive behavior can be broadly categorized into dynamical, micro-structural, thermodynamic, and stochastic approaches [3–7]. Notably, Lu *et al* demonstrated that two-level random telegraph noise (RTN) in the high-resistance state (HRS) of a Pd/TaO_2/Pd-based resistive random-access memory (RRAM) device arises from variable-range hopping between oxygen vacancy centers [8]. Similarly, studies by Botond *et al* have revealed that the current-to-noise ratio exhibits a universal dependence on device resistance, with a significant shift in noise behavior when transitioning from diffusive to ballistic conduction [9].

Despite substantial scientific interest in these noise characteristics, several fundamental questions remain unresolved. For instance, it is unclear whether diffusive processes in memristors are universal across different device platforms or specific to certain architectures and operational regimes. Additionally, the nature of long-range temporal correlations in conductance at a fixed voltage remains poorly

doi:10.1088/978-0-7503-6169-9ch7 © IOP Publishing Ltd 2025. All rights, including for text and data mining (TDM), artificial intelligence (AI) training, and similar technologies, are reserved.

understood. Differences in fluctuation characteristics between the low-resistance state (LRS) and HRS further add to the complexity of these systems.

At its core, stochasticity in memristive systems reflects the presence of inherent unpredictability during the resistance-switching processes [10–12]. For example, when a memristor transitions between states in response to an applied voltage, the exact timing and final resistance value can vary, even under seemingly identical conditions [13]. This randomness plays a dual role: while it poses challenges for precision and repeatability, it also opens avenues for leveraging probabilistic computation, particularly in fields such as stochastic neural networks and random number generation [10].

Moreover, the presence of stochasticity has profound implications for designing memristive devices and systems. Engineers and researchers must account for this variability when integrating memristors into circuits and ensure that the overall system behavior remains robust despite individual device unpredictability. Techniques such as statistical modeling, error correction algorithms, and adaptive feedback mechanisms are often employed to mitigate the effects of stochasticity while capitalizing on its potential benefits [14].

While the stochastic behavior of memristive systems introduces complexity in their operation, it also enriches their functional repertoire. By carefully managing and exploiting this inherent randomness, researchers can unlock innovative applications that harness both the deterministic and probabilistic aspects of memristive devices, further solidifying their role in next-generation computing paradigms [3].

In figure 7.1(a), classical computing operates on the deterministic principles of Boolean logic and binary data representation, where each computational state is precisely defined as either a 0 or a 1. This determinism is supported by well-defined voltage margins that distinguish logical states and ensure robustness against noise or minor fluctuations [4]. Classical systems rely on high-precision hardware and error correction mechanisms to achieve reliable computations. This precision, while foundational to traditional computing, comes at the cost of increased hardware

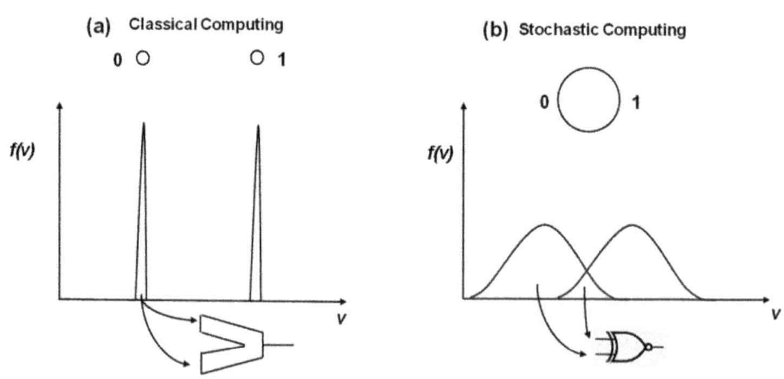

Figure 7.1. (a) Classical computing with well-defined margins. (b) Stochastic computing leveraging quantum uncertainty for error tolerance and simplified hardware [7].

complexity, energy consumption, and limits in scalability as the size and speed of circuits continue to grow. In figure 7.1(b), stochastic computing introduces a novel paradigm that embraces randomness and uncertainty as inherent features of computation rather than viewing them as errors to be mitigated. Inspired by principles from quantum mechanics, such as uncertainty and probabilistic behavior, stochastic computing processes information using probabilistic representations. Data is encoded in streams of random or pseudo-random bits, and operations are performed on probabilities rather than deterministic binary values [14]. This enables reduced hardware complexity and enhanced error tolerance.

Quantum uncertainty is harnessed to simplify computation and improve energy efficiency. For instance, stochastic computing can tolerate variations and noise in physical hardware, making it suitable for approximate computing tasks, neuromorphic systems, and machine learning. By leveraging randomness, this approach also aligns with emerging quantum technologies, where stochasticity is an intrinsic property of qubit behavior [15]. Figures 7.1(a) and (b) contrast the rigidity of classical computing's deterministic nature with the flexibility and efficiency of stochastic computing, showcasing the potential for simpler, error-tolerant hardware and novel computational models inspired by quantum mechanics. This shift from well-defined precision to probabilistic processing is a critical step toward future computing paradigms, particularly in areas requiring scalable, low-power solutions [16].

Resistive switching: The presence of stochasticity in memristive systems fundamentally impacts the understanding and utilization of their resistance state evolution, particularly during transitions between the high resistance state (HRS) and low resistance state (LRS). These transitions, pivotal for the functionality of memristors in applications such as non-volatile memory and neuromorphic computing, are inherently unpredictable due to several intrinsic and extrinsic factors [17].

Material imperfections: Memristive devices are fabricated from materials that often contain defects or structural irregularities. These imperfections create localized variations in the device's electric field, leading to randomized filament formation or dissolution during resistance switching. This randomness directly contributes to variations in the timing and outcomes of state transitions [18]. For instance, the stochastic growth of conductive filaments in oxide-based memristors is heavily influenced by atomic-scale inhomogeneities within the material matrix.

Thermal fluctuations: The operation of memristive devices is significantly affected by thermal energy. During switching events, local heat generation can induce random motion of charge carriers (e.g. ions or electrons), altering the energy landscape and introducing variability in transition dynamics. The influence of thermal fluctuations becomes particularly pronounced at nanoscale dimensions, where energy barriers for state transitions are comparable to thermal energy levels [19].

Non-deterministic processes: The process of switching between HRS and LRS often involves quantum tunneling and other probabilistic phenomena at the atomic and molecular scales. These effects further amplify the unpredictability of switching behavior, in particular under variable environmental conditions such as temperature and electric field strength [20].

The stochastic behavior of memristive devices presents both opportunities and challenges:

Opportunities: Stochasticity can be harnessed in applications requiring variability, such as in probabilistic computing or stochastic neural networks, where randomness is a feature rather than a limitation [18].

Challenges: For conventional applications, such as reliable data storage, managing and mitigating stochasticity is essential to ensure consistency and predictability. This involves strategies such as material engineering to reduce defects and achieve more uniform device behavior, thermal management to minimize fluctuations, and development of error correction techniques and adaptive algorithms to compensate for inherent variability. The stochasticity in memristive system adds a layer of complexity, blending deterministic operations with probabilistic behavior [14]. Understanding and controlling these stochastic factors are critical to unlocking the full potential of memristive devices across diverse technological domains.

Resistance levels: The inherent stochasticity in memristive systems introduces both challenges and unique opportunities, significantly impacting their performance and potential applications.

Inconsistent device behavior: Even in stable high- or low-resistance states, memristors exhibit slight variations in resistance due to inherent noise or fluctuations. These inconsistencies hinder the precise and repeatable operation of memristive devices, complicating their use in accurate and reliable computing or memory tasks [20].

Complex predictability: Controlling and predicting the behavior of stochastic systems during computation is inherently complex. This unpredictability poses hurdles in applications that demand high accuracy and deterministic performance, such as conventional memory systems and digital logic circuits [15].

Device variability: The variability in switching behaviors, due to random migration of ions or formation of conductive filaments, further challenges the reliability of memristors in large-scale applications such as dense crossbar arrays [16].

Opportunities offered by stochasticity using memristive device are as follows:

Neuromorphic computing: Stochasticity aligns closely with the probabilistic and adaptive nature of biological neural processes. In neuromorphic systems, this randomness facilitates the replication of learning and memory mechanisms observed in the human brain, making memristors well-suited for such architectures [17].

Stochastic computing: Stochasticity in memristors can be leveraged for probabilistic and statistical computations. This approach could enable energy-efficient computing, in particular for tasks that do not require high precision, potentially consuming less power than traditional binary logic systems [18].

Random number generation: The intrinsic randomness of memristive devices makes them ideal for generating high-quality random numbers for cryptography and probabilistic algorithms [14].

Noise suppression circuits: Harnessing inherent noise in memristors could lead to innovative designs for circuits that actively suppress unwanted noise [11].

Examples of stochastic behavior:

Metal filament memristors: These devices rely on the formation and dissolution of metallic filaments to switch resistance states. The stochastic nature of filament growth introduces random fluctuations in switching thresholds and timing, affecting the overall system behavior [13].

Oxide-based memristors: In these devices, stochasticity arises from the migration of ions and defects within the oxide material. This migration leads to variations in resistance and switching behavior, particularly under varying thermal and electrical conditions [21].

Research is actively focused on mitigating the adverse effects of stochasticity while capitalizing on its potential for novel applications. Strategies include the following:

Material improvements: Reducing imperfections and optimizing ion mobility to minimize variability [10].

Algorithmic adaptation: Developing algorithms that can tolerate or even exploit randomness [12].

Hybrid architectures: Integrating memristors with conventional electronics to balance precision and adaptability [13].

By addressing these challenges and opportunities, memristive systems hold promise for revolutionizing areas such as neuromorphic computing, advanced memory systems, and unconventional computing paradigms [16].

Memristive devices belong to a novel category of electronic components characterized by their ability to retain resistance states based on the history of applied voltage. This intrinsic memory property, coupled with stochastic behavior at nanoscale dimensions, enables these devices to execute in-memory computing and logic operations with potential advantages in speed, energy efficiency, and density compared to traditional CMOS technology [17].

Stochasticity, the inherent randomness in physical processes, is a key feature of memristive systems. It arises from various sources, including material imperfections, quantum effects, and thermal fluctuations. While traditionally considered a challenge, this stochasticity can be harnessed as a resource for innovative computing paradigms [18].

Synchronization, the coordinated behavior of two or more systems, is a fundamental phenomenon observed in natural and technological contexts. Traditional synchronization methods often rely on external control signals or highly precise initial conditions, which are susceptible to noise and scalability challenges. In contrast, stochasticity-enabled synchronization leverages inherent randomness, such as noise, to synchronize chaotic or nonlinear systems [19].

The convergence of memristive properties and stochastic synchronization opens exciting possibilities:

Noise-induced synchronization: By utilizing stochastic fluctuations, memristive systems can achieve robust synchronization without external precision control, enhancing scalability and resilience [20].

Probabilistic computing: Memristive stochasticity enables the realization of probabilistic computing, offering solutions for optimization problems and neural network training [13].

Chaos-based applications: Harnessing chaotic behavior in memristive systems, synchronized via stochasticity, can lead to advances in secure communication, random number generation, and unconventional computing [15].

Neuromorphic computing: Stochastic synchronization in memristive networks can mimic the variability and adaptability of biological neural systems, paving the way for energy-efficient artificial intelligence [20].

Stochasticity in memristive systems not only redefines how randomness is perceived in electronic devices but also provides a fertile ground for exploring computing paradigms that are robust, efficient, and adaptable to the demands of emerging technologies [21].

7.2 Noise induced synchronization

The exploration of noise-induced synchronization through memristive devices represents an exciting and rapidly evolving field at the intersection of neuromorphic computing and nonlinear dynamics [12]. Memristive devices, as a class of nonlinear electrical components, possess a unique memory effect, where their resistance changes in response to the magnitude and polarity of the applied current. This property makes them ideal candidates for applications in artificial neural networks (ANNs) and neuromorphic computing, effectively mimicking synaptic plasticity observed in biological brains [13].

Synchronization, a phenomenon where two or more oscillators or dynamical systems align their states to a common frequency or phase, is prevalent in natural systems from the synchronized flashing of fireflies to the coordinated firing of neurons in the brain. Within this framework, noise-induced synchronization emerges as a counterintuitive mechanism where noise, traditionally viewed as a disruptive force, facilitates synchronization in dynamical systems [14].

Recent research has delved into utilizing memristive devices to achieve noise-induced synchronization in AANs. By integrating memristive synapses, these networks exhibit robust synchronization capabilities even under noisy conditions [15]. This breakthrough underscores the potential of memristive devices to enhance resilience and energy efficiency in neuromorphic systems.

The experimental validation of these properties, as illustrated in figure 7.2, employs an electrical characterization set-up using the Arc One instrument. This set-up enables precise measurement and analysis of the dynamic behavior of memristive devices under varying conditions, providing critical insights into their

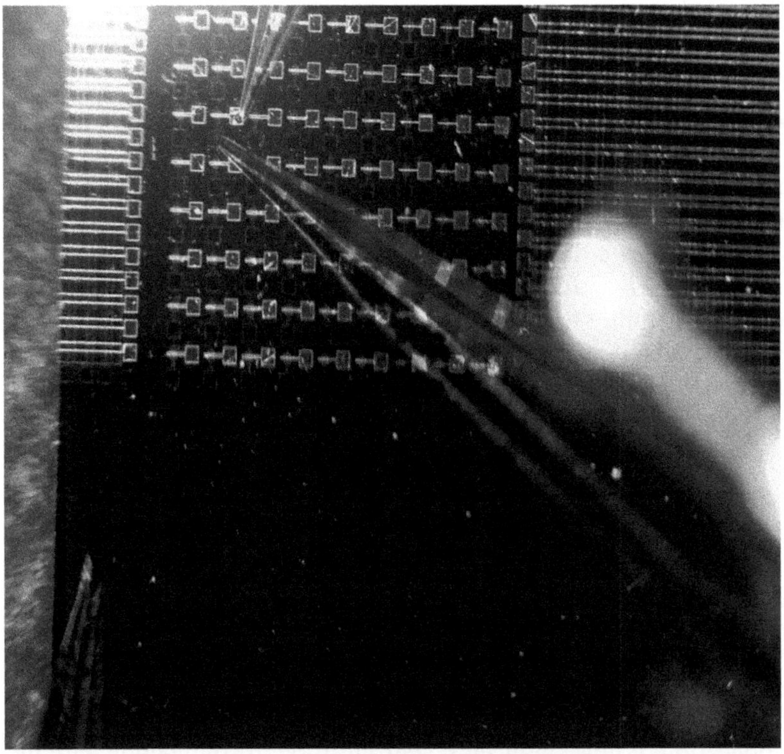

Figure 7.2. Electrical characterization of a memristive crossbar array using the Arc One system.

role in noise-induced synchronization and advancing the design of next-generation computing systems [16].

Advantages of noise-induced synchronization with memristive devices:

Adaptive learning and plasticity:

- Memristive synapses can modulate their resistance based on the timing and strength of input signals, emulating biological synaptic plasticity [11].
- This adaptability allows ANNs to learn and dynamically adjust their synchronization behavior in response to environmental changes [12].

Energy efficiency:

- Noise-induced synchronization minimizes the need for external control mechanisms, reducing energy consumption [13].
- Memristive devices inherently operate at lower power compared to traditional CMOS components, making them ideal for energy-constrained systems [14].

Robustness to noise:

- Unlike conventional systems that view noise as disruptive, this approach leverages noise as a constructive force to achieve synchronization [15].
- The ability to function in noisy environments enhances the resilience of neuromorphic systems [16].

Scalability and density:
- Memristive devices, due to their nanoscale size and high integration density, are well-suited for scaling up complex networks [17].
- Their ability to synchronize large-scale coupled systems opens avenues for advanced neuromorphic architectures [18].

Enhanced dynamical properties:
- Exploiting noise as a synchronization driver enables systems to achieve a common state despite initial differences, providing stability in chaotic or nonlinear dynamics [19].
- This capability is crucial for applications such as real-time processing in adaptive systems and secure communications [20].

Neuromorphic computing applications:
- Noise-induced synchronization in memristive systems paves the way for innovative applications, including real-time pattern recognition, decision-making systems, and brain-inspired computing models [21].

By incorporating memristive devices into coupled systems, researchers are redefining how noise is utilized in computing, transforming it into a resource for synchronization and learning. This innovative approach holds immense promise for the development of robust, adaptive, and energy-efficient artificial neural networks, advancing the boundaries of neuromorphic and nonlinear computing paradigms [22].

The application of noise-induced synchronization in conjunction with memristive devices offers a transformative approach to circuit design, significantly reducing complexity and enhancing operational efficiency. This streamlined methodology arises from the intrinsic properties of memristive devices, which eliminate the need for external control signals or intricate synchronization mechanisms [23].

Simplified circuit design:
- Memristive devices inherently adapt and learn from input signals, enabling self-synchronization without external controls [12].
- This property reduces the need for additional components, resulting in simpler and more compact circuit architectures [13].

Intrinsic noise tolerance:
- By leveraging noise as a driving force for synchronization, the system inherently accommodates and benefits from noise, traditionally considered destabilizing [11].
- This resilience ensures reliable synchronization even in environments where noise is unavoidable, enhancing the robustness of practical implementations [14].

Enhanced efficiency:
- The self-synchronizing behavior of memristive devices minimizes energy consumption by reducing the reliance on external synchronization mechanisms [17].
- The approach is well-suited for energy-constrained applications, such as edge computing and IoT devices [17].

Scalability to large networks:
- The methodology is adaptable across various memristive devices and circuit configurations, enabling the synchronization of large-scale networks [11].
- This scalability supports advanced applications, including neuromorphic computing and distributed systems [10].

Broader applicability:
- The deliberate incorporation of noise as a constructive element expands the usability of memristive synchronization to diverse contexts, including pattern recognition, secure communication, and real-time adaptive systems [16].

Resilience to disturbances:
- The system's ability to synchronize autonomously in noisy and dynamic environments ensures consistent performance under real-world conditions [20].

This novel use of noise-induced synchronization not only simplifies the design and deployment of circuits but also positions memristive systems as a robust and energy-efficient solution for emerging technologies. The methodology's adaptability and scalability make it particularly suitable for applications where simplicity, resilience, and efficiency are paramount, such as neuromorphic computing, AI-driven systems, and complex network synchronization [21].

By turning noise into an ally rather than an adversary, researchers are unlocking new possibilities for innovative, streamlined circuit designs and paving the way for practical, high-performance computing systems.

7.3 Stochastic computing

The conventional method of transferring data between memory and processing units in computing systems often results in high energy consumption and latency, which contributes to the well-known von Neumann bottleneck. This limitation hampers the overall performance and efficiency of traditional computing architectures. However, memristive devices offer a promising solution by enabling in-memory computation (IMC), where both data storage and processing occur within memory cells, eliminating the need for time-consuming data transfer between separate units [13].

One of the key innovations that memristive technology enables is memristor-aided logic (MAGIC). MAGIC is designed specifically for IMC, allowing logical operations such as NOR and NOT to be performed natively within memory cells. This approach offers several advantages [14]:

Parallelism: By performing logical operations within memory, MAGIC allows parallel execution of multiple operations, significantly boosting processing efficiency.

Energy efficiency: Reducing the need for data transfers between memory and processing units leads to substantial energy savings.

Simplified architecture: MAGIC minimizes the need for complex hardware architectures, contributing to reduced circuit complexity.

Stochastic computing, which uses probabilistic representations for arithmetic functions, is particularly suitable for applications requiring complex arithmetic such as multiplication. Stochastic computing is more resilient to faults and noise than traditional binary computing, making it ideal for environments where these factors are prevalent. Memristive systems, with their inherent randomness and noise tolerance, align naturally with stochastic computing, offering increased robustness and simplicity in executing tasks such as multiplication [24].

MAGIC's ability to perform NOR and NOT operations within memory aligns well with stochastic computing, which excels at performing complex arithmetic functions such as multiplication. This makes memristive devices particularly advantageous for data-intensive applications such as digital signal processing (DSP) and convolutional neural networks (CNNs). Stochastic computing allows for faster and more energy-efficient multiplication, which is crucial in these applications, as traditional binary multipliers tend to be slower and more power-hungry [25].

Despite the advantages, memristive technology still faces challenges, particularly in the context of stochastic computing and MAGIC. These include:

Non-linearity and variability: Memristive devices are susceptible to variations in resistance and non-ideal behavior, which may impact the reliability of computations.

Scalability: As memristive devices scale down in size, ensuring consistent performance and managing noise-induced synchronization in large networks becomes more complex.

Integration with existing architectures: Incorporating memristive logic into traditional computing systems requires overcoming integration challenges with established silicon-based technologies.

Nevertheless, memristive technology holds immense promises for solving the von Neumann bottleneck, in particular with the integration of MAGIC and stochastic computing. Continued advancements in memristive materials, noise management, and circuit integration will likely lead to further breakthroughs in energy-efficient, high-performance computing systems [17].

Memristors, while promising, are not yet fully mature and exhibit process variations, non-idealities, and sensitivity to faults and noise, which can compromise the reliability of fixed-point binary methods. These issues pose significant challenges in achieving consistent performance, particularly in environments where stability is critical. However, stochastic computing presents a compelling alternative, offering a more robust approach to computation in the presence of noise and faults [16].

Stochastic computing and its advantages:

Stochastic computing is based on simplifying complex calculations by converting input data into independent bit streams, where each bit represents a probability rather than a fixed value. These uncorrelated bit streams are then fed into an AND gate, and the output generates logical 1s with a probability equal to the product of the input streams. This probabilistic approach enables the execution of operations, such as multiplication, in a simplified and noise-resilient manner, making stochastic computing a natural fit for scenarios where traditional fixed-point binary methods face limitations [14].

Advantages of stochastic computing:

Noise resilience: Stochastic computing is inherently more robust to noise and faults, offering increased reliability in unstable environments compared to binary systems.

Simplification of complex operations: Stochastic computing simplifies complex operations, such as multiplication, by using bit streams and probability-based logic, reducing computational complexity [17].

Energy efficiency: By eliminating the need for precise bit-level computation, stochastic computing can be more energy-efficient, particularly in tasks that do not require absolute precision but rather approximate results [18].

Integration of memristive devices with stochastic computing:

Memristive devices, with their inherent randomness and nonlinear behavior, align well with the principles of stochastic computing. The unpredictability of memristive devices can be leveraged to perform stochastic operations directly within the hardware, facilitating efficient, high-performance computations in tasks such as random number generation and probabilistic decision-making [19].

Synergy between memristive devices and stochastic computing:

Randomness for probabilistic calculations: Memristors, with their noise tolerance and variability, contribute to the generation of probabilistic outputs required in stochastic computing [20].

Efficient calculations: The integration of memristors into stochastic circuits allows for native computation of complex functions, making the system faster and more energy-efficient than traditional binary methods, particularly in data-intensive tasks [21].

Resilient computing: Memristive-based stochastic computing can maintain functionality even in noisy or fault-prone environments, offering a significant advantage over conventional computing architectures.

Simulations and applications: Recent simulations have shown that memristor-based stochastic computing outperforms traditional binary methods in terms of both speed and energy efficiency. This innovation is particularly beneficial for data-intensive tasks such as digital signal processing, CNNs, and other applications requiring high computational power. By leveraging the inherent properties of memristive devices, researchers have demonstrated that stochastic computing can handle complex calculations with greater efficiency and reliability [22].

The integration of memristive devices with stochastic computing represents a significant breakthrough in memristor-based computing, offering a novel approach to addressing challenges such as fault tolerance, energy efficiency, and computational speed. While memristive technology still faces hurdles related to process variation and non-ideal behavior, the potential for native stochastic computing provides a promising avenue for advancing next-generation neuromorphic computing and data-heavy applications [23]. As research progresses, the ability to harness memristive devices for probabilistic and efficient computation will likely revolutionize areas where traditional computing struggles to meet the demands of complexity and noise resilience.

Zamarreño-Ramos *et al* (2011) and Querlioz *et al* (2011) proposed a pulsing scheme to implement spike-timing-dependent plasticity (STDP) in memristive synapses (figure 7.3(a)). Presynaptic spikes generate rectangular voltage pulses (green) applied to the presynaptic terminal, while postsynaptic spikes produce shorter pulses (blue) at the postsynaptic terminal. The resulting voltage drop, defined as presynaptic minus postsynaptic potential, governs synaptic changes (figure 7.3(b)). Postsynaptic spikes alone induce long-term depression (LTD), whereas a postsynaptic spike following a presynaptic spike within τ drives long-term potentiation (LTP). Presynaptic spikes alone cause no plasticity. Thus, the memristor conductance follows an STDP rule.

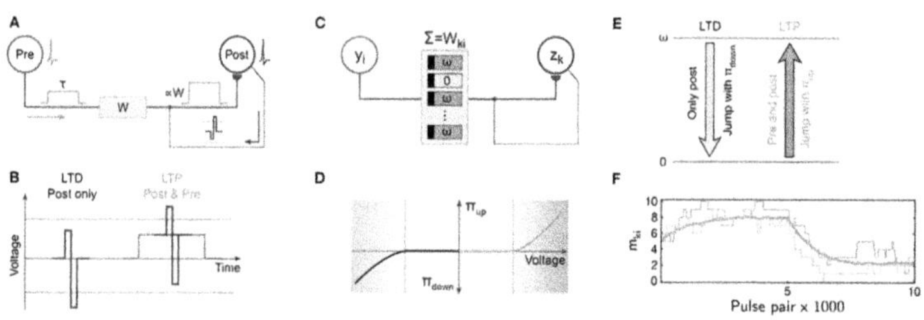

Figure 7.3. Compound memristive synapse model with stochastic memristors. (A) STDP pulsing scheme. Input spikes elicit a rectangular voltage trace (green, left) that is sent to the presynaptic terminal of the memristor synapse. Post-synaptic spikes elicit a brief voltage pulse (blue) which is sent back to the synapse. (B) Solitary postsynaptic spikes trigger LTD since the voltage exceeds the lower threshold of the memristor. Simultaneous pre- and post-synaptic spikes trigger LTP since the voltage exceeds the upper threshold. (C) Compound memristive synapse model. A synapse is composed of M bistable memristors operating in parallel. Each memristor can either be active (weight ω) or inactive (weight 0). The total synaptic weight W_{ki} between input neuron Y_i and network neuron z_k is the sum of the individual memristor weights. (D) Bistable memristors switch stochastically between the active and inactive state depending on the applied voltage difference across its terminals. Switching to the active state (inactive state) occurs with probability π_{up} (π_{down}) if a certain threshold voltage (dotted line) is exceeded. (E) Summary of stochastic transitions for compound-synapse STDP. (F) In an STDP pairing experiment, the stabilizing weight dependence of compound synapse plasticity governs convergence to a dynamic equilibrium. 10 000 plasticity pulses were applied to a synapse with $M = 10$ constituents. During the first half, 80% (20%) of the events were of LTP (LTD) type. During the second half, the probability for LTP (LTD) events was inverted to 20% (80%). Thin lines: number of active memristors $m_{ki}(t)$ for two example simulation runs. Thick line: Average $\langle m_{ki(t)} \rangle$ over 100 runs. The average weight converges to a dynamic equilibrium. Reproduced from [39] CC BY 4.0.

A synapse model is proposed in which **M bistable memristors** operate in parallel to form a single synaptic weight W_{ki} between the ith input neuron y_i and the kth network neuron z_k (figure 7.3(c)). Each memristor has two stable states: a high-conductive (active) state and a low-conductive (inactive) state. Since the conductance of inactive devices is negligible compared to the active ones, the overall weight is determined mainly by the active memristors.

Figure 7.3(d) shows a simplified model of stochastic switching in individual memristors under the STDP pulsing scheme. This leads to stochastic plasticity in compound memristive synapses, summarized in figure 7.3(e) as compound-synapse STDP.

Figure 7.3(f) illustrates how such a compound synapse converges stochastically to a dynamic equilibrium during an STDP pairing experiment. In this example, the synapse contains $M = 10$ bistable switches, each with switching probabilities $\pi_{\text{up}} = \pi_{\text{down}} = 0.001$. The same parameters are later applied in the network-level simulations.

WTA post-learning behavior: The WTA network behavior shows how, after learning, some neurons spike in response to specific patterns while others become silent. This post-learning behavior is a direct reflection of the stochastic nature of the learning process. In the WTA framework, only the strongest responses (the 'winners') are allowed to spike, while weaker responses are suppressed (table 7.1). This helps the network focus on the most relevant features in the input patterns, leading to efficient classification or recognition [28].

The stochastic nature of the learning process refers to the fact that synaptic weights adjust randomly in the early stages, but over time, the network stabilizes as it converges to a state where the spiking behavior becomes more deterministic based on the learned patterns. Some neurons may remain silent because they either no longer have sufficient weight connections to trigger a spike or because other neurons become more specialized in representing the input patterns [29].

Context in conventional computing (CMOS technology): In conventional CMOS technology, the process of adapting to patterns and making decisions based on learned information is typically managed by complex, predefined algorithms. This contrasts with the more stochastic and adaptive learning process exhibited by the WTA network, where synaptic weights are dynamically adjusted based on the input data, and output is determined through probabilistic spiking behaviors [30]. Unlike traditional computing, which depends on rigid and structured binary logic, this spiking network, driven by memristive devices and stochastic computing principles, allows for more flexible, fault-tolerant, and efficient learning and decision-making processes.

Table 7.1. WTA performance under different conditions [10].

Parameter name	Parameter value and classification accuracy			
Output layer size	16	32	64	128
Accuracy	58.9%	64.2	73.9	78.4

This shift marks a significant departure from conventional approaches and highlights the potential of memristive-based systems in neuromorphic computing [31].

In conventional computing systems, particularly those based on CMOS technology, the ongoing trend of miniaturization presents significant challenges. As transistors shrink in size, problems such as increased power leakage and variations in operational characteristics have become more pronounced. These issues lead to reliability concerns and higher power consumption, undermining the performance gains typically expected from smaller transistor sizes. The constant push for miniaturization also exacerbates thermal management and cross-talk between increasingly smaller components [12].

To address these challenges, researchers are exploring two primary approaches:

Utilization of novel materials: The first strategy focuses on the exploration and implementation of novel materials that can improve transistor performance. For example, graphene and carbon nanotubes are being investigated as alternatives to traditional silicon. These materials have the potential to enhance transistor speed and reduce power consumption, offering higher electrical conductivity and lower resistance compared to conventional materials [32]. However, significant challenges remain in integrating these materials into existing semiconductor processes, particularly with respect to connectivity, scalability, and cost.

Development of new computer components: The second approach aims to move beyond traditional transistor-based architectures by developing entirely new components that can bypass the limitations of CMOS technology. One of the most promising innovations in this area is the use of memristors within crossbar structures. Memristors are non-volatile devices that store information about the electricity flow passing through them, allowing them to retain memory without the need for constant power [33]. This feature makes them highly suitable for advanced memory systems and offers a potential solution to the von Neumann bottleneck in computing.

Digital memristors are specialized devices that store binary information by modulating their resistance: they represent '1' with low resistance and '0' with high resistance. The key advantage of digital memristors is their ability to rapidly and reliably switch between these two states, making them ideal for use in memory and logic circuits. This switching is achieved through a programming pulse of a specific voltage and duration, which changes the state of the memristor [14]. Reading the stored information is accomplished by connecting the memristor to a resistor and voltage supply, from which the current can be measured to determine the stored value.

Memristors offer several advantages over traditional memory devices [34]:

Compact size: Memristors are smaller than conventional memory technologies such as DRAM or flash memory, allowing for denser storage.

Swift switching: The ability to quickly change states makes them ideal for fast access memory, which is critical in modern computing tasks.

Non-volatility: Unlike volatile memory (e.g. RAM), memristors retain data even when the power is turned off, providing a reliable long-term storage solution.

Combining memristors with CMOS circuits: Researchers are also investigating the integration of memristors with traditional CMOS circuits to combine the best of both worlds. Memristors can offer non-volatile memory storage, while CMOS circuits continue to handle conventional logic operations. By integrating memristors into existing CMOS technology, systems can achieve higher memory density and energy efficiency, providing a more sustainable and powerful computing solution [30]. This hybrid approach leverages the non-volatile memory properties of memristors and the mature logic capabilities of CMOS, addressing both memory and processing requirements simultaneously.

The challenges posed by miniaturization in conventional CMOS technology are driving researchers to explore innovative approaches for enhancing computer components. The use of novel materials holds promise for improving transistor performance, while the development of memristive components, particularly within crossbar structures, offers a potential solution to many of the limitations faced by traditional computing systems. Memristors, in particular digital memristors, provide a compelling advantage for next-generation memory and logic circuits, and their integration with CMOS systems could mark a significant step forward in creating more efficient, reliable, and scalable computing architectures [32].

7.4 The effect of perturbation on memristive switching

Memristive devices, particularly memristors, are revolutionary components in the realm of computing and memory systems. These devices are unique in their ability to recall and adjust resistance based on the history of applied voltage, offering substantial potential for applications such as memory storage, computational tasks, and neuromorphic computing [14]. However, like all electronic devices, memristors are vulnerable to perturbations, external disruptions or disturbances that can significantly impact their performance and reliability [20].

In the context of memristive switching, perturbation refers to the intentional introduction of disturbances or variations in the electrical properties of a memristor. These disturbances can arise from several sources, including [24]:

Temperature variations: Fluctuations in temperature can cause changes in the resistance of memristors, influencing their switching behavior.

Voltage spikes: Sudden increases in voltage can affect the stability of the memristor's state, causing unintended changes in resistance.

Electromagnetic interference (EMI): External electromagnetic fields can introduce noise that may disrupt the resistance modulation process in memristors.

These perturbations can have a detrimental effect, particularly in applications where reliability and accuracy are paramount, such as information storage or precise calculations. When memristive devices are subjected to such disturbances, their switching process may become unstable, leading to errors, data corruption, or failures in computations [18].

7.4.1 Investigating the effect of perturbation

Understanding the effects of perturbation on memristive switching is essential for optimizing memristor performance [16]. By carefully studying how various perturbations influence the resistance levels and state transitions, researchers can improve the stability and reliability of memristor-based systems.

Perturbation is a powerful tool that can be employed to [12]:

Modulate resistance levels: Perturbations can influence the switching characteristics of memristors, such as the speed of state transitions and the precision of resistance changes [14].

Improve the precision of state transitions: Controlled perturbations can be applied to ensure that memristors switch between desired resistance states more reliably, contributing to more accurate operations in computing tasks [18].

The dual role of perturbation: Perturbation can be a disruptor or enhancer. While perturbations are typically viewed as negative influences in electronic systems, they can, in some cases, enhance the performance of memristive devices. This phenomenon occurs when specific types of noise or disturbances are leveraged intentionally to improve the functionality of memristors [22].

Noise-induced switching: Certain types of random noise or perturbations can accelerate the switching process of memristors, leading to faster data processing and more responsive systems. In this sense, perturbation transforms chaos into opportunity [21].

Enhanced memory retention: Perturbations, particularly those involving controlled temperature fluctuations or voltage pulses, may also improve the retention characteristics of memristors, making them more suitable for non-volatile memory applications. This enhanced memory retention could be valuable for building brain-inspired computing systems that require robust and efficient memory storage [24].

Noise-induced synchronization: In systems such as neuromorphic computing, perturbations in the form of noise can play a role in synchronizing the behavior of memristive neurons or networks, potentially leading to more energy-efficient computations that mimic the behavior of biological systems [22].

7.4.2 Perturbation-driven advancements for memristive systems

Ongoing research is focused on exploring the impact of perturbations on memristive switching and leveraging them for robust device operation [21]. By understanding and controlling these external influences, researchers aim to develop strategies for:

- Increasing the reliability of memristive systems, ensuring consistent performance even in the presence of temperature or voltage fluctuations.
- Enhancing the energy efficiency of memristor-based systems, which could contribute to the development of low-power computing devices.
- Building secure memory systems. Perturbations, if harnessed correctly, could play a role in protecting data integrity, making memristive devices suitable for secure memory chips that resist tampering or interference.

- The interactions between perturbations and memristive devices lay the groundwork for the next generation of memristor-based technologies. Understanding how perturbations influence switching dynamics will be crucial for developing memristors that are both reliable and power-efficient. Ongoing research includes [20, 25].
- Exploring novel perturbation techniques to improve the switching speed and precision of memristors.
- Investigating how electromagnetic interference and temperature fluctuations affect the stability of memristor-based systems and developing methods to mitigate these effects.
- Developing neuromorphic computing systems where perturbations can be utilized for enhanced performance in tasks such as pattern recognition, machine learning, and data processing.

The successful integration of perturbations into memristive devices could revolutionize computing technologies, paving the way for more resilient, efficient, and advanced systems that harness the benefits of noise and randomness rather than relying solely on traditional, deterministic designs.

Kumar *et al* have reported that surface perturbations significantly influence the resistive switching (RS) behavior of nanoscale Y_2O_3 memristors by altering the formation and characteristics of conductive filaments (CFs) [35]. Their study highlights that when an external voltage is applied between the top electrode (TE) and bottom electrode (BE), oxygen vacancies migrate, forming CFs that dictate the device's resistance states. As observed, higher surface roughness leads to abrupt RS behavior due to localized CF formation, resulting in lower switching voltages (V_{SET} and V_{RESET}), which aligns with previous findings. However, Kumar *et al* noted that at excessive surface perturbation levels, non-uniform CF heights can cause failures in the RESET process, similar to what Kim *et al* previously reported. Additionally, their study indicates that increasing perturbation height leads to a gradual decrease in the ON–OFF ratio, as the shorter CFs reduce the effective filament radius while increasing device current and temperature. Thus, as Kumar *et al* have demonstrated, optimizing surface perturbation height is crucial for controlling switching characteristics and improving the overall performance and reliability of memristors.

Figure 7.4 illustrates the device schematic, highlighting the SET and RESET processes under surface perturbations. Figures 7.4(a) and (b) depict schematics with flat surfaces. To systematically analyse the impact of surface perturbations, five different perturbation levels (0.1, 0.2, 0.5, 1.0, and 1.5 nm) were introduced over the bottom electrode's surface, which subsequently affected the material layers above (figure 7.4(c)).

The electrical responses obtained from memristors with varying surface roughness levels are depicted in figure 7.5. The RS behavior in these devices can be explained as follows.

When an external voltage bias is applied between the TE and the BE in a sandwich structure with an oxide switching layer, oxygen ions or vacancies migrate due to the electric field established between the electrodes. The accumulation of charge carriers (oxygen vacancies) alters the memristor's resistance, thereby

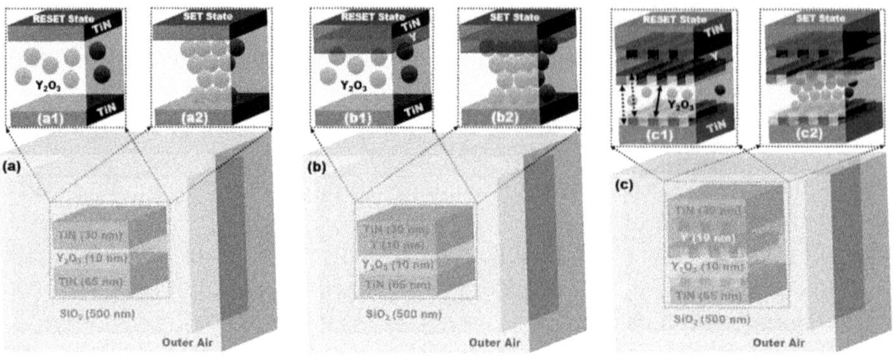

Figure 7.4. Three-dimensional (3D) memristor structure used in COMSOL Multiphysics with associate external device environment comprising (a) TiN/Y_2O_3/TiN, (b) TiN/Y_2O_3/Y/TiN, and (c) TiN/Y_2O_3/Y/TiN-based memristors with surface perturbation.

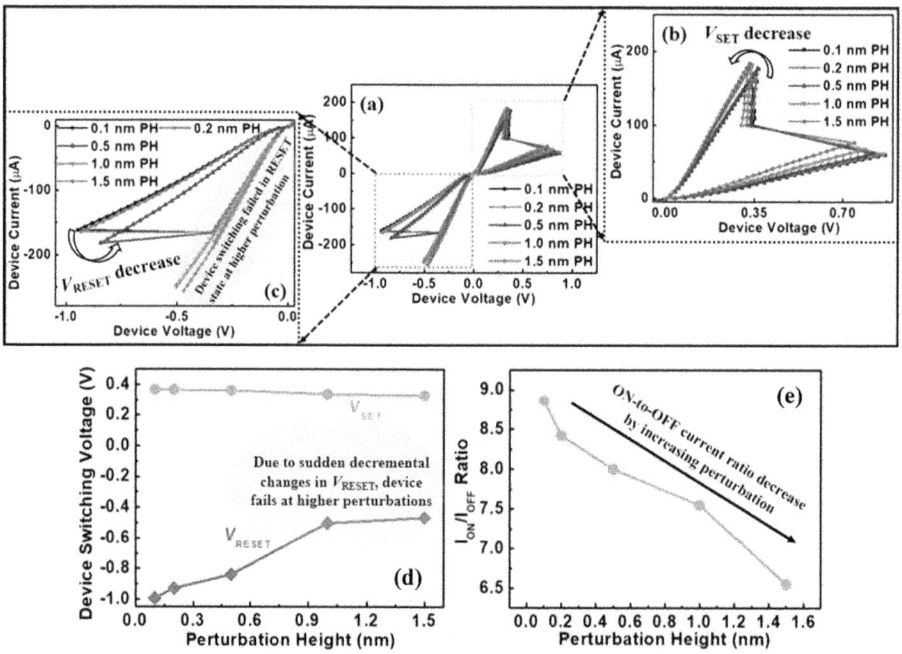

Figure 7.5. Resistive switching responses of the memristor under varied heights of surface perturbations: (a) full hysteresis loop, (b) RS loop under positive applied voltage, and (c) RS loop under negative applied voltage. (d) Effect of surface perturbation height over the device switching voltage, and (e) ON/OFF current ratio.

modulating current conduction within the device. The presence of needle-like structures over the BE further reduces the effective distance to the TE, leading to accelerated carrier movement compared to flat surfaces. As a result, devices with higher surface roughness exhibit abrupt RS due to localized CFs and show relatively lower switching voltages (figures 7.5(b)–(d)).

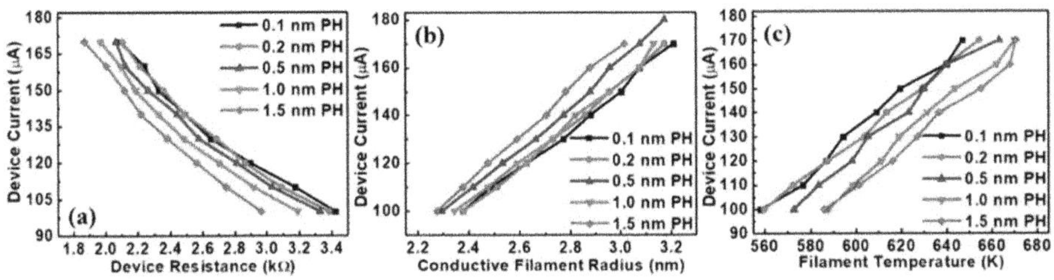

Figure 7.6. Effect of surface perturbation height on the (a) device resistance versus device current, (b) CFs radius versus device current, and (c) CFs temperature versus device current.

While higher surface perturbations lower the switching voltage, excessive perturbation disrupts the RESET process due to non-uniform CF heights, as shown in figure 7.5(b). This failure mechanism is consistent with experimental observations by Kim *et al* [36]. Additionally, surface perturbations significantly affect the ON/OFF ratio of the memristor. As seen in figure 7.5(b), the current ratio decreases almost linearly with increasing perturbation height.

A detailed study on the effects of surface perturbation height on key performance parameters device current, CF radius, and temperature is presented in figure 7.6. The findings include:

(i) **Device current** (figure 7.6(a)): Increased perturbation height modulates device resistance, influencing overall current flow.

(ii) **CF radius** (figure 7.6(b)): Higher perturbations lead to shorter CF lengths, reducing the effective radius due to instantaneous current flow.

(iii) **CF temperature** (figure 7.6(c)): Shorter CF lengths result in higher device current, subsequently increasing CF temperature due to enhanced current density.

This study by Kumar *et al* highlights the significant role of surface perturbations in determining the RS characteristics and overall performance of nanoscale Y_2O_3 memristors.

7.4.3 Top electrode perturbation

Top electrode perturbation (TEP) is a technique used to influence the properties of memristive devices by introducing controlled disturbances specifically to their top electrode. Memristive devices, which are non-volatile memory devices that exhibit resistance-switching behavior, hold great promise for applications in neuromorphic computing, data storage, and logic operations [20]. Their unique ability to retain information in the form of resistance states makes them valuable for next-generation computing systems. The top electrode plays a critical role in determining the switching characteristics of memristors, and by introducing perturbations at this electrode, researchers can fine-tune the memristive behavior to optimize performance for specific applications [22].

The role of the top electrode in memristive switching. Memristors are two-terminal devices that exhibit resistance switching based on the history of applied voltage, which enables them to store information in the form of resistance states. These devices typically have a top electrode (often made of a conductive material) and a bottom electrode, with the memristive material located between them. The top electrode is particularly important because it directly influences the electric field distribution across the device and the formation or dissolution of filaments that lead to resistance changes [14]. The perturbation of the top electrode allows researchers to manipulate the voltage thresholds required to switch between resistance states, modify the ON/OFF resistance ratio, and improve the switching endurance of the device. These modifications can lead to significant improvements in device performance, energy efficiency, and reliability [26].

Objectives and benefits of top electrode perturbation. TEP offers a dynamic approach for controlling the behavior of memristive devices. By selectively adjusting the electrical characteristics at the top electrode, researchers can induce various beneficial changes in the device's switching behavior. Some of the potential benefits and objectives of TEP include [27]:

- **Modifying the switching threshold voltage**: By perturbing the top electrode, it is possible to modify the voltage levels required to switch the memristor between its HRS and LRS. This enables the fine-tuning of device performance for specific applications, such as low-power memory or high-speed switching circuits [28].
- **Enhancing ON/OFF resistance ratio**: TEP can help optimize the resistance ratio between the high and low states of the memristor. A higher ON/OFF resistance ratio is desirable for clearer state differentiation, improving the device's reliability in storing information and performing logical operations [29].
- **Improving switching endurance**: The longevity or endurance of memristors, i.e. how many times they can be cycled between resistance states without degradation can be influenced by perturbing the top electrode. This enhancement is critical for increasing the device's lifespan, making it more suitable for long-term memory applications [30].
- **Enabling multilevel switching**: Memristors typically switch between two distinct resistance states (ON and OFF), but with TEP, it is possible to achieve multilevel switching. This allows memristors to store more than one bit of information in a single device by having multiple resistance states, thereby increasing memory density and data storage capacity [31].
- **Inducing memristor oscillators**: TEP can also be used to generate oscillations in memristive devices, transforming them into memristor oscillators. This can be particularly useful in applications such as signal processing, where oscillations are needed for frequency generation or modulation [32].
- **Fine-tuning responsiveness**: Perturbing the top electrode allows for more precise control over the response time and switching speed of the memristor. This fine-tuning makes the device more adaptable to varying circuit requirements, such as faster response in high-speed computing or optimized signal processing [33].

Applications of top electrode perturbation in memristive devices. The ability to control the switching characteristics of memristive devices through TEP opens up a wide range of possibilities in memory storage and computational circuits. Some potential applications include [34]:

- **Optimizing neuromorphic systems**: In neuromorphic computing, where memristors are used to mimic synaptic behavior in artificial neural networks, TEP can help adjust the synaptic weights to match specific learning patterns. This level of control is essential for building systems that closely resemble biological brains in terms of adaptability and learning [37].
- **Memory storage**: TEP can be used to enhance non-volatile memory devices by improving the reliability and endurance of the memristor, allowing it to be used for high-density, long-lasting data storage [38].
- **Signal processing**: In signal processing applications, TEP can be leveraged to control the switching characteristics of memristors used in circuits that require dynamic response times or oscillation generation, such as filters, modulators, and signal generators [36].
- **Fault-tolerant computing**: TEP can also be applied to enhance the robustness of memristor-based systems by improving their tolerance to external disturbances, ensuring more reliable operation in environments prone to noise or other perturbations [37].

While the top electrode perturbation technique offers numerous advantages, there are also challenges associated with its implementation:

- **Complexity in precise control**: Achieving precise control over the perturbation at the top electrode may require advanced techniques and equipment [17].
- **Integration with existing systems**: Integrating memristors with TEP into traditional CMOS systems might pose challenges in terms of compatibility and design complexity [22].
- **Long-term reliability**: It is important to ensure that perturbations do not inadvertently degrade the device over time, particularly in high-endurance applications [14].

TEP is a powerful technique for influencing the behavior of memristive devices by controlling the electrical characteristics at the top electrode. This approach allows researchers to fine-tune key properties of memristors, such as switching thresholds, resistance ratios, and endurance, while enabling exciting applications such as multilevel switching and memristor oscillators. The ability to dynamically adjust these parameters opens up new possibilities for energy-efficient memory storage, neuromorphic computing, and signal processing, making TEP an essential tool in the development of advanced memristive systems [25].

The top electrode is one of the metal layers in this structure; by perturbing the top electrode, researchers try to influence the electrical characteristics of the memristor. This perturbation can involve altering the voltage applied to the electrode or introducing external factors that impact the switching behavior. The goal is to gain better control over the resistance states of the memristor allowing for precise manipulation and optimization of its performance. Reliability concerns arise because external disturbances can interfere with the intended operation of memristive devices [23]. For instance, variations in the environment, electrical noise or unintended voltage fluctuations may lead to undesired changes in the resistance states of the memristor. This in turn can result in data corruption or errors in computations if the memristor is used for memory storage or as a computational element. Researchers are actively exploring techniques to mitigate the impact of TEP on memristive devices. This includes the development of protective measures, adaptive control algorithms, and improved materials that enhance the stability and reliability of memristors under varying conditions. Researchers are working to overcome these challenges with the goal of realizing the complete potential of memristive devices in emerging technologies such as neuromorphic computing, non-volatile memory storage, and advanced electronic systems.

7.4.4 Bottom electrode perturbation

Memristors typically consist of two electrodes separated by a thin insulating layer, and the resistive switching occurs at this interface. The bottom electrode specifically refers to one of these terminals, and perturbation involves the purposeful introduction of controlled changes to this electrode. This manipulation can take various forms, such as altering the electrical potential, applying thermal stimuli, or inducing chemical modifications. The significance of studying bottom electrode perturbation lies in its potential to unveil fundamental insights into the behavior and performance of memristive systems. The researcher's objective is to analyse specific alterations to the bottom electrode that affect the resistive switching mechanism which is essential for determining the memory-like behavior of the device.

This detailed exploration is crucial for several reasons. First, the impact of bottom electrode perturbation aids in optimizing the functionality and reliability of memristors. It provides a deeper comprehension of the intricate interplay between material properties, electrode configurations, and external stimuli. Second, the development of non-volatile memory technologies, where memristors hold promise for high-density and energy-efficient storage [24]. Moreover, the investigation into bottom electrode perturbation contributes to the advancement of neuromorphic computing, a field that draws inspiration from the human brain's architecture. By manipulating the bottom electrode, researchers can potentially enhance the device's synaptic properties, paving the way for more efficient and brain-like computing systems. In essence, the detailed scrutiny of bottom electrode perturbation in memristive systems represents a crucial step in harnessing the full potential of these devices for future electronic applications, ranging from memory storage to neuromorphic computing.

Memristive devices are innovative components known for their ability to retain resistance states, holding significant promise for the future of electronics. However, it is crucial to understand and control their behavior for effective use. A key concern is bottom electrode perturbation (BEP), where changes in the properties of the bottom electrode can impact the performance and reliability of these devices. BEP involves changes caused by factors such as ionic and electronic migration, high temperatures, and mechanical stress during switching, leading to adverse effects such as changes in voltage requirements and device degradation. Manipulating the electrical characteristics of memristors through intentional BEP seeks precise control over resistance states, enabling optimization and customization of device performance. Researchers address reliability concerns by exploring protective measures, adaptive control algorithms, and materials enhancing stability [25]. Understanding the physics and mechanisms behind resistance switching is crucial for effective strategies to mitigate perturbations. The reliability of memristive devices is vital for successful integration into electronic systems, particularly in applications such as non-volatile memory storage and neuromorphic computing. Robust countermeasures against BEP aim to ensure consistent and dependable operation, maximizing the potential of memristors in next-generation technologies.

7.5 Applications and future directions

In addressing the intricacies introduced by stochasticity within memristive systems, the innate randomness inherent to these systems presents substantial opportunities for pioneering functionalities [14]. This section examines both extant applications [25] and prospective future avenues that strategically leverage stochasticity.

7.5.1 Neuromorphic computing

The variability in memristors complements the stochastic behavior of biological neurons, with their randomness or unpredictability. The combination of the variability in memristors and the stochastic nature of biological neurons makes memristors well-suited for emulating the learning and memory processes in the human brain. In other words, memristors, with their inherent variability, can mimic the way our brains learn and remember information [26]. This alignment has led to advancements in the development of neuromorphic computing systems. This involves designing computer systems inspired by the structure and functioning of the human brain. These neuromorphic computing systems utilize memristors that are capable of executing complex tasks such as pattern recognition and image classification. Thus, the unique characteristics of memristors combined with their alignment with the stochastic nature of biological neurons contributes to the development of advanced computing systems that can perform complex tasks such as recognizing patterns and classifying images.

7.5.2 Pattern recognition

Pattern recognition in memristive devices with stochasticity involves leveraging the inherent variability or randomness within memristive systems, arising from factors such as manufacturing imperfections, to enhance the identification of patterns within weak signals. Memristive devices, which exhibit resistance changes based on applied voltages, benefit from the phenomenon of stochastic resonance, where controlled noise amplifies the recognition of faint patterns [27]. This proves particularly useful in scenarios with low signal-to-noise ratios, such as image and pattern recognition tasks, as the stochastic behavior in memristive systems contributes to improved accuracy and reliability in detecting intricate patterns within the input signals.

7.5.3 Hardware security

In the realm of hardware security applications, strategically capitalizing on the stochastic nature of memristive devices emerges as a promising avenue to fortify resilience against diverse forms of attacks. Stochasticity, referring to the inherent variability or randomness within memristive systems, can be intentionally harnessed to introduce an element of unpredictability into the hardware. This deliberate infusion of randomness serves to reduce vulnerability to attacks relying on deterministic patterns or predictability. Within the domain of hardware security, where safeguarding sensitive information holds utmost importance, the incorporation of stochastic elements into memristive systems becomes instrumental in establishing a robust defense mechanism [28]. This is particularly evident in cryptographic systems and secure communication protocols, where leveraging the stochasticity of memristive devices can substantially enhance hardware resilience. The introduction of controlled randomness adds a layer of complexity, making it significantly more challenging for adversaries to exploit vulnerabilities or decipher encrypted information. In essence, the utilization of memristive stochasticity contributes to fortifying the security landscape, providing an additional layer of protection crucial for safeguarding sensitive applications and upholding the integrity of hardware-based security measures.

7.5.4 Stochastic computing

The approach being discussed allows for the efficient execution of probabilistic and statistical computations. In simpler terms, it means that calculations involving probabilities and statistics can be performed effectively using this method [29]. In comparison to traditional deterministic computing, which follows strict rules and produces the same output for a given set of inputs, stochastic computing is being considered. Stochastic computing involves randomness in its operations and offers potential benefits in terms of power consumption and hardware simplicity. The advantages mentioned, such as lower power consumption and simplified hardware, suggest that using stochastic computing, which embraces randomness, can be more energy-efficient and require less complex hardware than traditional deterministic computing. The applications of this approach are varied and can be found in different fields [30]. Examples include Monte Carlo simulations, which are a method for solving mathematical problems using random sampling, financial modeling, which often involves dealing with uncertainties and probabilities, and machine learning algorithms, where probabilistic computations are essential.

7.5.5 Random number generation

The forefront of research now delves into the realm of memristive devices endowed with stochasticity for random number generation (RNG), representing an avant-garde pursuit to harness the intrinsic variability of memristive systems for the creation of genuinely random numbers [31]. In stark contrast to pseudo-random number generators relying on algorithms and seed values, memristive systems introduce a novel dimension of unpredictability owing to their inherent stochastic behavior, stemming from fabrication variations and material properties. The exploration of memristive stochasticity for RNG holds immense potential, particularly in domains where authentic randomness is paramount, such as cryptography, secure communication protocols, and simulations. In cryptography, the foundation of secure encryption keys relies on truly random numbers, augmenting the robustness of cryptographic algorithms against sophisticated attacks [32]. Likewise, in secure communication, the integration of genuinely random numbers contributes to the fortification of encryption schemes. Furthermore, in simulations that demand unpredictability, the utilization of memristive system-based RNG emerges as a valuable tool. As ongoing research progresses in this direction, the integration of memristive systems for RNG stands poised to redefine the landscape of randomness generation, ushering in a new era of security and reliability across a diverse spectrum of applications.

7.5.6 Noise suppression circuits

By strategically leveraging the principles of stochasticity, researchers are actively engaged in designing circuits based on memristive systems. The primary objective of this work is to proactively manage and diminish the impact of noise fluctuations within electronic systems. This collaborative initiative is propelled by the expectation that the successful integration of these memristor centric circuits could result in enhancements of the signal integrity and complete performance across a wide spectrum of electronic devices. The focal point of this concerted effort lies in addressing and proficiently controlling noise disturbances within electronic systems [33]. The envisioned memristive system-based circuits aspire to not only manage noise but also to elevate the reliability and efficiency of electronic operations. This is anticipated to make substantial contributions to the progress and evolution of electronic technology.

7.5.7 Exploring novel applications

The unique characteristics inherent in stochastic memristive systems persistently drive research efforts towards exploring memristive stochastic behavior for many applications that extend beyond its current boundaries. Potential areas of interest span the development of self-aligned circuits and the application of encryption techniques rooted in the establishment of reconfigurable and adaptive hardware systems [34]. These areas represent promising avenues where the distinctive properties of stochastic memristive systems can be leveraged to introduce innovative solutions and advancements, expanding their utility and impact across diverse technological domains.

7.6 Conclusion

The approach of stochastic memristive systems holds versatile applicability across diverse domains, spanning Monte Carlo simulations, modeling, and machine learning algorithms. It has significance in enhancing computational performance, and provides innovative solutions for tackling complex problems. Particularly in tasks involving probabilistic and statistical computations, integrating stochasticity into memristive systems offers a more effective solution. The emphasis here is on the transformative impact of introducing stochastic elements, extending beyond computational enhancements. The use of stochasticity in memristive systems has the potential to reshape the landscape of artificial intelligence, aiming for a more authentic replication of the intricate workings of the human brain in learning and memory emulation. This envisions a promising trajectory for the evolution of AI, highlighting continuous innovation in memristive systems [37]. Exploring new applications and refining existing ones are identified as crucial paths to push the boundaries of these systems in computing. Anticipating a dynamic field, ongoing advancements are expected to redefine the capabilities and possibilities of memristive systems, in a new era of computational potential. In addition to exploring the transformative impact of stochasticity, the underlying mechanisms which make these applications effective, researchers are delving into the intricate interplay between stochastic elements and the inherent characteristics of memristive systems, explaining the compatibility of enhanced computational work. Specific examples and case studies, such as the use of stochastic memristive devices in Monte Carlo simulations for modeling random processes, probabilistic learning algorithms for pattern recognition, and stochastic neural networks for uncertainty-aware decision making, showcase remarkable results achieved through the integration of stochasticity. These applications provide concrete instances where memristive systems not only enhance computational efficiency but also outperform traditional approaches in handling complex tasks involving variability, randomness, and high-dimensional data [37, 38]. While acknowledging substantial benefits, the discussion also addresses challenges and considerations associated with incorporating stochasticity into these systems. This balanced perspective adds depth to the explanation, fostering a comprehensive understanding of the complexities involved [38]. Theoretical implications of stochasticity are discussed, backed by empirical evidence, providing a practical and nuanced view. This comprehensive approach contributes to a more holistic understanding of how stochasticity shapes the future of memristive systems and their applications across various domains.

BEP in memristive systems encapsulates a sophisticated exploration into the nanoscale intricacies of memristors, devices that exhibit unique resistive switching behavior. Within this domain, the emphasis is specifically placed on the deliberate manipulation of the bottom electrode, a key element in the architecture of memristive systems. Memristors are characterized by their capacity to retain and alter their resistance states, a phenomenon critical for applications in non-volatile memory and neuromorphic computing. The bottom electrode is integral to this functionality, forming one of the interfaces where resistive switching occurs.

Perturbation refers to the intentional and controlled disturbance or modification of the bottom electrode used in experimental techniques [38]. The nature of perturbation can vary widely, encompassing electrical perturbations involving the application of voltage or current, thermal perturbations through controlled heating, and chemical perturbations involving targeted material modifications.

The mechanisms governing resistive switching, and consequently the performance of memristive devices, are strongly influenced by the structural and interfacial properties of the bottom electrode, which dictate charge transport, defect dynamics, and the stability of conductive filaments. Researchers seek to decipher how alterations to the bottom electrode influence the intricate interplay of charge carriers, defects, and interfaces, aiming to optimize the reliability, stability, and speed of memristors [20]. In the realm of non-volatile memory, insights gained from studying bottom electrode perturbation contribute to the development of more efficient and high-density storage solutions. Furthermore, the findings hold relevance for neuromorphic computing, where mimicking synaptic behaviors is crucial for building brain-inspired computational architectures. As the exploration of bottom electrode perturbation advances, it is leading to the discovery of novel phenomena and the development of innovative strategies for tailoring memristive systems to specific applications [37]. The continuous refinement of understanding in this area promises to open new possibilities in electronics, shaping the landscape of future computing and memory technologies.

Bibliography

[1] Yang J J, Strukov D B and Stewart D R 2012 Memristive devices for computing *Nat. Nanotechnol.* **8** 13–24

[2] Humood K, Saylan S, Mohammad B and Abi Jaoude M 2021 Effect of the compliance current on the retention time of Cu/HfO_2-based memristive devices *J. Electron. Mater.* **50** 4397–406

[3] Ielmini D 2011 Modeling the universal set/reset characteristics of bipolar RRAM by field- and temperature-driven filament growth *IEEE Trans. Electron Devices* **58** 4309–17

[4] Kim S *et al* 2013 Physical electro-thermal model of resistive switching in bi-layered resistance-change memory *Sci. Rep.* **3** 1680

[5] Karpov V G, Niraula D, Karpov I V and Kotlyar R 2017 Thermodynamics of phase transitions and bipolar filamentary switching in resistive random-access memory *Phys. Rev. Appl.* **8** 024028

[6] Agudov N V *et al* 2020 Nonstationary distributions and relaxation times in a stochastic model of memristor *J. Stat. Mech.* **2020** 024003

[7] Linn E, Siemon A, Waser R and Menzel S 2014 Applicability of well-established memristive models for simulations of resistive switching devices *IEEE Trans. Circuits Syst.* I **61** 2402–10

[8] Al-Shedivat M, Naous R, Cauwenberghs G and Salama K N 2015 Memristors empower spiking neurons with stochasticity *IEEE J. Emerg. Sel. Top. Curcuits Syst.* **5** 242–53

[9] Vincent A F *et al* 2015 Spin-transfer torque magnetic memory as a stochastic memristive synapse for neuromorphic systems *IEEE Trans. Biomed. Circuits Syst.* **9** 166–74

[10] Naous R, Al-Shedivat M and Salama K N 2016 Stochasticity modeling in memristors *IEEE Trans. Nanotechnol.* **15** 15–28

[11] Jun M, Wenkang X, Ping Z and Ge Z 2019 Synchronization between memristive and initial-dependent oscillators driven by noise *Physica* A **536** 122598

[12] Xu Y, Jia Y, Ma J, Alsaedi A and Ahmad B 2017 Synchronization between neurons coupled by memristor *Chaos, Solitons Fractals* **104** 435–42

[13] Alam M R, Najafi M H, Taherinejad N, Imani M and Gottumukkala R 2022 Stochastic computing in beyond von-Neumann era: processing bit-streams in memristive memory *IEEE Trans. Circuits Syst. Express Briefs* **69** 2423–7

[14] Lammie C, Eshraghian J K, Lu W D and Azghadi M R 2021 Memristive stochastic computing for deep learning parameter optimization *IEEE Trans. Circuits Syst. Express Briefs* **68** 1650–4

[15] Alam M R, Najafi M H and TaheriNejad N 2021 Exact stochastic computing multiplication in memristive memory *IEEE Design Test* **38** 36–43

[16] Knag P, Lu W and Zhang Z 2014 A native stochastic computing architecture enabled by memristors *IEEE Trans. Nanotechnol.* **13** 283–93

[17] Agrawal A *et al* 2020 Revisiting stochastic computing in the era of nanoscale nonvolatile technologies *IEEE Trans. Very Large Scale Integr. VLSI Syst.* **28** 2481–94

[18] Stathopoulos S, Serb A, Khiat A, Ogorzałek M and Prodromakis T 2019 A memristive switching uncertainty model *IEEE Trans. Electron Devices* **66** 2946–53

[19] Yang Y, Huang and Probing R 2018 Memristive switching in nanoionic devices *Nat. Electron.* **1** 274–87

[20] Zidan M A, Strachan J P and Lu W D 2018 The future of electronics based on memristive systems *Nat. Electron.* **1** 22–9

[21] Hongjian L, Lifeng M, Zidong W, Yurong L and Fuad E A 2020 An overview of stability analysis and state estimation for memristive neural networks *Neurocomputing* **391** 1–12

[22] Alawad M and Lin M 2019 Survey of stochastic-based computation paradigms *IEEE Trans. Emerg. Top. Comput.* **7** 98–114

[23] Soman S and Suri M 2016 Recent trends in neuromorphic engineering *Big Data Anal.* **1** 15

[24] Li J *et al* 2023 Sparse matrix multiplication in a record-low power self-rectifying memristor array for scientific computing *Sci. Adv.* **9** eadf7474

[25] Liu S, Wang Y, Fardad M and Varshney P K 2018 A memristor-based optimization framework for artificial intelligence applications *IEEE Circuits Syst. Mag.* **18** 29–44

[26] Cui J and Qiu Q 2016 Towards memristor based accelerator for sparse matrix vector multiplication *IEEE Int. Symp. on Circuits and Systems (ISCAS) (Montreal)* pp 121–4

[27] Bojnordi M N and Ipek E 2016 Memristive Boltzmann machine: a hardware accelerator for combinatorial optimization and deep learning *IEEE Int. Symp. on High Performance Computer Architecture (HPCA)* pp 1–13

[28] Sun Z and Huang R 2021 Time complexity of in-memory matrix-vector multiplication *IEEE Trans. Circuits Syst. Express Briefs* **68** 2785–9

[29] Li C *et al* 2018 Large memristor crossbars for analog computing *IEEE Int. Symp. on Circuits and Systems (ISCAS) (Florence, Italy)* pp 1–4

[30] Li J *et al* 2023 A memristive neural network based matrix equation solver with high versatility and high energy efficiency *Sci. China Inf. Sci.* **66** 122402

[31] Yu J, Nguyen H A D, Xie L, Taouil M and Hamdioui S 2018 Memristive devices for computation-in-memory *Design, Automation & Test in Europe Conf. & Exhibition (DATE) (Dresden, Germany)* pp 1646–51

[32] Ma W, Zidan M A and Lu W D 2018 Neuromorphic computing with memristive devices *Sci. China Inf. Sci.* **61** 060422

[33] Kumar S *et al* 2024 Investigation of filament formation and surface perturbation in nanoscale-Y_2O_3 memristor: a physical modeling approach *J. Electron. Mater.* **53** 2965–72

[34] Kim H D, Yun M J, Hong S M, Park J H, Jeon D S and Kim T G 2014 Impact of roughness of bottom electrodes on the resistive switching properties of platinum/nickel nitride/nickel 1 × 1 crossbar array resistive random access memory cells *Microelectron. Eng.* **126** 169

[35] Bao H *et al* 2022 Toward memristive in-memory computing: principles and applications *Front. Optoelectron.* **15** 23

[36] Liu H, Sun S, Liu J, Li Q, Diao J and Li Z 2021 Binary memristive synapse based vector neural network architecture and its application *IEEE Trans. Circuits Syst. Express Briefs* **68** 772–6

[37] Fyrigos I A, Ntinas V, Sirakoulis G C, Dimitrakis P and Karafyllidis I 2019 Memristor hardware accelerator of quantum computations *26th IEEE Int. Conf. on Electronics, Circuits and Systems (ICECS) (Genoa, Italy)* pp 799–802

[38] Karafyllidis I G, Sirakoulis G C and Dimitrakis P 2019 Memristive quantum computing simulator *IEEE Trans. Nanotechnol.* **18** 1015–22

[39] Bill J and Legenstein R 2014 A compound memristive synapse model for statistical learning through STDP in spiking neural networks *Front Neurosci.* **8** 412

IOP Publishing

Resistive Switching Systems for In-Memory Computation and Artificial Intelligence

Shaibal Mukherjee

Chapter 8

Integration of neuromorphic chips at the system level

8.1 Introduction to neuromorphic computing

Neuromorphic chips at the system level are a class of non-volatile memory devices whose electrical resistance depends on the history of the applied voltage and current. This means their resistance can be adjusted based on the amount and direction of the electric current that passes through them. Memristive systems can 'remember' the last resistance state even when the power is turned off [1], which makes them suitable for emulating synaptic connections in neural networks [2]. The integration of neuromorphic chips at the system level represents an advancement in computing, as in intelligent systems it closely emulates the intricate functionality of the human brain [3]. Neuromorphic computing has emerged as a highly promising paradigm, offering unprecedented potential for the development of cognitive systems capable of learning, adaptation, and complex pattern recognition. Among the hardware components which facilitate the efficient processing of neural inspired algorithms [4], memristive devices have emerged as key players, attracting considerable attention. Memristive devices exhibit unique properties that enable the emulation of synaptic behavior, mimicking the fundamental building blocks of neural networks with remarkable fidelity. The allure of memristive devices stems from their ability to facilitate dense, high-speed, and low-power signal processing [5], thus offering a compelling solution for the demanding requirements of neuromorphic computing architectures.

In this context, the integration of neuromorphic chips at the system level represents a crucial step forward, bridging the gap between theoretical concepts and practical realizations. By seamlessly integrating neuromorphic chips into larger computing systems, researchers can harness the full potential of these innovative technologies that allow groundbreaking applications in diverse domains, including

doi:10.1088/978-0-7503-6169-9ch8 © IOP Publishing Ltd 2025. All rights, including for text and data mining (TDM), artificial intelligence (AI) training, and similar technologies, are reserved.

artificial intelligence, robotics, and healthcare [6]. As researchers continue to push the boundaries of neuromorphic computing, integration of neuromorphic chips at the system level remains a central focus for developing next-generation intelligent systems that are not only powerful and efficient but also inherently adaptive. One promising direction is the use of memristive crossbar array (MCA)-based integration, which enables neuromorphic computation through efficient handling of inputs, outputs, and synaptic updates. In such architectures, the MCA manages a wide range of input–output mappings while maintaining synaptic weights across both internal and external domains. With full 8-bit input precision, these systems can support accurate output data collection, making them particularly useful for tasks such as image decomposition and other simulation-driven applications. This highlights the potential of MCAs to enhance the robustness and versatility of neuromorphic platforms [1].

Figure 8.1 shows the biological process of synapse function, where an axon from one neuron meets the dendrites of another neuron. It also highlights the signaling processes, such as neurotransmitter release and receptor activation, that enable communication between neurons, which is essential for processes such as learning and memory in the brain. Neuromorphic computing endeavors to mirror the structural and operational working of the human brain through hardware implementation. This innovative approach offers potential solutions to the challenges

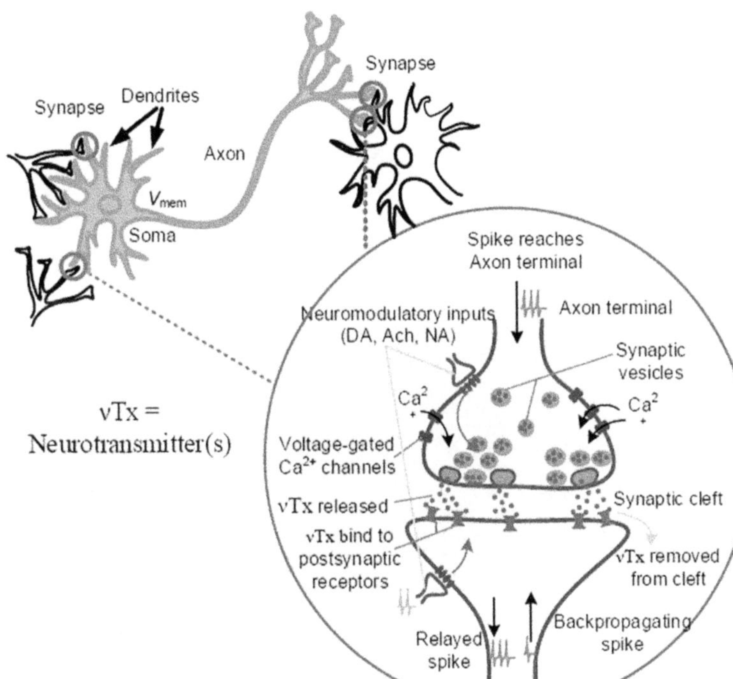

Figure 8.1. The synapse is created where the axonal terminal meets dendrites, with certain signaling mechanisms illustrated. (Adapted from [1]. CC BY 4.0.)

faced by conventional computers, including their high energy demands and struggles with tasks such as pattern recognition [6, 7]. At the heart of this field are memristive devices, which exhibit the distinctive property of having their electrical resistance modulated by the history of voltage or current stimuli they have experienced. This memory-dependent adaptability makes memristive devices highly suitable for emulating the synaptic functionalities of the human brain [8]. Neuromorphic computing, inspired by the structure and functionality of the human brain, is a cutting-edge approach to computing that aims to mimic the brain's efficient information processing capabilities. One key component of neuromorphic computing is the use of memristive devices, which are electronic components with memory properties that can mimic synaptic connections in the brain. Researchers and engineers are prepared to harness the capabilities of memristive devices in intelligent system design, paving the way for exceptional levels of performance, efficiency, and versatility [9].

8.1.1 Neuromorphic computing with memristive devices

Neuromorphic computing is an innovative approach to designing computational systems that mimic the structure and function of the human brain. By utilizing memristive devices, which are components that can change their resistance based on the voltage and current that has passed through them, neuromorphic systems can achieve highly efficient and parallel processing capabilities. Memristive devices are particularly well-suited for simulating synaptic weights in neural networks, allowing for more energy-efficient and scalable implementations of artificial intelligence and machine learning models [10]. This combination holds the promise of creating more powerful, adaptive, and efficient computing systems that can handle complex tasks with greater work. Figure 8.2 describes a synaptic set-up in a neuromorphic system where 16 individual bistable resistive RAMs (RRAMs) (devices that can retain two distinct resistance states) are arranged in a 4×4 grid, simulating a dendritic structure. The arrangement of these RRAMs helps to model how synaptic

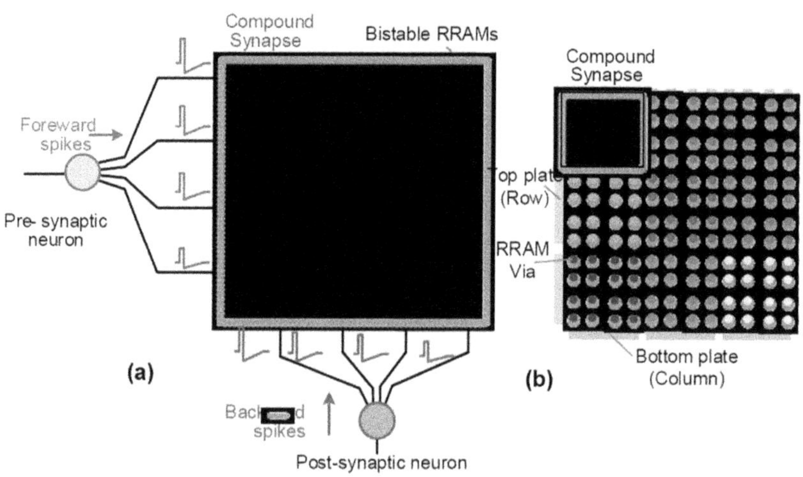

Figure 8.2. A complex synapse featuring 16 bistable RRAMs arranged in parallel within a 4×4 dendritic set-up, as depicted in the layout configuration. (Adapted from [1]. CC BY 4.0.)

connections operate in biological systems, with the ability to store and adjust synaptic weights through resistance changes. The figure highlights the potential for such architectures to enable parallel processing and energy-efficient learning mechanisms in neuromorphic computing.

8.1.1.1 Synaptic emulation

Memristive devices are a class of electronic components that possess unique properties which make them highly effective in replicating the behavior of synapses, which are the connections between neurons in the brain. Synapses play a crucial role in transmitting signals and facilitating communication between neurons, enabling the brain to process information and learn from experience [11]. In neuromorphic computing systems, which aim to mimic the structure and function of the human brain using electronic circuits, memristors serve a pivotal role. These devices have the capability to mimic the synaptic weights of biological neurons. Synaptic weight refers to the strength or ability of the connection between two neurons, determining the signals that are transmitted across the synapse. Adjusting the resistance of memristors can replicate the varying strengths of synaptic connections observed in the brain. This ability to mimic synaptic weights enables the creation of artificial neural networks (ANNs) within neuromorphic computing systems [12]. ANNs are computational models inspired by the biological neural networks of the brain. They consist of interconnected nodes, or artificial neurons, organized in layers. Memristors integrated into these networks act as analogy of biological synapses, modulating the flow of information between artificial neurons based on the strength of their connections. With memristors emulating synaptic weights, ANNs can learn and adapt to input patterns, similar to the human brain's ability to process and respond to stimuli [13]. Through a process known as synaptic plasticity, which involves the strengthening or weakening of synaptic connections in response to activity, ANNs can adjust their internal parameters to optimize performance and improve accuracy in tasks such as pattern recognition, data classification, and decision-making [14]. In essence, memristive devices enable neuromorphic computing systems to harness the principles of synaptic plasticity, paving the way for the development of intelligent systems that can mimic the learning capabilities of the human brain. This convergence of electronics and neuroscience holds promise for advancing fields such as artificial intelligence, cognitive computing, and brain-inspired computing [15].

8.1.1.2 Parallel processing

Memristive devices are a groundbreaking technology that facilitate parallel processing, a fundamental aspect of neuromorphic computing. In traditional computing, tasks are usually executed one after the other in a sequential way. However, human brains, with their intricate neural networks composed of billions of interconnected neurons, operate differently. They process information in parallel, meaning multiple computations occur simultaneously across the neural network. The memristive devices mimic the behavior of synapses in the brain, the connections between neurons where information is transmitted. Leveraging the memristive properties of these devices enables the construction of parallel processing architectures [16]. This means that instead of facing tasks sequentially as in traditional computers, memristive-based systems can perform multiple operations at the same time like the brain synapses processes information. Parallel processing architectures implemented with memristive devices bring about substantial enhancements in computational efficiency and speed. By harnessing the power of parallelism, tasks that would have taken considerable time in a traditional computing set-up can be executed much faster, leading to advancements in various fields such as artificial intelligence, scientific simulations, and data analysis. In essence, memristive devices allow for a computing paradigm that closely mimics the efficiency of the human brain, providing new possibilities for innovation and technological advancement [17].

8.1.1.3 Low power consumption

Neuromorphic computing leverages memristive devices that offer a paradigm shift in computational architecture, notably distinguished by its incomparable advantage of low power consumption, a feat unattainable by traditional computing methodologies. At the heart of this innovation lies the remarkable property of memristors—their ability to retain resistance states even in the absence of a power supply. This intrinsic characteristic revolutionizes energy dynamics in computational systems. In traditional computing architectures, power consumption remains a universal challenge as constant energy supply is required to sustain operations [18]. Conversely, memristive devices consume minimal energy to maintain synaptic weights. This efficiency stems from their unique property of retaining resistance states independently, thereby eliminating the need for continuous power supply. Consider the implications of such efficiency in modern computing—with the increase of data driven applications demanding increasingly sophisticated processing capabilities, conventional systems strain under the weight of accelerating power demands [19]. In contrast, neuromorphic computing powered by memristors offers sustainability and resource optimization. Furthermore, the energy-efficient nature of memristive neuromorphic architectures extends beyond simple operational computation. This universal approach aligns effortlessly with the global imperative for sustainable technological advancement. In essence, the superiority of neuromorphic computing with memristive devices indicates a transformative epoch in computational efficiency by surpassing the limitations of traditional architectures and promoting energy-efficient design [20].

8.1.1.4 Adaptive learning

Memristive devices act as artificial synapses, forming the foundation of adaptive learning algorithms in neuromorphic systems. Much like their biological counterparts, they enable efficient, continuous learning and dynamic adaptation to incoming information, thereby bridging the gap between hardware and brain-inspired intelligence [21]. This dynamic feature highlights a field of cognitive functions crucial for a countless number of applications, from pattern recognition to decision-making, forcing neuromorphic computing to the foreground of intelligent system design. At the heart of this capability lies the intrinsic behavior of memristors, which emulate the synaptic plasticity observed in biological neural networks. Synaptic plasticity, the ability of synapses to strengthen or weaken over time in response to activity, is a fundamental mechanism underpinning learning and memory in the brain [22]. Memristive devices replicate this phenomenon by modulating their electrical resistance based on the intensity and frequency of input signals, thereby mirroring the synaptic efficacy changes essential for learning. The integration of memristors into neuromorphic architectures enables the realization of adaptive learning algorithms that mimic the brain's ability to continuously adapt and refine its synaptic connections. These algorithms leverage the synaptic plasticity afforded by memristive devices to iteratively adjust the strengths of connections (synaptic weights) between artificial neurons in response to input stimuli [23]. Through this iterative process, the system refines its internal representation of patterns in the data, enhancing its ability to recognize, classify, and make decisions with increasing accuracy over time. This adaptability is indispensable for tasks characterized by evolving environments, dynamic datasets, and the influx of new information. In pattern recognition applications, for example, the ability to adapt synaptic weights enables the system to discern subtle variations in input patterns, thereby improving classification accuracy and robustness against noise or variability. Similarly, in decision-making scenarios, adaptive learning algorithms empower the system to assimilate new insights and update its decision-making criteria, ensuring relevance and efficacy in real-time contexts [24]. Moreover, the continuous learning capability facilitated by memristive devices enables neuromorphic systems to mimic the incremental learning process observed in biological organisms. This property is particularly advantageous in scenarios where the system operates in open-ended environments with evolving tasks or objectives, as it can seamlessly integrate new knowledge and experiences without the need for explicit reprogramming or retraining. The integration of memristive devices and adaptive learning algorithms is the essence of neuromorphic computing, allowing artificial systems with the capacity for autonomous, aware adaptation [25]. By emulating the plasticity and adaptability inherent in biological neural networks, these systems transcend the constraints of static programming paradigms, paving the way for intelligent machines capable of dynamic, data driven decision-making in complex and ever-changing environments.

8.1.1.5 Biological plausibility

Neuromorphic computing, empowered by memristive devices, represents a revolutionary approach to artificial intelligence that aspires to replicate the intricacies of the human brain in computational models, endeavoring to emulate not only the structural organization of the brain but also its fundamental mechanisms of information processing and learning. By harnessing the principles of neural architecture and synaptic plasticity, memristive-based neuromorphic systems hold the promise of human-like cognitive capabilities and mastering complex cognitive tasks with extraordinary efficiency and adaptability [26]. Central to the biologically inspired paradigm of neuromorphic computing is the concept of neural emulation. Different to conventional computing methodologies that rely on rigid, predefined algorithms, neuromorphic systems seek to model the dynamic interactions between neurons, synapses, and circuits, mirroring the decentralized, parallel processing architecture of the brain. Memristive devices play a pivotal role in this endeavor, serving as the building blocks that mimic the synaptic connections between biological neurons. Crucially, memristors emulate the synaptic plasticity observed in biological synapses, enabling them to modulate their electrical resistance based on their history of electrical activity [27]. The ability of biological synapses to strengthen or weaken in response to neuronal activity is known as long-term potentiation (LTP) and long-term depression (LTD).

As illustrated in figure 8.3, the exceptional properties of 2D materials, such as low power consumption, gate tunability, compatibility with hetero-integration, and high flexibility, position them as promising candidates for artificial synaptic devices, enabling energy-efficient neuromorphic computing. By leveraging these emerging materials, fundamental synaptic functions such as short-term plasticity (STP), LTP, paired-pulse facilitation (PPF), and spike-timing-dependent plasticity (STDP) can be effectively implemented in ANNs. Furthermore, due to their excellent electrostatic coupling, 2D materials facilitate advanced functionalities, including precise tuning of synaptic states, accelerated synaptic learning, and hetero-synaptic cooperation. These capabilities are challenging to achieve in conventional memristors due to their inherent structural limitations [27].

Another significant characteristic of a memristive system is its ability to transition from short-term memory (STM) to long-term memory (LTM), which is effectively captured by the proposed analytical model. As illustrated in figure 8.4(a), the memristive device is subjected to 20 consecutive input pulses with a +4 V amplitude and a 40% duty cycle. Initially, each electrical stimulus increases the device's conductivity, followed by a decay due to spontaneous diffusion. However, when

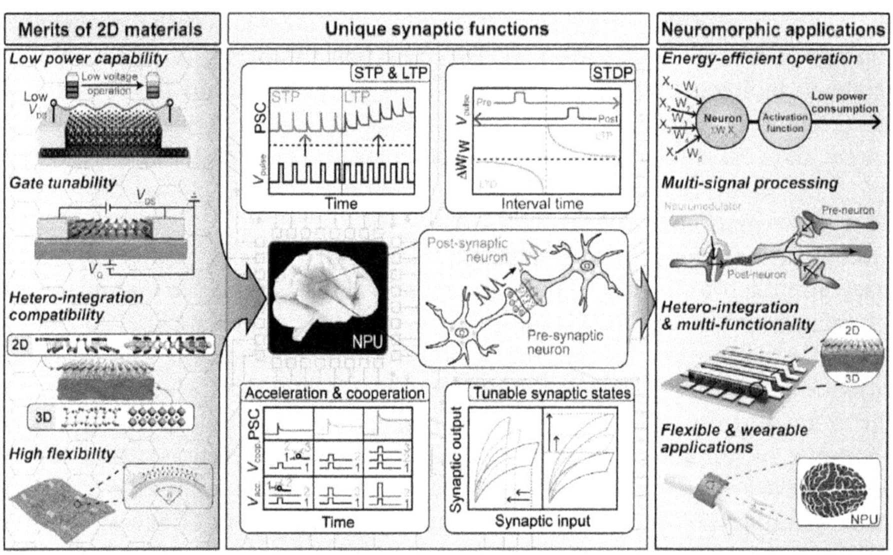

Figure 8.3. Perspectives and potential applications of neuromorphic computing enabled by the distinctive properties of 2D materials. (Reproduced with permission from [27]. Copyright 2020 John Wiley and Sons.)

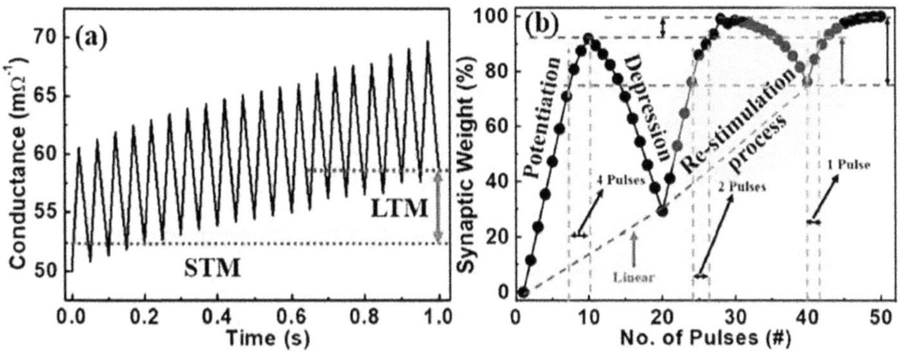

Figure 8.4. (a) The transition from STM to LTM, where conductance changes in response to successive stimulation pulses. (b) The potentiation and depression processes, including the effects of restimulation. (Reproduced with permission from [28]. Copyright 2022 IOP Publishing.)

the time interval between successive stimulations is relatively short, ranging from 5 to 30 ms, an overall increase in conductance is observed despite the decay, as shown in figure 8.4(a). This effect arises from the competition between diffusion and ion migration [28]. Additionally, the stabilization of the switching process and the persistence of LTM indicate the formation of new synaptic connections and modifications in the pulse shape and size, providing additional pathways for synaptic transmission. Over time, LTM gradually fades, demonstrating that synaptic connections weaken, although at a much slower rate than the decay observed in STM [28].

Figure 8.4(b) illustrates the synaptic plasticity behavior of the memristive device in terms of potentiation and depression processes [28]. Under a positive electrical stimulus, the synaptic weight or normalized conductance of the memristive device continuously strengthens, whereas a negative stimulus gradually weakens it. Furthermore, figure 8.4(b) highlights the restimulation process following the initial potentiation and depression stages, where fewer electrical stimuli are required to reach the same level of memory learning. This behavior closely resembles the learning mechanisms observed in biological systems, facilitating a more efficient relearning process [28].

The artificial synapse's potentiation and depression characteristics are replicated by applying input voltage pulses. Figure 8.5(a) illustrates the potentiation (P) process, where the device conductance gradually increases under the influence of 50 consecutive positive pulses with an amplitude of +1.3 V and a pulse width (PW) of 10 ms. Conversely, figure 8.5(b) depicts the depression (D) process, where 50 negative pulses with an amplitude of −1.0 V and a PW of 10 ms are applied, leading to a reduction in conductance. The read voltage pulse (V_R) used in these measurements is 0.1 V.

Figure 8.5(c) and (d) present the combined plot of potentiation and depression along with the normalized current distribution. The nonlinearity (NL) factor for the P and D processes is calculated to be 0.67 at pulse number (n) = 25. The NL factor is normalized with respect to total plasticity and ranges from 0 to 1 during a synaptic

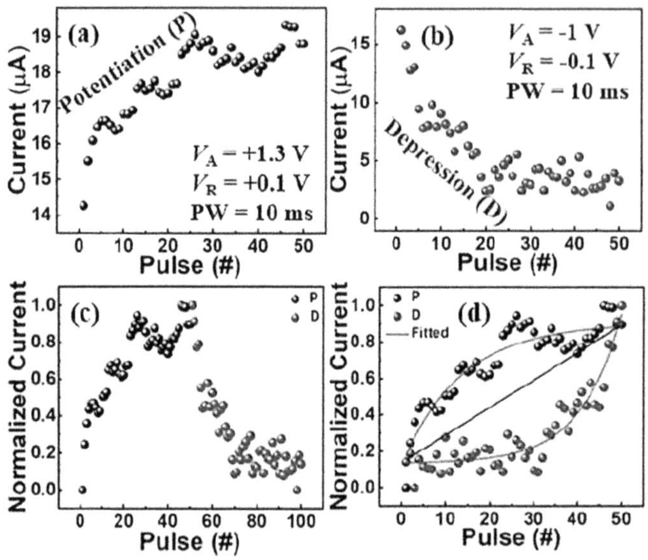

Figure 8.5. (a) Potentiation, (b) depression, and (c) and (d) normalized current distribution representing the synaptic behavior of the MCA. The input pulse parameters are provided in the insets of (a) and (b). (Reproduced with permission from [29]. Copyright 2023 IEEE.)

weight update sequence consisting of an equal number (*N*) of successive P pulses and D pulses. Ideally, in a perfectly linear synaptic weight update, the NL value would be 0 [29], aligning with the black linear reference line in figure 8.5(d). The obtained memristive device characteristics closely match the potentiation and depression behaviors observed in biological synapses [29].

By emulating these synaptic dynamics, memristive-based neuromorphic systems can encode and store information in a manner similar to the brain's synaptic memory, facilitating learning and adaptation over time. Furthermore, the parallelism inherent in neuromorphic architectures, coupled with the energy-efficient properties of memristive devices, enables the efficient processing of large-scale neural networks. This scalability and energy efficiency are crucial for tackling complex cognitive tasks that demand massive computational resources, such as image recognition, natural language processing, and autonomous decision-making [30]. The pursuit of human-like cognitive abilities through memristive-based neuromorphic computing extends beyond mere emulation of brain structure and function. It encompasses the aspiration to imbue artificial systems with the capacity for perception, learning, reasoning, and decision-making attributes traditionally associated with human intelligence. By harnessing the power of memristors to emulate synaptic plasticity and neural dynamics, neuromorphic systems have the potential to exhibit cognitive traits akin to human cognition, including adaptability, context-sensitivity, and creativity. In essence, neuromorphic computing with memristive devices represents a convergence of neuroscience, engineering, and computer science, aimed at unlocking the mysteries of the human brain and controlling its computational process. By striving for biologically plausible computational models, researchers seek not only to advance the frontiers of artificial intelligence but also to deepen our understanding of the principles underlying cognition and consciousness. In doing so, they pave the way for a future where machines possess human-like cognitive abilities, revolutionizing industries, transforming societies, and reshaping the very fabric of human–machine interaction [22–25].

8.2 Neuromorphic characteristics

Neuromorphic computing aims to replicate the neural architecture and operational processes of the human brain, creating more efficient and intelligent systems for information processing. A crucial technological enabler in this paradigm is the memristive crossbar array, which takes advantage of the unique properties of memristors to offer a compact, energy-efficient, and highly parallel computing architecture [30]. Unlike traditional digital components, memristors are capable of storing data as analog values, similar to the strength of synaptic connections in biological neural networks. This feature enables a more nuanced form of data representation that overcomes the limitations inherent in binary systems. Memristors' ability to adjust resistance based on voltage inputs offers a continuous, dynamic method for encoding information, reflecting the inherent flexibility of the brain's synaptic connections.

One of the key advantages of memristors is their ability to exhibit STDP, a learning mechanism inspired by biological systems. STDP allows the memristive device to adjust its resistance based on the timing of voltage spikes, which determines the strength of the synaptic connection between neurons [5]. This ability to modulate synaptic strength according to the temporal relationships between spikes enables memristive systems to mimic the adaptive learning processes of the human brain, providing a biologically inspired approach to computation. By leveraging these dynamic properties, neuromorphic systems can perform real-time learning and adaptation, much like the human brain.

The architecture of memristive crossbar arrays is designed to support high connectivity, akin to the dense synaptic networks found in biological neural systems. This architecture enables a large number of synaptic connections to be integrated within a small physical footprint. Memristive crossbar arrays can be scaled to nanometer dimensions, making them well-suited for tasks requiring intensive data processing, such as pattern recognition, image analysis, and real-time analytics [13]. The high-density and parallel processing capabilities of these arrays enable the simultaneous execution of multiple computations, resulting in dramatic improvements in both speed and efficiency. By mimicking the parallel nature of biological neural networks, memristive systems can tackle complex problems more efficiently than traditional architectures.

In addition to their computational efficiency, memristors are known for their energy efficiency. Being non-volatile devices, memristors retain information without requiring power, which significantly reduces energy consumption. This non-volatility allows memristive systems to retain data without constantly refreshing memory, unlike conventional systems. Furthermore, in-memory analog computation can be executed directly within the memristive crossbar arrays, eliminating the energy costs typically associated with transferring data between processing and memory units [18]. This reduction in energy overhead aligns with the goal of energy-efficient computing, in particular for applications in edge devices and Internet of Things (IoT) systems, where low power consumption is paramount.

Memristive systems also align with the Hebbian learning principle, where the simultaneous activation of presynaptic and postsynaptic neurons strengthens their connection. This feature supports the development of self-organizing and adaptive computing systems that can adjust their behavior based on input data and interactions. By executing learning algorithms directly within the memristive crossbar arrays, these systems can learn in real time, without relying on external computational resources. This localized learning approach enhances the overall efficiency and responsiveness of the system [9].

The inherent redundancy and connectivity of the memristive crossbar architecture also provide fault tolerance, which is a critical aspect for ensuring reliable operation in practical applications. Even in the event of hardware failures or errors, the system can continue functioning, ensuring robustness and minimizing downtime. Additionally, advanced error correction techniques can be integrated into the system to further enhance computational accuracy and resilience [7].

In conclusion, memristive crossbar arrays offer transformative potential for neuromorphic computing. By combining low power consumption, high-density parallel computation, and adaptive learning capabilities, these arrays represent a foundational technology for the next generation of intelligent systems. Their ability to mimic the structure and function of biological neural networks positions them as a key enabler of advanced computing architectures that can power applications ranging from artificial intelligence to cognitive computing, and beyond [11].

8.3 System-level integration challenges

System-level integration involves addressing a spectrum of interconnected challenges across hardware, software, communication protocols, and overarching system architecture. A detailed exploration of these challenges is provided below, highlighting their nuances and potential solutions [4].

Integrating complex systems from multiple vendors presents several challenges related to compatibility, scalability, security, and performance, which must be addressed to ensure seamless interoperability. These systems often utilize different technologies, standards, and communication protocols, which can lead to integration difficulties [3]. Ensuring that these disparate components work together seamlessly requires careful consideration of both hardware and software aspects. The main challenge lies in ensuring that the different components can interact effectively despite their differences in architecture and functionality. For example, integrating proprietary technologies might require custom solutions such as specialized adapters or middleware, which can add complexity and cost to the system integration process.

One of the primary approaches to overcome these compatibility and interoperability issues is the adoption of standardized interfaces and communication protocols.

Standards, such as communication protocols for the IoT, can provide a unified way for disparate components to communicate and exchange data, ensuring consistency across the entire system. Additionally, middleware plays a critical role in bridging the gap between incompatible systems by acting as an intermediary layer that translates and facilitates communication between different system components. Middleware can help manage data flow, standardize communication, and make it easier to integrate systems that might otherwise be incompatible. Furthermore, implementing custom application programming interfaces (APIs) and adapters is another viable solution. These tools allow proprietary systems to communicate by providing a layer that translates between the technologies involved, making it easier to integrate systems with differing architectures [11].

As the system grows in complexity, the number of interactions and dependencies between components increases, leading to potential inefficiencies and performance degradation. For instance, as more components are added, the system may become harder to manage, requiring additional maintenance and troubleshooting. To manage this complexity, a modular design approach can be adopted. This involves breaking down the system into smaller, independent modules that can be developed, tested, and maintained separately. Modular design improves the scalability of the system and allows for easier management of resources and updates [13]. Additionally, advanced simulation tools can be used early in the design process to predict and address potential integration issues before they arise. Simulation environments allow developers to test the system's behavior in a virtual setting, helping identify bottlenecks, performance issues, and integration conflicts. This proactive approach allows for more efficient and effective integration efforts. Moreover, adopting an iterative integration strategy, where components are integrated and tested incrementally, can ensure that each module works as expected before proceeding to the next phase. This approach minimizes risks and allows for quicker identification and resolution of issues [15].

Scalability is another critical challenge in system integration, as systems must be capable of handling fluctuating workloads while maintaining performance and reliability. When systems scale up, new bottlenecks may emerge in terms of data throughput, network capacity, or computational resources, affecting overall system performance. Conversely, scaling down a system can lead to the loss of key functionality. To address these challenges, elastic architectures can be employed. These architectures enable systems to scale dynamically, adjusting resources according to workload demands. This elasticity can be achieved through cloud-based infrastructure or on-premise solutions that offer on-the-fly resource allocation based on real-time needs. Additionally, load balancing techniques are essential to distribute workloads evenly across available resources, preventing any single component from becoming a performance bottleneck. Proper load balancing ensures that the system operates efficiently even under peak demand. Another important aspect of scalability is future-proof planning, where the system is designed with potential future growth in mind. This involves considering not only the current needs but also how the system may need to scale as technology advances and usage patterns change [17].

Security and privacy are major concerns when integrating systems from different vendors, as increased integration typically results in a larger attack surface. Systems become more vulnerable to unauthorized access and data breaches as more components are connected and more data are exchanged between them. To mitigate these risks, it is critical to implement robust security measures such as data encryption. Encrypting data both at rest and in transit ensures that sensitive information remains protected even if intercepted or accessed by unauthorized parties. Additionally, implementing access control mechanisms, such as role-based or attribute-based access control, ensures that only authorized users or systems can interact with sensitive components. This provides an added layer of security by restricting access to critical systems based on user roles or attributes. Regular security audits and penetration testing are also necessary to identify and address vulnerabilities. These audits help ensure that the system is resilient to new and emerging threats and that vulnerabilities are addressed before they can be exploited [18].

Reliability and fault tolerance are key considerations in system integration, as failures in one component can often lead to cascading failures that affect the entire system. This is particularly important in mission-critical applications where up-time is essential. To improve system reliability, redundancy can be introduced at various levels. Redundant components, whether in hardware or software, act as backups in case of failure, ensuring that the system continues to function even if one part fails. Error detection and correction mechanisms also play a vital role in maintaining system reliability. These systems automatically detect errors in real time and correct them before they lead to performance degradation or failure. Additionally, failover mechanisms can be implemented, allowing the system to automatically switch to backup components in the event of a failure, minimizing downtime and maintaining service availability [19].

Testing and validation are vital to ensure that the integrated system works as intended under a wide range of conditions. Given the complexity of modern systems, exhaustive testing is often impractical, which makes it important to use automated testing tools for regression and performance testing. These tools help ensure that the system's core functionality remains intact even as new features are added or existing components are updated. Scenario simulation is another valuable technique, allowing the system to be tested under real-world conditions, including stress tests and performance under load. This helps identify potential failure points and ensure that the system can handle extreme scenarios. Validation frameworks are also essential to ensure that the system complies with regulatory, functional, and performance requirements. By implementing these frameworks, developers can guarantee that the system meets the necessary standards before deployment.

In real-time applications, maintaining synchronization and precise timing across components is crucial, particularly in distributed computing environments. To address timing challenges, time-triggered communication protocols such as time-sensitive networking (TSN) can be used. These protocols enable synchronized communication between different system components, ensuring that all parts of the system remain in sync, which is particularly important in mission-critical applications, such as industrial control systems or autonomous vehicles.

Additionally, global clocks and centralized or distributed clock synchronization mechanisms help maintain consistency across distributed systems. These clocks ensure that all nodes in the system are synchronized to the same time reference, which is essential for coordinated operations. Minimizing latency is another critical aspect of real-time systems. Latency optimization strategies, such as optimizing network design and communication paths, help reduce delays and ensure timely data processing [21].

Power efficiency is a growing concern in integrated systems, in particular for portable devices or edge systems where power consumption is limited. To address power efficiency challenges, dynamic power management techniques can be employed, allowing the system to adjust its power usage based on workload demands. This reduces power consumption during idle periods while maintaining performance when required. Low-power components, such as energy-efficient processors and memory devices, can further reduce overall system power consumption. Effective thermal management is also essential to prevent overheating and maintain system stability. This can include using cooling solutions such as heat sinks, fans, or passive cooling methods to keep the system at optimal operating temperatures [8].

Cost and timeliness are often challenges in large-scale system integration projects, where unforeseen complexities can lead to budget overruns and delays. Detailed planning, including risk assessments and contingency measures, is essential to mitigate these challenges. Agile development methodologies can be adopted to allow for iterative progress and quick adaptation to changes, ensuring that issues are addressed promptly and that the project stays on track. Resource allocation must also be carefully managed to avoid delays, ensuring that sufficient resources are available throughout the project lifecycle [10].

Finally, stakeholder collaboration is critical to the success of system integration. Miscommunication or conflicting priorities among stakeholders can derail integration efforts, making it important to maintain clear and consistent communication. Centralized communication platforms and frequent progress check-ins help ensure that all stakeholders remain aligned throughout the integration process. Clear documentation is also essential to provide a record of all decisions, changes, and updates made during the integration process, ensuring that all team members and stakeholders have access to up-to-date information [22]. Addressing these system integration challenges requires a comprehensive, multidisciplinary approach that combines technical expertise, effective project management, and strong collaboration among stakeholders. By adopting strategies such as modular design, standardized interfaces, security best practices, and proactive testing, organizations can successfully navigate these challenges and achieve successful system-level integration.

8.3.1 Integration challenges in neuromorphic computing

Integration challenges in neuromorphic computing stem from the complex task of replicating the functionality of biological neural networks within hardware and software systems. One of the most significant hurdles in this integration process is the co-design of hardware and software components. Neuromorphic systems require highly specialized architectures that are capable of efficiently executing neural network computations, particularly in models such as spiking neural networks (SNNs) or recurrent neural networks (RNNs). These architectures must be tailored to mimic the biological processes of the brain, which is a nontrivial task. A critical aspect of integration involves ensuring these custom hardware designs work seamlessly with existing software frameworks used for neural network training and inference [17]. However, the lack of compatibility between traditional machine learning tools, which are optimized for von Neumann-based systems, and neuromorphic hardware complicates this process. As a result, new frameworks or significant adaptations to existing ones are necessary to bridge this gap and facilitate efficient integration.

The diversity of neural network topologies further amplifies the integration challenge. Each network topology, whether it is an SNN, a feedforward model, or a more complex architecture such as a deep recurrent network, comes with distinct requirements in terms of data flow, memory access, and computational processes. Ensuring the efficient operation of such diverse networks within a unified neuromorphic system demands highly modular and adaptable designs. This modularity is essential for accommodating the unique requirements of different neural network models. Moreover, memory systems play a crucial role in this context, as they must support the efficient storage and retrieval of synaptic weights and model parameters. Traditional memory technologies such as DRAM and SRAM are not designed for these specialized needs, often leading to insufficient performance [13]. This limitation has driven the exploration and development of novel memory solutions, including RRAM and phase-change memory (PCM), which offer non-volatile, energy-efficient storage that aligns with the requirements of neuromorphic computing.

Energy efficiency is another central pillar of neuromorphic computing. Biological brains operate with remarkable energy efficiency, processing vast amounts of information while consuming minimal power. Achieving similar energy efficiency in artificial systems remains a significant challenge, particularly when scaling systems for practical applications. Neuromorphic hardware must incorporate low-power components and adopt energy-aware design strategies, such as dynamic voltage scaling and power gating, to reduce overall energy consumption. These strategies must be carefully balanced with the need for high computational performance to effectively handle complex tasks, including real-time analytics, decision-making, and adaptive learning. Energy-efficient designs are particularly important for portable applications such as robotics and IoT devices, where power constraints are often stringent [14].

Scalability and connectivity are also essential considerations for deploying neuromorphic systems at scale. The dense connectivity of biological neural networks where every neuron is connected to many others presents a significant challenge when replicating this structure in hardware. Achieving similar connectivity in neuromorphic systems requires scalable communication protocols and interconnects that can support low latency and high bandwidth. Additionally, as neuromorphic processors are integrated into larger systems, such as robotics platforms or IoT networks, the need for domain-specific adjustments becomes more pronounced. Each application may demand customized solutions for communication, resource allocation, and task management to ensure that neuromorphic components work optimally within the broader system [11].

Validation and testing of neuromorphic systems are particularly challenging due to the stochastic nature of spiking behavior and the inherent complexity of neuromorphic architectures. Traditional testing methods are not sufficient to evaluate the performance and reliability of neuromorphic systems. Therefore, advanced testing methodologies, including hardware-in-the-loop simulations, are essential to assess the behavior of the system in real-world scenarios. These simulations must account for the dynamic and unpredictable nature of neural network activity, which requires specialized tools and techniques. Furthermore, comprehensive error detection and correction mechanisms must be in place to ensure that neuromorphic systems can function reliably under a range of conditions, including noisy environments and hardware aging [8].

Addressing these integration challenges requires interdisciplinary collaboration, involving expertise from neuroscience, computer engineering, materials science, and software development. This collaboration will facilitate the design of systems that are both functional and efficient while adhering to the principles of neuromorphic computing. Partnerships between academia, industry, and research institutions are critical for driving innovation and accelerating progress in the field. Moreover, the development of open-source platforms and shared resources can foster collaboration across different sectors and provide valuable insights for addressing complex integration issues. By tackling these challenges head-on, neuromorphic computing holds the potential to revolutionize fields such as robotics, artificial intelligence (AI), and sensor networks, paving the way for intelligent, energy-efficient systems that closely mimic the processing capabilities of the human brain [16].

8.3.2 Compatibility with existing system architectures

Integrating neuromorphic computing into existing systems presents a series of unique challenges, primarily due to the need for compatibility with established architectures, protocols, and workflows. Many industries have made significant investments in traditional computing infrastructures, creating a situation where seamless interoperability between neuromorphic technologies and these systems becomes a critical concern. Neuromorphic systems, designed to mimic brain-like processing, often require specialized hardware such as massively parallel processing units and innovative memory architectures that can store synaptic weights. Traditional systems, which were not designed with these advanced requirements in mind, require the development of new interfaces and protocols to bridge the gap between neuromorphic and conventional components [2].

On the software side, the existing frameworks used for neural network training and inference may not be directly applicable to neuromorphic hardware. These frameworks are typically optimized for von Neumann architectures, which follow a sequential, centralized processing model. In contrast, neuromorphic systems operate using event-driven, parallel processing approaches that often involve SNNs or other bio-inspired mechanisms. This significant departure from traditional approaches necessitates substantial modifications to existing tools or, in some cases, the creation of entirely new ones. For instance, compilers, simulators, and optimization algorithms need to be reimagined to work within the unique operational paradigms of neuromorphic systems. Developers will need to be equipped with the skills to adapt to new programming models, such as those suited for SNNs, where communication between neurons occurs through discrete spikes rather than continuous signals [5].

The compatibility challenges extend beyond hardware and software to include system-level integration. Ensuring that data formats, communication protocols, and interfaces can operate seamlessly across traditional and neuromorphic platforms is essential. This integration is particularly challenging when considering real-world deployments, where neuromorphic systems need to be incorporated into existing infrastructures such as sensor networks, data pipelines, and control systems. These systems often involve a range of legacy technologies and standards, making the alignment of operational parameters, data flow, and performance requirements a complex task. Ensuring performance consistency during integration requires careful coordination to maintain system stability while accommodating new technologies [13].

To address these integration challenges, a concerted effort from researchers, engineers, and industry stakeholders is necessary. The development of standardized interfaces and protocols is a crucial step toward achieving compatibility and fostering easier integration. Open standards, for example, can help unify diverse systems, enabling smoother communication between neuromorphic and traditional components. Additionally, providing migration strategies and transition frameworks for organizations looking to adopt neuromorphic computing can help reduce the barriers to adoption. These frameworks could include hybrid architectures, which leverage the complementary strengths of both traditional and neuromorphic systems during the transitional phase. Hybrid systems would allow organizations to take advantage of the existing infrastructure while gradually incorporating neuromorphic elements to enhance performance and energy efficiency [11].

Ultimately, overcoming these compatibility challenges is vital for the broader adoption of neuromorphic computing. It requires collaborative innovation to harmonize new technologies with existing ecosystems, ensuring that the transformative potential of neuromorphic systems can be fully realized across various industries, including robotics, artificial intelligence, autonomous vehicles, and beyond. This approach will allow neuromorphic computing to offer its distinct advantages, such as energy efficiency, scalability, and adaptability, within the framework of existing technological and organizational structures [13].

8.4 Techniques for exploiting memristive devices

The exploration of techniques for exploiting memristive devices in neuromorphic computing delves deeply into the complexities of integrating these devices into computational frameworks to harness their unique properties for synaptic computations [19]. Memristive devices, characterized by their nonlinear resistive behavior and ability to store analog resistance states, hold significant potential for emulating the functionalities of biological synapses within neural networks [25]. These devices are central to neuromorphic computing due to their resemblance to synaptic behavior, allowing for efficient data storage and processing within a unified framework. However, their integration into computational systems involves addressing several intricate technical challenges and optimizing their design for specific applications [4].

One prominent technique involves leveraging memristive devices as analog synapses in ANN implementations. Memristive devices can encode synaptic weights in their resistance states, enabling parallel processing and reducing energy consumption during computation. This analog approach allows for the representation of continuous weight values, which is closer to the functionality of biological synapses compared to the binary weights in conventional digital systems. The use of memristive devices for synaptic weight storage and computation could lead to breakthroughs in energy-efficient and highly parallel neuromorphic systems. However, achieving this requires overcoming challenges associated with device variability, nonlinear conductance characteristics, and limited endurance. For example, variations in resistance states due to fabrication inconsistencies or operational aging can lead to inaccuracies in weight storage, which affects the overall performance of neural network computations. Advanced calibration techniques, including adaptive tuning algorithms and feedback control mechanisms, are essential to ensure precise encoding and retrieval of synaptic weights [11].

Another significant avenue explores the use of memristive devices' non-volatility and low-power operation for implementing persistent memory and state retention mechanisms in neuromorphic systems. The inherent ability of memristive devices to maintain their resistance states without requiring a continuous power supply makes them ideal for energy-efficient and fault-tolerant computational paradigms. This property is particularly advantageous in edge computing and IoT applications, where power efficiency is critical. Nonetheless, ensuring the reliability of memristive-based memory arrays in the face of noise, environmental perturbations, and aging effects remains a major challenge. Techniques such as error correction codes (ECC), redundancy in array design, and noise-tolerant programming algorithms have been proposed to mitigate these issues. Additionally, research into advanced materials and device structures aims to enhance the endurance and stability of memristive devices under repeated operation cycles [5].

Memristive devices also enable the realization of unconventional computing architectures inspired by the brain's principles of plasticity and self-organization [28]. These architectures leverage the dynamic conductance modulation of memristive devices to emulate synaptic plasticity and implement learning mechanisms directly in hardware. For example, LTP and LTD key processes in synaptic learning can be mimicked by gradually altering the resistance states of memristive devices through controlled electrical pulses. This approach has profound implications for creating adaptive, self-learning systems capable of performing tasks such as pattern recognition, decision-making, and real-time learning. However, designing and optimizing neuromorphic circuits that incorporate memristive devices requires careful consideration of factors such as learning stability, energy dissipation, and computational overhead. Additionally, achieving the desired learning dynamics involves the co-design of algorithms and hardware that can fully exploit the analog nature of memristive devices while ensuring compatibility with digital processing environments [12].

In summary, the exploration of techniques for utilizing memristive devices in neuromorphic computing represents a cutting-edge frontier in research. These efforts aim to develop efficient, adaptive, and brain-inspired computational systems that leverage the unique properties of memristive devices. However, addressing the challenges associated with device variability, reliability, and system-level integration is critical for unlocking their full potential. Future advancements in memristive-based neuromorphic computing will require interdisciplinary collaboration across fields such as materials science, device physics, computer architecture, and machine learning. Such collaborations will accelerate the development of next-generation neuromorphic platforms that can deliver unprecedented energy efficiency, scalability, and functionality for a wide range of applications [22].

8.4.1 Design considerations for integrating memristive device

Integrating memristive devices into computational systems demands a comprehensive, multi-layered design strategy that addresses challenges and opportunities across the device, circuit, system, programming, and manufacturing levels. These devices, known for their nonlinear resistance behavior and ability to store analog values, offer transformative potential in areas such as neuromorphic computing, in-memory computation, and high-density storage. However, leveraging these unique properties requires tailored solutions to overcome their inherent limitations and ensure compatibility with existing technologies [20].

At the device level, memristive devices often exhibit variability in their resistance states due to manufacturing inconsistencies, environmental factors, and aging effects. This variability can lead to reduced computational accuracy and system reliability. To address these challenges, calibration techniques and adaptive algorithms are essential for maintaining precision. Material optimization plays a critical role in improving switching characteristics, reducing resistance drift, and enhancing scalability. Furthermore, reliability concerns, such as limited write endurance, necessitate advanced solutions such as wear-leveling algorithms, error-correcting codes (ECC), and robust device architectures that ensure long-term performance [21].

At the circuit level, designing interfaces that effectively integrate memristive devices with traditional electronics is key. These circuits must handle the conversion between the analog operation of memristive devices and the digital nature of conventional systems while maintaining signal integrity. Noise reduction, power management, and efficient energy distribution are critical considerations. Architectural innovations, such as crossbar arrays and current-mode circuits, can facilitate high-density integration and parallel computation, maximizing the potential of memristive networks [11].

At the system level, creating hybrid architectures that combine traditional processors with memristive arrays is essential for enabling in-memory computation and reducing the data transfer bottleneck. Fault tolerance mechanisms, such as redundancy and self-repair systems, are necessary to address the susceptibility of memristive arrays to device failures. Collaboration between hardware and software design teams is vital for co-optimizing system performance and ensuring seamless operation. By designing systems that leverage the unique strengths of memristive devices, it becomes possible to achieve significant gains in efficiency and performance [9].

Effective programming and control strategies are crucial for harnessing the potential of memristive devices. Techniques such as pulse-width modulation, voltage control, and iterative write–verify processes enable precise programming of resistance states. These strategies must account for the nonlinear behavior and variability of memristive devices while minimizing energy consumption. Additionally, the development of software frameworks, APIs, and simulation tools tailored to memristive systems is essential to facilitate broader adoption and ease of use in diverse applications [8].

Memristive devices also introduce novel computational paradigms, such as analog computing and spiking neural networks. Optimizing data representation to align with these paradigms is critical. For instance, encoding information through resistance levels or leveraging intrinsic properties for parallel processing can significantly enhance computational efficiency. Carefully designed algorithms that exploit the analog and parallel capabilities of memristive devices can further accelerate their adoption in advanced computing applications, including machine learning and neuromorphic systems [17].

Finally, scaling memristive technology to large-scale, commercially viable systems presents challenges such as interconnect complexity, heat dissipation, and manufacturability. Addressing these issues requires close collaboration with manufacturers to refine fabrication techniques and integrate memristive devices into existing production lines. Establishing industry standards and benchmarks for performance, reliability, and scalability will also be critical in accelerating adoption and ensuring the widespread implementation of memristive systems [19].

By addressing these challenges holistically at every level of design, memristive devices can be successfully integrated into computational systems. This will unlock their potential to drive transformative applications across artificial intelligence, data storage, and scientific computing. The convergence of advancements in materials science, circuit design, and system architecture will enable the creation of next-generation computing platforms that deliver unprecedented efficiency, scalability, and functionality [21].

8.4.2 Trade-offs between different design choices

In the complex realm of computational system design, trade-offs between design choices are not just unavoidable, they are integral to the decision-making process. These trade-offs arise from the intricate interplay of competing objectives, limited resources, and the specific requirements of diverse applications. Successfully navigating these trade-offs demands a deep understanding of system-level priorities and a strategic approach to optimization [23].

One of the most significant trade-offs is between performance and power consumption. High-performance systems, which offer increased computational speed and processing power, often require higher energy inputs. This increased power consumption not only escalates operational costs but also generates excessive heat, necessitating advanced cooling mechanisms. To address this, designers employ power-efficient strategies, such as dynamic voltage and frequency scaling (DVFS), which dynamically adjusts the voltage and clock frequency based on workload demands, and low-power architectures, which are specifically optimized to minimize energy usage. The challenge lies in ensuring these techniques do not degrade critical performance metrics, such as processing speed or system responsiveness, particularly in power-sensitive domains such as mobile and embedded systems [24].

Another essential trade-off involves area efficiency versus design complexity. Adding advanced features or functionalities to a system often results in increased design complexity, which requires more physical space on a chip. This can lead to higher manufacturing costs and challenges in maintaining yield during fabrication. To address this, optimization techniques such as layout compaction, multi-layer routing, and modular design principles are employed to minimize the chip area while preserving the desired functionality. Designers must also ensure that the added complexity does not compromise manufacturability or reliability [25].

The tension between flexibility and specialization represents another pivotal trade-off. Flexible, general-purpose systems, such as those built on field-programmable gate arrays (FPGAs) or general-purpose processors, provide adaptability across a broad range of applications. However, their performance and efficiency often lag behind specialized solutions. For example, application-specific integrated circuits (ASICs) are highly optimized for specific tasks, such as machine learning inference or signal processing, delivering superior performance and energy efficiency for those tasks. However, ASICs lack the versatility to accommodate other applications, making them less suitable for dynamic or evolving workloads. Balancing this trade-off requires careful evaluation of the system's intended use cases and long-term adaptability [26].

Other trade-offs include latency versus throughput, where reducing the time delay for individual task processing may impact the system's ability to handle high volumes of tasks simultaneously. In such scenarios, designers must prioritize based on application demands—for instance, real-time applications such as video streaming often prioritize low latency, while batch processing systems focus on maximizing throughput. Similarly, achieving higher accuracy in computations or predictions frequently increases design complexity, requiring more sophisticated algorithms, higher-resolution data paths, or increased computational resources. This necessitates a judicious selection of algorithms and hardware components to strike a balance between precision and efficiency [31].

Scalability versus cost is another pressing concern, in particular in distributed or cloud-based systems. Ensuring that a system can scale seamlessly to handle growing workloads often requires significant investment in infrastructure, such as additional servers or storage solutions. However, cost constraints may limit scalability, requiring creative solutions such as virtualization, resource pooling, and adaptive load balancing to achieve optimal performance without excessive expenditure [31].

Finally, systems that operate in safety-critical domains, such as autonomous vehicles, aerospace, or medical devices, face the trade-off between safety and performance. Incorporating robust safety mechanisms, such as redundancy, fault-tolerant designs, and real-time monitoring, can introduce performance overheads. Designers must carefully manage these trade-offs to ensure reliability without compromising the system's operational goals [23].

Navigating these trade-offs requires a methodical and iterative approach. Techniques such as multi-objective optimization, which simultaneously evaluates multiple competing objectives, play a crucial role in identifying the best compromises. Iterative design refinements and application-driven decision-making enable designers to adjust priorities based on evolving needs. Modern tools, such as hardware–software co-design frameworks, simulation environments, and performance modeling techniques, allow for a comprehensive exploration of design trade-offs. By leveraging these tools, designers can achieve optimal outcomes that align with user requirements, technological constraints, and market demands, ensuring a balanced and effective system design [31].

8.5 Neuromorphic chip design and implementation

The design and implementation of neuromorphic chips represent a groundbreaking advancement in computational hardware, drawing inspiration from the brain's neural architecture and its operational principles. These chips aim to replicate key features of biological neural systems, such as parallel processing, low power consumption, and adaptive learning, through a collaborative approach integrating neuroscience, computer engineering, and advanced semiconductor technology. A pivotal aspect of neuromorphic chip design is the development of specialized hardware architectures optimized for neural network computations. These architectures typically incorporate massively parallel processing units such as SNNs or neuromorphic cores, designed to emulate the spiking behavior of biological neurons and synapses. Such designs also include advanced memory structures such as crossbar arrays or memristive devices, which store synaptic weights and network parameters directly within the hardware, enabling efficient data access during neural network training and inference. Additionally, scalable interconnects and three-dimensional integration techniques enhance connectivity, mimicking the brain's dense synaptic networks [14].

Neuromorphic chips stand out for their hardware-integrated learning mechanisms, allowing real-time adaptation and self-organization without relying on external software-based training. These systems implement synaptic plasticity, including Hebbian learning and STDP, which dynamically adjust synaptic weights in response to activity. This is coupled with event-driven processing, where computations are triggered asynchronously by discrete events, mirroring the energy-efficient information handling of biological systems. To support these features, efficient hardware accelerators are designed to facilitate critical operations such as spike-based communication and synaptic updates, optimizing the system's computational throughput [16].

Energy efficiency is a cornerstone of neuromorphic chip design, achieved through innovative approaches such as asynchronous computing, which eliminates the need for a global clock, reducing energy waste. Approximate computing further enhances efficiency by trading off precision for power savings, leveraging neural networks' inherent tolerance to minor inaccuracies. In-memory processing is another key strategy, integrating computation within memory units to minimize energy-intensive data transfers [11].

As neuromorphic systems scale, they face challenges such as increased complexity and error susceptibility. To address this, robust interconnects, error detection and correction mechanisms, and fault-tolerant architectures are employed. These systems often include inherent redundancy, enabling elegant degradation and continued operation even in the face of hardware failures or computational noise [5].

The realization of neuromorphic chips requires interdisciplinary collaboration across neuroscience, semiconductor engineering, and algorithm development. Neuroscience provides insights into brain functionality, guiding biologically plausible designs, while semiconductor advancements enable the fabrication of dense, efficient hardware. Algorithmic innovations leverage neuromorphic architectures for cutting-edge applications such as pattern recognition, autonomous robotics, and real-time data analytics. By fusing biology-inspired principles with state-of-the-art engineering, neuromorphic chips pave the way for intelligent systems that mimic the cognitive and learning abilities of the human brain, heralding a transformative shift in computational paradigms [8].

8.6 Applications and future directions

The integration of neuromorphic chips at the system level holds significant promise across various applications and points toward intriguing future directions in computing.

Figure 8.6 presents a two-layer crossbar RRAM synapse array integrated with peripheral complementary metal-oxide-semiconductor (CMOS) neurons. It highlights critical components and their roles in neuromorphic computing, as explained below:

Winner-take-all (WTA) bus: Figure 8.6(a) demonstrates the implementation of the WTA mechanism, a key feature in neuromorphic systems that mimics biological competition between neurons. The WTA bus allows the system to identify and select the most active neuron while suppressing less active ones, ensuring efficient signal processing and reducing noise or redundancy. By implementing this competitive dynamic, the system can prioritize certain outputs over others, which is particularly beneficial in tasks such as pattern recognition, classification, or decision-making. The WTA bus, integrated with CMOS neurons, enhances computational efficiency and ensures only the most relevant signals are propagated through the network [14].

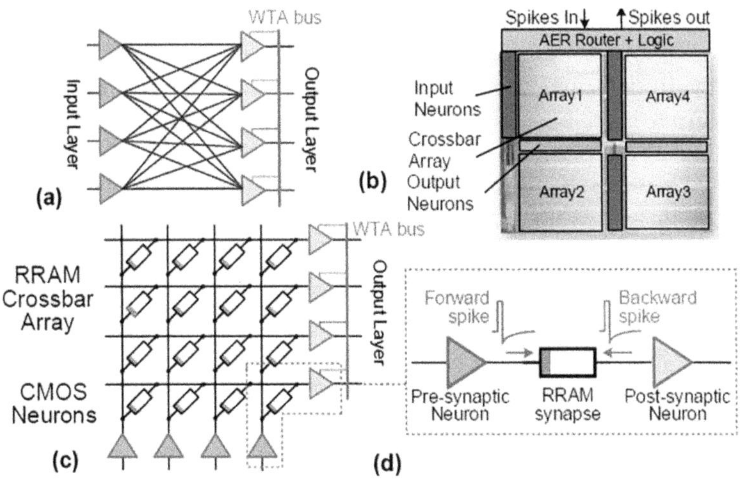

Figure 8.6. A crossbar RRAM synapse array with two layers, coupled with peripheral CMOS neurons incorporating (a) a WTA bus, (b) spike input and output with the input neurons using a crossbar array, (c) an RRAM crossbar with CMOS neurons, and (d) forward spikes and backward spikes with an RRAM synapse.

Spike inputs and outputs with input neurons using the crossbar array: Figure 8.6 (b) highlights how the system processes spike-based signals. The input neurons generate action potential-like spikes, which act as the primary mode of communication in the neuromorphic network. These spikes are then transmitted through the crossbar array, facilitating interaction between the neurons and the synaptic weights stored in the RRAM devices. The output spikes, generated after processing, carry information downstream to subsequent layers or components in the system. This spike-based communication mimics biological neural systems, enabling asynchronous and energy-efficient signal transmission. By leveraging spikes for input and output, the system aligns closely with brain-inspired computing paradigms [19].

RRAM crossbar with CMOS neurons: Figure 8.6(c) focuses on the integration of the RRAM crossbar array and CMOS neurons. The RRAM crossbar functions as the synaptic array, where each RRAM device at the intersection of the crossbar acts as a programmable synapse. These synapses store and modulate weights, which determine the strength of the connection between neurons. The CMOS neurons complement the RRAM crossbar by performing computational tasks such as generating, transmitting, and integrating spikes. This integration allows for seamless interaction between memory and computation, essential for efficient neuromorphic processing. The figure emphasizes how this set-up enables real-time data processing and adaptive learning through weight updates within the RRAM synapse array [11].

Forward spikes and backward spikes with RRAM synapse: Figure 8.6(d) illustrates the bidirectional spike propagation in a neuromorphic system utilizing RRAM synapses. Forward spikes represent the signals that propagate from the input neurons through the RRAM crossbar to the output neurons during normal inference or computation. These spikes carry information about input data and are used to compute the neural network's output. In contrast, backward spikes refer to the feedback signals sent from the output layer back to the synaptic array. These are typically used during training or adaptation processes to adjust the synaptic weights stored in the RRAM devices. Such feedback might follow a biologically inspired learning rule, such as STDP, where the timing of spikes determines the strength of synaptic updates. This dual spike propagation (forward and backward) highlights the RRAM synapse's role in both computation and learning, enabling real-time updates and efficient neuromorphic processing [7].

These components, working in synergy, illustrate a biologically inspired neuromorphic system that combines the competitive dynamics of WTA, efficient spike-based communication, and the powerful memory-computation capabilities of RRAM and CMOS integration. This design offers a scalable and energy-efficient architecture for applications in artificial intelligence, such as pattern recognition, classification, and adaptive learning [6].

8.6.1 Applications

8.6.1.1 AI and machine learning

Neuromorphic chips represent a groundbreaking frontier in the realm of AI and machine learning (ML). These chips have the potential to spark a profound revolution by providing highly efficient hardware solutions for a wide array of tasks, including but not limited to pattern recognition, natural language processing (NLP), and decision-making. At the heart of their transformative power lies their unique ability to emulate the architecture of the human brain. Unlike conventional processors, which rely on sequential processing, neuromorphic chips are designed to perform parallel processing, mirroring the parallelism observed in the human brain's neural networks. This parallelism allows neuromorphic chips to excel in handling complex computational tasks with remarkable efficiency. One of the most significant applications of neuromorphic chips lies in the field of deep learning, where they demonstrate exceptional prowess in both training and inference tasks [13]. Deep learning algorithms, which are pivotal in powering many AI applications, often require massive computational resources for tasks such as training complex neural networks and making predictions based on learned patterns. Neuromorphic chips, with their ability to execute parallel computations akin to the brain's neural networks, offer a compelling solution for accelerating these processes while minimizing energy consumption. In essence, neuromorphic chips hold the promise of ushering in a new era of AI and ML applications characterized by unprecedented efficiency and scalability. By harnessing the principles of neural processing, these chips have the potential to propel advancements in various fields, ranging from healthcare and autonomous vehicles to cybersecurity and robotics. As research and development in neuromorphic computing continue to advance, we can anticipate even greater strides towards the realization of intelligent systems that emulate the remarkable capabilities of the human brain [19].

8.6.1.2 Robotics and autonomous systems

Integrating neuromorphic chips into robotics and autonomous systems represents a significant advancement that holds the potential to revolutionize their cognitive capabilities. These chips, inspired by the architecture of the human brain, offer a promising avenue for imbuing robots with enhanced intelligence, enabling them to make real-time decisions and exhibit adaptive behavior in dynamic environments. One of the key advantages of neuromorphic chips lies in their ability to process information in a manner akin to the human brain. Unlike traditional processors, which rely on sequential processing, neuromorphic chips leverage parallel processing, mirroring the parallelism observed in neural networks [11]. This parallel architecture allows them to handle complex computational tasks with remarkable efficiency and speed, making them well-suited for applications in robotics and autonomous systems.

One of the primary ways in which neuromorphic chips can benefit robotics is through sensor fusion. Robots equipped with multiple sensors, such as cameras, LiDAR, radar, and other environmental sensors, generate vast amounts of data about their surroundings. Processing and interpreting this sensory data in real time are essential for robots to navigate their environment, identify objects, and make informed decisions. Neuromorphic chips excel in this regard, as they can efficiently integrate and process diverse sensory inputs, enabling robots to perceive and understand their environment more effectively. Moreover, neuromorphic chips enable robots to exhibit adaptive behaviour by learning from their interactions with the environment. Traditional robotic systems often rely on pre-programmed algorithms or static decision-making rules, limiting their ability to adapt to changing circumstances [24]. In contrast, neuromorphic chips support the implementation of machine learning algorithms that enable robots to learn and improve their performance over time. By continuously analysing sensory data and adjusting their behaviour based on feedback, robots equipped with neuromorphic chips can adapt to new situations, optimize their actions, and autonomously navigate complex environments. Furthermore, the energy efficiency of neuromorphic chips makes them particularly well-suited for deployment in battery-powered robotic systems. Their low power consumption and parallel processing capabilities enable robots to perform complex cognitive tasks while conserving energy, extending their operational lifespan and autonomy. In summary, integrating neuromorphic chips into robotics and autonomous systems offers a promising pathway to enhance their cognitive capabilities. By leveraging parallel processing, sensor fusion, and adaptive learning, these chips enable robots to perceive, interpret, and respond to their environment in a manner that approaches human-like intelligence [16]. As research and development in neuromorphic computing continue to advance, we can expect to see increasingly sophisticated robotic systems that can autonomously navigate and interact with the world in more intelligent and adaptive ways.

8.6.1.3 Neuroscience and brain–machine interfaces

Neuromorphic chips serve as a groundbreaking platform for delving into neural dynamics and advancing the field of brain–machine interfaces (BMIs), which hold immense promise for decoding neural signals and establishing real-time interactions between machines and the brain. These chips represent a paradigm shift in computational neuroscience and neuroengineering, offering researchers a powerful tool to simulate neural networks and delve into the intricacies of brain functions. One of the most remarkable aspects of neuromorphic chips is their ability to mimic the behaviour of biological neurons and synapses [15]. Unlike conventional digital processors, which operate using binary logic and sequential processing, neuromorphic chips emulate the parallel processing and distributed connectivity observed in the brain. This unique architecture enables them to replicate the dynamics of neural networks more accurately, providing researchers with a platform to study complex phenomena such as synaptic plasticity, neuronal spiking, and network dynamics. One of the primary applications of neuromorphic chips lies in the development of BMIs, which establish direct communication pathways between the brain and external devices. These interfaces hold tremendous potential for restoring lost sensory or motor function in individuals with neurological disorders or injuries. By decoding neural signals and translating them into actionable commands, BMIs can enable individuals to control prosthetic limbs, communicate through thought alone, or even regain sensory feedback from artificial sensors [11]. Neuromorphic chips play a pivotal role in the development and optimization of BMIs by providing a platform for modeling and simulating neural circuits. Researchers can use these chips to construct biologically plausible models of the brain, incorporating features such as spiking neurons, synaptic plasticity, and network connectivity. By interfacing these models with external sensors and actuators, they can create closed-loop systems that respond to neural activity in real time, enabling bidirectional communication between the brain and external devices. Furthermore, neuromorphic chips offer insights into the underlying mechanisms of neurological disorders and brain function. By simulating neural circuits and perturbing them in controlled experiments, researchers can elucidate the neural basis of diseases such as epilepsy, Parkinson's disease, and Alzheimer's disease. These insights pave the way for the development of novel therapeutic interventions, such as closed-loop deep brain stimulation or targeted drug delivery, which can modulate neural activity and alleviate symptoms of neurological disorders. In summary, neuromorphic chips represent a transformative technology with far-reaching implications for neuroscience, neuroengineering, and biomedical research. By providing a platform for studying neural dynamics, developing BMIs, and unraveling the mysteries of brain function, these chips are poised to revolutionize our understanding of the brain and unlock new avenues for treating neurological disorders and enhancing human–machine interactions.

8.6.1.4 Edge computing and the Internet of Things

Neuromorphic chips represent a cutting-edge technology and are increasingly gaining attention for their potential in edge computing applications, particularly within the realm of IoT devices. These chips offer a unique combination of low power consumption and real-time processing capabilities, making them exceptionally well-suited for deployment in edge computing environments. At the core of their appeal is their ability to emulate the parallel processing and efficiency of the human brain, which allows them to execute complex computational tasks with minimal energy expenditure [26]. This characteristic is particularly advantageous in edge computing scenarios, where devices often operate with limited power resources, such as battery-powered sensors or mobile gadgets. By leveraging neuromorphic chips for local data processing, IoT devices can conserve energy and extend their battery life, thereby enhancing their operational lifespan and reducing maintenance requirements. Furthermore, neuromorphic chips excel at real-time processing, enabling them to analyse data streams and make decisions instantaneously. In edge computing, this capability is invaluable for applications that demand rapid response times, such as autonomous vehicles, smart surveillance systems, or industrial automation. By performing computation locally on the device, rather than relying on remote servers or cloud infrastructure, neuromorphic chips minimize latency and ensure timely responses to critical events. This not only enhances the overall efficiency of IoT systems but also improves their responsiveness and reliability in dynamic environments. Moreover, by offloading computation to the edge, neuromorphic chips help alleviate the burden on network bandwidth and reduce data transmission overheads. In traditional cloud-based architectures, IoT devices often rely on sending large volumes of raw sensor data to centralize servers for processing and analysis. This approach not only consumes significant bandwidth but also introduces delays associated with data transmission and server-side processing. In contrast, edge computing with neuromorphic chips enables devices to preprocess data locally and transmit only relevant insights or actionable information to the cloud, thereby reducing network congestion and optimizing resource utilization [11]. Overall, the integration of neuromorphic chips into edge computing architectures holds immense potential for revolutionizing IoT systems. By combining low power consumption, real-time processing capabilities, and reduced latency, these chips enable IoT devices to perform sophisticated computation at the edge, enhancing their efficiency, responsiveness, and autonomy. As the demand for intelligent IoT applications continues to grow, neuromorphic chips are poised to play a crucial role in shaping the future of edge computing and ushering in a new era of smart, interconnected devices.

8.6.2 Future directions

8.6.2.1 Hybrid architectures

In envisioning the future of computing systems, there is a growing interest in integrating neuromorphic chips with traditional computing architectures to harness the complementary strengths of both approaches. These hybrid architectures have the potential to revolutionize the way we design and deploy computational systems, offering a powerful combination of energy efficiency, cognitive capabilities, computational power, and flexibility. Neuromorphic chips, inspired by the architecture and functioning of the human brain, excel in tasks that involve pattern recognition, real-time processing, and adaptive learning. Their ability to mimic the parallel processing and synaptic plasticity of biological neural networks makes them ideally suited for applications requiring cognitive capabilities, such as sensor fusion, decision-making, and autonomous behaviour. However, while neuromorphic chips offer impressive energy efficiency and cognitive prowess, they may lack the raw computational power and flexibility of traditional processors, particularly in tasks requiring complex algorithmic computation or numerical processing. On the other hand, traditional computing architectures, such as CPUs and GPUs, are well-established for their computational power, versatility, and programmability [17]. These processors excel in executing a wide range of algorithms, from numerical simulations and scientific computing to graphical rendering and artificial intelligence. They provide the raw computing horsepower needed to tackle complex computations and handle large datasets efficiently. However, traditional processors often consume more power and struggle with tasks that require real-time processing, adaptability, or cognitive functions. By integrating neuromorphic chips with traditional computing architectures, hybrid systems can leverage the best of both worlds. Neuromorphic chips can handle cognitive tasks, such as sensor data processing, pattern recognition, and decision-making, with remarkable energy efficiency and real-time responsiveness. Meanwhile, traditional processors can complement neuromorphic chips by providing the computational muscle needed for algorithmic computation, numerical processing, and general-purpose computing tasks. Together, these components form a symbiotic relationship, where each play to its strengths, resulting in more versatile, adaptive, and efficient computing systems. In practical terms, hybrid architectures could be implemented in various domains, including robotics, autonomous vehicles, healthcare, finance, and telecommunications [5]. For example, in a robotics application, neuromorphic chips could be used for sensor fusion, environment perception, and adaptive control, while traditional processors handle higher-level planning, navigation, and decision-making tasks. Similarly, in autonomous vehicles, neuromorphic chips could process sensor data in real-time to detect obstacles, pedestrians, and road signs, while traditional processors manage navigation, route planning, and vehicle dynamics. Overall, the integration of neuromorphic chips with traditional computing architectures represents a promising frontier in computer science and engineering. By combining the energy efficiency and cognitive abilities of neuromorphic chips with the computational power and flexibility of traditional processors, hybrid architectures enable the development of more versatile, adaptive, and intelligent systems capable of addressing a wide range of complex tasks and challenges. As research and development in this field continue to advance, hybrid computing systems are poised to play a pivotal role in shaping the future of technology and innovation.

8.6.2.2 Bio-inspired computing

Researchers are delving into bio-inspired computing paradigms by drawing significant inspiration from the brain's intricate structure and dynamic functionality. The goal is to develop neuromorphic systems that mimic the brain's neural architecture

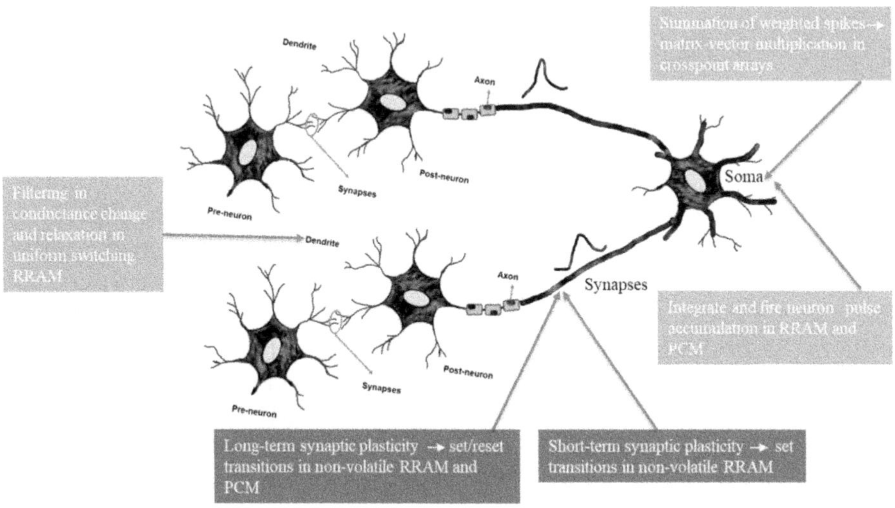

Figure 8.7. Bio-inspired computing using RRAM.

and processes, leading to breakthroughs in computational efficiency and adaptability. These innovative systems aim to replicate key principles observed in biological brains, including neuromodulation, plasticity, and self-organization, to tackle complex tasks with heightened proficiency, as shown in figure 8.7 [18]. Neuromodulation could enable systems to adjust their processing pathways dynamically, plasticity could lead to hardware that learns and optimizes its performance over time, and self-organization could allow systems to independently develop optimal structures and pathways. Future neuromorphic systems, by incorporating these principles, are expected to surpass current computing paradigms in both efficiency and robustness, revolutionizing fields such as artificial intelligence, robotics, and data processing with their sophisticated pattern recognition, decision-making, and problem-solving capabilities [25]. Figure 8.7 illustrates the concept of bio-inspired computing implemented using RRAM technology. This approach mimics the functioning of biological neural systems by leveraging the unique properties of RRAM devices, which act as artificial synapses in neuromorphic architectures. The figure likely depicts how RRAM enables essential neural functions such as synaptic plasticity (learning and memory), spike-based communication, and energy-efficient computation. By replicating key characteristics of biological systems, such as adaptability and parallel processing, RRAM-based architectures provide a foundation for developing scalable, efficient, and brain-inspired computing systems designed to handle complex tasks in artificial intelligence and machine learning.

8.6.2.3 Neuromorphic hardware accelerators

As the field of neuromorphic computing continues to advance and mature, one exciting possibility on the horizon is the development of dedicated hardware accelerators optimized for specific tasks. These specialized accelerators could represent a significant step forward in the realm of edge computing and IoT applications, offering high-performance solutions tailored to meet the demands of real-time processing, sensor data analysis, anomaly detection, and adaptive control. One of the key advantages of dedicated hardware accelerators is their ability to efficiently execute specific computational tasks by leveraging the unique architectural features of neuromorphic chips. Unlike general-purpose processors, which are designed to handle a wide range of algorithms and computations, these accelerators can be finely tuned and optimized for functions, resulting in improved performance, lower power consumption, and reduced latency [19]. For example, in IoT applications, where devices often operate with limited computational resources and power constraints, dedicated neuromorphic accelerators could offer significant benefits. By offloading sensor data processing, anomaly detection, and real-time control tasks to specialized hardware, these accelerators can enable IoT devices to analyse data locally, make intelligent decisions autonomously, and respond rapidly to changing environmental conditions, all while conserving energy and bandwidth. Moreover, dedicated accelerators optimized for specific tasks can facilitate the development of more efficient and robust edge computing solutions. For instance, in industrial automation settings, where real-time monitoring and control are crucial, neuromorphic accelerators could be employed to process sensor data from manufacturing equipment, detect anomalies or faults in real time, and adjust operational parameters accordingly to optimize efficiency and productivity. Furthermore, in applications such as cybersecurity and autonomous vehicles, where rapid decision-making and response times are paramount, dedicated hardware accelerators could play a vital role in enhancing system performance and reliability. By specializing in tasks such as threat detection, anomaly recognition, and adaptive control, these accelerators can help mitigate security risks, improve situational awareness, and enhance overall system resilience. In summary, the emergence of dedicated hardware accelerators optimized for specific tasks represents an exciting development in the evolution of neuromorphic computing. By harnessing the power of specialized hardware to execute critical functions efficiently and effectively, these accelerators have the potential to unlock new opportunities for edge computing, IoT applications, and beyond. As research and development in this area continue to progress, we can expect to see increasingly sophisticated and versatile hardware solutions that further advance the capabilities of neuromorphic computing and drive innovation across a wide range of domains.

8.6.2.4 Neuromorphic computing in space exploration

Neuromorphic chips hold immense promise for revolutionizing space exploration by introducing advanced capabilities for autonomous decision-making and adaptive control in spacecraft and rovers. This technology has the potential to significantly enhance the efficiency, flexibility, and autonomy of space missions, enabling exploration in environments that are distant, challenging, and often inaccessible to human intervention. One of the key advantages of neuromorphic chips in the context of space exploration is their ability to emulate the brain's architecture and perform parallel processing. This parallel processing capability enables rapid analysis of the vast amounts of data collected by spacecraft sensors, allowing for real-time decision-making and response to dynamic environmental conditions [19]. For example, neuromorphic chips could enable spacecraft to autonomously navigate through complex terrain, avoid hazards, and adapt their trajectory in response to unexpected obstacles or changes in mission objectives. Moreover, neuromorphic chips can facilitate sensor fusion, enabling spacecraft and rovers to integrate data from multiple sensors, including cameras, spectrometers, and radar, to build comprehensive situational awareness of their surroundings. This enhanced perception capability allows for more accurate navigation, hazard detection, and scientific observation, ultimately improving the success and scientific yield of space missions. Additionally, the low power consumption and energy efficiency of neuromorphic chips make them well-suited for space applications where power and resources are limited. By reducing the computational workload on spacecraft and enabling onboard processing of sensor data, neuromorphic chips can help conserve energy, extend mission duration, and minimize reliance on ground-based communication and control systems [23]. Furthermore, neuromorphic chips enable adaptive control algorithms that can dynamically adjust spacecraft operations based on changing mission requirements or environmental conditions. For example, in the case of long-duration missions or missions to distant planets, neuromorphic-based adaptive control systems can optimize power usage, thermal management, and communication protocols to maximize mission success and spacecraft longevity. Overall, the integration of neuromorphic chips into spacecraft and rovers has the potential to revolutionize space exploration by enhancing autonomy, adaptability, and intelligence. By leveraging the advanced capabilities of neuromorphic computing, future space missions can achieve greater efficiency, autonomy, and scientific discovery, paving the way for unprecedented advancements in our understanding of the cosmos and our ability to explore and inhabit other worlds. Future missions may leverage neuromorphic systems to process data in real time, adapt to changing environments, and optimize resource utilization in space habitats and exploration vehicles. The integration of neuromorphic chips at the system level opens exciting possibilities across a wide range of applications, from AI and robotics to neuroscience and edge computing. Future directions in this field include hybrid architectures, bio-inspired computing, specialized hardware accelerators, and applications in space exploration, paving the way for more efficient, adaptable, and intelligent computing systems.

Bibliography

[1] Saxena V, Wu X, Srivastava I and Zhu K 2018 Towards neuromorphic learning machines using emerging memory devices with brain-like energy efficiency *J. Low Power Electron. Appl.* **8** 34

[2] Amit D J and Fusi S 1994 Learning in neural networks with material synapses *Neural Comput.* **6** 957–82

[3] Sun B *et al* 2023 Memristor-based artificial chips *Am. Chem. Soc.* **18** 14–27

[4] Hu M, Li H, Chen Y, Wu Q, Rose G S and Linderman R W 2014 Memristor crossbar-based neuromorphic computing system: a case study *IEEE Trans Neural Netw. Learn. Syst.* **25** 1864–78

[5] Jeong Y and Lu W 2018 Neuromorphic computing using memristor crossbar networks: a focus on bio-inspired approaches *IEEE Nanatechnol. Mag.* **12** 6–18
[6] Sun S Y, Xu H, Li J, Li Q and Liu H 2019 Cascaded architecture for memristor crossbar array based larger-scale neuromorphic computing *IEEE Access* **7** 61679–88
[7] Adam G C, Hoskins B D, Prezioso M, Merrikh-Bayat F, Chakrabarti B and Strukov D B 2017 3-D memristor crossbars for analog and neuromorphic computing applications *IEEE Trans. Electron Devices* **64** 312–8
[8] Li Z *et al* 2015 An overview on memristor crossabr based neuromorphic circuit and architecture *2015 IFIP/IEEE Int. Conf. on Very Large Scale Integration (VLSI-SoC) (Daejeon, Korea (South))* pp 52–6
[9] Li Y *et al* 2018 Review of memristor devices in neuromorphic computing: materials sciences and device challenges *J. Phys. D: Appl. Phys.* **51** 503002
[10] Fernando B R, Qi Y, Yakopcic C and Taha T M 2020 3D memristor crossbar architecture for a multicore neuromorphic system *2020 Int. Joint Conf. on Neural Networks (IJCNN) (Glasgow, UK)* pp 1–8
[11] James A P and Chua L O 2021 Analog neural computing with super-resolution memristor crossbars *IEEE Trans. Circuits Syst.* I **68** 4470–81
[12] Xia L *et al* 2018 MNSIM: simulation platform for memristor-based neuromorphic computing system *IEEE Trans. Comput. Aided Des. Integr. Circuits Syst.* **37** 1009–22
[13] Xia Q and Yang J J 2019 Memristive crossbar arrays for brain-inspired computing *Nat. Mater.* **18** 309–23
[14] Burr G W *et al* 2016 Neuromorphic computing using non-volatile memory *Adv. Phys.* X **2** 89–124
[15] Truong S N and Min K S 2014 New memristor-based crossbar array architecture with 50-% area reduction and 48-% power saving for matrix-vector multiplication of analog neuromorphic computing *J. Semicond. Technol. Sci.* **14** 356–63
[16] Jiang H *et al* 2018 Pulse-width modulation based dot-product engine for neuromorphic computing system using memristor crossbar array *2018 IEEE Int. Symp. on Circuits and Systems (ISCAS) (Florence, Italy)* pp 1–4
[17] Hu M *et al* 2016 Dot-product engine for neuromorphic computing: programming 1T1M crossbar to accelerate matrix-vector multiplication *Proc. of the 53rd Annual Design Automation Conf. (DAC'16), Association for Computing Machinery (New York, NY)* pp 1–6
[18] Lu C *et al* 2024 Self-rectifying all-optical modulated optoelectronic multistates memristor crossbar array for neuromorphic computing *Nano Lett.* **24** 1667–72
[19] Ismail M, Chand U, Mahata C, Nebhen J and Kim S 2022 Demonstration of synaptic and resistive switching characteristics in W/TiO_2/HfO_2/TaN memristor crossbar array for bioinspired neuromorphic computing *J. Mater. Sci. Technol.* **96** 94–102
[20] Taha T M, Hasan R and Yakopcic C 2014 Memristor crossbar based multicore neuromorphic processors *27th IEEE Int. System-on-Chip Conf. (SOCC) (Las Vegas, NV)* pp 383–9
[21] Wen W *et al* 2015 An EDA framework for large scale hybrid neuromorphic computing systems *Proc. of the 52nd Annual Design Automation Conf. (DAC'15). Association for Computing Machinery (New York, NY)* pp 1–6
[22] Tao T *et al* 2023 Modeling and analysis of spike signal sequence for memristor crossbar array in neuromorphic chips *IEEE Trans. Circuits Syst.* I **70** 2271–82
[23] Liu C *et al* 2016 A memristor crossbar based computing engine optimized for high speed and accuracy *IEEE Computer Society Annual Symp. on VLSI (ISVLSI) (Pittsburgh, PA)* pp 110–5

[24] Hasan R and Taha T M 2014 Enabling back propagation training of memristor crossbar neuromorphic processors *Int. Joint Conf. on Neural Networks (IJCNN) (Beijing, China)* pp 21–8

[25] Park S O *et al* 2022 Experimental demonstration of highly reliable dynamic memristor for artificial neuron and neuromorphic computing *Nat. Commun.* **13** 2888

[26] Liu B *et al* 2014 Reduction and IR-drop compensations techniques for reliable neuromorphic computing systems *IEEE/ACM Int. Conf. on Computer-Aided Design (ICCAD) (San Jose, CA)* pp 63–70

[27] Huh W, Lee D and Lee C H 2020 Memristors based on 2D materials as an artificial synapse for neuromorphic electronics *Adv. Mater.* **32** 2002092

[28] Gautam M K, Kumar S and Mukherjee S 2022 Y_2O_3-based memristive crossbar array for synaptic learning *J. Phys. D: Appl. Phys.* **55** 205103

[29] Kumar S *et al* 2022 Y_2O_3-based crossbar array for analog and neuromorphic computation *IEEE Trans. Electron Devices* **70** 473–7

[30] Zhu Y *et al* 2020 Statistical training for neuromorphic computing using memristor-based crossbars considering process variations and noise *Design, Automation & Test in Europe Conference & Exhibition (DATE) (Grenoble, France)* pp 1590–3

[31] Yang F *et al* 2021 Vertical organic nanocrystal arrays for crossbar memristors with tuning switching dynamics toward neuromorphic computing *Smart Mat* **2** 99–108

IOP Publishing

Resistive Switching Systems for In-Memory Computation and Artificial Intelligence

Shaibal Mukherjee

Chapter 9

Memristive systems in image processing and artificial intelligence

9.1 Introduction to memristive systems

Memristive systems, which harness the groundbreaking technology of memristors, represent a significant paradigm shift in computational hardware, particularly for image processing and artificial intelligence (AI) applications. Memristors, or memory resistors, are two-terminal, non-volatile devices that can modulate electrical current flow while retaining a history-dependent state of charge [1]. This unique feature makes them exceptionally well-suited for high-density, low-power computational tasks, particularly those that involve the processing and analysis of large-scale datasets, such as images. By leveraging these capabilities, memristive systems can deliver enhanced performance and efficiency in handling complex computational workloads [2].

Figure 9.1 illustrates the development hierarchy of artificial perception systems, which focus on bridging and integrating biological principles with system-level engineering to create next-generation intelligent sensory systems. Figure 9.1 emphasizes how artificial perception systems are evolving by mimicking biological sensory processes, such as vision, hearing, and touch, through advanced engineering techniques. These systems are designed to replicate the way biological organisms perceive and interact with their environment, enabling machines to recognize patterns, make decisions, and learn from sensory inputs. The integration of biological principles, such as neural processing and sensory mechanisms, with cutting-edge system engineering, paves the way for the development of intelligent systems that can adapt to complex real-world scenarios. The hierarchy shows how progress is being made at various levels, from mimicking the simplest biological sensory mechanisms to creating more sophisticated systems capable of performing tasks requiring human-like perception and cognition. This progression marks a

doi:10.1088/978-0-7503-6169-9ch9 © IOP Publishing Ltd 2025. All rights, including for text and data mining (TDM), artificial intelligence (AI) training, and similar technologies, are reserved.

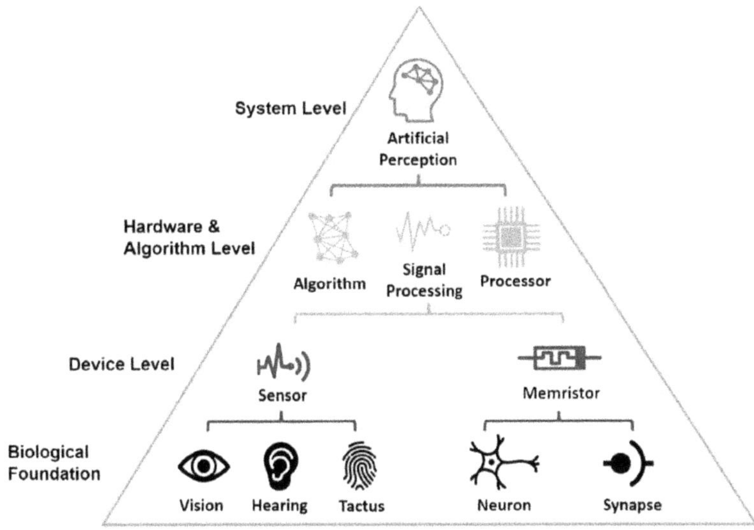

Figure 9.1. The development hierarchy of artificial perception systems bridges and integrates biological principles with system-level engineering to create next-generation intelligent sensory systems. Reproduced from [22] John Wiley & Sons. Copyright 2020 The Authors. Published by WILEY-VCH Verlag GmbH & Co. KGaA, Weinheim.

critical step toward developing more autonomous and intelligent machines in fields such as robotics, healthcare, and AI.

9.1.1 Image decomposition techniques

Image decomposition plays a vital role in image processing, enabling the breakdown of complex images into simpler components for analysis, enhancement, or representation. These methods allow us to isolate specific features, such as textures, colors, or edges, and study their properties independently. The choice of decomposition method depends on the specific application, whether it involves frequency analysis, feature extraction, or compression.

In 2D discrete wavelet transform (2D-DWT), an image is processed through high-pass and low-pass filters based on the desired decomposition level (DL). To achieve image compression using 2D-DWT, downsampling is applied to extract approximation coefficients that retain only the low-frequency components. The low-pass filter (LPF) smooths the image by averaging the coefficients, whereas the high-pass filter (HPF) captures the detailed coefficients, highlighting finer image features [9].

Each DL produces separate frequency sub-bands, where the approximation coefficients from the previous level serve as input for the next decomposition. At every decomposition step, four sub-bands are generated: LL, LH, HL, and HH. The LL sub-band contains approximation coefficients with low-frequency components, preserving the majority of the image's information. The LH sub-band extracts horizontal features, the HL sub-band captures vertical details, and the HH sub-band highlights diagonal features. The number of decomposition levels determines the number of transformation stages, influencing the computational complexity, as

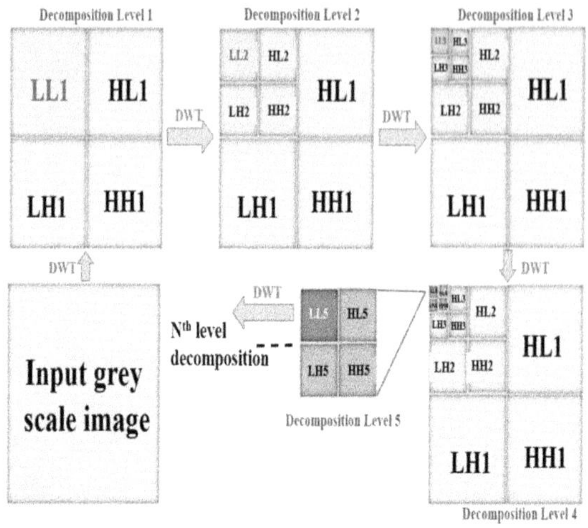

Figure 9.2. Stepwise decomposition process of an image.

shown in figure 9.2. A higher number of decomposition levels leads to greater compression efficiency while reducing processing complexity [9, 10].

In the spatial domain, decomposition typically focuses on pixel-level details. This can involve separating images into individual color channels such as RGB or YUV for tasks such as segmentation and correction. For instance, block-based decomposition divides an image into smaller regions for localized processing, commonly used in JPEG compression or texture analysis. Such methods provide a straightforward way to handle spatial variations within images but may struggle with tasks requiring frequency or multiscale analysis.

Frequency domain techniques provide a different perspective by representing images in terms of their spatial frequency components. The Fourier transform is a cornerstone of this approach, converting an image into a spectrum of frequencies where low frequencies represent smooth areas, and high frequencies correspond to edges and details. This technique is invaluable in filtering noise or enhancing edges. Similarly, the wavelet transform enables multi-resolution analysis, capturing both spatial and frequency information simultaneously, making it ideal for tasks such as denoising or image compression. Other methods such the discrete cosine transform (DCT) are optimized for compression and underpin standards such as JPEG.

Matrix and subspace decomposition techniques, such as singular value decomposition (SVD) and principal component analysis (PCA), are widely used for dimensionality reduction and feature extraction. SVD decomposes an image into matrices that capture its essential structure while discarding less significant details, aiding in noise reduction or compression. PCA, on the other hand, identifies the most critical components of an image in terms of variance, which is particularly useful in tasks such as face recognition. These techniques reveal insights into the underlying structure of images that are not immediately apparent in their raw form.

In contrast, multiscale decomposition methods such as Gaussian and Laplacian pyramids analyse images at different scales, capturing structures of varying sizes.

This approach is beneficial for applications such as image blending, where smooth transitions between images are crucial, or super-resolution, where finer details are reconstructed. Morphological decomposition, focusing on shapes and structures, offers another dimension for tasks such as object detection or texture analysis.

Modern advancements have introduced machine learning-based methods for image decomposition. Deep learning models, including convolutional neural networks (CNNs) and autoencoders, can automatically learn complex decomposition strategies tailored to specific applications. For instance, CNNs extract hierarchical features that are instrumental in tasks such as segmentation or object detection. Similarly, autoencoders encode images into compact latent spaces, enabling applications such as denoising or image generation.

Image decomposition techniques provide a toolkit for transforming and understanding images at various levels of abstraction. Whether focusing on spatial details, frequency components, or learned representations, these methods are integral to a wide range of applications, from medical imaging and remote sensing to photography and computer vision. By breaking images into manageable parts, we can uncover patterns, enhance details, or compress information effectively, paving the way for innovations in both academic research and industrial applications.

9.1.2 Wavelet based decomposition techniques

Wavelet decomposition is a transformative approach in image processing that allows for the analysis of images at multiple resolutions. It operates by breaking down an image into sub-components that capture both its spatial and frequency characteristics. Unlike traditional methods such as the Fourier transform, which focus solely on global frequency information, wavelet decomposition provides localized information about where specific frequency changes occur within an image. This dual spatial–frequency representation makes wavelet decomposition highly effective for tasks such as image compression, denoising, and feature extraction.

The technique revolves around wavelets, which are small, oscillating functions that decay rapidly to zero. These wavelets are used as building blocks to analyse images hierarchically, starting from coarse approximations of the image and moving towards finer details. The process begins with filtering the image using low-pass and high-pass filters. The LPF captures the smooth, low-frequency content, while the HPF isolates the edges and high-frequency details. The result is a set of sub-bands that divide the image into four components: approximations (LL), horizontal details (LH), vertical details (HL), and diagonal details (HH). The LL sub-band, which contains the most significant information, is further decomposed in subsequent levels to create a multi-resolution representation.

This multi-resolution analysis provides a structured view of the image, enabling a range of applications. For example, in image compression, the energy of the image is concentrated in the LL sub-band, allowing high-frequency components to be quantized or discarded with minimal loss of quality. This principle is the foundation of standards such as JPEG2000. In denoising, noise predominantly resides in high-frequency components, and wavelet decomposition enables selective thresholding to suppress noise while preserving critical features. Similarly, edge detection and texture analysis benefit from the ability to focus on high-frequency sub-bands that emphasize transitions and patterns.

One of the major advantages of wavelet decomposition is its adaptability. It captures features at varying scales, making it well-suited for analysing complex structures within images. Furthermore, its ability to represent both spatial and frequency information simultaneously makes it a superior choice for applications requiring localized analysis. However, the technique is not without challenges. Selecting an appropriate wavelet family, such as Haar, Daubechies, or Symlets, is critical and task dependent. Additionally, multi-level decomposition can be computationally intensive, and improper thresholding during tasks such as denoising or compression may lead to visual artifacts.

The wavelet decomposition stands out as a versatile and powerful tool in image processing. By offering a detailed, multiscale breakdown of an image, it opens possibilities for effective image representation, enhancement, and analysis. Its applications span diverse fields, from medical imaging and satellite imagery to multimedia processing, underscoring its significance in modern computational techniques.

Memristive devices are renowned for their ability to offer high density storage, low power consumption, and rapid switching capabilities [3]. These properties make them particularly well-suited for implementing neuromorphic computing architectures, which mimic the brain's neural networks. In image processing and AI, memristive systems can significantly enhance performance and efficiency by providing novel ways to store and manipulate data.

Figure 9.3 provides an overview of the development trends in neuromorphic computing performance, highlighting key challenges and advancements. Figure 9.3(a)

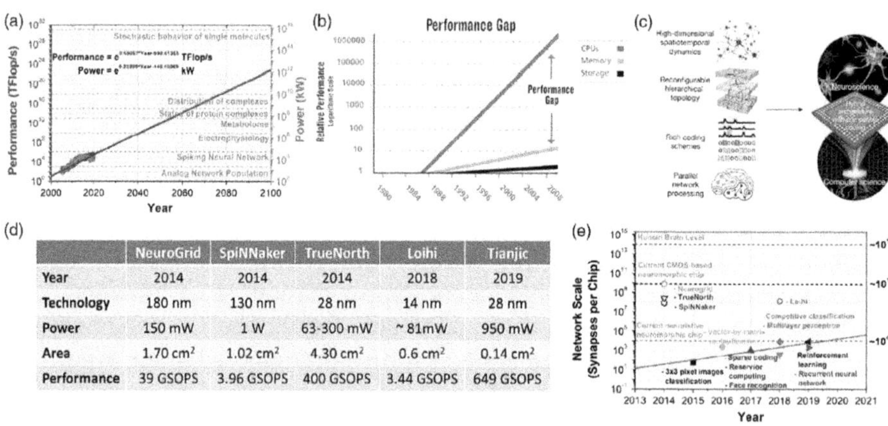

	NeuroGrid	SpiNNaker	TrueNorth	Loihi	Tianjic
Year	2014	2014	2014	2018	2019
Technology	180 nm	130 nm	28 nm	14 nm	28 nm
Power	150 mW	1 W	63-300 mW	~ 81mW	950 mW
Area	1.70 cm^2	1.02 cm^2	4.30 cm^2	0.6 cm^2	0.14 cm^2
Performance	39 GSOPS	3.96 GSOPS	400 GSOPS	3.44 GSOPS	649 GSOPS

Figure 9.3. Development overview of neuromorphic computing performance trends. (a) Performance and power consumption of top supercomputers. (b) Memory gap in modern systems. (c) Design philosophy of a typical neuromorphic chip. (d) Key parameters of CMOS-based neuromorphic chips. (e) Exponential scaling in memristive neuromorphic chips development. Reproduced from [22] John Wiley & Sons. Copyright 2020 The Authors. Published by WILEY-VCH Verlag GmbH & Co. KGaA, Weinheim.

illustrates the performance and power consumption of top supercomputers, showing the increasing computational power of these systems, alongside the growing energy demands, which emphasizes the need for more energy-efficient models such as neuromorphic systems. Figure 9.3(b) highlights the memory gap in modern systems, showing the growing disparity between processing power and memory bandwidth. This gap underscores the necessity for new memory architectures, such as memristive systems, which offer high-speed, in-memory processing to alleviate this bottleneck. Figure 9.3(c) presents the design philosophy of a typical neuromorphic chip, focused on creating energy-efficient, highly parallel circuits that emulate brain-like processing, ideal for tasks such as pattern recognition. In figure 9.3(d), the key parameters of CMOS-based neuromorphic chips are outlined, demonstrating the limitations of traditional CMOS systems, such as scalability and energy efficiency, which are increasingly addressed by memristive technologies. Finally, figure 9.3(e) showcases the exponential scaling in the development of memristive neuromorphic chips, emphasizing their rapid advancements in performance and power efficiency. This highlights the potential of memristive systems to overcome the challenges faced by CMOS-based chips and to revolutionize neuromorphic computing with improved scalability and reduced power consumption.

9.1.2.1 Image compression

One critical area where memristive systems can make a significant impact is in image compression. Traditional image compression algorithms, such as JPEG and PNG, depend on complex mathematical transformations to reduce file sizes, which can be computationally intensive and energy consuming. Memristive systems have the potential to enhance these processes significantly by enabling more efficient data storage and retrieval. By leveraging the unique memory capabilities of memristors, new compression algorithms can be developed that offer higher compression ratios while consuming less energy and providing faster processing times. Memristors can store and process data simultaneously, which eliminates the need for extensive data transfers between the memory and the processing unit. This integrated approach not only speeds up the compression process but also reduces the overall energy consumption [2]. Furthermore, the non-volatile nature of memristors ensures that the compressed data remain intact even when the power is turned off, enhancing data reliability and integrity. These advantages make memristive systems particularly suitable for applications requiring large-scale image data processing, such as in medical imaging, satellite imagery, and multimedia storage [11].

Exploiting the high parallelism, non-volatility, low power consumption, and compact structure of memristors, a single-device design has been demonstrated to store image data at 6-bit precision while supporting functions such as compression, convolution, and filtering. A memristor-based image compression framework is shown in figure 9.4 [5], incorporating the effects of the 2D discrete wavelet transform. It employs three crossbar arrays: a computational array for multiply -accumulate operations, an intermediate array for storing transform coefficients, and a final array for retaining the compressed image. Compression is achieved by

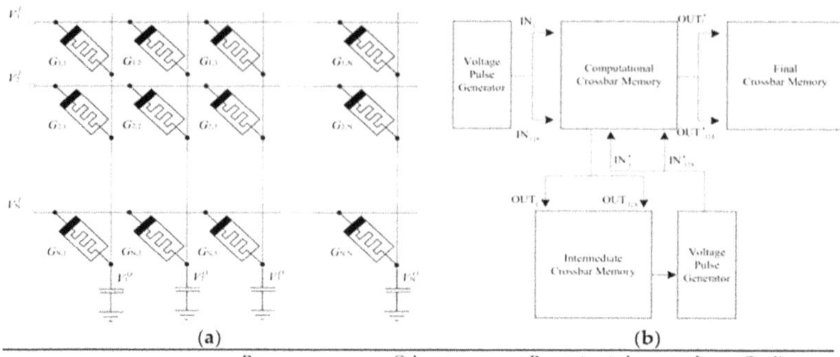

	Row Transformation	Column Transformation	Reconstructed Image	Image Quality Metrics
Conventional Computing (8 bits)				PSNR =57.24 dB SSIM =0.9994 CW-SSIM=1
Conventional Computing (5 bits)				PSNR = 35.81 dB SSIM = 0.9739 CW-SSIM =0.993
Memristor-based Computing (32-levels)				PSNR =33.29 dB SSIM =0.8853 CW-SSIM=0.9983

(c)

Figure 9.4. Application of crossbar array based on memristor in image compression. (a) memristor crossbar array; (b) image compression framework; (c) image compression result. Reproduced from [5] CC BY 4.0.

mapping input pulses to memristive conductance values and distributing them across the arrays.

Figure 9.5 presents a visualization of reconstructed images from the Kodak dataset, which were generated by the proposed model. The model's performance is evaluated using mean squared error (MSE) loss, a common loss function for image reconstruction tasks, ensuring that the pixel-wise differences between the reconstructed and original images are minimized. The optimization of the model is controlled by a parameter, denoted as λ, which is set to 0.01. This parameter likely plays a role in balancing regularization terms or controlling the weight of different components within the loss function to improve the quality of the reconstructed images. This highlights how well the proposed model reconstructs images from the Kodak dataset, showcasing the effectiveness of the optimization strategy. The reconstructed images provide a clear representation of the model's ability to retain important visual features while minimizing reconstruction errors.

We now examine a study on the gate-induced current modulation properties of a one-transistor–one-resistor (1T1R) pixel, highlighting its potential applications in memristor-based circuits and operations such as kernel processing for image computation. The first demonstration involves measuring the current–voltage (I–V) characteristics of the 1T1R pixel in both high- and low-resistance states. Measurements are performed by applying a fixed read voltage of 0.2 V while varying the gate voltage (V_G) between 2 and 10 V [4]. The high- and low-resistance states represent distinct storage conditions within the memristor, serving as the basis for encoding binary logic levels (0 and 1) or multiple analog levels required for

Figure 9.5. A visualization of the reconstructed images from the Kodak dataset, generated by the proposed model. The model is optimized using MSE loss, with the λ parameter set to 0.01. Reprinted by permission from Springer Nature Customer Service Centre GmbH: Springer-Verlag GmbH Germany, *Machine Vision and Applications*, [11], copyright (2024).

computation. This shows how the *I–V* characteristics evolve as the memristor's resistance is gradually tuned using continuous gate-induced modulation. By adjusting the gate voltage, the resistance can be controlled precisely, allowing for gradual changes in the current, essential for applications such as neuromorphic computing, where continuous weight adjustment is needed.

Figure 9.6 illustrates the gate-induced current modulation properties of a 1T1R pixel for kernel operations. Figure 9.6(a) shows the *I–V* characteristics of the 1T1R pixel at high and low resistance states, measured at a fixed reading voltage of 0.2 V and gate voltages (V_G) of 2 and 10 V. This highlights the change in resistance under different gate conditions, which is crucial for controlling the memristor's behavior. Figure 9.6(b) demonstrates the continuous electrical tuning of the memristor, where gate-induced modulation is used to alter the *I–V* response over time, showcasing the dynamic adjustability of the memristor's resistance. Figure 9.6(c) provides a discretized plot with 64 current states (6 bits) adjusted by V_G, along with an inset showing the 1T1R pixel circuit controlled via an indium zinc oxide (IZO) thin-film transistor (TFT), emphasizing fine-grained resistance control. Figure 9.6(d) displays both constant and incremental external bias pulse schemes, which demonstrate linear weight updates in the memristor, highlighting its application in neuromorphic and machine learning tasks. Figures 9.6(e) and (f) further illustrate incremental weight update properties at gate voltages ranging from 2 to 10 V, showing how the resistance can be incrementally tuned using constant and incremental pulse schemes. Figure 9.6(g) presents the circuit diagram of a 3 × 3 1T1R array, where IZO TFTs and HfO_2 memristors are connected in series, with color variations indicating the resistances of the memristors. Figure 9.6(h) shows how a Gaussian blur kernel with a sigma value of 1.1 is implemented via the memristive crossbar array, where current values from the 3 × 3 array demonstrate the application of image processing tasks, such as Gaussian blurring, using the 64 discretized states. Finally, figure 9.6(i) illustrates the *in situ* monitoring of programmed states during measurements at fixed read and gate voltages of 0.2 and 5 V, respectively, ensuring precise control and

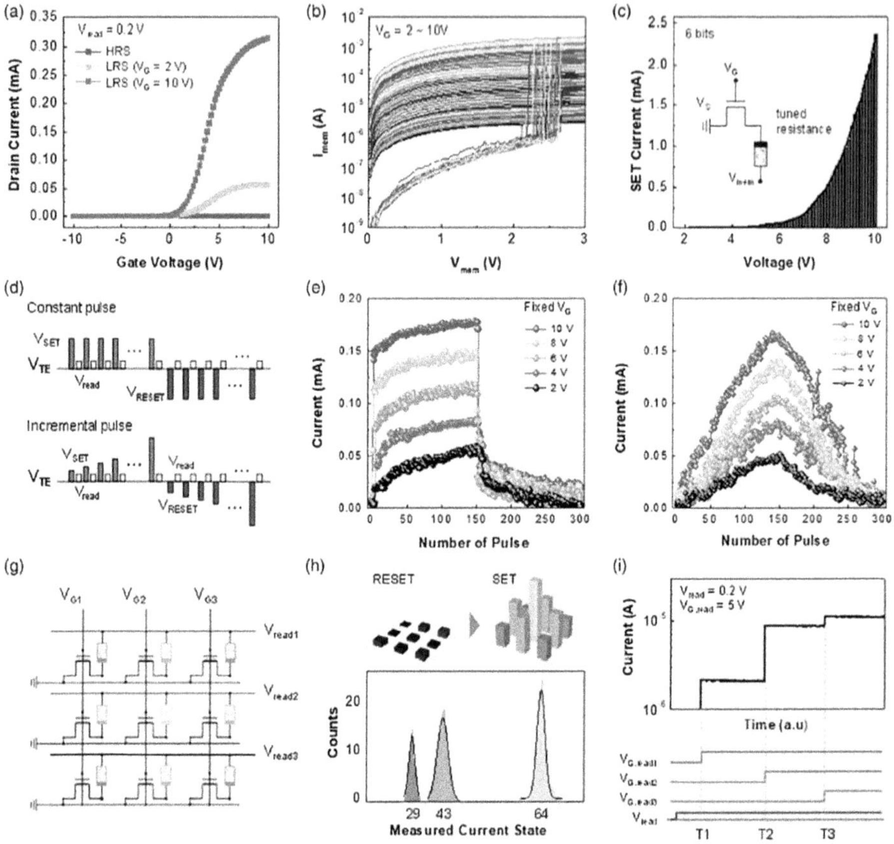

Figure 9.6. Gate-induced current modulation properties for kernel operations: (a) *I–V* characteristics of the 1T1R pixel at high and low resistance states measured with a fixed reading voltage of 0.2 V and gate voltages (V_G) of 2 V and 10 V. (b) *I–V* characteristics of the 1T1R pixel obtained during continuous electrical tuning of the memristor using gate-induced modulation. (c) Discretized plot showing 64 current states (6 bits) adjusted by V_G, with the inset illustrating the 1T1R pixel circuit and resistance control via the IZO TFT. (d) Constant and incremental external bias pulse schemes demonstrating linear weight updates in the memristor. The incremental weight update properties of the 1T1R pixel are shown using (e) constant and (f) incremental pulse schemes at V_G ranging from 2 to 10 V. (g) Circuit diagram of a 3 × 3 1T1R array connected in series with IZO TFTs and HfO_2 memristors, with color variations representing the proposed resistances of the memristor. (h) Gaussian blur kernel with a sigma value of 1.1 implemented via the memristive crossbar array, demonstrated through measured current values from the 3 × 3 array based on calibrated 64 linearly discretized states. (i) *In situ* monitoring of programmed states in the 1T1R array during measurements performed at a fixed read voltage (V_D) and gate voltage (V_G) of 0.2 and 5 V, respectively. (Reproduced from [7]. CC BY 4.0.)

real-time monitoring of the memristive system's behavior. This highlights the potential of the 1T1R memristive array in performing kernel operations and dynamic image processing tasks through fine control of resistance states.

This illustrates how the gate voltage can be used to achieve 64 discretized current states (equivalent to 6 bits). These states represent different resistance levels controlled by the IZO TFT integrated into the 1T1R circuit (as shown in the inset).

This fine control over resistance allows for multi-bit storage, making the memristor suitable for analog computation and in-memory processing tasks. Another example demonstrates two external bias pulse schemes—constant and incremental—that allow for linear updates of the memristor's weight values. These schemes are critical for training memristor-based neural networks, where precise control overweight updates is needed to converge on an optimal solution [5].

Further, figure 9.6 shows how the incremental weight updates are achieved using a constant pulse scheme, with V_G ranging from 2 to 10 V. The constant pulse scheme maintains a consistent and predictable change in the memristor's resistance with each pulse. Similarly, weight updates using an incremental pulse scheme are also demonstrated, allowing for finer control and enabling smaller resistance changes per pulse, advantageous for precision applications. A circuit diagram depicts a 3 × 3 array of 1T1R cells connected in series with IZO TFTs and HfO_2 memristors, where color variations represent different resistance states within the memristors [4]. This configuration is used in image processing tasks such as convolution, where multiple kernels can be applied in parallel.

The Gaussian blur kernel with a sigma value of 1.1 is implemented through this 3 × 3 crossbar array. The measured current values from the array correspond to the kernel's operation, demonstrating how a blurring effect can be achieved via calibrated resistance states. The 64 linearly discretized states enable precise tuning, allowing for accurate image filtering directly in hardware. Finally, the *in situ* monitoring of programmed states in the 1T1R array during measurements with fixed read and gate voltages ($V_D = 0.2$ V and $V_G = 5$ V) is demonstrated. This real-time monitoring ensures that the programmed states remain stable and consistent during operation, crucial for reliability in applications such as in-memory computing. These collectively demonstrate how the 1T1R structure can be used for both digital and analog computations, showcasing its potential in neuromorphic circuits, in-memory computing, and image processing tasks. The ability to finely tune resistance levels and implement complex kernels such as Gaussian blur highlights the versatility and applicability of this approach in advanced computational systems [12].

9.1.2.2 Biomedical image processing

In the biomedical field, image processing is fundamental to disease diagnosis and treatment planning, impacting patient outcomes significantly. Medical imaging techniques such as MRI, CT scans, and x-rays generate vast amounts of data that require precise and efficient analysis [13]. Memristive systems offer promising advancements in this domain by providing faster and more accurate image processing capabilities. Memristors can be employed to develop advanced filtering and enhancement techniques that are crucial for the early detection of diseases. These techniques can improve the clarity and quality of medical images, making it easier for healthcare professionals to identify and analyse critical features [6–10]. For instance, memristors' unique ability to perform computations directly in-memory allows for real-time image enhancement and noise reduction, which are essential for accurate diagnostics. Moreover, memristive systems can support the development of sophisticated neural networks tailored for medical image analysis. These memristive-based neural networks can be trained to detect tumors, lesions, or other abnormalities in medical images with exceptional precision. By leveraging the high-density and low-power attributes of memristors, these neural networks can process large volumes of imaging data quickly and efficiently, facilitating timely and accurate diagnoses. In practice, this means that a memristive system could scan an MRI or CT image, enhance its features, filter out noise, and highlight potential areas of concern, all in a fraction of the time it would take traditional systems. This increased speed and accuracy can lead to earlier disease detection, allowing for timely intervention and potentially better patient outcomes. Additionally, the low power consumption of memristive systems makes them ideal for portable medical devices, enabling advanced diagnostic capabilities in remote or resource-limited settings [7]. This can expand access to high-quality medical care and diagnostic services to a broader population.

Figure 9.7 illustrates the application of different methods for edge detection on a CT image, comparing traditional techniques with a proposed memristor-based approach. The original source image, figure 9.7(a), is first processed using the Laplacian of Gaussian (LOG) operator, figure 9.7(b), which combines Gaussian smoothing and Laplacian filtering to detect edges, although it may introduce

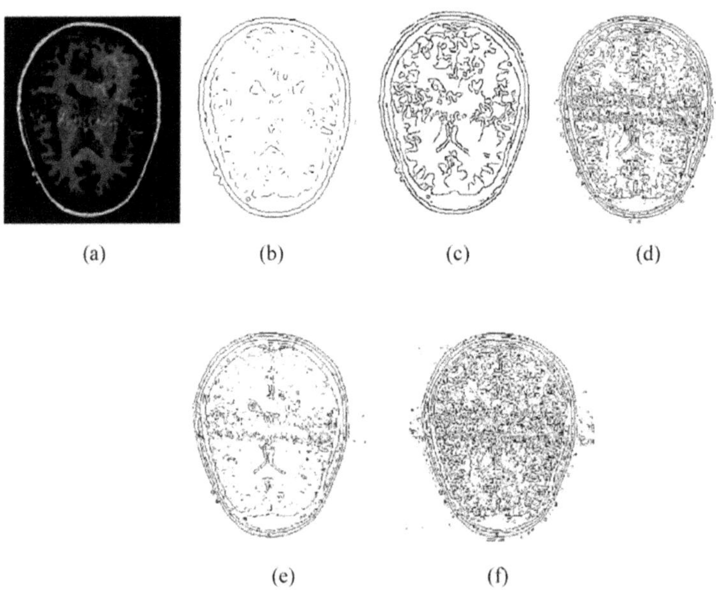

Figure 9.7. Applying various methods to extract the edges of the CT image: (a) source image; (b) edge extraction using the LOG operator; (c) edge extraction using the Canny operator; and (d)–(f) edge extraction using the proposed M-PCNN method with different memristor parameters. Reprinted from [8], Copyright (2017), with permission from Elsevier.

noise-related artifacts. The Canny operator, known for its precision, is then applied in figure 9.7(c), producing sharper edges with better noise resistance and fewer false positives due to its multi-stage process involving gradient computation and edge tracking by hysteresis. Figure 9.7(d)–(f) demonstrates edge extraction using the proposed memristor-based pulse-coupled neural network (M-PCNN) method with varying memristor parameters. The M-PCNN, inspired by neural network models, leverages the unique properties of memristors to perform adaptive edge detection, enabling fine-tuning of parameters to enhance edge sharpness, continuity, and clarity. This approach offers greater flexibility compared to traditional methods, making it suitable for capturing detailed edge features in medical imaging [8]. The comparison highlights how the M-PCNN's customizable edge detection can provide more accurate and noise-resistant results, making it a valuable tool for medical image analysis. Figure 9.8 illustrates the detection of mode collapse in generative adversarial networks (GANs) used for x-ray image synthesis. Mode collapse refers to a phenomenon where the GAN generates limited variations of synthetic images, often resulting in repetitive patterns and a lack of diversity in the generated data. This highlights red areas within the synthetic x-ray images, which indicate regions where repeated patterns occur. These repeated patterns, such as the consistent depiction of the lungs, suggest that the model is generating similar features across multiple synthetic images, pointing to a lack of variation in the generated samples.

Furthermore, the suppression of chest bones is another indicator of mode collapse. The absence or underrepresentation of important anatomical features, such as chest bones, in the synthetic images suggests that the GAN is not capturing the full diversity of real x-ray images, further confirming the presence of mode

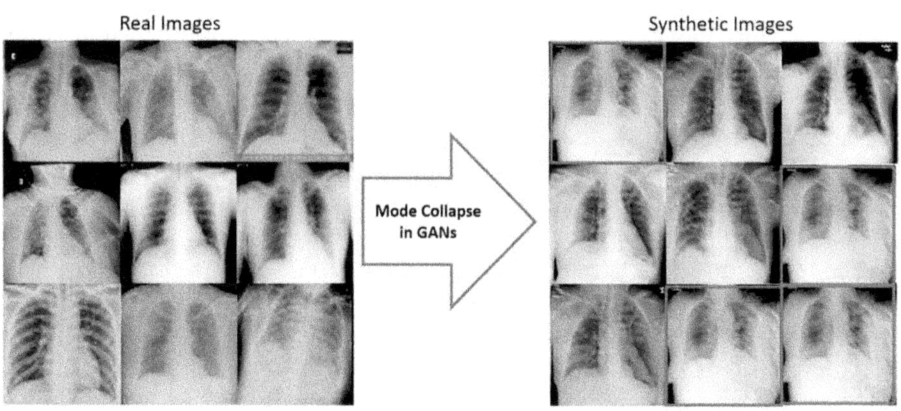

Figure 9.8. Detection of mode collapse in GANs for x-ray image synthesis. The highlighted red areas indicate repeated patterns in synthetic x-ray images, with similar feature distributions, such as the lungs. Additionally, the suppression of chest bones points to the presence of a mode collapse issue in GANs. (Reproduced from [13]. CC BY 4.0.)

collapse. The detection of these repeated patterns and missing features is crucial for diagnosing and addressing mode collapse in GANs, particularly when generating synthetic medical images such as x-rays. This underscores the importance of identifying and mitigating mode collapse to improve the quality and diversity of generated synthetic images.

9.1.2.3 Agriculture image processing

Memristive systems also hold significant promise in the agricultural sector, where image processing plays a vital role in monitoring crop health and detecting diseases. Modern agriculture increasingly relies on advanced imaging techniques, such as those captured by drones or satellites, to gather detailed information about large farming areas. These images can reveal crucial insights about the condition of crops, including signs of pest infestations, nutrient deficiencies, water stress, and other factors that can affect yield. Memristor-based systems can enhance the analysis of these agricultural images by offering real-time, precise, and energy-efficient processing capabilities. These systems can be integrated into drones and satellites to analyse images directly as they are captured, providing immediate feedback to farmers. This immediate analysis can help identify early signs of issues affecting crop health, such as the distinct patterns of pest infestations or the subtle color changes indicative of nutrient deficiencies. The unique properties of memristors, such as their ability to perform computations directly in-memory and their low power consumption, make them ideal for these applications. They can process large volumes of image data quickly and with minimal energy, which is particularly important for drones and satellites that rely on limited power sources. For instance, a memristive system could be deployed on a drone flying over a field [9]. As the drone captures images of the crops, the memristor-based processor could analyze these images in real-time, detecting areas where plants are under stress or where pests might be present. This real-time capability means that farmers can receive alerts and actionable insights almost immediately, enabling them to take timely actions such as applying pesticides, adjusting irrigation, or adding fertilizers. This timely intervention can significantly improve crop health and productivity. By addressing issues as soon as they are detected, farmers can prevent minor problems from escalating into major ones, leading to increased yields and reduced losses. Additionally, the efficient use of resources such as water and fertilizers can be optimized, promoting more sustainable farming practices. Moreover, memristive systems can be trained to recognize a wide range of crop health indicators, adapting to different types of crops and environmental conditions [10]. This flexibility allows for broader application across various agricultural settings, from large-scale industrial farms to smaller, more specialized agricultural operations [14].

The framework consists of four main components: leaf object detection (Step 1), feature extraction network training (Step 2), index library construction (Step 3), and plant image retrieval (Step 4) (see figure 9.9). Each module is introduced briefly here, with technical details provided later.

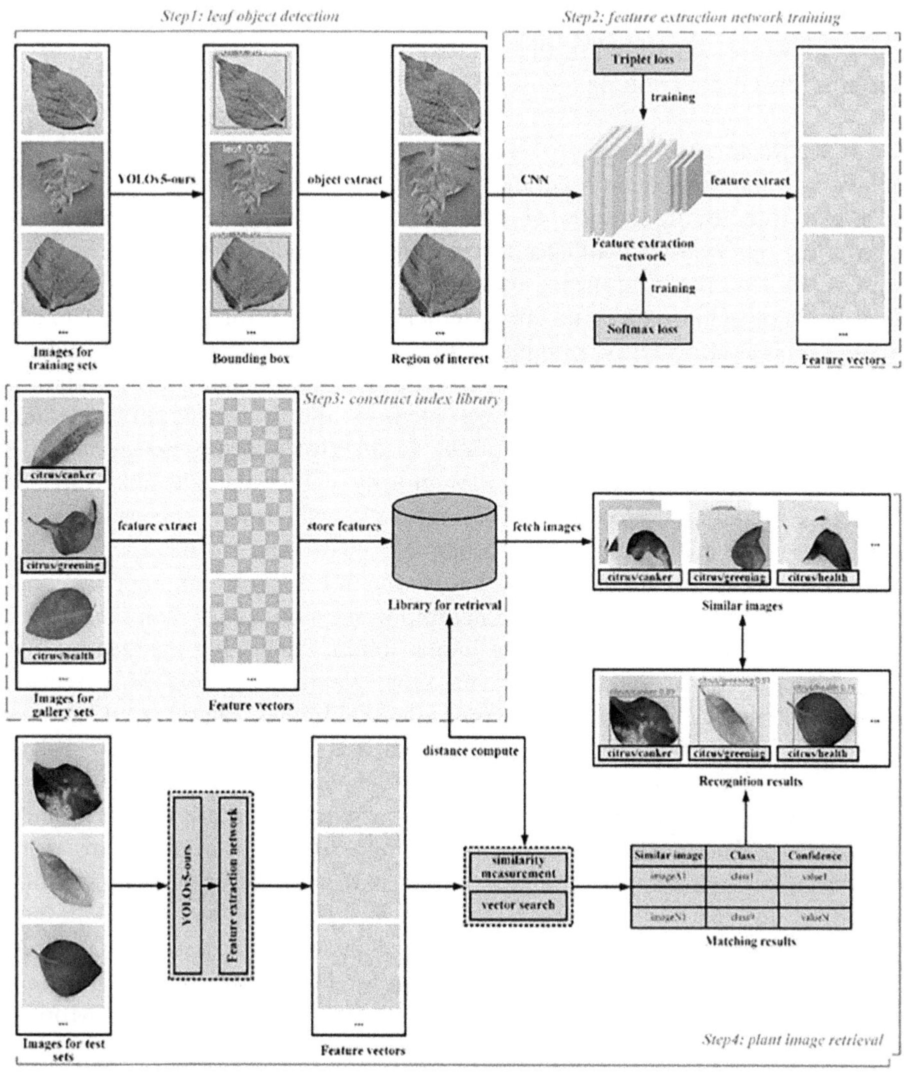

Figure 9.9. The framework of the retrieval system. Reproduced from [15] CC BY 4.0.

Leaf object detection predicts the bounding boxes of individual leaves, while the feature extractor generates feature vectors for each detected region. These two models are trained independently using different datasets and can therefore be developed separately.

In real-world leaf disease retrieval systems, the number of categories is often large or undefined. To enable fast retrieval, nearest-neighbor search is performed between query feature vectors and those stored in the index library. Thus, before deployment, all images are converted into feature vectors and organized by category to form the index library. When a new disease category appears, its images can simply be added to the database, allowing the system to recognize it without additional retraining.

9.1.2.4 Artificial intelligence

Machine learning and deep learning, critical components of modern AI, benefit immensely from the integration of memristive systems. These advanced memory devices offer significant advantages in creating more efficient and powerful neural networks. By incorporating memristors into AI hardware, we can achieve unprecedented levels of performance and energy efficiency. Memristors, with their ability to store and process information simultaneously, enable neural networks to handle vast amounts of data at incredibly high speeds. Traditional systems often face bottlenecks due to the constant data transfer between memory and processing units, leading to increased latency and power consumption. Memristive systems, however, mitigate these issues by performing computations directly within the memory, drastically reducing the need for data movement. This results in much faster processing times and significantly lower energy consumption, making them ideal for large-scale machine learning and deep learning tasks. One of the most promising applications of memristors in AI is the development of neuromorphic chips. These chips are designed to mimic the synaptic functions of the human brain, facilitating the creation of AI systems that can learn and adapt in real-time. Neuromorphic chips leverage the unique properties of memristors to replicate the brain's neural networks more accurately, enabling more advanced and efficient learning algorithms [3, 7–10]. This capability is crucial for developing AI systems that require continuous learning and decision-making, such as autonomous vehicles, robotics, and advanced recommendation systems. The integration of memristors into AI hardware also allows for the development of more compact and power-efficient devices. For example, portable AI applications, such as wearable health monitors and mobile AI assistants, can greatly benefit from the reduced power consumption and enhanced processing capabilities of memristive systems. These devices can operate for longer periods without needing frequent recharging, offering more convenience and reliability to users. Moreover, memristive systems support the implementation of complex deep learning models that were previously limited by hardware constraints. High-dimensional data, such as images, audio, and video, can be processed more efficiently, leading to better performance in tasks such as image recognition, natural language processing, and predictive analytics. The ability to handle such data-intensive applications with greater speed and accuracy opens new possibilities for AI innovation and deployment. Furthermore, the adaptability of memristive systems enhances the robustness and versatility of AI applications. These systems can be tailored to various learning paradigms, including supervised, unsupervised, and reinforcement learning, providing a broad foundation for diverse AI research and development efforts. Their capability to perform real-time learning and decision-making is particularly valuable in dynamic environments where AI systems must constantly adapt to new information and changing conditions [16].

9.1.2.5 Edge detection and correction

Edge detection is a crucial and foundational task in image processing, with applications spanning from object recognition to image segmentation and beyond. It involves identifying the boundaries or edges within an image, which are essential for understanding the structure and content of visual data. Accurate edge detection is vital for tasks such as object recognition, where distinguishing between different objects based on their contours and shapes is necessary, and for image segmentation, where precise delineation of regions within an image allows for detailed analysis and classification. Memristive devices offer significant advancements in edge detection algorithms by enabling operations that are both energy-efficient and high-speed. Traditional edge detection algorithms often rely on complex mathematical operations and extensive data transfer between memory and processing units, which can be computationally intensive and power-hungry. Memristors, with their ability to perform in-memory computations, address these challenges by allowing edge detection processes to occur directly within the memory. This integration reduces the need for frequent data transfers, thereby accelerating processing times and minimizing power consumption [2, 10]. By utilizing memristive systems, edge detection algorithms can be optimized to operate with greater efficiency. Memristors can handle the large amounts of data required for processing high-resolution images with reduced latency, enabling real-time edge detection in dynamic environments. This capability is particularly advantageous in applications that require fast and accurate image analysis, such as autonomous driving, where detecting the edges of road signs, lanes, and obstacles in real-time is critical for safe navigation. In addition to enhancing the speed and efficiency of edge detection, memristive systems also play a role in improving the accuracy of image analysis tasks through edge correction [10]. Once edges are detected, they may sometimes be noisy or imprecise due to various factors such as image quality or sensor limitations. Memristive devices can be employed to refine and correct these detected edges by applying advanced filtering and enhancement techniques. This post-processing step helps to smooth out irregularities and enhance the clarity of the edges, resulting in more accurate and reliable image analysis [9]. For instance, memristive systems can implement adaptive filters that adjust based on the characteristics of the detected edges, correcting distortions and sharpening the boundaries to match the true contours of objects. This refined edge information is essential for high-quality object recognition and image segmentation, where precise delineation of features leads to better performance in identifying and classifying different elements within an image. Moreover, the compact size and low power requirements of memristive devices make them suitable for integration into various imaging hardware, including portable devices and embedded systems. This allows for efficient edge detection and correction in a wide range of applications, from medical imaging and industrial inspection to consumer electronics and surveillance systems [17].

Figure 9.10 illustrates the memristive crossbar array (MCA) architecture designed for image storage and retrieval. In this system, memristors are placed at each intersection or cross point of the crossbar architecture, forming the core of the

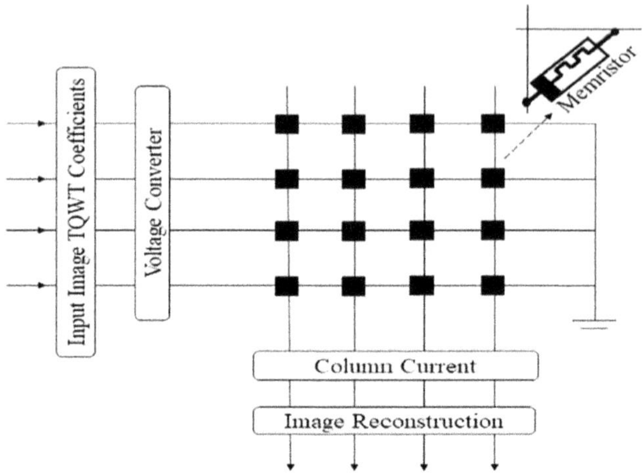

Figure 9.10. MCA for image storage and retrieval. The memristor, which is placed at each cross point in the crossbar architecture is magnified by its circuit symbol.

storage mechanism. This also provides a magnified view of one of the memristors at a cross point, displaying its corresponding circuit symbol to emphasize its role within the array.

The crossbar structure facilitates efficient storage and retrieval by leveraging the memristive devices' ability to store information through their resistance states, which can be dynamically adjusted based on the voltage or current applied. This enables the system to store image data in a compact and non-volatile manner, with each memristor acting as a memory element [12]. The memristor's resistance at each cross point encodes the image data, allowing for high-density storage. When retrieving the image, the resistance states of the memristors are read, and the stored data are used to reconstruct the image.

The use of memristive crossbar arrays in image storage offers significant advantages, such as high-speed data retrieval and low power consumption, making them ideal for large-scale image storage applications. The highlights both the physical architecture and the essential role of the memristors, showcasing their potential for efficient image processing and storage in future memory systems.

9.1.2.6 Image construction applications

In various applications that involve image construction and reconstruction, such as medical imaging, remote sensing, and computer graphics, memristive systems present notable advantages due to their unique properties and high-speed processing capabilities. These applications often deal with scenarios where images must be constructed or reconstructed from incomplete, noisy, or corrupted data. Memristive systems can significantly enhance the quality and efficiency of these processes. In medical imaging, accurate image reconstruction is critical for effective diagnosis and treatment planning. Medical imaging modalities such as MRI, CT scans, and

PET scans often produce data that can be incomplete or corrupted due to various factors, such as patient movement or limitations in imaging technology. Memristive systems can help address these challenges by leveraging their ability to perform high-speed, in-memory computations. By using memristors, advanced reconstruction algorithms can be implemented to process and correct incomplete or noisy medical images [9]. For instance, memristive systems can execute sophisticated filtering and interpolation techniques that fill in missing data and reduce noise. This results in clearer, more detailed images that enhance diagnostic accuracy. Improved image quality can lead to better identification of anomalies, more precise localization of medical conditions, and more informed treatment decisions, ultimately improving patient outcomes [11].

For compressing the reconstructed output image (see tables 9.1 and 9.2), threshold values corresponding to different compression percentages have been applied. As the decomposition level (DL) increases, a noticeable degradation in image quality occurs. An input image with a resolution of 512 × 512 is compressed at the first DL, resulting in a 256 × 256 resolution approximation image. At the second DL, the resolution is further reduced to 128 × 128, which remains acceptable for diagnostic purposes. However, at the third, fourth, and fifth DL, the resolution decreases to 64 × 64, 32 × 32, and 16 × 16, respectively. At the fifth DL, the reduction to 16 × 16 significantly impacts image quality, leading to increased noise and reduced clarity, making it unsuitable for practical applications. This is further confirmed by the values of PSNR snd Ssim as depicted in table 9.1.

In remote sensing, images are often captured from satellites or drones, and the data may be affected by atmospheric conditions, sensor limitations, or other distortions. Memristive systems can offer substantial benefits in reconstructing high-quality images from such data. The high-speed processing capabilities of memristors enable real-time correction and enhancement of images, which is crucial for applications such as environmental monitoring, agricultural assessment, and disaster management. For example, in satellite imagery, memristive systems can be used to reconstruct clear and accurate images from noisy or partially obscured data [9]. This enhanced image quality allows for better analysis of land use, tracking of environmental changes, and assessment of natural disasters. Accurate remote sensing images are essential for making informed decisions and developing effective strategies for managing resources and responding to crises.

In computer graphics, particularly in rendering and image synthesis, accurate image construction from limited or abstract data is often required. Memristive systems can improve the efficiency and quality of rendering processes by enabling rapid computation and real-time adjustments. This capability is beneficial in applications such as virtual reality, gaming, and digital content creation. Memristors can be used to implement advanced algorithms for image synthesis and reconstruction, including techniques such as texture mapping, shading, and image-based rendering. These algorithms require processing large amounts of data and performing complex calculations to produce realistic and high-quality visual content [8, 9]. The speed and efficiency of memristive systems facilitate faster

Table 9.1. Biomedical images (MRI and CT scan) with different DL.

Images	MRI		CT scan	
Decomposition levels	Haar wavelet	Biorthogonal wavelet	Haar wavelet	Biorthogonal wavelet
Original input image	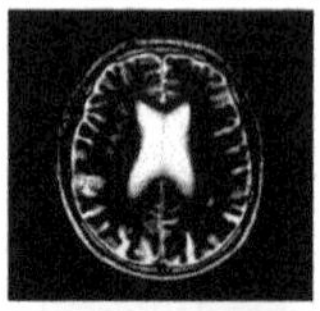	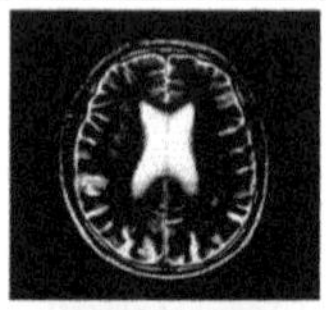	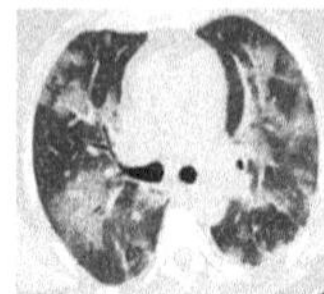	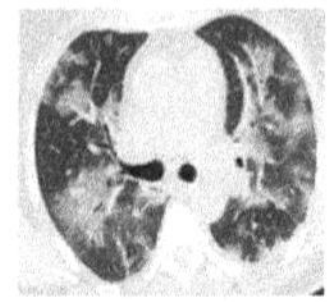
DL1	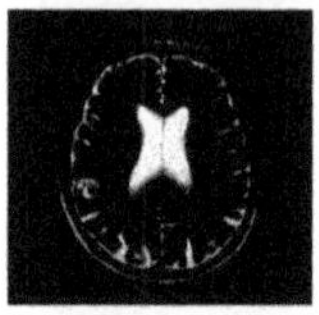	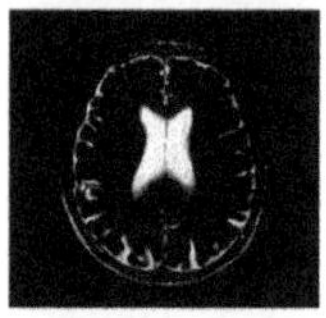	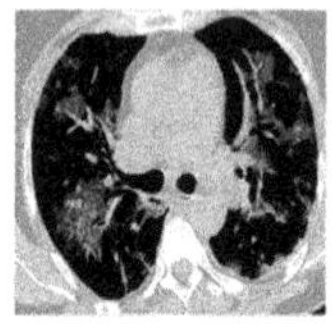	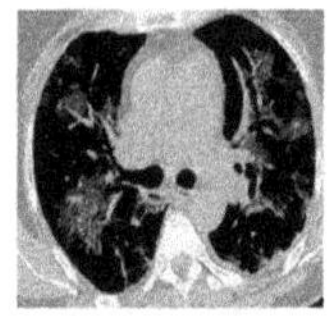
DL2	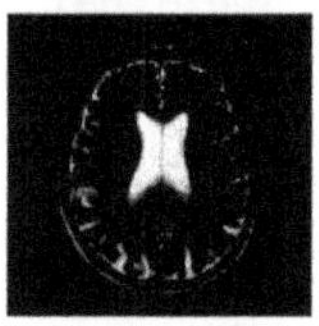		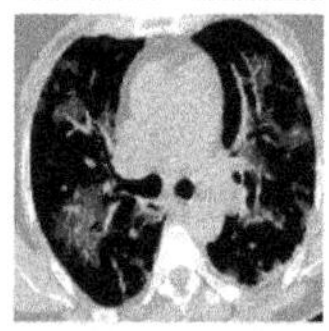	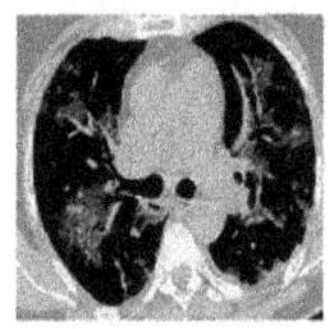
DL3	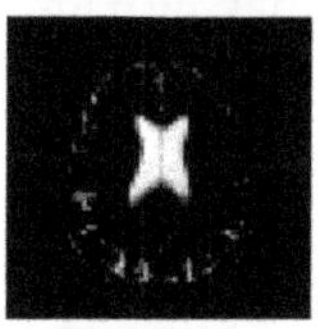	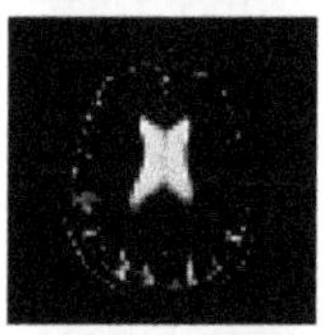	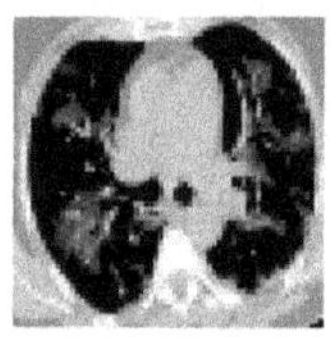	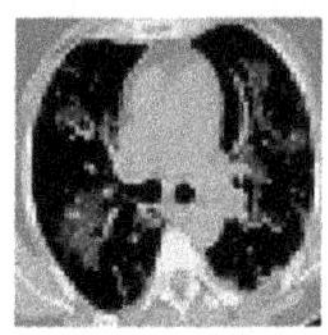
DL4	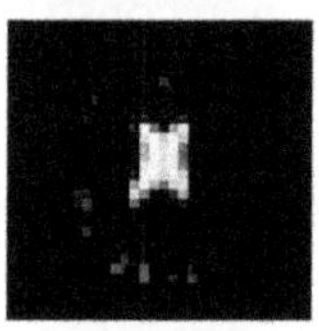		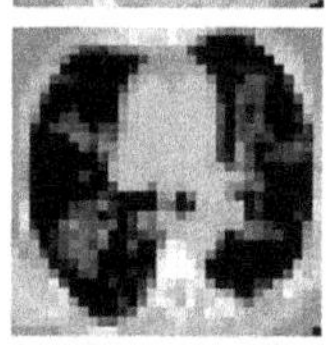	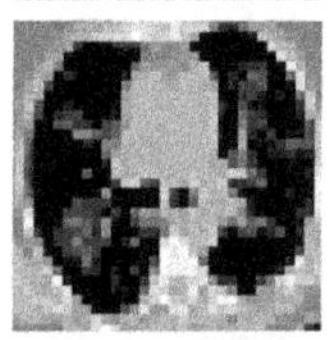
DL5			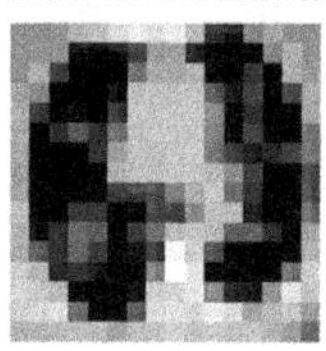	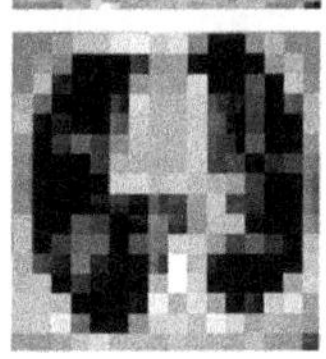

rendering times and more detailed images, enhancing the visual experience and enabling more immersive and engaging graphics [3].

Despite their proposal, integrating memristive systems into mainstream image processing and AI applications poses several challenges. These include the variability in memristor device characteristics, the need for advanced fabrication techniques, and the development of new algorithms optimized for memristive hardware. Future research is likely to focus on addressing these challenges,

Table 9.2. Input and output images obtained after decomposition using optimized tunable Q-factor wavelet transform (TQWT) parameters.

Images	Chest x-ray images 1	Chest x-ray images 2	CT scan	MRI
Input	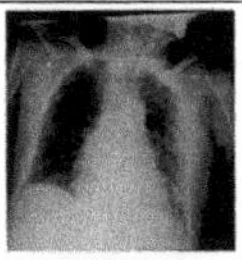	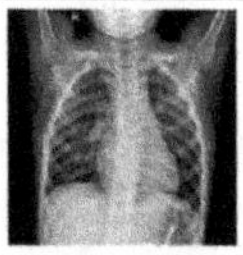	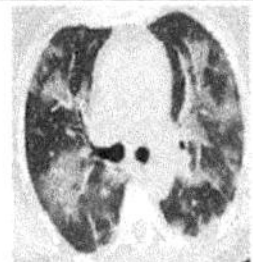	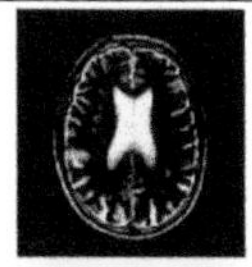
Reconstructed Output ($Q = 4$, $r = 3$, and $J = 2$)	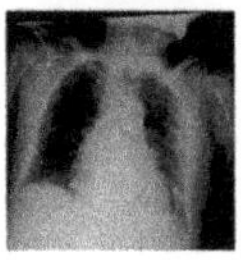	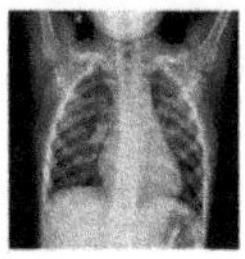	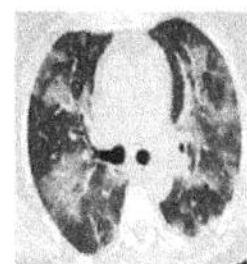	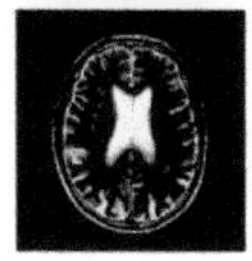
Quality Measures	PSNR = 50.4271 dB SSIM = 0.9946	PSNR = 47.3663 dB SSIM = 0.9968	PSNR = 43.4716 dB SSIM = 0.9936	PSNR = 42.4547 dB SSIM = 0.9971

improving the reliability and scalability of memristive devices, and exploring new application domains.

9.2 The working principle of memristors

Memristors function by altering their resistance based on the history of voltage and current that has passed through them. This characteristic allows them to store information in a way that is analogous to synapses in the human brain, making them an ideal component for neuromorphic computing systems [4]. In image processing, memristors can be used to create highly efficient and compact hardware accelerators for tasks such as filtering, edge detection, and pattern recognition. Memristive device applications in image processing are discussed below.

Figure 9.11 shows that an MCA-based model enables efficient storage of compressed images while consuming less power and occupying a smaller area compared to conventional technology that relies on application-specific integrated circuits (ASICs) for biomedical image storage [9]. The decomposed image coefficients are stored in the MCA by mapping their values to corresponding voltage levels. As illustrated in the figure, these mapped voltages are applied to the crossbar array along the rows. For image reconstruction, column currents are collected and utilized to perform the inverse wavelet transform operation. Additionally, the storage mechanism and a digital microscope image of the fabricated MCA demonstrate that the deposited material layers are precisely aligned to form cross-point structures [10]. A key advantage of the presented analytical model is that it provides valuable insights for designers and engineers when developing MCA-based systems for various real-time applications. This model allows designers to assess the accuracy and efficiency of MCA-based architectures, offering a deeper understanding of their behavior and interactions.

Memristors play a crucial role in image processing by leveraging their unique properties for efficient computation and storage. In image storage and retrieval,

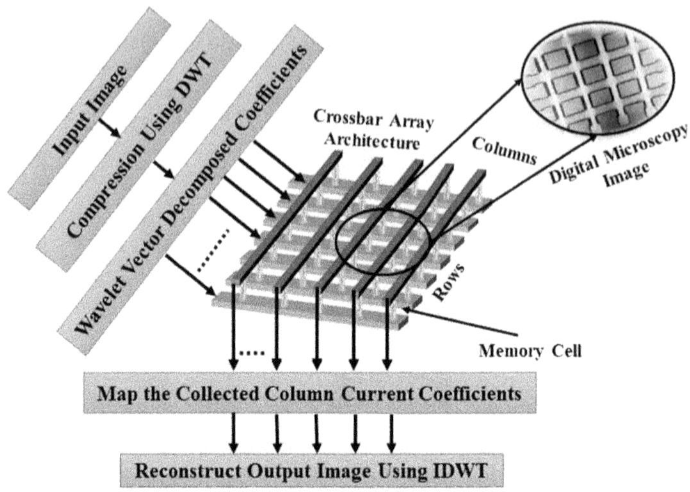

Figure 9.11. Image pixel values in form of vectors stored in MCA-based device, and a digital microscope image of a section of the fabricated MCA which shows that the deposited material layers have perfectly aligned with each other to form a cross-point structure.

memristors enable high-density, non-volatile memory arrays, ensuring long-term data retention even in the absence of power. Their ability to perform analog computations directly in-memory makes them highly effective for edge detection, a fundamental image processing task used to identify boundaries within images, reducing the need for extensive data transfer between memory and processing units [5, 6]. Similarly, in image filtering, memristors accelerate convolution operations by executing them in parallel, enhancing image quality and feature extraction while minimizing energy consumption. Additionally, in pattern recognition, which is essential for applications such as facial recognition and automated surveillance, memristors can be integrated into neuromorphic systems to mimic the brain's parallel processing capabilities, improving the efficiency and accuracy of recognition algorithms. These capabilities make memristors a promising technology for advancing real-time image processing applications [7–11].

Advantages of memristors in image processing are as follows:

Energy efficiency: Memristors are known for their exceptionally low power consumption, in particular when compared to traditional memory and processing units. This energy efficiency makes memristors particularly well-suited for use in battery-operated and portable image processing devices [9]. By minimizing power requirements, memristors can extend battery life and enhance the overall performance of portable electronics, ensuring that these devices can operate for longer periods without frequent recharging. This advantage is crucial for applications that require continuous image processing capabilities on-the-go, such as in mobile phones, wearable devices, and remote sensing equipment.

High density: The compact size and high packing density of memristors enable the development of highly efficient and space-saving image processing systems that boast substantial storage capacities. This means that more memory cells can be integrated into a smaller area, allowing for the creation of devices that are not only powerful but also compact and lightweight [1]. These characteristics are particularly advantageous in applications where space is at a premium, such as in mobile and wearable technology. By incorporating memristors, these systems can handle large volumes of image data without compromising on size, making them ideal for advanced imaging tasks in portable and embedded devices.

Non-volatility: Memristors possess the remarkable ability to retain data even when power is removed, ensuring the integrity and longevity of stored information. This non-volatile nature eliminates the need for frequent data refreshing, which is a common and often resource-intensive requirement in traditional volatile memory systems such as DRAM [2]. In volatile memory, data must be constantly refreshed to prevent loss, consuming additional power and processing resources. In contrast, memristors maintain data stability without such demands, leading to more efficient and reliable memory solutions. This feature is particularly beneficial for applications that require long-term data storage and uninterrupted operation, such as in critical medical imaging systems, archival image databases, and various portable electronic devices. By reducing the need for continuous power and data management, memristors contribute to lower overall energy consumption and enhanced system performance.

Speed: Memristors have the unique capability to perform computations directly within the memory itself, which significantly reduces the latency typically associated with transferring data between separate memory and processing units. In traditional computing architectures, data must constantly move back and forth between the processor and the memory, creating a bottleneck that can slow down processing speed. However, with memristors, this data movement is minimized because both storage and computation occur in the same place [3]. This integration allows for much faster processing times as it eliminates the delays caused by data transfer. Consequently, systems utilizing memristors can achieve higher overall processing speeds, making them especially suitable for real-time image processing tasks and other applications that demand rapid computation. This capability not only enhances performance but also leads to more efficient use of energy and resources, contributing to the development of faster, more responsive, and power-efficient computing systems.

While memristors offer numerous advantages, several challenges remain before they can be widely adopted in image processing applications. These include variability in device fabrication, limited endurance, and the need for advanced algorithms that can fully exploit the capabilities of memristors. Future research is focused on improving the reliability and scalability of memristor-based systems, developing hybrid architectures that combine memristors with traditional processing units, and exploring new applications in real-time image processing and artificial intelligence. Memristors represent a promising technology for advancing the field of image processing. Their unique properties, such as low power consumption, high density, and in-memory computation capabilities, make them well-suited for a range of image processing tasks. Continued research and development are expected to overcome current challenges and unlock the full potential of memristors, paving the way for more efficient and powerful image processing systems [18].

9.3 Image compression using memristive systems

Image compression is an essential component of digital image processing, designed to minimize the data required to represent an image without compromising its quality excessively. This is increasingly important in a digital world dominated by high-resolution imagery, where efficient storage and transmission are critical. Traditional compression methods, such as JPEG and PNG, reduce data by eliminating redundancies within the image. However, with the advent of memristive systems, a novel and more efficient paradigm for image compression has emerged, harnessing the unique capabilities of these devices [4].

Memristors, non-volatile resistive memory devices, offer a distinct advantage due to their ability to adjust and retain resistance values even when power is off. This property enables them to perform both storage and computation simultaneously, mimicking the behavior of biological synapses in the human brain. By combining memory and processing in a single unit, memristive systems reduce the need for data transfer between separate processing and storage units, making them particularly well-suited for applications such as image compression. The analog nature of memristors adds another layer of efficiency, as they can handle complex mathematical operations directly in-memory, a feature central to their use in image compression [5].

The process of memristive-based image compression begins with the representation of the image in matrix form, where each pixel's intensity is mapped to a specific resistance value in a memristive array. This mapping leverages the memristor's ability to store analog values, creating a compact and efficient representation of the image. Next, matrix decomposition techniques such as singular value decomposition (SVD) or principal component analysis (PCA) are employed to break the image matrix into smaller components. Memristors excel in these tasks due to their capability to store and compute data directly within the array, significantly reducing the computational overhead compared to traditional methods [6].

Once decomposed, the system applies thresholding, where low-energy components of the matrix those contributing minimally to the image's visual quality are discarded. Memristors, with their adjustable resistance, can dynamically adapt to different thresholds, enabling tailored compression levels based on specific requirements. Finally, the compressed image is reconstructed by combining the retained components. The non-linear properties of memristors ensure that the reconstruction process preserves critical image features while minimizing data loss, offering a balance between compression efficiency and image quality [7].

Despite its promise, memristive-based image compression faces several challenges. Fabrication variability is a significant concern, as inconsistencies in memristor manufacturing can lead to variations in performance and compression quality. Additionally, memristors are inherently sensitive to noise, which can introduce errors during compression and reconstruction. To address this, robust error correction techniques must be developed. Another challenge is the integration of memristive systems with existing digital infrastructure, which requires overcoming compatibility issues with current hardware and software architectures [8].

The memristive-based image compression represents a cutting-edge approach that leverages the unique properties of memristors for efficient data reduction. As memristor technology continues to mature, its potential to revolutionize image processing is immense. It offers the possibility of creating energy-efficient, high-performance systems for storing, processing, and transmitting digital images, making it a promising frontier in the evolution of digital technologies [9].

9.4 Biomedical image processing

Biomedical image processing plays a pivotal role in accurate diagnosis, treatment planning, and medical research. Traditionally, this field has relied on digital processing techniques that demand substantial computational resources to manage the large volumes of data produced by imaging modalities such as MRI, CT, and X-ray. Memristors, a new class of non-volatile resistive memory devices, offer an innovative approach to biomedical image processing by enabling in-memory computing, which can significantly enhance speed, energy efficiency, and processing capabilities [1].

Memristors are two-terminal devices characterized by a unique property known as memristance, where their resistance changes according to the history of voltage and current applied. This allows them to 'remember' past states, making them inherently suitable for non-volatile memory applications. Unlike traditional/conventional memory devices that require continuous external power to preserve data, memristors can retain information even when the power is turned off. This non-volatile nature makes them highly valuable for a broad range of applications, particularly in biomedical systems, where reliable, energy-efficient, and high-density storage is critical [2].

Furthermore, memristors have the ability to perform both logic and memory functions within the same physical device. This is a significant departure from traditional von Neumann architectures, which separate the memory and processing units. In von Neumann systems, data must be transferred back and forth between the memory and processor, creating latency and limiting efficiency, particularly in applications involving large-scale data processing such as medical image analysis. Memristors, by integrating memory and logic functions in the same unit, eliminate this bottleneck, allowing for more efficient, parallel, and energy-saving computation [4].

9.4.1 Integration of memristors in biomedical image processing systems

In biomedical image processing, the role of advanced computational tools is paramount for enhancing the accuracy and speed of image analysis, particularly in medical imaging modalities such as MRI, CT scans, x-rays, and histopathology.

Memristive systems, with their ability to execute both memory and computational tasks in-memory, offer a transformative approach to improving these systems [6].

Below are key ways in which memristors can enhance various aspects of medical image processing:

Noise reduction: Medical images are often corrupted by noise due to various factors, including imaging device limitations, environmental conditions, or patient movement. This noise can severely impact the quality of the images, making it harder for clinicians to make accurate diagnoses. Memristive systems can play a crucial role in implementing noise reduction algorithms, such as filtering, directly within the memory. The analog nature of memristors allows for real-time, efficient, and parallel processing of large datasets, enabling faster and more effective noise suppression. By executing filtering algorithms directly in-memory, memristive systems avoid the latency introduced by data transfer between processing units and memory, offering a solution for near-instantaneous noise reduction [7].

Image segmentation: Segmentation is a critical task in medical image processing that involves partitioning an image into meaningful regions. For example, in cancer diagnosis, segmentation algorithms can separate tumors from healthy tissue, facilitating accurate assessment. Memristive arrays are particularly well-suited for executing segmentation algorithms, such as edge detection and thresholding, with high parallelism. Memristive systems can handle these complex algorithms much more efficiently and with lower power consumption compared to traditional digital systems. The ability to process data directly in-memory not only speeds up the segmentation process but also enables real-time or near-real-time segmentation capabilities, which is essential for urgent medical diagnoses where speed is crucial [9].

Pattern recognition and feature extraction: Pattern recognition and feature extraction are essential steps in medical image analysis. Identifying specific patterns, such as cancerous cells in histopathology images or abnormalities in brain scans, requires advanced algorithms capable of recognizing subtle differences in pixel values. Memristive neuromorphic systems essentially neural networks that are based on memristors are uniquely positioned to address these challenges. By mimicking the adaptive behavior of biological synapses, memristor-based neural networks can be trained to recognize complex patterns and anomalies in medical images (see table 9.2). The in-memory processing capabilities of memristive systems mean that these tasks can be performed with greater efficiency, speed, and accuracy compared to traditional digital systems. This reduces the time required for diagnosis and improves the overall reliability of pattern recognition [11].

Image compression: Medical imaging generates large volumes of high-resolution data, which poses significant challenges in terms of storage and transmission. This is particularly problematic in telemedicine, where images need to be transmitted over networks with limited bandwidth. Memristors can be used to implement image compression algorithms, which reduce the size of the data while preserving crucial diagnostic information. In traditional systems, compression and decompression operations require separate processing units and memory, leading to increased latency and power consumption. Memristive systems, on the other hand, can execute compression algorithms directly within the memory, leading to significant improvements in efficiency and reducing the resource requirements for transmitting and storing medical images [13].

Image reconstruction: In imaging modalities such as MRI and CT, raw data are captured in the form of signals and must undergo a reconstruction process to create the final image that clinicians can analyze. This reconstruction often involves complex computational tasks, such as Fourier transforms and interpolation, which can be computationally expensive. Memristor-based systems can accelerate this reconstruction process by performing the necessary computations directly within the memory. This reduces the time required to generate high-quality images from raw data, facilitating faster diagnoses. Moreover, the parallel processing capabilities of memristive systems allow them to handle the large-scale computations involved in image reconstruction with lower power consumption and reduced computational overhead [5].

Memristive systems are uniquely positioned to address several challenges in biomedical image processing, offering a significant advantage over traditional computing architectures. By integrating memory and computational tasks in the same physical unit, memristors eliminate the bottleneck of data transfer between memory and processing units, enabling more efficient and faster processing of medical images. Their ability to perform tasks such as noise reduction, image segmentation, pattern recognition, image compression, and image reconstruction with high parallelism and energy efficiency makes them an ideal candidate for next-generation biomedical imaging systems [7]. As research in memristive technologies continues to evolve, their potential to revolutionize medical image analysis and improve diagnostic accuracy and speed will become increasingly apparent, ultimately enhancing healthcare outcomes. Memristors offer a groundbreaking approach to biomedical image processing by combining memory and computation in a single device, leading to enhanced performance, energy efficiency, and scalability. As research and development in memristor technology continue to progress, these devices have the potential to revolutionize how medical images are processed, ultimately improving patient care and advancing medical research [11].

Figure 9.12 illustrates the comprehensive process of image encryption and decryption, highlighting various aspects of visual and statistical analysis to evaluate the encryption scheme's effectiveness. The first component with the plaintext image, figure 9.12(a), represents the original image before encryption, which typically exhibits clear patterns and relationships among neighboring pixels. This image serves as the input to the encryption process and is analysed to establish baseline characteristics such as pixel intensity distributions and correlations [20]. Following encryption, the resulting ciphertext image, figure 9.12(b), is presented. This image is a visually scrambled version of the plaintext, designed to obscure the original content completely. An effective encryption scheme ensures that the ciphertext appears entirely random, devoid of any discernible patterns or structures that might reveal information about the plaintext.

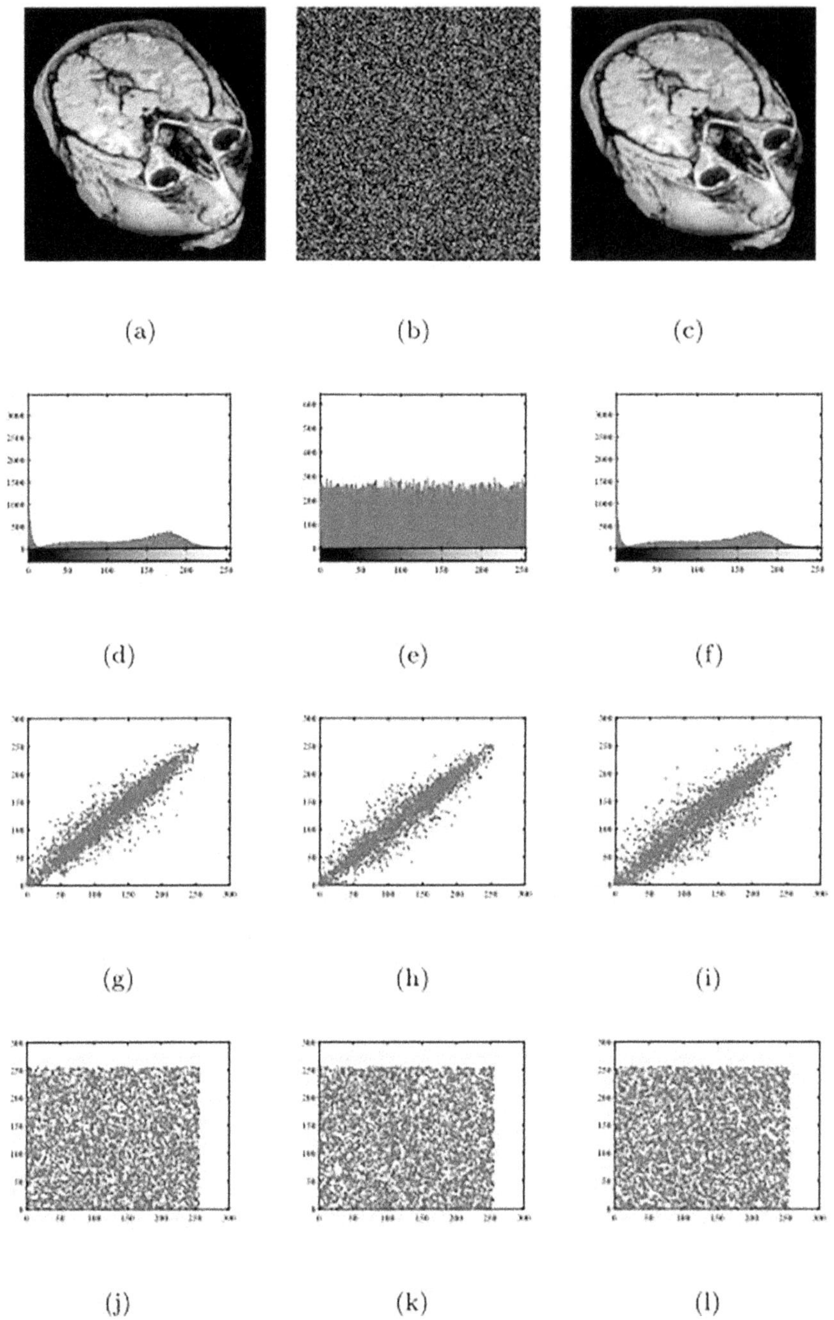

Figure 9.12. The encryption and decryption process includes the following images, histograms, and correlation analyses: (a) plaintext image, (b) ciphertext image, (c) decrypted image, (d) histogram of the plaintext image, (e) histogram of the ciphertext image, (f) histogram of the decrypted image, (g) horizontal correlation before encryption, (h) vertical correlation before encryption, (i) diagonal correlation before encryption, (j) horizontal correlation after encryption, (k) vertical correlation after encryption, and (l) diagonal correlation after encryption. (Reproduced with permission from [20]. Copyright 2024 Elsevier.)

The decryption process, which reverses the encryption to recover the original image, produces the decrypted image in figure 9.12(c). Ideally, this image should closely match the plaintext image, confirming the accuracy and reliability of the encryption–decryption algorithm. Any deviations in the decrypted image might indicate weaknesses or errors in the cryptographic process [5]. To further analyze the statistical transformations, the histograms of the images are provided. The histogram of the plaintext image, figure 9.12(d), shows the distribution of pixel intensity values in the original image, typically reflecting natural image content with identifiable peaks and valleys. In contrast, the histogram of the ciphertext image, figure 9.12(e), should appear uniformly distributed if the encryption effectively masks the original intensity patterns, indicating randomness. The histogram of the decrypted image, figure 9.12(f), should closely resemble that of the plaintext image, demonstrating successful reconstruction of the original pixel intensity distribution after decryption.

To assess the impact of encryption on pixel relationships, this includes correlation analyses before and after encryption. The horizontal (figure 9.12(g)), vertical (figure 9.12(h)), and diagonal (figure 9.12(i)) correlations before encryption measure the relationships between neighboring pixels in the plaintext image. Natural images usually exhibit strong correlations in all directions, as adjacent pixels tend to have similar intensities [7]. However, after encryption, the horizontal (figure 9.12(j)), vertical (figure 9.12(k)), and diagonal (figure 9.12(l)) correlations in the ciphertext image are expected to be minimal or non-existent. This lack of correlation demonstrates the encryption scheme's ability to disrupt the inherent spatial relationships within the image, ensuring that the ciphertext is secure and resistant to attacks aimed at exploiting these relationships.

Figure 9.12 provides a detailed visual and statistical analysis of the encryption and decryption process. It validates the encryption algorithm by showing that the plaintext image's content is thoroughly obscured in the ciphertext, while the decrypted image faithfully reconstructs the original content. The uniformity in the ciphertext histogram and the loss of correlations after encryption underscore the scheme's strength in concealing the image's statistical properties, making it robust against cryptographic attacks [13].

9.5 Artificial intelligence and memristive systems

AI has brought about a paradigm shift across various sectors such as healthcare, finance, transportation, and many others. By enabling machines to learn from vast amounts of data and perform tasks that traditionally required human cognition, AI has revolutionized the way we approach complex problems. However, as AI models become more sophisticated and scale up in terms of complexity and data requirements, the computational demands on current systems have significantly increased. Processing large datasets and running advanced algorithms have become more resource-intensive, creating a need for hardware that can handle these growing demands in a more efficient manner. To address these needs, emerging technologies

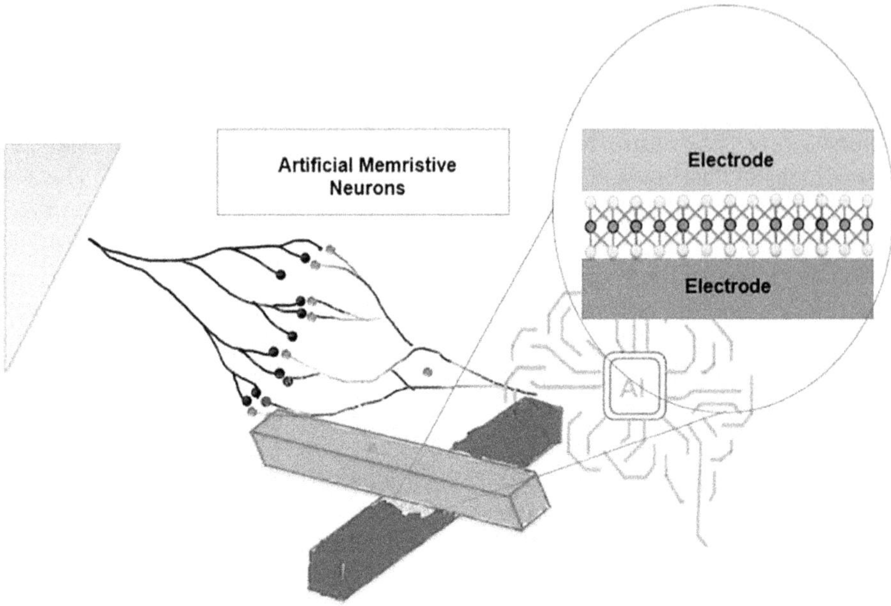

Figure 9.13. Artificial memristive neurons using memristive devices.

such as memristive systems are providing groundbreaking solutions, offering new possibilities for AI hardware, as shown in figure 9.13. Memristive systems, a class of non-volatile memory devices, have gained considerable attention due to their potential to transform AI computing by enabling in-memory computing, offering energy-efficient processing, and supporting neuromorphic architectures [14].

9.5.1 Memristive systems and their unique properties

At the heart of memristive systems lies the memristor, a two-terminal electronic device whose resistance can change based on the electrical signals (voltage or current) applied to it. This property allows memristors to store and process information in ways that are akin to how biological synapses function in the human brain. Unlike traditional digital devices such as transistors, memristors are non-volatile, meaning they retain their state even when the power is turned off. This non-volatility makes memristors an excellent choice for persistent memory storage. In addition to storing information, memristors also perform computational tasks by adapting their resistance based on input signals, providing a way to integrate both memory and computation into a single device. This integration marks a significant departure from the limitations of conventional computing systems and creates the potential for new, more efficient architectures that could power the next generation of AI technologies [16].

9.5.2 In-memory computing

Traditional computing architectures, such as the von Neumann architecture, rely on the separation of memory and processing units. In these systems, data must frequently be transferred between the memory and the processor to perform computations. This constant back-and-forth transfer creates a bottleneck, known as the 'memory wall', which limits the efficiency and speed of data-intensive AI tasks. Memristive systems offer a solution to this bottleneck through in-memory computing, where both data storage and processing are conducted within the memory cells themselves. This integration significantly reduces the need for data transfers, thereby minimizing latency, power consumption, and computational overhead. By performing computations directly within the memory, memristive systems offer an extremely efficient platform for AI tasks, particularly those that require rapid data processing and massive parallelism, as shown in figure 9.13 [17].

9.5.3 Neuromorphic computing

Neuromorphic computing aims to replicate the structure and functionality of biological neural networks, allowing machines to process information in a way that mimics human brain activity. Memristors are particularly well-suited for this task because their resistance can adapt based on the input signals, much like the way synaptic strength changes in response to neural activity. This ability to change state allows memristive systems to 'learn' by adjusting their resistance to stimuli, a process known as synaptic plasticity. This makes memristors the ideal building blocks for neuromorphic chips, which are designed to handle tasks such as pattern recognition, sensory processing, and real-time decision-making. Neuromorphic systems powered by memristors are not only more energy-efficient than traditional computing hardware but also have the potential to process data in ways that are closer to human cognitive functions. By mimicking the brain's processes, memristive systems open the door to highly efficient, brain-like computing architectures [18].

9.5.4 Accelerating machine learning algorithms

One of the most computationally demanding aspects of AI is the training of machine learning models, in particular deep learning networks. These networks require extensive matrix operations, such as weight updates and multiplications, which involve handling vast amounts of data and substantial computational resources. Memristive arrays are particularly well-suited for this task, as they can perform these matrix operations directly within the memory, enabling highly parallel processing. By eliminating the need to transfer data between memory and processing units, memristive systems can drastically improve the speed and energy efficiency of training deep learning models. This parallelization speeds up the training process and reduces the overall computational power required, which is especially important for training large-scale neural networks. This improvement not only accelerates machine learning algorithms but also has a significant environmental benefit, as it reduces the carbon footprint associated with AI model training [19].

9.5.5 Edge AI applications

As AI continues to evolve, there is increasing demand for deploying AI capabilities on edge devices such as smartphones, Internet of Things (IoT) devices, and autonomous vehicles. These devices operate under constraints such as limited power, small form factor, and connectivity challenges. Memristive systems offer an ideal solution for these challenges due to their compact size and low power consumption. By enabling computation to occur directly on the device (local computation), memristive systems reduce the need for continuous cloud connectivity, making them well-suited for edge AI applications. These systems allow edge devices to perform complex computations such as real-time object detection, speech recognition, and predictive maintenance without relying on constant data transfer to the cloud. This capability is critical for applications that require real-time processing and decision-making in resource-constrained environments [20].

9.5.6 Transformative potential for AI hardware

Memristive systems represent a transformative leap in AI hardware by bridging the gap between the growing computational demands of AI models and the limitations of traditional computing architectures. The ability to perform in-memory computing, emulate biological synaptic functions, accelerate machine learning algorithms, and support energy-efficient edge AI applications positions memristors as a key technology in the evolution of AI hardware. As research and development in memristive systems continue to advance, these technologies are expected to play an integral role in the next generation of AI solutions, enabling faster, more efficient, and sustainable computing. Memristive systems not only hold the potential to redefine AI computation but also to unlock new possibilities across industries, from healthcare and transportation to robotics and smart devices. Through their ability to provide both computational power and memory in a single device, memristive systems are set to address some of the key challenges faced by current AI technologies, paving the way for a future where AI is both more intelligent and more efficient [21].

Bibliography

[1] Hu X, Feng G, Duan S and Liu L 2017 A memristive multilayer cellular neural network with applications to image processing *IEEE Trans. Neural Netw. Learn. Syst.* **28** 1889–901

[2] Zhang Y, Cui M, Shen L and Zeng Z 2021 Memristive fuzzy deep learning systems *IEEE Trans. Fuzzy Syst.* **29** 2224–38

[3] Miranda E and Sune J 2020 Memristors for neuromorphic circuits and artificial intelligence applications *Materials* **13** 938

[4] Mehonic A *et al* 2024 Roadmap to neuromorphic computing with emerging technologies *APL Mater* **12** 10

[5] Ji X, Dong Z, Zhou G, Lai C S, Yan Y and Qi D 2021 Memristive system based image processing technology: a review and perspective. *Electronics* **10** 3176

[6] Hu X, Feng G, Duan S and Liu L 2017 A memristive multilayer cellular neural network with applications to image processing *IEEE Trans. Neural Netw. Learn. Syst.* **28** 1889–901

[7] Lee H S, Baek Y, Lin Q, Minsu Chen J, Park M, Lee D, Kim S and Lee K 2021 Efficient defect identification via oxide memristive crossbar array based morphological image processing. *Adv. Intell. Syst.* **3** 2000202

[8] Zhu S, Wang L and Duan S 2017 Memristive pulse coupled neural network with applications in medical image processing *Neurocomputing* **227** 149–57

[9] Jyoti K, Sushma S, Yadav S, Kumar P, Pachori R B and Mukherjee S 2023 Automatic diagnosis of COVID-19 with MCA-inspired TQWT-based classification of chest x-ray images *Comput. Biol. Med.* **152** 106331

[10] Jyoti K *et al* 2032 Memristive crossbar array-based computing framework via DWT for biomedical image enhancement *IEEE Trans. Emerg. Top. Comput.* **12** 766–79

[11] Zhang Y and Lin K 2024 End-to-end optimized image compression with the frequency-oriented transform *Mach. Vis. Appl.* **35** 27

[12] Zhang J *et al* 2025 Blind image deconvolution by generative-based kernel prior and initializer via latent encoding *European Conference on Computer Vision* (Cham: Springer)

[13] Saad M M, O'Reilly R and Rehmani M H 2024 A survey on training challenges in generative adversarial networks for biomedical image analysis *Artif. Intell. Rev.* **57** 19

[14] Almeida F and Hesham A S 2024 Detecting three different diseases of plants by using CNN model and image processing. *J. Electr. Syst.* **20** 1519–25

[15] Peng Y and Wang Y 2022 Leaf disease image retrieval with object detection and deep metric learning *Front. Plant Sci.* **13** 963302

[16] Huang Y *et al* 2024 Memristor-based hardware accelerators for artificial intelligence *Nat. Rev. Electr. Eng.* **1** 286–99

[17] Pan S *et al* 2024 End-to-end edge detection on self-rectifying resistive memory array *J. Mater. Chem. C* **12** 19180–19190

[18] Yang C *et al* 2024 Memristor-based bionic tactile devices: opening the door for next-generation artificial intelligence *Small* **20** 2308918

[19] Xiong L *et al* 2024 Dynamic behavior analysis, color image encryption and circuit implementation of a novel complex memristive system *Optoelectron. Lett.* **20** 183–92

[20] Leng X, Wang X and Zeng Z 2024 Memristive Hopfield neural network with multiple controllable nonlinear offset behaviors and its medical encryption application *Chaos Solit. Fract.* **183** 114944

[21] Yadav M S, Varshney K and Rawat B 2024 Memory switching versus threshold memory switching: finding a promising synaptic device for brain-inspired artificial learning systems *ACS Appl. Eng. Mater.* **2** 2131–42

[22] Ji X, Zhao X, Tan M C and Zhao R 2019 Artificial perception built on memristive system: visual, auditory, and tactile sensations *Adv. Intell. Syst.* **2** 1900118

www.ingramcontent.com/pod-product-compliance
Ingram Content Group UK Ltd.
Pitfield, Milton Keynes, MK11 3LW, UK
UKHW051924100926
8556IPUK00021B/1351

9 780750 361705